THE CHALLENGE OF J.

McMaster New Testament Studies

The McMaster New Testament Studies series, edited by Richard N. Longe-necker, is designed to address particular themes in the New Testament that are of concern to Christians today. Written in a style easily accessible to ministers, students, and laypeople by contributors who are proven experts in their fields of study, the volumes in this series reflect the best of current biblical scholarship while also speaking directly to the pastoral needs of people in the church today.

The Challenge of
Jesus' Parables

Edited by

Richard N. Longenecker

WILLIAM B. EERDMANS PUBLISHING COMPANY
GRAND RAPIDS, MICHIGAN / CAMBRIDGE, U.K.

© 2000 Wm. B. Eerdmans Publishing Co.
255 Jefferson Ave. S.E., Grand Rapids, Michigan 49503 /
P.O. Box 163, Cambridge CB3 9PU U.K.

Printed in the United States of America

05 04 03 02 01 00   7 6 5 4 3 2 1

Library of Congress Cataloging-in-Publication Data

The challenge of Jesus' parables / edited by Richard N. Longenecker.
p.   cm.   — (McMaster New Testament studies)
Proceedings of the 4th annual H. H. Bingham Colloquium in New Testament,
held June 22-23, 1998, at McMaster Divinity College.
Includes bibliographical references.
ISBN 0-8028-4638-6 (pbk.: alk. paper)
1. Jesus Christ — Parables.   I. Longenecker, Richard N.   II. H. H. Bingham Colloquium
in New Testament (4th: 1998: McMaster Divinity College).   III. Series.

BT375.2.C45   2000
226.8'06 — dc21
00-020304

Contents

v

Contributors

Stephen C. Barton Senior Lecturer in New Testament, Department of Theology, University of Durham, Durham, England

Craig A. Evans Professor of New Testament and Director of the Graduate Program in Biblical Studies, Trinity Western University, Langley, BC

Richard T. France Rector of the United Benefice of Wentnor, Ratlinghope, Myndtown, Norbury, More, Lydham and Snead, Bishop's Castle, Shropshire, England

Donald A. Hagner George Eldon Ladd Professor of New Testament, Fuller Theological Seminary, Pasadena, California

Morna D. Hooker The Lady Margaret's Professor of Divinity Emerita, and Fellow of Robinson College, University of Cambridge, Cambridge, England

Sylvia C. Keesmaat Senior Member in Biblical Studies and Hermeneutics, Institute for Christian Studies, Toronto, Ontario

Michael P. Knowles G. F. Hurlburt Professor of Preaching, McMaster Divinity College, McMaster University, Hamilton, Ontario

Walter L. Liefeld Professor Emeritus of New Testament, Trinity Evangelical Divinity School, Deerfield, Illinois

Richard N. Longenecker Distinguished Professor of New Testament, McMaster Divinity College, McMaster University, Hamilton, Ontario

CONTRIBUTORS

Allan W. Martens Adjunct Professor of New Testament, Tyndale College and Seminary, Toronto, Ontario

Klyne R. Snodgrass Paul W. Brandel Professor of New Testament Studies, North Park Theological Seminary, Chicago, Illinois

Robert H. Stein Ernest and Mildred Hogan Professor of New Testament Interpretation, Southern Baptist Theological Seminary, Louisville, Kentucky

Stephen I. Wright Director, College of Preachers, London, England

Preface

THIS IS THE fourth volume in the McMaster New Testament Studies series, sponsored by McMaster Divinity College, Hamilton, Ontario, Canada. The series is designed to address particular themes in the New Testament that are (or should be) of crucial concern to Christians today. The plan is to prepare and publish annual symposium volumes, with the contributors being selected because of their proven expertise in the areas assigned and their known ability to write intelligibly for readers who are not necessarily academics. Each article included in these symposium volumes, therefore, will evidence first-class biblical scholarship, but will also be written in a manner capable of capturing the interest of intelligent lay people, theological students, and ministers. In purpose, the articles will be both scholarly and pastoral. In format, they will be styled to reflect the best of contemporary, constructive scholarship, but in a way that is able to be understood by and speaks to the needs of alert and intelligent people in the church today.

This fourth volume in the MNTS series focuses on the parables of Jesus as presented in the Synoptic Gospels. It is a topic that is central for an understanding of Jesus and his ministry. It is also important for an appreciation of how the canonical evangelists treated the traditions about Jesus at their disposal. More than that, however, the teachings of Jesus' parables form, in large part, the heart of the Christian gospel, and so are integral to all of our Christian lives and ministries.

The topic has, of course, been treated extensively throughout the history of the Christian church, both by scholars and preachers — with interest in these parables having actually increased in our day, both on the part of those who read them academically and those who read them devotionally. Nonetheless, we believe that Jesus' parables need a more responsible scholarly treatment and better personal applications than they usually receive in either scholarly writings or the popular press. So we have prepared this fourth MNTS volume with the hope that it will prove to be of help to many earnest Christians who seek to think and live in a more Christian fashion, and thereby have a positive impact on the church at large.

Our heartfelt thanks are expressed to Dr. William H. Brackney, Principal and Dean of McMaster Divinity College, and to the faculty, administration, and boards of the college, for their encouragement and support of the entire project. Likewise, we express our deep appreciation to the family of Herbert Henry Bingham, B.A., B.Th., D.D., a noted Canadian Baptist minister and administrator of the previous generation, which has generously funded the fourth annual "H. H. Bingham Colloquium in New Testament" at McMaster Divinity College, held during June 22-23, 1998. It was at that colloquium that the authors of the present volume presented their papers and received criticism from one another, from the editor, and from others in attendance, before then reworking and polishing their papers, as necessary, prior to final editing and the normal publication process. Most heartily, however, we thank those who have written articles for this volume, for they have taken time out of busy academic schedules to write in a more popular fashion — in many cases, distilling from their academic publications material of pertinence for the Christian church generally. And we thank Bill Eerdmans and the Wm. B. Eerdmans Publishing Company for their continued support of the series.

THE EDITOR

Introduction

THE PARABLES OF JESUS are commonly assumed to be simple stories, told in an engaging manner and easily understood by almost everyone. People can still be heard to say, "Give us only the parables, and the Christian religion will be more readily welcomed, more quickly understood, and more easily assimilated." But Jesus' parables, while seemingly simple in their story lines, set before their modern readers a number of complex and significant challenges: challenges having to do with (1) Jesus' purpose in telling these parables, (2) how they were used by the canonical evangelists in their Gospels, and (3) the depth and breadth of meaning that they possess — but also, and probably more important, (4) our being awakened anew to the radical message that they proclaim.

The word "parable" *(parabolē)* appears forty-eight times in the Synoptic Gospels (seventeen times in Matthew, thirteen in Mark, and eighteen in Luke). It is entirely absent in John's Gospel and is missing in the rest of the New Testament as well, except for two uses in Hebrews 9:9 and 11:19 that are without importance for a discussion of Jesus' parables. The word has various shades of meaning in the Synoptic Gospels and can be understood to refer to a number of ways in which Jesus both taught and ministered. John's Gospel, however, presents Jesus as speaking in extended discourses, not in sayings or parables, though parabolic forms may underlie some of the Johannine discourses (e.g., 10:1-5; perhaps also 3:29; 8:35; 11:9-10, and 12:24).

What follows in this book are thirteen articles written by thirteen first-rate New Testament scholars that attempt to understand the parables of Jesus as portrayed in the Synoptic Gospels on their own terms and to set out the challenge of their teachings anew — all the while profiting from the great amount of study that has already transpired and seeking to use the tools of contemporary New Testament scholarship in a responsible manner. The articles build on the scholarly expertise of their respective authors. But they are presented in a manner that is intended to be understood by intelligent lay people, theological students, and ministers. Each article has a Selected Bibliography of no more than sixteen entries for further study, with many of the works cited being foundational for the article itself. All of the articles, however, are devoid of discussion-type footnotes which either interact with competing positions or bring in subsidiary materials. Even documentary-type footnotes are held to a minimum, and then only set in abbreviated form in parentheses in the text when felt to be absolutely necessary.

The organization of Jesus' parables into particular subject groups, as well as the wording of the captions for these groups, is simply for pedagogical purposes. Such groupings, admittedly, are somewhat artificial, and such captions somewhat anachronistic. Jesus did not structure his teaching in terms of our modern categories. Nor did the evangelists incorporate Jesus' parables into their Gospels to conform to our modern analyses. Nonetheless, it is hoped that — while the parables should undoubtedly be understood as something of a "seamless garment" in their general contours and thrust — such groupings and captions will prove useful for a more detailed analysis.

Unabashedly, the authors of this volume have taken certain critical stances and used a variety of interpretive methods in their respective treatments. The only criterion they have followed is that of greatest compatibility with the material being studied. It is expected that their academic expertise will be evident in what they write. More than that, however, it is hoped that through their efforts the teaching of Jesus in his extant parables and the proclamation of the evangelists in their portrayals of those parables will be better presented than is usually the case. And what is prayed for is that by such a truer and abler presentation, Christians will be instructed and challenged to live more genuine lives as Jesus' followers and the Christian church will be benefited in carrying out the tasks of its God-given mission.

THE EDITOR

PART I

History, Genre, and Parallels

From Allegorizing to Allegorizing: A History of the Interpretation of the Parables of Jesus

KLYNE R. SNODGRASS

IN NO OTHER AREA of New Testament study is a history of interpretation so crucial as it is with the parables of Jesus. Here a history of interpretation is virtually a prerequisite for understanding (1) the issues that must be addressed and (2) the tendencies that appear in many of today's treatments. It is a story that has been told repeatedly and in much greater detail by others than is possible here (see, for example, the works by Blomberg, Jones, Kissinger, Perrin, and Stein in the bibliography). Nonetheless, one cannot do a serious study of the parables without first setting out and interacting with such a history of interpretation. For these seemingly simple stories of Jesus, which are widely seen to be gems of articulation about life and God, have proven to be anything but simple.

1. Theological Allegorizing

The primary interpretive issue with regard to Jesus' parables has always been the extent to which the details of the stories are to be taken as relevant for a proper understanding. From the earliest days and throughout most of the church's history, Jesus' parables have been allegorized — that is, people have read into them various features of the church's theology, with many of those features often having little to do with Jesus' own intent.

The best-known example of such theological allegorization is Augustine's interpretation of the Parable of the Good Samaritan (Luke 10:30-37), where virtually every item is given a theological significance: (1) the man is Adam; (2) Jerusalem is the heavenly city; (3) Jericho is the moon, which stands for our mortality; (4) the robbers are the devil and his angels, who strip the man of his immortality and beat him by persuading him to sin; (5) the priest and Levite are the priesthood and the ministry of the Old Testament; (6) the good Samaritan is Christ; (7) the binding of the wounds is the restraint of sin; (8) the oil and wine are the comfort of hope and the encouragement to work; (9) the donkey is the incarnation; (10) the inn is the church; (11) the next day is after the resurrection of Christ; (12) the innkeeper is the apostle Paul; and (13) the two denarii are the two commandments of love, or the promise of this life and that which is to come (summary from *Quaestiones Evangeliorum* 2.19).

Such allegorizing of texts was not limited to the church. It is found frequently in the writings of the Jewish philosopher-theologian Philo, was used by various Hellenistic interpreters of Homer and Plato, and appears in some of the *pesharim* or interpretive treatments of Scripture found in the Dead Sea Scrolls at Qumran, like that of 1QpHab 12.2-10 (on Hab 2:17). In the church this "Alexandrian exegesis" went hand in hand with the belief that Scripture could yield a fourfold meaning: a literal meaning; an allegorical-theological meaning; an ethical meaning; and a heavenly meaning, which reflected future bliss. So, for example, Thomas Aquinas took God's statement of Gen 1:3, "Let there be light," to refer literally to creation, but also allegorically to mean "Let Christ be born in the church," ethically to mean "May we be illumined in mind and inflamed in heart through Christ," and with regard to heaven to mean "May we be conducted to glory through Christ" (see his *Commentary on the Epistle to the Galatians* 4:7).

In the history of parable interpretation, therefore, it is not surprising to find commentators asserting with respect to the Parable of the Hidden Treasure (Matt 13:44) either that Christ is the treasure, who is hidden in the field of Scripture, or that the treasure is doctrine, which is hidden in the field of the church. Competing allegories could coexist without difficulty. Similarly, Gregory the Great understood the three times that the owner came looking for fruit in the Parable of the Barren

4

Fig Tree (Luke 13:6-9) to represent (1) God's coming before the law was given, (2) his coming at the time the law was written, and (3) his coming in grace and mercy in Christ. He also understood the vinedresser to represent those who rule the church, and the digging and dung to refer to the rebuke of unfruitful people and the remembrance of sins (see his *Forty Gospel Homilies*, 31). Allegorizing, in fact, was the primary method for the interpretation of Jesus' parables from at least the time of Irenaeus to the end of the nineteenth century (for numerous other examples, see Wailes, *Medieval Allegories*). Unfortunately, it still occurs all too often in modern preaching.

Some Church Fathers and Reformers, of course, protested such allegorizing. Tertullian and Luther did, at least to some degree. Likewise, John Chrysostom and John Calvin voiced opposition to allegorical exegesis — though, at times, allegorizing continued to creep into their own treatments (cf. D. Steinmetz, "Calvin and the Irrepressible Spirit," *Ex Auditu* 12 [1996] 94-107). Chrysostom's comment on the Parable of the Vineyard Workers is still good advice:

> The saying is a parable, wherefore neither is it right to inquire curiously into all things in parables word by word, but when we have learnt the object for which it was composed, to reap this, and not to busy one's self about anything further. (*The Gospel of Matthew*, Homily 64.3)

Some caution, however, needs to be exercised in our evaluations of those who allegorized, for people like Augustine were not ignorant. Those who engaged in allegorical interpretation assumed (1) that life had a relation to the text and (2) that the text had power to direct their lives. Such assumptions, of course, are highly laudatory. Furthermore, they did not base their doctrinal formulations on allegorical exegesis, but sought to establish controls in order to prevent excesses by limiting those who could participate in such interpretations and by setting up boundaries within which that interpretation should operate (cf. Steinmetz, "Calvin and the Irrepressible Spirit," 97).

Still, allegorizing is no legitimate means of interpretation. It obfuscates the message of Jesus and replaces it with the teaching of the church. Such an interpretive procedure assumes that one knows the truth before reading a text, and then finds that truth paralleled by the text being read — even if the text is about another subject.

5

2. Historical, Non-Allegorizing Approaches

Theological allegorizing of the parables came largely to an end in scholarly circles during the latter part of the nineteenth century and throughout most of the twentieth century, principally through the work of Adolf Jülicher, C. H. Dodd, and Joachim Jeremias — even though, as we will see, they were not always consistent.

Adolf Jülicher

Although others before him had argued against the abuses of allegorizing, Adolf Jülicher's two volumes on the parables of Jesus in 1888 and 1899 sounded the death knell for theological allegorizing as a legitimate hermeneutical tool and radically affected the interpretation of Jesus' parables thereafter. In his war against allegorizing, Jülicher denied that Jesus used allegory at all (which he defined as a series of related metaphors) or incorporated any allegorical traits into his stories (where a point in a story "stands for" something else in reality). Allegory was too complex for the simple Galilean preacher. Rather, Jesus' stories contained self-evident comparisons that did not need interpretation. All allegorizing interpretations of the parables, therefore, must be viewed as being illegitimate.

Furthermore, Jülicher insisted, where allegory or allegorical traits do appear in the stories — such as in the Parable of the Sower or the Parable of the Wicked Tenants — the evangelists are to blame. For the evangelists misunderstood the parables, assumed that they had a concealing function (e.g., Mark 4:10-12), and turned them into dark and mysterious sayings (*Gleichnisreden Jesu*, 1.44-70 and 80-81). Paradoxically, however, Jülicher retained confidence about the genuineness of the parable tradition, and he knew that parables in "Hellenistic scribal learning" were sometimes enigmatic (*cf. ibid.*, 1.42).

In Jülicher's view, a parable is an expanded simile, whereas an allegory is an expanded metaphor. Simile and parable are features of literal speech, and so are easily understood. Metaphor and allegory, however, are non-literal; they say one thing and mean another. Therefore, they are to be seen as features of indirect speech, which hide meaning and need to be decoded. Jülicher allowed no mingling of parable and allegory, no "mixed forms."

Furthermore, in Jülicher's understanding there could be no positing of several points of comparison between an image *(Bild)* and the object *(Sache)* portrayed, as happens with allegory. Jesus' parables had only one point of contact (one *tertium comparationis*) between an image and its object. His purpose was not to obscure, and so his parables cannot be viewed as allegories. Rather, Jesus' parables should be seen as enunciating only one somewhat general religious maxim — or, perhaps more accurately said, some pious moralism about God and the world.

Jülicher's impact on the study of parables was not limited to his discussion of allegory. He also distinguished between various types of parables: "similitudes" (as the Parable of the Leaven), "parables" proper, and "example stories" (as the Parable of the Good Samaritan). These distinctions — along with that of allegory — are still used today, though there is considerable debate about whether allegory and example story are, in fact, legitimate categories. Also, by arguing that the evangelists had altered Jesus' parables, Jülicher opened the door for attempts to reconstruct the original version of the parables (for his reconstruction of the Parable of the Banquet in Matt 22:1-14 and Luke 14:15-24, see *Gleichnisreden Jesu*, II.431; note also his admission that this parable has numerous correspondences between image and object [*ibid.*, 432]). Such reconstructions are fairly common among scholars today, even when those who make them complain about their hypothetical character.

Attacks on Jülicher's position came quickly and have continued right to the present. Among the first was Paul Fiebig, who argued that Jülicher had derived his understanding of Jesus' parables from Greek rhetoric rather than from the Hebrew world, where allegorical parables and mixed forms were common (*Altjüdische Gleichnisse und die Gleichnisse Jesu* [Tübingen: Mohr-Siebeck, 1904]; *Die Gleichnisreden Jesu im Lichte der rabbinischen Gleichnisse des neutestamentlichen Zeitalters* [Tübingen: Mohr-Siebeck, 1912]). And in contemporary treatments of the parables, as we will see, scholars who focus on a Jewish background for the parables object to Jülicher's reductionistic views and reject the idea that any literature is self-interpreting. In fact, it may fairly be said that the more attention one pays to Jewish parables, the less impressed one is with Jülicher's explanations.

Furthermore, many scholars have called attention to the confusion that exists between "allegory" and "allegorizing" in Jülicher's treatment of the issues. Hans-Josef Klauck (*Allegorie und Allegorese in synoptischen*

Gleichnistexten [Münster: Aschendorff, 1978]), for example, speaks of Jülicher as having thrown out allegory, which is a literary form, whereas the real problem is that of allegorizing, which is an interpretive procedure of reading into material a theology not originally intended. And others, particularly Madeleine Boucher (*The Mysterious Parable* [Washington: Catholic Biblical Association of America, 1977]) and John Sider (*Interpreting the Parables* [Grand Rapids: Zondervan, 1995]), have argued that allegory is not a literary genre at all, but a way of thinking that can be present in various genres.

Few today accept Jülicher's definition of parable, for most view a parable as an expansion of a metaphor and not a simile (e.g., H. Weder, *Die Gleichnisse Jesu als Metaphern* [Göttingen: Vandenhoeck & Ruprecht, 1978]). And virtually no one accepts his claim that the parables present us with only rather general religious maxims. Several scholars, in fact, have pointed out that Jülicher's reaction against allegory only reflects a nineteenth-century distaste for the allegories that were written during the sixteenth through the eighteenth centuries (e.g., Mary Ford, "Towards the Restoration of Allegory," *St. Vladimir's Theological Quarterly* 34 [1990] 162-63). And others have mounted frontal attacks against many of Jülicher's views (e.g., Maxime Hermaniuk, Matthew Black, Raymond Brown, John Drury, and Craig Blomberg), particularly against his treatments of metaphor and allegory (cf. esp. C. L. Blomberg, *Interpreting the Parables* [Downers Grove: InterVarsity, 1990]).

Even so, Jülicher's conclusions have had surprising staying power — continuing on in the scholarly and popular psyches right down to the present, despite the inadequacy of his views. People often still speak of a parable as having only one point and are suspicious of any feature that may have allegorical significance. And even when aware of the inadequacy of Jülicher's arguments, many scholars are still caught in the vortex of his procedures and conclusions. It is as if once the seeds of the attack on the allegorizing of the church were scattered, they cannot be collected again for reevaluation but must be allowed to germinate without hindrance.

C. H. Dodd and Joachim Jeremias

The Dodd and Jeremias era of parable studies extends from 1936, with the appearance of Dodd's *The Parables of the Kingdom*, to roughly 1970 —

though Jeremias's *The Parables of Jesus* (1963) is still influential. Jeremias's work was an extension of Dodd's, and both were dependent on Jülicher. Both tried to understand the parables in their historical and eschatological contexts, even though they differed in their respective understandings of eschatology. Both viewed the parables as realistic first-century peasant stories and sought to explain the cultural setting of the individual parables. But in seeking to recover the original situations in which Jesus spoke, both Dodd and Jeremias also tried to remove the allegorical features found in the evangelists' presentations of the parables.

At least a third of Dodd's small book is not explicitly on the parables, but is concerned more generally with Jesus and the kingdom. Dodd understood Jesus' message in terms of "realized eschatology" — that is, that the kingdom of God had already arrived. His treatments of the parables are relatively brief and often quite straightforward. But Dodd believed that later Gospel tradition had, at certain points, obscured Jesus' original message by reorienting his original realized eschatology to ethical issues and a futuristic eschatology. For example, the Parable of the Talents (Matt 25:14-30//Luke 19:11-27) was originally about the conduct of the Pharisees, but was changed to address matters of moral responsibility and to speak about the second advent of Christ (*Parables*, 146-53). Likewise, parables about the end time, such as that of the Ten Virgins (Matt 25:1-13) and those regarding the harvest (Mark 4:26-29; Matt 13:24-30), were not originally about a coming end time, but about the crisis of Jesus' earthly ministry.

Jeremias extended Dodd's work in detail. He provided historical and cultural evidence for understanding the parables and, guided by the canons of form criticism, sought to ascertain a parable's original form by stripping away the allegorical features and other additions that had been supplied by the early church. Almost a third of his book discusses ten areas where changes made by the church need to be addressed and rectified in order to return to the original utterances of Jesus — these secondary, non-original matters having to do, invariably, with the contexts, introductions, conclusions, and interpretive comments connected with the stories as they now appear in the Synoptic Gospels. Such shortened, de-allegorized versions of Jesus' parables are close to the versions of the parables found in the *Gospel of Thomas*, a collection of sayings of Jesus that probably dates from the second century (although the question of date is debated).

9

While granting the presence of the kingdom in Jesus' ministry, Jeremias described Jesus' message as an eschatology that was in the process of realization. In his parables Jesus presented people with a crisis of decision and invited them to respond to God's mercy. Thus the parables are often viewed as a vindication of Jesus' offer of the gospel to the poor.

Jeremias's influence has been so strong that Norman Perrin once asserted that all future interpretations of the parables would have to be interpretations of them as Jeremias analyzed them (*Jesus and the Language of the Kingdom*, 101)! Few today, however, would make such a claim. Rather, many contemporary scholars hold that just as Jülicher's work was foundational, but aberrant, so Jeremias's work, while significant, is fatally flawed. At the very least, one must double-check all of Jeremias's claims, for some of them will not stand up to investigation.

One further point should also be made. While both Dodd and Jeremias attempted to remove allegory from Jesus' parables, both of them also brought allegorical interpretations back into consideration when they discussed the meaning of the parables. For example, Jeremias held that Jesus could not have uttered the Parable of the Banquet (Luke 14:7-14) as an allegory of the feast of salvation, but that he may, nonetheless, well have had it in mind (*Parables*, 69)! Such duplicity led Matthew Black to accuse Dodd of running with the allegorical hare and yet hunting with the Jülicher hounds ("The Parables as Allegory," *Bulletin of the John Rylands Library* 42 [1960] 283). Such inconsistency often occurs among those who overreact against allegory.

3. Existentialist, Artistic, and Initial Literary Approaches

Since about 1970 a mood has prevailed among New Testament scholars that feels the historical, eschatological approaches of people like Dodd and Jeremias to be insufficient. The beauty and the power of Jesus' parables is considered to have been lost, or at least seriously curtailed. Attention has turned to hermeneutical and aesthetic concerns.

Several persons and movements have attempted to go beyond the work of Dodd and Jeremias. Yet while seeking something more than the merely historical, most of these approaches still follow their predecessors in method by first stripping off those features of the parables that are thought to be allegorical or interpretive additions.

Existentialist Approaches

As part of the "New Hermeneutic," Ernst Fuchs, along with his students Eta Linnemann and Eberhard Jüngel, brought the concerns of existentialism and the insights of a particular understanding of language to bear on the interpretation of the parables. Fuchs and Jüngel, however, are not principally important in the study of the parables because of their exegesis of specific parables. Rather, they are significant because of their application of their understanding of language to the interpretation of the parables generally.

For Fuchs, existence is essentially linguistic. He argues for what he calls "the language-character of existence" (*Studies of the Historical Jesus*, 211), and he asserts that "the real content of language . . . is . . . being itself" (*ibid.*, 222). Language does not merely describe. It enacts; it imparts! Language has the power to bring into being something that was not there before the words were spoken. To call someone a brother, for example, does not make him one, but it admits that person as a brother and establishes community (*ibid.*, 209-10).

The parables are such "language events" (*Sprachereignisse*). This concept is similar to the idea of "performative utterances," which emphasizes the power of language to accomplish and enact. For Fuchs, parables are analogies, and in analogy lies the very language power of existence. The purpose of an analogy is not to increase the knowledge that one has. Rather, an analogy functions to shape one's attitude. Thus Jesus' parables have the power to bring to expression the reality to which they point. In his parables, Jesus' understanding of his own situation enters language in a special way so that his existence is available to his hearers. The parables, therefore, are a summons to this existence; and to respond, one must allow oneself to be laid hold of by Jesus' existence (*ibid.*, 220).

Fuchs and his colleagues were also part of "the new quest for the historical Jesus," and so they placed heavy emphasis on understanding Jesus and his mission. The parables are verbalizations of Jesus' understanding of his situation in the world. Understandably, therefore, one of the main features of Linnemann's *Parables of Jesus* (London: SPCK, 1966), which stands as much in the Jeremias tradition as it does in the new hermeneutic, is her attempt to hear the parables as Jesus' original audience would have heard them.

Much can be said by way of evaluating the views of Fuchs, Linnemann, and Jüngel with respect to the parables of Jesus. Pertinent critiques have been set forth by Jack Dean Kingsbury ("Ernst Fuchs' Existentialist Interpretation of the Parables," *Lutheran Quarterly* 2 [1970] 380-95; *idem*, "The Parables of Jesus in Current Research," *Dialog* 11 [1972] 101-7) and Anthony C. Thiselton ("The Parables as Language-Event," *Scottish Journal of Theology* 23 [1970] 437-68), as well as by Norman Perrin and Warren Kissinger (see bibliography). For my part, I believe the importance of their stance is in forcing people to consider language and its effect more seriously than before. For the parables of Jesus are, in fact, language events that create both new worlds and the possibility of a changed existence.

Artistic Approaches

If Fuchs and his colleagues were still concerned with the situation of the historical Jesus, the same cannot be said for those who today emphasize the artistic character of the parables. Existential concerns still rank high on the agenda of current artistic approaches. But a focus on the historical situation of Jesus has been deemphasized.

Many interpreters in the past have commented on the artistic character of the parables, including C. H. Dodd (cf. *Parables*, 195). But they had not made this a major factor for interpretation. Geraint Vaughn Jones in 1964, however, sought to widen the relevance of the parables by emphasizing their artistic and literary character and to highlight the way that they mirror human experience — that is, "to transpose them into the field of symbols of our permanent human experience" (*Art and Truth of the Parables*, xi). He attempted to distinguish between symbol and allegory, the former being present in the parables, and accepted that Jesus told allegorical stories. Yet despite seeking a wider relevance for the parables, he considered only eight of the fifty parables he studied to be candidates for a wider interpretation — viewing nineteen of them, in fact, to be strictly limited by their historical reference (*ibid.*, 141-43).

Dan Via, who was heavily influenced by existentialist interpreters like Fuchs, argued in 1967 that the parables are not bound by their author's intent (cf. his *The Parables*), and so expressed less interest in Jesus' original situation. The parables are aesthetic works that should be interpreted as texts in their own right. They must be viewed as being autonomous. They address the present because in their patterns is an understanding of existence that calls for decision.

Both Jones and Via sought to recover the humanity of the parables and to highlight their universal appeal to the human condition. Jones, however, was willing to say that some of Jesus' parables were allegories, whereas Via spent considerable effort (as many had before him) trying to distinguish parable and allegory. Yet even Via granted that parables may have allegorical correspondences and argued against a "one point" approach. Via also emphasized that parables cannot be completely translated into another form (cf. *Parables*, 32-56). And this understanding, as we will see, has become increasingly important in more recent studies.

Via divided the parables of the Gospels into "tragic" and "comic" parables, with "comic" connoting a sense of positive movement. His procedure for the interpretation of the parables has three divisions: (1) historico-literary criticism; (2) literary existential analysis, which is usually the longest section; and (3) existential-theological interpretation. The lessons he draws from the parables sometimes seem strikingly similar to Jülicher's pious maxims, though with an existential twist. But are we really to believe that the Parable of the Wicked Tenants is only a parable of "unfaith" that teaches that sin is a person's self-centered effort to reject any and all limitations that God imposes (cf. *Parables*, 137)?

Initial Literary Approaches

Robert Funk's 1966 *Language, Hermeneutic, and Word of God* is perhaps the most influential work on the parables of the last few decades (though only pages 124-222 deal directly with the parables themselves). He too was heavily influenced by the German existentialist theologians, but he brought a literary focus that they did not have. Adapting Dodd's definition of parable, he emphasized four basic points: (1) that a parable is a simile or metaphor, which may remain simple or be expanded; (2) that the metaphor or simile is drawn from common life; (3) that the metaphor arrests the hearer by its vividness or strangeness; and (4) that the application is left imprecise to tease the hearer into making his or her own application (*ibid.*, 133).

Contrary to Jülicher, however, Funk understood a parable not as an extension of a simile, but as an extension of a metaphor. Furthermore, he did not view metaphors as inferior to similes in their communicative abilities. Quite the opposite: if similes illustrate, metaphors create meanings (*ibid.*, 137). Furthermore, a metaphor cannot be closed off to only one particular meaning, since it is incomplete until the hearer is drawn into it as a participant. Therefore, a parable cannot be reduced to a single meaning, as Jülicher claimed in reducing the lessons of the parables to pious moralisms or as Dodd and Jeremias did in distilling a single eschatological point. For since metaphors are bearers of the reality to which they refer, and a parable is an extended metaphor, parables cannot be reduced to ideas and are not expendable once their meaning has been derived.

Metaphors — and therefore parables — remain open-ended with a potential for new meanings. Even in their original contexts they were heard by diverse audiences, and so had the capacity for various ideas. In asserting a potential for new meanings in the parables, Funk, however, is not arguing for an unbridled creation of meaning. For in his understanding, the original telling had an intent that served as a control over every reinterpretation. Furthermore, Funk's emphases on "everydayness" and "vividness or strangeness" — which were the second and third points in Dodd's definition — may seem somewhat contradictory. But Funk shows that everydayness points to the ways that parables address human existence, whereas strangeness points to the ways in which parables shatter the familiar. Paradox, therefore, is intrinsic to Jesus' parables. And the *Gospel of Thomas*, as Funk views it, is to be seen as sometimes superior to the canonical Gospels.

Several of Funk's points have been well-received by scholars today. That parables are extended metaphors and that they cannot be translated into ideas and then discarded are commonplace themes among contemporary interpreters. Likewise, his focus on reader response and his insistence on paradox are accepted by many, as is also his high valuation of the *Gospel of Thomas*.

Following the direction of Funk's work is John Dominic Crossan's *In Parables: The Challenge of the Historical Jesus* (New York: Harper & Row, 1973). The stated purpose of Crossan's book is to render explicit all that is contained in a phrase drawn from Günther Bornkamm: that "the parables are the preaching itself and are not merely serving the purpose of a lesson quite independent of them" (cf. Bornkamm's *Jesus of Nazareth* [New York: Harper & Row, 1960], 69). Not surprisingly, Crossan, following Paul Ricoeur, distinguishes between an allegory and a parable — arguing that an allegory can always be translated into a text that can be understood by itself, which renders the allegory useless, whereas myth and metaphor cannot be reduced to "clear language" (*Parables*, 11).

14

The metaphors that Crossan is interested in are not ones that simply illustrate information, but those in which participation precedes information. He argues against a linear view of time and for a permanent eschatology — that is, for an eschatology that emphasizes "the permanent presence of God as the one who challenges the world and shatters its complacency repeatedly" (*ibid.*, 26). Furthermore, he believes there are three parables that provide us with a key to the understanding of all the others, for they show the deep structure of the kingdom: the Treasure (Matt 13:44); the Pearl (Matt 13:45); and the Great Fish (*Gospel of Thomas*, Logion 8). Also, he divides the parables into three categories that correspond to the "three modes of the kingdom's temporality": (1) parables of advent; (2) parables of reversal; and (3) parables of action.

Crossan offers detailed analyses of the parables, usually favoring the *Gospel of Thomas* and ending up with shortened versions, after eliminating the introductions, the interpretations, and the conclusions that he thinks were added by the church. The parables of reversal, for example, are understood to have been changed into example stories by the early church. Creative reinterpretation of Jesus' parables by the primitive church, in fact, is a stated presupposition of Crossan's work (cf. *Parables*, 5), and so necessitates the work of scholarly reconstruction. The meanings that Crossan assigns to the parables are sometimes creative and helpful, but at other times are quite unconvincing — for example, his suggestion that the Parable of the Wicked Tenants is an immoral story about people who acted quickly on an opportunity (*ibid.*, 96).

In the decade between 1970 and 1980, "structuralist" approaches dominated the study of the parables, especially in the "Parables Seminar" of the Society of Biblical Literature and the early issues of *Semeia* (which is appropriately subtitled *An Experimental Journal for Biblical Criticism* and published by the SBL). Funk, Via, and Crossan were all participants in the Parables Seminar, and they have continued to be active in many of the later developments of parables research as well.

A structuralist approach to the parables is not concerned with historical meaning or the author's intent. Rather, structuralists seek to compare both the surface and the deep structures of the texts themselves, highlighting matters having to do with movements, motives, functions, oppositions, and resolutions within those texts. At times structuralist analyses have been suggestive. Most of the time, however, structuralist studies only dripped with technical jargon and provided little additional insight.

Not surprisingly, structuralism quickly faded from the scene. Norman Perrin's negative assessment was fully justified: "The contribution this [the literary-structuralist approach] may make to the understanding and interpretation of this or any parable is by no means either obvious or immediate" (*Jesus and the Language of the Kingdom*, 180, see also 181).

The work of Madeleine Boucher in *The Mysterious Parable* (1977), however, is quite unlike the mainstream of studies that take a literary approach. In my estimation, this brief book is one of the most significant treatments of the parables ever written. For from her expertise in literary criticism, she has provided a devastating critique of Jülicher, sane discussions of parable and allegory, and a helpful treatment of Mark's supposed theory on the purpose of parables in Mark 4.

Boucher argues, as does John Sider (see his *Interpreting the Parables* [1995]) and a number of other literary specialists, that allegory is not a literary genre at all, but a way of thinking. In one fell swoop, therefore, she sets aside all previous discussions that have attempted to distinguish between a parable and an allegory. She finds, in fact, nothing inherently objectionable about the presence of allegorical features in the parables of the Gospels, for parables can be either simple or complex and are often mysterious. And her explanation of the redactional shaping of Mark 4 and of the theology operative in that chapter is superb.

Other literary approaches today question the legitimacy of the distinction between an image and its object in the parables, as well as the search for a *tertium comparationis* (cf., e.g., H. Weder, *Die Gleichnisse Jesu als Metaphern* [Göttingen: Vandenhoeck & Ruprecht, 1978], 97). Such questioning is almost a by-product of an emphasis on the irreducibility of metaphor and parable. For if a metaphor cannot be reduced to non-metaphorical language, but must be participated in, one cannot set aside an image to find its object.

4. Studies Emphasizing Palestinian Culture and the Jewish Parables

From at least as early as C. A. Bugge (*Die Haupt-Parabeln Jesu* [Giessen: Ricker'sche Verlagsbuchhandlung, 1903]) and Paul Fiebig (*Altjüdische Gleichnisse und die Gleichnisse Jesu* [Tübingen: Mohr-Siebeck, 1904]; cf. also his *Die Gleichnisreden Jesu im Lichte der rabbinischen Gleichnisse des neutestamentlichen Zeitalters* [Tübingen: Mohr-Siebeck, 1912]), some scholars had argued for the importance of recognizing the Jewish origin of Jesus' parables. And in the last three decades this focus has received major attention from several directions.

J. Duncan M. Derrett, a specialist in ancient oriental law, is one scholar who has drawn attention to the importance of Palestinian culture for interpreting Jesus' parables. Derrett has published a number of articles — many of them on the parables — which seek to show the significance of first-century Jewish culture for an understanding of the New Testament generally (see his *Law in the New Testament* [London: Darton, Longman and Todd, 1976]; also his *Studies in the New Testament*, 2 vols. [Leiden: Brill, 1977, 1978]). Derrett's studies are never boring. He brings information from the rabbinic material and from a variety of other ancient sources in order to display attitudes and presumptions of the ancient Jews about such things as contracts, ownership issues, employer-employee relations, and social relations — that is, about the everyday situations from which the parables were formed. The material he presents is always helpful, though, it needs to be also noted, the conclusions he draws sometimes stretch credulity. Few, for example, would accept his view that the Parable of the Wicked Tenants alludes to the story of the expulsion from the garden in Genesis 3 (cf. *Law*, 310-12) or that the Parable of the Banquet is an artistic midrash on Zeph 1:1-16 (cf. *Law*, 126-29). Nonetheless, so much background material for the parables is brought together by Derrett that his work should not be ignored.

Another scholar who draws attention to Palestinian cultural features is Kenneth Bailey, who also engages in a detailed analysis of the literary structure of each parable that he treats (cf. *Finding the Lost: Cultural Keys to Luke 15* [St. Louis: Concordia, 1992]; see also his *Poet and Peasant: A Literary Cultural Approach to the Parables in Luke* [Grand Rapids: Eerdmans, 1976], and his *Through Peasant Eyes: More Lucan Parables, Their Culture and Style* [Grand Rapids: Eerdmans, 1980]). Bailey interprets the parables not only from research in ancient Jewish sources, but also from what he learned of the Palestinian mindset as a missionary in Lebanon and from examining Arabic and Syriac translations of the parables. Unfortunately, one cannot always assume that the attitudes and practices of modern, peasant life in either Lebanon or Palestinian are the same as they were in Jesus' day, or that such modern contexts should be taken as keys to the interpretation of Jesus' parables. Nonetheless, Bailey's work is valuable, even though it must be used with caution.

Quite different in their focus on Jewish origins are several works that directly compare ancient Jewish parables with those of Jesus. Asher Feldman (*The Parables and Similes of the Rabbis* [Cambridge: Cambridge University Press, 1924]) and W. O. E. Oesterley, (*The Gospel Parables in the Light of Their Jewish Background* [New York: Macmillan, 1936]), among others, did preliminary work in this area. To date, at least 1,500 rabbinic parables have been collected. And in the last two decades at least eight books have appeared that analyze these rabbinic parables and their relevance for an understanding of the parables of Jesus, with that of David Flusser (*Die rabbinischen Gleichnisse und der Gleichniserzähler Jesus,* Teil 1: *Das Wesen der Gleichnisse* [Bern: Peter Lang, 1981]) being the most significant.

Flusser's work, as well as that of the other scholars who focus on parables within Judaism, challenges the conclusions not only of Jülicher, but also of Jeremias, of reader-response approaches, and of much of contemporary New Testament scholarship. Flusser acknowledges that a thoroughgoing editing of Jesus' parables by the evangelists has taken place, but he is nonetheless optimistic about the reliability of the parables as they are set out in the Gospels. He argues (1) that the contexts of the parables are usually correct, and (2) that the introductions and conclusions to the parables are both necessary and usually derive from Jesus himself. He views the *Gospel of Thomas* as dependent on the Synoptic Gospels and as being unimportant for researching the words of Jesus. Furthermore, he asserts that the parables are not realistic, but pseudo-realistic — that is, that while Jesus' parables build on the features of everyday life, they go well beyond those everyday, realistic features in making their points.

Of the other studies that have recently been published analyzing Jewish parables vis-à-vis the parables of Jesus, the most important (in English) are those by Brad H. Young (*Jesus and His Jewish Parables* [New York: Paulist, 1989]), Harvey K. McArthur and Robert M. Johnston (*They Also Taught in Parables* [Grand Rapids: Zondervan, 1990]), and David Stern (*Parable in Midrash: Narrative and Exegesis in Rabbinic Literature* [Cambridge, MA: Harvard University Press, 1991]). Comparing the structure of Jesus' parables with the structure of the rabbinic parables reveals that explanations usually accompany not only the parables of Jesus but also those of the rabbis — which, of course, raises questions about the ease with which New Testament scholars have deleted the explanations in the Gospels. Stern, in fact, argues directly against Jülicher's notion, which has often been adopted by others, that parables do not require an interpretation. He rightly insists that no literature is self-interpreting (cf. his "Jesus' Parables from the Perspective of Rabbinic Literature," in *Parable and Story in Judaism,* ed. C. Thoma and M. Wyschogrod [New York: Paulist, 1989], 45-51).

Two words of caution, however, need to be expressed with regard to this "Jewish" approach to the study of the parables. The first has to do with some of the conclusions reached. Sometimes studies focusing on the Jewish parables find it necessary to go out of their way to defend against either an anti-Semitism or a disparagement of the Jewish parables, as if they were inferior. Given the insensitivity and hyperbole of some Christian scholars, this is not surprising and may be necessary.

A second word of caution regarding method needs also to be expressed. For while comparison with the rabbinic parables is absolutely necessary, numerous pitfalls exist in using the rabbinic materials. The most obvious problem, of course, is the late date of the rabbinic parables. Virtually no Jewish parables, other than those in the Old Testament and one found to date in the Dead Sea Scrolls, can be demonstrated to be older than the parables of Jesus, and so with rabbinic parables we are dealing with material that is later than the Gospels. Furthermore, while the rabbinic parables are similar in form and content to those of Jesus, unlike Jesus' parables they were used to support the rabbis' exegetical interpretations and explanations of Scripture. Suggestions of dependence between the rabbis and Jesus, or *vice versa,* should probably be ignored, for direct dependence in either direction is unlikely (see further the article by Craig A. Evans, "Parables in Early Judaism," in the present volume).

One other comment needs here also to be made. For while numerous studies exist on the relation of the Gospel parables to Jewish parables, relatively little has been done by way of studying Graeco-Roman parables and their relevance for our understanding of Jesus' parables. This is a serious lacuna that needs to be filled.

5. The Return of Allegory, Allegorizing, and Polyvalence

From approximately 1980 to the present, several discernible shifts have taken place in the study of the parables. Most of these have been influenced principally by literary criticism.

Somewhat surprisingly, allegory has resurfaced in a much more positive light. Craig Blomberg in *Interpreting the Parables* (1990), for example, argues that we need to recognize that Jesus' parables are allegories, and that a parable may have more than one correspondence between an image and the reality depicted. A parable, in fact, can be expected to have at least as many correspondences as it has main characters. His argument is legitimate, if one accepts that allegory is a literary genre. In my opinion, however, it is better to view allegory as a literary mode rather than a genre, and so to view parables as proportional analogies (as argued by Mary Ford, "Towards the Restoration of Allegory," and John W. Sider, *Interpreting the Parables*). Nonetheless, I agree that parables may be allegorical and have more than one point.

In several of his later writings, John Dominic Crossan has radically altered his earlier views on the parables and advocated a much more positive view of allegory. His appreciation for the usefulness of allegory, however, is quite different from that of Blomberg. For Crossan's concern is less with the question of correspondences and more with issues having to do with reader-response, in which a text's meaning is determined by the interaction of the reader with the text (see his *Cliffs of Fall* [New York: Seabury, 1980], esp. 96-97; and "Parable, Allegory, and Paradox," in *Semiology and the Parables*, ed. D. Patte [Pittsburgh: Pickwick, 1976], 247-81, esp. 271-78).

Increasingly Crossan has emphasized that parables are paradoxes and that they are polyvalent, capable of multiple meanings. For since they can be read in multiple contexts, they possess the capability of multiple meanings. Polyvalent narration reveals the play of the various plots across many levels of reality. Thus an interpreter of parables must be one who plays with a narrative in its various contexts, and the possibilities are without limit. This emphasis on polyvalence, which has become popular in the last few decades, is the fruit of seeds planted by Robert Funk and Dan Via, as well as, to some degree, by G. V. Jones.

In *Perspectives on the Parables* (Philadelphia: Fortress, 1979), Mary Ann Tolbert offers a defense of polyvalent interpretation that assists us in understanding the movement. For in that work she argues for multiple meanings on the basis of the fact that competent scholars, who use the same methods, have reached equally valid but different interpretations (*ibid.*, 30). She admits that the specific contexts of the Gospel parables limit their interpretation, but also notes that sometimes the Gospel writers themselves place the same parable in different contexts (*ibid.*, 52-55). She does not disparage the allegorizing exegesis that existed prior to the Enlightenment; on the contrary, she calls attention to the challenge and excitement that it provided ancient preachers (*ibid.*, 63-64). She views interpretation as a creative act, as an art rather than a skill. She also seeks to preserve the integrity of the parables, but at the same time to allow the interpreter to choose the particular context in which each of the parables is to be read (*ibid.*, 68-71) in order to "exploit" the polyvalency of the parable (*ibid.*, 93).

For example, on one reading, using the terms of Freudian psychology, Tolbert interprets the Parable of the Prodigal Son as speaking to the wish of every individual for harmony and unity within. The younger son corresponds to Freud's *id*, the elder brother to the *superego*, and the father to the *ego* (*ibid.*, 102-7). Alternatively, but still in line with Freud, she sees the parable as speaking about the painful nature of emotional ambivalence. The excessive love of the father betrays hostility toward the prodigal, while the anger of the elder brother is displaced onto the father. Both interpretations she views as being legitimate. Or to take another example, Daniel Patte offers three competing, but in his estimation equally valid, interpretations of the Parable of the Unforgiving Servant ("Bringing Out of the Gospel-Treasure What Is New and What Is Old: Two Parables in Matthew 18–23," *Quarterly Review* 10 [1990] 79-108). Clearly we have moved a long way from Jülicher. While Augustine might not have understood the interpretive conclusions, he would certainly have enjoyed the process!

A word of caution is necessary, for people use "polyvalence" in different ways. Craig Blomberg uses the term to point to a depth of meaning that is present in the parables, but he means by it reading the parables from the multiple perspectives of the characters within the stories. He is not interested in reading the parables in contexts other than those provided by the Gospel writers (see his "Poetic Fiction, Subversive Speech, and Proportional Analogy in the Parables," *Horizons in Biblical Theology* 18 [1996] 123). This is quite different from the way others, like Tolbert, use "polyvalence" to refer to multiple meanings the reader may assign parables from reading them in various contexts.

That Jesus' parables have depth, far-reaching implications, and are not reducible to simple explications are valid observations. But those who argue for polyvalent readings in various non-Gospel contexts have, it seems to me, not been reflective enough about their practice. For in adapting and retelling the parables in new contexts, they have ceased being hearers of the parables and have become tellers of the parables instead.

Susan Wittig's advocacy of polyvalent readings reveals what really is happening. She grants that the original teller of the Gospel parables had a meaning system in mind and that from the sender's [i.e., the author's] perspective multiple signifieds are wrong. Still, she argues that what was originally signified by the parable becomes a secondary signifier, which leads to multiple meanings. Her argument is: "From another, more objective point of view [i.e., other than the author's], what is demonstrated here is the ability to semantically alter a parabolic sign by embedding it within another belief-system and validating the new significance by reference to those beliefs" ("A Theory of Polyvalent Reading," in *SBL 1975 Seminar Papers*, vol. 2, ed. G. MacRae [Missoula: Scholars, 1975], 169-83; quotation from p. 177).

Embedding parables in another belief system was exactly what Augustine was doing. When one does this, however, one is no longer interpreting the parables of Jesus. One is, rather, reflecting on the significance of his parables in another system, however close or far away. Meditating on the parables is perfectly legitimate. But it is far different from discerning the intent of Jesus. Part of the difficulty is, of course, our multiple uses of the word "meaning." And it is for this reason that I prefer to talk about the "function" of the parables in the teaching of Jesus and of the "significance" of that function for us today.

6. Reduction to Banality

The charge of banality against many modern treatments of the parables — that is, of reducing the parables of Jesus to worn-out conventions or simplistic statements, with their messages being drearily predictable — is not new. It was leveled against Jülicher's pious religious maxims, and Norman Perrin spoke of the surprising banality of Dan Via's conclusions (cf. Perrin, *Jesus and the Language of the Kingdom*, 154). Indeed, Jülicher himself claimed that Jesus' parables were originally about "trifling matters," and that they had only been given more theological meanings by the evangelists (see his "Parables," *Encyclopedia Biblica* [New York: Macmillan, 1902], III. 3566). And tendencies to reduce the parables to the level of banality continue today.

One such example is Bernard B. Scott's *Hear Then the Parable* (1989), which is one of the more comprehensive treatments of the parables of the

Synoptic Gospels in recent years. Scott stands in the Jeremias tradition of reducing the parables to an earlier form. Unlike Jeremias, however, he does not seek the original words or *ipsissima verba* of Jesus, but the original structures or *ipsissima structura* of the parables. In his opinion, people did not memorize words; rather, when first hearing the parables they memorized structures. Like Jeremias, he views the *Gospel of Thomas* as an early and often superior source of the Jesus tradition.

Scott accepts that the parables as originally given had a number of allegorical features, though he seeks to remove the allegorical additions that he believes have been inserted by tradition. Allegorical features in the parables, he asserts, open them up to polyvalence. His method is first to analyze the "performance" of a parable by each evangelist as he works back to the simplest form. Second, he analyzes how the originating structure effects meaning; and third, he analyzes the parable's juxtaposition to the kingdom to discover how the parable challenges conventional wisdom.

The first part of Scott's book offers a number of helpful insights regarding parables in general. His interpretations, however, regularly reduce the parables to rather simplistic statements, which are often reminiscent of Jülicher's reduction of the parables to pious moralisms. In the end, one wonders — if, indeed, the intent of the parables was so evasive and general — why the stories were ever remembered. Why, it must be asked, was the Parable of the Pharisee and the Toll Collector ever remembered? In Scott's view, it is not an example story and has no lesson. Rather, it subverts the system that sees the kingdom of God in terms of the temple, and so places the holy outside the kingdom and the unholy inside the kingdom (*Hear Then the Parable*, 97). Likewise, the Parable of the Prodigal Son subverts the idea that the kingdom decides between the chosen and rejected, for the father rejects no one and both are chosen (*ibid.*, 125). And the Parable of the Wicked Tenants is understood to question whether the kingdom will go to the promised heirs, since *"in the plot the kingdom fails and the inheritance is in doubt"* (*ibid.*, 253, italics his).

Like Jülicher, Charles Hedrick explicitly says that Jesus' parables were banal and that it was the evangelists who inserted theological and kingdom significance into them in an attempt to make them relevant (cf. his *Parables as Poetic Fictions* [Peabody: Hendrickson, 1994]). Hedrick's views on the parables run counter to virtually all previous works. He argues that parables are not metaphors/symbols, that they do not reference the kingdom of God, and that they were poetic fictions that Jesus taught to stimulate thought. The specific circumstances of their original narration in the life of Jesus is irretrievably lost. The original stories were brief fictions that portrayed realistic aspects of first-century Palestinian life and were meant to be open to a range of possible meanings (*ibid.*, 3-8, 27, 35). The parables, therefore, are "potentially radical poetic fictions that competed with Judaism's paradigmatic narrative rigidity" (*ibid.*, 87).

With these assumptions, Hedrick proposes that the Parable of the Good Samaritan offers two responses to the injured man: the first, that of callous indifference; the second, outlandish benevolence. The first is wrong; the second is an impossible ideal. The parable is, in fact, a parody of the ideal of the righteous person in late Judaism (*ibid.*, 113, 115-16). The Parable of the Rich Fool, he believes, is about the laughingly inappropriate action of a rich man who tears down his barns when he should be harvesting. The parable is ultimately nihilistic and offers no hope, meaning, or theology (*ibid.*, 158-61). And with regard to the Parable of the Pharisee and the Toll Collector, the prayer of the toll collector assumes that one may rely on God's mercy without confession, repentance, or restitution. The reader is left with a frightening glimpse of two possible alternatives, neither of which is satisfying, and does not know in the end which person it is that God accepts (*ibid.*, 233-35).

William Herzog's *Parables as Subversive Speech* (Louisville: Westminster/John Knox, 1994) is quite different from the works of Scott and Hedrick, but the procedure and the results are much the same. Herzog assumes that the parables are not theological or moral stories, but political and economic ones. The scenes they present are codifications about how exploitation expressed itself in the ancient world. The work of Paulo Freire, the twentieth-century Brazilian pedagogue of the oppressed, is the lens that Herzog uses to read the New Testament parables. He sees Jesus using parables to present situations that were familiar to the rural poor and to encode the systems of oppression that controlled their lives and held them in bondage. The parables, therefore, were not a means of communicating theology and ethics, but of stimulating social analysis (*ibid.*, 27-28). They were discussion starters, and that is why the "conclusions" are often unsatisfying (*ibid.*, 259-61).

Since the parables are to be separated from their Gospel contexts, a new context must be found in which they are to be read. For Herzog it is the context of exploitation, a theory derived from his work on the Parable of the Vineyard Workers. The vineyard owner does not correspond to

God, but is a member of an oppressing elite class (*ibid.*, 96). In the Parable of the Wicked Tenants, the tenants are not wicked; rather, they are the original landowners who lost their land through usurpation and their action is an attempt to reassert their honorable status as heirs. In the end the parable codifies the futility of violence (*ibid.*, 112-13). The Parable of the Unforgiving Servant points to the hopelessness of looking for a messianic ruler and to the critical role played by "retainers" in an oppressive system. The parable proposes that neither the messianic hope nor the tradition of popular kingship can resolve the people's dilemma (*ibid.*, 148-49).

Undeniably, a number of recent studies have made helpful methodological contributions to an understanding of Jesus' parables. Nonetheless, the extent to which many modern critical approaches and assumptions have caused problems for parable interpretation is displayed by some recent interpretations of the Parable of the Widow and the Judge — all of which are liable to the charge of banality. Dan Via, for example, taking a Jungian approach, views this parable as presenting a problem in male psychology: The male ego refuses to respond to the anima, the archetype of a woman in a man's unconscious ("The Parable of the Unjust Judge: A Metaphor of the Unrealized Self," in *Semiology and Parables,* ed. D. Patte [Pittsburgh: Pickwick, 1976], 1-32). Herman Hendrickx applies the parable to the red tape and bureaucracy of today's society and to the bribery and venality of judges, as a result of which Christians should seek justice (*The Parables of Jesus* [San Francisco: Harper & Row, 1986], 231-32). Bernard Scott focuses on the widow's continued wearing down of the judge, viewing it as a metaphor for the kingdom — that is, it teaches that the kingdom keeps coming, keeps battering down opposition regardless of honor or justice, and may even come under the guise of shamelessness (*Hear Then the Parable,* 175-87). And Charles Hedrick argues that the parable presents the judge as a thoroughly honest man who in the end compromises his integrity for his own comfort, which should lead readers to reflect on the integrity of their own compromises (*Parables as Poetic Fictions,* 187-207).

More radically, William Herzog interprets the scene as a clear violation of Jewish legal practice, since only one judge is present. The widow refuses to be silent, and by her shameless behavior she achieves a just verdict. Thus, Herzog concludes, the oppressed must collude in their oppression for the system to work — and, by implication, suggests that they should refuse to accommodate to the system (*Parables as Subversive Speech,* 215-32). More radically still, Robert Price argues that this parable was originally an exemplary story and that it has been adulterated by Luke to keep women in submission. The parable, in his view, attests the bitterness of widows who have been mistreated by church officials. The unjust judge is the pastor, and the parable advises widows to get justice by the terrorism of nuisance (*The Widow Traditions in Luke-Acts: A Feminist-Critical Scrutiny* [Atlanta: Scholars, 1997], 191-201).

What is obvious in all of these attempts to interpret the Parable of the Widow and the Judge is that the more one cuts a parable from its contexts in the Gospels, the life of Jesus, and the theology of Israel, the more there exists a lack of control and the more subjectivity reigns. With the removal of the theology of the evangelists there has been introduced the ideology or sociology of the interpreter. Herzog asserted that it is "naive to assume that the form of any parable found in the Gospels coincides with the parable spoken by Jesus" (*Parables as Subversive Speech,* 46). But while, undoubtedly, the Gospel parables have been redactionally shaped by the evangelists, it seems far more naive to think that interpreters can abandon the Gospel contexts and ever hope to find the message of Jesus — particularly when correspondences exist between the parables and the non-parabolic teachings of Jesus. If the message of the parables is what many modern studies suggest, one wonders why the stories were ever originally told and — even more — why they were ever remembered.

7. Concluding Reflections

We have come full circle. For if the patristic and medieval interpreters allegorized the parables by reading into them their own theologies, modern scholarship is no less guilty in reading into them its own agenda. We have gone from allegorizing to allegorizing — in some cases, straying today even further from hearing the voice of Jesus. In fact, if some of the assumptions of our contemporary, more radical interpreters are correct, the average person surely cannot read the parables and come to an understanding of them. This is not to castigate everything done by interpreters today, for in many ways much good work has been done and many insights have been achieved — particularly, we believe, by scholars who have paid attention to the context of Jesus' ministry and to parallels that exist in the Jewish parables.

We stand at a time when, for all our modern insights into how figurative speech works, we need to readdress issues of method. Jülicher was certainly correct to react to the theological allegorizing of the church. A similar reaction, however, is needed against the sociological and ideological allegorizing of today. The blunder that Jülicher made in his assessment of allegory needs to be set aside. But also several questions of method deserve better answers than we have been given.

One of the important questions for current interpreters concerns the contexts in which the parables of Jesus have been placed by the evangelists. Clearly, many of Jesus' parables (but not all) would have been told several times. So we should probably not think of only one specific occasion for the telling of each of the parables. And to the degree that this is true, we should give up attempts to reconstruct a parable's original form.

The parables are stories with an intent in the context of Jesus' ministry, though they also have been framed by the evangelists to speak to the situations that they addressed. It is legitimate, therefore, to ask: To what degree in reading the parables do we see Jesus' intent and to what degree do we see the situation of the early church? But if the general contexts in which the evangelists have placed the parables are totally unreliable, I see little hope of finding the intent of Jesus.

Equally important are the explanations that often come at the conclusion of the parables. Is this common feature of Old Testament and Jewish parables true also of Jesus' parables, or were his parables left imprecise and without any clear indication of their intent? Do we hear in these explanations the voice of the church or the voice of Jesus?

Contemporary New Testament scholarship rightly resists the idea that the parables are reducible to abstract explanations, as if the stories could be distilled and then discarded. At the same time, the parables do point beyond themselves to other realities and can be explained in non-figurative speech — which is what all scholars attempt to do in writing books and articles on the parables. How do we do justice to the "language event" character of the parables, retain their force, and yet understand the theology they express without reducing them to pious (or not so pious) moralisms? The parables have an unquestionable depth. How can we legitimately appreciate their "field of meaning" within the intent of Jesus without turning them into polyvalent modeling clay?

That the parables are artistic and poetic must never be denied. Equally important, however, is the conviction that they are also historically and contextually based. In 1977 Madeleine Boucher had the good sense to say: "If the poetic structures in the parables became dominant, their power to achieve an effect in the hearer would then be lost" (*Mysterious Parable*, 16). Sadly, that has happened all too often. The parables derive their meaning from Jesus who told them, and they cannot legitimately be understood apart from the context of his ministry.

Can interpreters do justice to the variety of forms in Jesus' parabolic teaching? Frequently the category "parable" has been defined by a small number of examples. Such a practice, however, predetermines how other forms are assessed and interpreted. Peter Dschulnigg is correct to complain that previous parable theories have been shaped too little from the parables of Jesus themselves ("Positionen des Gleichnisverständnisses im 20. Jahrhundert," *Theologische Zeitschrift* 45 [1989] 347). Related to this is the question of realism: To what degree are the parables realistic, everyday occurrences, and to what degree are they pseudo-realistic, extravagant, or unrealistic? If predetermined to be realistic, any item not fitting the norm will be found offensive and excluded.

I am painfully aware of studies, both general and specialized, that have been omitted from our present survey — for example, the six volumes on the parables produced in 1835 by Edward Greswell (Jülicher was not the first to do a serious study of the parables), or modern studies by Jack Kingsbury, Charles Carlston, John Donahue, Jan Lambrecht, and numerous others. An enormous amount of work has been done on the parables. One might be tempted to say, as Geraint Jones did in 1964, "I doubt, moreover, if many further lines of interpretation can be explored than those which have already been established" (*Art and Truth of the Parables*, x). But that would be as wrong now as it was then, for work will and should continue. Perhaps, however, we have provided enough perspective so as not to repeat the errors of previous interpreters and to appreciate more fully something of the depth of Jesus' intent in these relentlessly engaging stories.

Selected Bibliography

Blomberg, Craig L. *Interpreting the Parables.* Downers Grove: InterVarsity, 1990.

————. "The Parables of Jesus: Current Trends and Needs in Research," in *Studying the Historical Jesus: Evaluations of the State of the Current*

Research, ed. B. D. Chilton and C. A. Evans. Leiden: Brill, 1994, 231-54.

Boucher, Madeleine. *The Mysterious Parable*. Washington: Catholic Biblical Association of America, 1977.

Dodd, C. H. *The Parables of the Kingdom*. London: Nisbet, 1936.

Flusser, David. *Die rabbinischen Gleichnisse und der Gleichniserzähler Jesus*. Teil 1: *Das Wesen der Gleichnisse*. Bern: Peter Lang, 1981.

Fuchs, Ernst. *Studies of the Historical Jesus*. Naperville: Allenson, 1964.

Funk, Robert W. *Language, Hermeneutic, and Word of God*. New York: Harper & Row, 1966.

Jeremias, Joachim. *The Parables of Jesus*. London: SCM; New York: Scribner's, 1963.

Jones, Geraint Vaughn. *The Art and Truth of the Parables*. London: SPCK, 1964.

Jülicher, Adolf. *Die Gleichnisreden Jesu*, 2 vols. Freiburg: Akademische Verlagsbuchhandlung von J. C. B. Mohr, 1888, 1899.

Kissinger, Warren S. *The Parables of Jesus*. Metuchen, NJ: Scarecrow, 1979.

Perrin, Norman. *Jesus and the Language of the Kingdom*. Philadelphia: Fortress, 1976.

Scott, Bernard Brandon. *Hear Then the Parable: A Commentary on the Parables of Jesus*. Minneapolis: Fortress, 1989.

Stein, Robert H. *An Introduction to the Parables of Jesus*. Philadelphia: Westminster, 1981.

Via, Dan Otto, Jr. *The Parables*. Philadelphia: Fortress, 1967.

Wailes, Stephen L. *Medieval Allegories of Jesus' Parables*. Berkeley: University of California Press, 1987.

CHAPTER 2

The Genre of the Parables

ROBERT H. STEIN

THE STUDY OF THE PARABLES of Jesus has gone through a number of phases, focused on a number of issues, and developed a number of diverse methodologies. It is important, therefore, to understand how the genre "parable" has been defined during the past century and to clarify the nature of the parables as they appear in the Synoptic Gospels.

1. The Modern Discussion

The modern discussion of parables and of the genre "parable" was introduced by Adolf Jülicher in 1888 in his two-volume *Die Gleichnisreden Jesu.* In treating Jesus' parables, Jülicher followed Aristotle's *Rhetoric* in dividing this literary form into (1) "similitude" *(Gleichnis)*, (2) "parable" in the narrow sense *(Parabel)*, and (3) "exemplary story" *(Beispielerzählung)*. A similitude he defined as a brief narrative of a typical, real-life event, which is usually told in the present tense. Examples of this he found in Mark 4:21-22 ("the Light Hidden under a Basket"), Mark 4:26-29 ("the Seed Growing by Itself"), Luke 15:4-10 ("the Lost Sheep and the Lost Coin"), and Matt 24:32-33 ("the Fig Tree"). He defined a parable as a fictitious narrative involving a particular, one-time event or situation. Examples of this he found in Luke 15:11-32 ("the Prodigal Son"), Matt 20:1-16 ("the Workers in the Vineyard"), and Matt 25:14-30 ("the Talents"). Unlike similitudes, parables are usually told in the past tense. An example story Jülicher de-

30

fined as a story that functions as a model for correct behavior. He found four of these in the Gospels: Luke 10:30-35 ("the Good Samaritan"); Luke 12:16-21 ("the Rich Fool"); Luke 16:19-31 ("the Rich Man and Lazarus"); and Luke 18:10-14 ("the Pharisee and the Tax Collector").

This sharp distinction between similitudes and parables, however, has rightly been called into question as being somewhat arbitrary. Some similitudes could easily be classed as parables, while some parables could be labeled similitudes. For example, are Matt 7:24-27 ("the Wise and Foolish Builders") and Luke 11:5-8 ("the Friend at Midnight") similitudes or parables? Common to all of Aristotle's three subspecies of this literary genre is the comparison made between two unlike things.

Jülicher also followed Aristotle (*Rhetoric* 2.20) in equating fables with parables (*Gleichnisreden Jesu* 1.98). The issue of whether fables should be included in the genre of parables ultimately centers on how one defines "fable." For if one defines a fable broadly as a narrative that sheds light on human experience or behavior, then fables are very much like parables (cf. Beavis, "Parable and Fable," 473-98). But if one uses the more common definition of a fable as being a story about animals, plants, or inanimate objects, then equating fables with parables in the New Testament is illegitimate, since there are no such animal or plant stories in the teachings of Jesus. Two clear examples of fables, of course, are to be found in the Old Testament, in Judg 9:8-15 and 2 Kings 14:9. And though neither is specifically referred to as a *mashal* or parable, they both should be considered as such. Nonetheless, if we determine our definition and understanding of the genre of the parables from the New Testament, then fables cannot be included.

A major contribution of Jülicher involved his discussion of the difference between parables and allegories. He defined a parable as being an extended simile, whereas an allegory was a series of extended metaphors. Because a parable was an extended simile, Jülicher concluded that it could contain only a single point of comparison. In interpreting a parable, therefore, one should not search for various meanings, but for *the* meaning. Details in a parable simply provide local color and interest. They do not possess meaning in themselves, but only contribute to *the* meaning of the text. Consequently, they contain no point of comparison. On the other hand, an allegory incorporates numerous metaphors that possess various meanings. And each of these metaphors with its respective meaning can and should be interpreted.

For Jülicher, therefore, the parables of Jesus are to be seen as extended similitudes that possess only a single point of comparison or *tertium comparationis*. When he came across allegorical details in the parables, he attributed them to the early church and not to Jesus. Parables are furthermore to be understood as being self-explanatory. They are themselves interpretations, and so should be seen as aids to understanding (*Gleichnisreden Jesu* 1.73). Thus there is no need to interpret them. In fact, any parable that requires interpretation would be an extremely poor one, and so would totally fail in its purpose (*ibid.*, 1.74). Allegories, on the other hand, have to be decoded. For whereas parables illuminate, allegories disguise.

Jülicher's absolute distinction between parables and allegories is generally not accepted today. Literature, like reality, does not fit into neat, arbitrary categories. What we find, instead, is a continuum between "single point parables" and "detailed allegories." In between there exist parables and story-like comparisons that contain allegorical details, which, while not detailed allegories, are also not simple parables.

Jülicher himself acknowledged that some parables in the Gospels possess allegorical details, but he attributed all of these details to the work of the early church. Nevertheless, the fact of the presence of such allegorical details in some of the Gospel parables indicates that "parables" and "allegories" — at least in the mind of the early church — were not viewed as being radically different or separate literary forms. And there is no reason to assume that Jesus saw them as separate and mutually exclusive literary forms either.

As for the claim that parables are self-explanatory and antithetical to interpretations, we need to note that the teasing nature of some parables suggests that at times they function as riddles. Riddles are not always self-evident. Nonetheless, parables serve well as riddles even when they have to be explained, as Nathan's parable in rebuke of David illustrates (cf. 2 Sam 12:1-4 for the parable and 12:5-13 for the explanation). The Old Testament contains a number of such riddle parables that are then explained (cf. 2 Sam 14:6-7 [8-21]; 1 Kings 20:39-40 [41-42]; Isa 5:1-6 [7]; Ezek 15:2-5 [6-8]; 17:2-10 [11-21]; see also Judg 9:7-15 [16ff.]; 2 Kings 14:9 [10]). Likewise, the New Testament has many parables that appear with an accompanying interpretation (cf. Mark 3:23-26 [27]; 4:3-9 [13-20]; 4:21 [22]; 4:24 [25]; 7:14-15 [18-23]; 12:1-9 [10-11]; 13:28 [29], 34 [32-33, 35-37]; Matt 11:16-17 [18-19]; 13:24-30 [37-43], 47-48 [49-50]; 18:23-34

[35]; 20:1-15 [16]; 21:28-31a [31b-32]; 22:11-13 [14]; 25:1-12 [13]; Luke 4:23b [23c]; 7:41-42 [43-47]; 10:30-35 [36-37]; 11:5-7 [8]; 12:16-20 [21], 35-38 [40], 39 [40]; 13:25-27 [28-30]; 14:8-10 [11], 28-30 [33], 31-32 [33]; 15:4-6 [7], 8-9 [10]; 16:1-8a [8b-13]; 17:7-9 [10]; 18:2-6 [1, 7-8], 9-14a [9, 14b]; 19:12-27 [11]).

Regardless of whether one views some, most, or all of the interpretations in the Gospels as secondary, their presence indicates that at least some early interpreters of Jesus' parables saw such appended interpretations as not being impossible, unnecessary, or contrary to the genre of parables. For them, it seems, they were integral parts of the parables. Furthermore, it should be noted that rabbinic parables frequently are — and, in fact, often need to be — followed by interpretations. Thus the view that interpretations are antithetical to the genre of parables turns out to be a theoretical bias that has been belied in practice.

The threefold division of parables into "similitudes," "parables" in the narrow sense, and "exemplary stories" has been followed by a number of writers. Bultmann, for example, used Jülicher's categories, although he subdivided the first (i.e., similitudes) into three parts: "figurative sayings" or *Bildwörter* (e.g., Mark 4:21-22, "the Light Hidden under a Basket"; Matt 5:14, "a City Set on a Hill"); "metaphors" (e.g., Matt 7:3-5, "the Speck and the Log"; Matt 7:13-14, "the Narrow Gate"); and "similitudes" proper (e.g., Mark 4:26-29, "the Seed Growing Secretly"; Luke 15:4-10, "the Lost Sheep and the Lost Coin"). Bultmann's final two categories are "parables" (e.g., Luke 15:11-32, "the Prodigal Son"; Matt 20:1-16, "the Workers in the Vineyard"; Matt 25:14-30, "the Talents") and "exemplary stories" (i.e., Luke 10:30-37, "the Good Samaritan"; Luke 12:16-21, "the Rich Fool"; Luke 16:19-31, "the Rich Man and Lazarus"; Luke 18:10-14, "the Pharisee and the Tax Collector"). These categories correspond exactly with those of Jülicher. In fact, many of the parables listed by Bultmann as examples of these two last categories are the same as listed by Jülicher (*History of the Synoptic Tradition,* 166-79).

C. H. Dodd also followed Jülicher and grouped the parables of the Gospels into three main categories: "figurative sayings" or simple metaphors (e.g., Matt 5:14, "a City Set on a Hill"; Matt 15:14, "a Blind Man Guiding a Blind Man"; Luke 12:33, "Purses that Do Not Wear Out"); "similitudes" (e.g., Mark 4:21-22, "the Light Hidden under a Basket"; Mark 13:28-29, "the Fig Tree"; Matt 7:3-5, "the Speck and the Log"); and "parables proper" (e.g., Luke 15:4-10, "the Lost Sheep and the Lost Coin";

Luke 15:11-32, "the Prodigal Son"; Matt 20:1-16, "the Workers in the Vineyard"). Although Dodd refers to these three categories of parables in the same way as Jülicher and Bultmann, even using the German names *Gleichnis* and *Parabel* for the latter two (*Parables of the Kingdom*, 5-7), he defines them a bit differently and sometimes includes in one category materials that Jülicher and Bultmann included in another. Dodd clearly saw that the categories or classes into which one divides the parables were somewhat arbitrary, noting that "it cannot be pretended that the line can be drawn with any precision between these classes of parable — figurative sayings, similitudes, and parables proper" (*ibid.*, 7).

Whereas Dodd accepted a certain amount of arbitrariness in the classification of the parables according to the categories of Greek rhetoric, with every proposed category possessing a degree of fluidity, it was Joachim Jeremias who questioned this whole procedure. More than Jülicher, Bultmann, or Dodd, Jeremias recognized that the parables of Jesus were rooted in a Jewish milieu. So he argued that the categories drawn from Aristotle do not fit well the parables of Jesus. And because of the broad nature of the Hebrew *mashal*, which the Greek Old Testament (the Septuagint) and the Greek New Testament translate as "parable," Jeremias viewed any attempt to fit Jesus' parables into the categories of Greek rhetoric as "fruitless labour in the end" (*Parables of Jesus*, 20). All such attempts result in forcing on them a different and foreign literary genre.

2. A New Approach

In the latter third of the twentieth century the historical paradigm governing parable study gave way to a new approach. Dodd and Jeremias had focused attention on the study of the parables in light of the situation of Jesus (i.e., the first *Sitz im Leben*). And redaction critics had studied them in light of the situation of the evangelists (i.e., the third *Sitz im Leben*). But these historical interests were swept aside by the new approach, which advocated a literary rather than a historical paradigm.

Furthermore, this new approach was wedded to an existential philosophy and to a deconstructionist and/or reader-oriented hermeneutic. As Richard Eslinger notes: "The watershed in parables research derived from modern literary analysis which located parable within the range of metaphor" ("Preaching the Parables," 27). Consequently, the genre of the parables was understood not as a vehicle that served to bear the meaning of its author, but as an ontological entity that could not be interpreted or broken down into a meaning component. As metaphors, parables could not be reduced to an interpretation or an illustration. For as ontological entities, they are irreducible.

"Metaphors" and "parables" (the latter understood as a subset of metaphor) were also sharply distinguished from "similes" and "allegories" (the latter understood as a subset of simile). Previously, little difference had been seen between metaphors and similes other than the use of the particles "like" or "as." Aristotle had said: "The simile is a metaphor, for there is very little difference" (*The Art of Rhetoric*, 1.406b). And Quintilian asserted: "On the whole metaphor is a shorter form of simile" (*Institutio Oratoria*, 8.6.8). Now, however, an enormous chasm was seen as separating these two literary forms, with each of them functioning in radically different ways. Thus similes and allegories, which were claimed to operate on a lower level, were seen as merely describing and bearing information, being dead illustrations that presuppose understanding. Metaphors and parables, on the other hand, which were claimed to be living and transforming entities, were viewed as actually creating understanding and meaning.

In this new approach a metaphor and a parable are attributed unusual power, being almost divine-like in quality. Simile and allegory, because they deal with what is expressible, can be reduced to literal and abstract interpretations. But metaphor and parable are untranslatable because they deal with the inexpressible. They are not simply illustrations or bearers of meaning. They do not enhance or convey meaning. On the contrary, they interpret their readers! They create meaning by forcing the reader to participate in the parabolic event.

Understood in this manner, one experiences a language event in the reading of a parable. A person cannot study or seek to understand a parable. One can only experience it. Metaphor and parable are furthermore not simply *one way* of human knowing; rather, they are *the* way (cf. McFague TeSelle, *Speaking in Parables*, 62). They are the basic forms of all thought and language (*ibid.*, 52). Thus because of its almost ontological power, one does not simply read a parable. One "risks" it. For when one enters into the world of a parable, one is confronted with a reversal of expectations and compelled to respond. One "loses control" and is "torn apart" by a parable. In fact, when people are confronted by a parable they find that it "shatters their world," "calls existence into question," and "causes them to risk all."

Another consequence of this new approach to parables is the rejection of the idea that a parable possesses a single meaning. As literary works, parables are self-standing works of art that possess lives of their own. They possess power and beauty within themselves independent of their origin and are capable of creating many new "meanings" or language events. This independent nature of the parables is often described by such terms as "autonomous," "autotelic," "polyvalent," or "plurisignificant." A parable, therefore, cannot be limited to a single, correct meaning, but each parable through its regenerating power produces many different, but equally acceptable, impacts on a reader.

Much of the modern discussion of metaphor and parable is adorned with so much hyperbole and existentialist terminology that it is difficult to understand what is actually being said or meant. As a result, as Claus Westermann observes, "the simplicity of the parables is often no longer recognizable in the lofty heights of the abstract language of [the] . . . interpretation" (*Parables of Jesus*, 178-79). Frequently modern discussions reveal a great deal more about the proponents of these views than about the nature of a metaphor or a parable — or about how the original authors used them.

Yet is a parable really able to interpret us? How can an inanimate text interpret anyone or anything? What does it mean "to interpret?" Is interpretation not an aspect of thought and thinking? Can inanimate texts do this? The new approach clearly has attributed to an inanimate literary form an exclusively human characteristic — that is, the ability to interpret. On the other hand, if we explain the statement "metaphors interpret us" as a "personified metaphor," what do we mean by this new metaphor? Are we not, then, explaining one abstruse metaphor ("parables interpret us"), which we have used to explain another metaphor (which in the case of the biblical parables is far less abstruse), by still another metaphor ("personified metaphor")?

Much of the confusion in past discussions of the parables of Jesus appears to be due to the dual nature of communication. For all communication, whether oral or literary, involves both referential and commissive dimensions. Whereas the former is primarily informative in nature, the latter is primarily affective. And whereas the former seeks mainly to convey information, the latter seeks to convey emotion and bring about decision. No form of communication is simply informative or purely affective. Even an accountant's most sterile analysis and statistical report of people killed in automobile accidents during a certain period can affect people deeply, particularly if they have suffered a personal loss through one or more such accidents. Similarly, the most hyperbolic, metaphorical love poem does not only affect the reader but it also conveys information — at least this: that the poet loves the addressee of the poem!

The new approach is correct, in part, when it asserts that a parable cannot be reduced to an interpretation. Parables do not simply convey meaning. Nor do they simply clarify and illustrate. On the other hand, the new approach is incorrect when it claims that we cannot interpret a parable. It has been said that a parable, like a joke, cannot be explained. But a joke can be explained! Of course, the effectiveness of any joke is lost when it needs to be explained. Nevertheless, what a joke is seeking to say and do can be explained. What is being confused is the *meaning* of a joke and/or a parable (the referential dimension) and its *affective nature* (the commissive dimension). As Mary Ann Tolbert insists, we can and must interpret the parables (*Perspectives on the Parables*, 42).

A parable is both a vehicle and a message, and as such it possesses both informative and affective dimensions. Interpreters in the past have often so concentrated on the informative dimension that they lost sight of the powerful, affective nature of this literary form. An interpretation that begins "This parable means . . . ," if correct, can convey the meaning of a parable, but it cannot convey its affective dimension. It omits the commissive aspect and simply elucidates the parable's message in a didactic manner. Such barren and sterile referential language cannot convey the persuasive nature of the form of that message. Presently, however, this latter, affective dimension of a parable is being so emphasized by the new approach that the former, informative aspect is ignored and even denied.

Yet some advocates of the modern approach seem to be saying far more than that metaphor and parable are powerful literary forms. They appear, in fact, to attribute to this form itself the abilities and powers that traditionally have been associated with God himself. As John Donahue aptly observes: "The impression arises that at times salvation comes from metaphor alone!" (*Gospel in Parable*, 11). Yet can a parable really "transform?" Can it force its hearers to "risk" the parable, to "respond," to force them to participate in a language event? If a parable or a metaphor, in and of itself, can do this, how then can we have "dead" metaphors and parables? Why do not all metaphors and parables, since they possess this same literary form, equally transform and interpret their hearers? And why does not the same parable produce exactly the same effect on each hearer?

It is not a literary form *per se* that transforms hearers or produces in them a response. Rather, such effects are the result of the combination of (1) the persuasive and disarming nature of the literary form, (2) the truth of the divine message encapsulated in that form, (3) the convicting work of God's Spirit working through the particular vehicle and message, and (4) a human response. All of these factors in combination bring about transformation and "event." And of these factors, the literary form must be judged to be the most dispensable. For transformation and "event" can also take place through such forms as a command (e.g., Josh 24:15), an allegory (e.g., Mark 12:1-12), a prose portion (e.g., John 3:1ff.), or didactic material (e.g., Rom 3:21-31) — as long as the truthful nature of the message encapsulated in a particular literary form and the convicting work of God's Spirit working through that vehicle and message are present!

Parables function in two ways. They enhance communication and they assist persuasion — that is, they possess a referential dimension and a commissive dimension. They perform the latter by disarming their hearers and by piercing through defenses and resistance. They can do this because the analogy in a parable is different from the sensitive reality with which it is dealing. Through a parable Nathan was able to discuss the issue of David's murder of Uriah and his adultery with Uriah's wife, for the reality part of the parable was only recognized after the parable had been told and explained. How far would Nathan have gotten if he had said to David: "O King, I would like to talk to you about your adultery with Bathsheba and your murder of Uriah"? The nature of a parable, however, enabled the prophet to speak to David about both his adultery and his murder. For disarmed by the innocuous nature of the parable, David was open to judge honestly the issue at hand. And he found out too late that he was the man — that he was the one who, with his teeming flocks, had stolen another man's one ewe lamb!

3. The Basic Issue

Discussion of the genre of a parable in the abstract can lead only to arbitrary definitions of what one thinks a parable is and how it should function. On the other hand, if we seek to define the genre more objectively along the lines of how such classical writers as Aristotle or Quintilian understood a parable, we will again arrive at somewhat arbitrary definitions. Certainly to speak of the New Testament parables as autonomous, aesthetic works of art totally ignores their intimate tie with the one who told these parables. Christians over the centuries have not been interested in Jesus' parables because they have been enamored with anything so abstract as their literary genre. Rather, they have read, studied, investigated, and prayed over these parables precisely because they are the parables *of Jesus!*

Once we decide that we are interested in investigating the parables of Jesus, it becomes apparent that we are investigating the parables of one who lived and thought in a world governed by the Old Testament. Jesus' understanding of this genre was shaped by the Old Testament and early rabbinic *mashalim*, rather than by the Greco-Roman *fabellae* (cf. Beavis, "Parable and Fable," 493). And even if we grant a strong Hellenistic influence on the Palestinian culture of Jesus' day, the most direct influence on Jesus' understanding of the genre of the parables came from the Old Testament. It is, therefore, to this Old Testament influence that we must now turn.

4. The Genre of Parable in the Old Testament

The term used in the New Testament to describe the parables of Jesus is the Greek term *parabolē*. Yet while Jesus probably both understood and spoke Greek, his mother tongue was Aramaic. Thus to understand Jesus' use of parables we must focus on the Aramaic term that Jesus used, understand its semantic range, and come to appreciate how the genre described by that term functioned.

The Aramaic term that Jesus used (as in Mark 4:30; 13:28; Luke 4:23), which lies behind the Greek term *parabolē* found in the Gospels, is *mashal*. We know this because whenever the term *parabolē* appears in the Greek translation of the Hebrew Old Testament it translates the Hebrew *mashal*, except in Eccl 1:17. (In 2 Sam 23:3 and Ezek 19:14 the translators of the Septuagint apparently erred in using *parabolē* to translate a different Hebrew word that has the same consonants [*mashal*], but which means "to rule.") It becomes immediately apparent when one observes how *mashal* is used in the Old Testament that any simple definition of this genre ignores its breadth of meaning. In the Old Testament a *mashal* can refer to:

A Maxim or Proverb

"Like mother, like daughter." (Ezek 16:44)
"'Out of the wicked comes forth wickedness.'" (1 Sam 24:13 [24:14
in the Hebrew Bible and the LXX])

Cf. also 1 Sam 10:12; 1 Kings 4:32 (5:12 in the Hebrew Bible and the LXX);
Eccl 12:9; Ezek 12:22-23; 18:2-3. Other examples of a *mashal* serving as a
maxim or proverb in which the term is not translated by *parabolē* in the
Septuagint, but which nevertheless help us understand this use of *mashal*,
are: Job 13:12; Prov 1:1; 10:1; 25:1; 26:7, 9.

A Byword or Taunt

"You shall become an object of horror, a byword / taunt [*mashal*],
and a thing of ridicule among all the peoples where the LORD will
lead you." (Deut 28:37)
"You have made us a byword [*mashal*] among the nations, a laugh-
ingstock among the peoples." (Ps 44:14 [44:15 in the Hebrew Bible
and 43:15 in the LXX])

Other examples are: 2 Chron 7:20; Ps 69:11 (69:12 in the Hebrew Bible;
68:12 in the LXX); Jer 24:9; Mic 2:4; and Hab 2:6. Additional examples in
which *mashal* is not translated by *parabolē* in the Septuagint are Num
21:27-30; 1 Kings 9:7; Isa 14:3-4; and Ezek 14:8.

A Riddle

"I will open my mouth in a parable [*mashal* in the sense of a riddle];
I will utter dark sayings from of old." (Ps 78:2 [77:2 in the LXX])
"I will incline my ear to a proverb [*mashal* used in the sense of rid-
dle]; I will solve my riddle to the music of the harp." (Ps 49:4 [49:5
in the Hebrew Bible and 48:5 in the LXX])

Cf. also Prov 1:6 and Ezek 17:2ff. where *mashal* is a synonym for riddle.

A Parable

We find numerous examples of parables in the narrow sense in the Old Testament. As in the case of many of Jesus' parables where the term *parabolē* is not used (cf., e.g., Matt 18:23-35; 20:1-16; 25:1-13; Luke 10:30-35; 15:11-32; 16:1-8), so here the term *mashal* does not appear. Nevertheless, it is clear that the following parables are examples of *mashalim*: 2 Sam 12:1-4 (5-7), which can also be defined as a riddle; 14:6-7 (8-21); 1 Kings 20:39-40 (41-42); Isa 5:1-6 (7); 28:24-28; Ezek 15:1-5 (6-8); and Ezek 21:9-17.

An Allegory

Examples of allegory that are described by *mashal* and *parabolē* in the Hebrew and Greek Bibles are Ezek 17:2-10 (11-21), 20:45-49 [21:1-5 in the Hebrew Bible and the LXX], and 24:2-5. Other examples in which *mashal* and *parabolē* are not used but which nevertheless belong to this genre are Ezek 19:2-9, 10-14; 23:2-21.

Additional Dimensions of the Term 'Mashal'

A *mashal* in the Hebrew Old Testament, as well as a *parabolē* in the LXX, also designates "figurative discourses" (cf. Num 23:7-10, 18-24; 24:3-9, 15-19, 20, 21-22, 23-24), odes or poems (cf. Ps 49:4 [49:5 in the Hebrew Bible; 48:5 in the LXX]; 78:2 [77:2 in the LXX]), and "fables" (cf. Judg 9:7-15 [16ff.]; 2 Kings 14:9 [10]). In the last two examples the terms *mashal* and *parabolē* do not appear.

5. The Parables of Jesus

The parables of Jesus in the Gospels exhibit a similar breadth and semantic range of meaning as found in the Old Testament *mashal*. This is hardly surprising. Rather, it is what we should expect. For since the most formative influences in the life of Jesus were the Hebrew Scriptures (cf. Matt 5:17) and the Jewish world of the first century as shaped by those Scriptures, it is only natural that Jesus' understanding of a parable would follow the lines of the Old Testament *mashal*. Thus we find that the parables of Jesus include the following:

Maxims or Proverbs

> "He also told them a parable: 'Can a blind person guide a blind person? Will not both fall into a pit?'" (Luke 6:39)
> "Doubtless you will quote to me this proverb [*parabolē*], 'Doctor, cure yourself!'" (Luke 4:23)

Additional examples can be found in Mark 3:23-25 and 7:15-17. Cf. also Matt 6:22-23; 7:12, 17-18; 15:11; Mark 2:21, 22; and Luke 9:62 where the term *parabolē* does not appear, but which are nevertheless parables. Whereas a parable can be a proverb, this does not mean that every proverb can be classified as a parable. Only those proverbs in which a comparison of unlike things is found should be included in the genre "parable." Thus such passages as Matt 6:21, 34; 16:25; and Mark 6:4, while assuredly proverbs, are not parables.

Similes and Metaphors

In the Gospels we encounter numerous examples of similes and metaphors on the lips of Jesus. Although the new approach to parables has attributed a significant ontological difference to these two literary forms, the only literary difference between them is that in a simile there is an explicit comparison made that uses "like," "as," "as if," "seems," etc., whereas in a metaphor the comparison is implicit. Despite the claims made by the new approach for the separateness of these two literary forms, there seems to be little difference between a simile and a metaphor. The difference between "Jesus, as the Good Physician, went about healing the sick" and "The Good Physician went about healing the sick" is only the words "Jesus, as." The lack of these words does not cause the metaphor to "interpret" us or make us experience a "language event" any more than if these two words were present and the saying was a simile.

Although we do not find any similes or metaphors specifically called *parabolē* in the Gospels, the following could easily be referred to as parables:

(1) Simile

"See, I am sending you out like sheep into the midst of wolves; so be wise as serpents and innocent as doves" (Matt 10:16);

(2) Metaphor

"You are the light of the world." (Matt 5:14)

Should we include among the parables of Jesus every simile and every metaphor that he uttered? Basic to the genre of *mashal* and *parabolē* is the idea of a comparison between unlike things, and similes and metaphors are comparisons of unlike things! Leaving aside similitudes, which are extended similes, it may therefore be said that there are over sixty-seven examples of similes and metaphors in the Gospels (cf. Stein, *Method and Message of Jesus' Teachings,* 14-17).

Riddles

There are no examples in the Gospels of bywords or taunts such as found in the Old Testament. Nonetheless, the riddle-like nature of some of Jesus' parables is quite apparent.

"There is nothing outside a person that by going in can defile, but the things that come out are what defile." (Mark 7:15)

The lack of strict boundaries between the various classifications of parables in the Gospels can be seen by the fact that this passage is frequently classified as a proverb or figurative saying, and that it fits each of these classifications.

"We heard him say, 'I will destroy this temple that is made with hands, and in three days I will build another, not made with hands.'" (Mark 14:58)

The term *parabolē* is not used in this example, nor in Matt 13:52 or Luke 13:32-33.

Similitudes

A distinction is often made between similitudes and parables. The former are defined as simple comparisons involving pictures of typical occurrences of daily life, whereas parables are comparisons involving stories of singular events (cf. Stein, *Introduction to the Parables of Jesus,* 1981). In general this distinction is helpful, as long as it is not seen as rigid and absolute. Thus in Luke 15:3-7 we find a comparison that involves something typical of a shepherd's life:

> So he told them this parable, "Which one of you, having a hundred sheep and losing one of them, does not leave the ninety-nine in the wilderness and go after the one that is lost until he finds it? When he has found it, he lays it on his shoulders and rejoices. And when he comes home, he calls together his friends and neighbors, saying to them, 'Rejoice with me, for I have found my sheep that was lost.'" (Luke 15:3-7)

Likewise in Matt 13:33 there is portrayed a typical experience of a woman making bread:

> He told them another parable: "The kingdom of heaven is like yeast that a woman took and mixed in with three measures of flour until all of it was leavened." (Matt 13:33)

Other examples are Matt 13:31-32, 44, 45-46, and 52 (cf. 13:34-35); Mark 4:21-22, 26-29, and 30-32 (cf. 4:33-34); 13:28-29; Luke 5:36-38; 12:35-38; 15:8-10 (cf. 15:3). Compare also the following passages where, however, the term *parabolē* does not occur: Matt 7:24-27; 11:16-19; Mark 2:19-20; Luke 7:41-43; 12:39; 17:7-10.

Story Parables

Under this classification we refer to parables in the narrow sense — that is, to extended, fictional comparisons in story form that refer generally to a unique event. Story parables make up the most famous of Jesus' sayings. An example is the story parable of the persistent widow:

Then Jesus told them a parable about their need to pray always and not to lose heart. He said, "In a certain city there was a judge who neither feared God nor had respect for people. In that city there was a widow who kept coming to him and saying 'Grant me justice against my opponent.' For a while he refused. But later he said to himself, 'Though I have no fear of God and no respect for anyone, yet because this widow keeps bothering me, I will grant her justice, so that she may not wear me out by continually coming.'"

And the Lord said, "Listen to what the unjust judge says. And will not God grant justice to his chosen ones who cry to him day and night? Will he delay long in helping them? I tell you, he will quickly grant justice to them. And yet, when the Son of Man comes, will he find faith on earth?" (Luke 18:1-8)

Other examples that use the term *parabolē* include Luke 13:6-9 ("the Barren Fig Tree") and Luke 19:11-27 ("the Pounds"). Other even more familiar story parables that do not use the term *parabolē*, however, are Matt 20:1-16 ("the Gracious Employer"), Matt 25:1-13 ("the Wise and Foolish Maidens"), Matt 25:14-30 ("the Talents"), Luke 14:15-24 ("the Great Supper"), Luke 15:11-32 ("the Prodigal Son"), and Luke 16:1-8 ("the Shrewd Manager").

Example Parables

The distinction between story parables and example parables is somewhat arbitrary. Whereas a story parable functions as "an earthly story bearing a heavenly meaning," an example parable functions as an example that says either "Go and do likewise" (Luke 10:37) or "Go and do not do likewise." As a result, the meaning of the picture part of an example parable — that is, the analogy proper — lies much nearer to the surface and corresponds more closely to the reality that the analogy is teaching. This can be seen in the parable of the rich but foolish farmer:

Then he told to them a parable: "The land of a rich man produced abundantly. And he thought to himself, 'What should I do, for I have no place to store my crops?' Then he said, 'I will do this: I will pull down my barns and build larger ones, and there I will store all my grain and my goods. And I will say to my soul, "Soul, you have ample goods laid up for many years; relax, eat, drink, be merry." But God said to him, 'You fool! This very night your life is being demanded of you. And the things you have prepared, whose will they be?' So it is with those who store up treasures for themselves but are not rich toward God." (Luke 12:16-21)

Other examples in the Gospels where the term *parabolē* is found are Luke 14:7-11 ("the places at a feast") and Luke 18:9-14 ("the Pharisee and the publican"). Cf. also Luke 10:30-35 ("the good Samaritan"); Luke 16:19-31 ("the rich man and Lazarus"); and possibly Matt 18:23-35 ("the unforgiving servant") in which the term is not found.

Allegories

When we speak of the genre "parable" as including allegory, we are referring to allegory as a literary form, not as an exegetical method. This distinction between the literary form of allegory and the hermeneutical methodology of "allegorizing" must be kept clear (cf. Klauck, *Allegorie und Allegorese*). Allegory is a literary form found in both the Old Testament *mashal* and the New Testament *parabolē*. It originates with the original authors, who both used this literary form and intended their hearers to interpret the form as an allegory. "Allegorizing" is an exegetical method that originates with a reader who interprets an author's words in a manner that the author did not intend. It is therefore wrong to interpret story parables and example parables as allegories. This would be to "allegorize" these parables, for the reader would violate the intention of the author. On the other hand, it would also be wrong not to interpret an allegory as an allegory, for this would likewise violate the intention of the author.

In the Gospels there are several stories that in their present form are allegorical in nature. The Parable of the Tenants is a prime example:

Then he began to speak to them in parables. "A man planted a vineyard, put a fence around it, dug a pit for the wine press, and built a watchtower. Then he leased it to tenants and went to another country. When the season came, he sent a slave to the tenants to collect from them his share of the produce of the vineyard. But they seized him, and beat him, and sent him away empty-handed. Again he sent another slave to them.

This one they beat over the head and insulted. Then he sent another, and that one they killed. And so it was with many others — some they beat, and others they killed. He had still one other, a beloved son. Finally he sent him to them, saying, 'They will respect my son.' But those tenants said to one another, 'This is the heir; come, let us kill him, and the inheritance will be ours.' So they seized him, killed him, and threw him out of the vineyard. What then will the owner of the vineyard do? He will come and destroy the tenants and give the vineyard to others. Have you not read this Scripture: 'The stone that the builders rejected has become the cornerstone; this was the Lord's doing, and it is amazing in our eyes'?" When they realized that he had told this parable against them, they wanted to arrest him, but they feared the crowd. So they left him and went away. (Mark 12:1-12)

Other allegories are found in Mark 4:3-9 ("the Soils"); Matt 13:24-30 ("the Wheat and the Tares"); and Matt 21:1-10 ("the Marriage Feast"). In all of these examples the term *parabolē* is used to describe the allegory.

The issue of whether the allegorical interpretations associated with the parables of "the Soils" (Mark 4:13-20) and "the Wheat and Tares" (Matt 13:36-43) — as well, the allegorical details found in the parables of "the Wicked Tenants" and "the Marriage Feast" — are authentic is greatly debated. Yet even if every allegorical feature found in these parables and their interpretations were to be attributed to the early church and not to Jesus, the fact would remain that the genre "parable" found in the New Testament includes "allegory."

6. Conclusion

The term "parable" in the Bible possesses an extremely broad semantic range. It can refer to the three-word proverb "Physician, heal yourself" (Luke 4:23) or to a lengthy story parable such as the prodigal son (Luke 15:11-32). Lying at the core of the Old Testament *mashal* and the New Testament *parabolē* is a comparison of two unlike things. The comparison can be brief or extended, implicit (as in a metaphor, riddle, story, or example parable) or explicit (as in a simile, similitude, or allegory). The metaphysical-like distinctions attributed to certain of these forms are not only exaggerated but unwarranted. It is not the form of this genre that transforms the reader, but the divine truth that they contain. The fact that not just parables, but also similitudes and allegories found in the Bible, have been used by God to transform lives indicates that it is not primarily the form but the content that God uses to transform those who hear and respond.

The parables of the Bible possess a twofold nature. They contain both an informative dimension (the reality part) and an affective one (the picture part). Additional expressions used to distinguish the affective picture or metaphor from its informative content are: figurative meaning vs. literal meaning; vehicle vs. tenor; frame vs. focus; illustration vs. illustrated; subsidiary subject vs. principle subject; signifier vs. signified; or *Bildhälfte* vs. *Sachhälfte*. We can interpret into referential language the informative content of a parable, because this dimension can be expressed in non-metaphorical language. Thus the "meaning" of Jesus' parable of the prodigal son can be expressed as follows: "Jesus was saying to the Pharisees and scribes, 'Why are you so upset that God is showing mercy to outcasts and sinners in my ministry? Why are you not entering into the joy of the occasion? The kingdom of God has come!'" Such an explanation can, if correct, interpret the informative dimension of the parable. It neglects and loses entirely, however, the affective dimension of this parable, and a parable consists of both the message and the persuasive vehicle.

What the new approach has clearly observed about the parabolic genre is its affective dimension. Parables not only communicate information, they also disarm and persuade. It is not easy to resist the message of a parable. That is because its riddle-like nature requires involvement by the hearers and because the informative content it bears comes suddenly, usually before people are able to defend themselves against its message. Thus before David could defend himself against the informative dimension of Nathan's parable (2 Sam 12:1-4), the arrow-like, affective nature of the parable had already pierced his heart. We find a similar use of parables by Jesus in his attempt to disarm his hearers (cf. Matt 20:1-16; Luke 7:41-43; 10:30-35; 15:11-32).

Although the new approach has been helpful in bringing to our attention the affective nature of the parabolic genre, the extravagant nature and the magnitude of its claims for this genre must be rejected. For Jesus a parable served as a superb means of communication, but it was never an end in itself. Rather, it served as a vehicle by which Jesus sought to teach the divine message. This is clearly Mark's understanding when he states, "With many such parables he spoke the word to them, as they were able to hear" (Mark 4:33). It should be noted that the phrase "with many such parables" reveals that parables served as instruments or means by which Jesus taught the word of God. It is, therefore, an error to equate the means by which Jesus taught the word of God — that is, by the use of parables — with the transforming power and nature of that "word." It is also, however, an error for those who today proclaim that "word" not to make use of such an affective genre in their proclamation!

Selected Bibliography

Beavis, Mary Ann. "Parable and Fable." *Catholic Biblical Quarterly* 52 (1990) 473-98.

Brosend, William F., II. "The Limits of Metaphor." *Perspectives in Religious Studies* 21 (1994) 23-41.

Bultmann, Rudolf. *History of the Synoptic Tradition,* trans. J. Marsh. New York: Harper & Row, 1968.

Dodd, C. H. *The Parables of the Kingdom.* New York: Scribner's, 1961.

Donahue, John R. *The Gospel in Parable.* Philadelphia: Fortress, 1988.

Eslinger, Richard L. "Preaching the Parables and the Main Idea." *Perkins Journal* 37 (1983) 24-32.

Jeremias, Joachim. *The Parables of Jesus,* trans. S. H. Hooke. London: SCM; New York: Scribner's, 1963 (from 6th German edition).

Jülicher, Adolf. *Die Gleichnisreden Jesu.* Tübingen: Mohr, 1910.

Kjargaard, Mogens Stiller. *Metaphor and Parable.* Leiden: Brill, 1986.

Klauck, Hans-Josef. *Allegorie und Allegorese in synoptischen Gleichnistexten.* Münster: Aschendorff, 1978.

McFague TeSelle, Sallie. *Speaking in Parables: A Study in Metaphor and Theology.* London: SCM, 1975.

Meier, John P. *A Marginal Jew: Rethinking the Historical Jesus.* New York: Doubleday, 1991.

Siverns, L. E. "A Definition of Parable." *Theological Review* 9 (1988) 60-75.

Stein, Robert H. *An Introduction to the Parables of Jesus.* Philadelphia: Westminster, 1981.

———. *The Method and Message of Jesus' Teachings.* Louisville: Westminster, 1994.

Tolbert, Mary Ann. *Perspectives on the Parables: An Approach to Multiple Interpretations.* Philadelphia: Fortress, 1979.

Westermann, Claus. *The Parables of Jesus in Light of the Old Testament,* trans. F. W. Golka and A. H. B. Logan. Minneapolis: Fortress, 1990.

CHAPTER 3

Parables in Early Judaism

CRAIG A. EVANS

ACCORDING TO MARK 4:33-34a, Jesus "spoke the word to them with many such parables *(parabolai)*, as they were able to hear it; he did not speak to them without a parable *(parabolē)*." The Gospels give credence to Mark's claim, for the bulk of Jesus' teaching in the Synoptic Gospels is presented in the form of parables. Most of the articles in the present volume will be devoted to analyses of the meaning of those parables. Our task in this article, however, is to set out the data regarding parables in Early Judaism — in particular, to deal with matters having to do with the origins, forms, and functions of early Jewish parables.

Two major caveats, however, are immediately in order. For if by "early Jewish parables" we mean parables of the first century, then, apart from the parables of Jesus, there are very few that can with certainty be dated to this period. Furthermore, the character of the parables derived from the Jewish world — whether from shortly before the time of Jesus, during his time, or afterwards — are not exactly comparable to those of Jesus in the Synoptic Gospels. Nonetheless, we should not assume that Jesus was the only Jewish teacher of his day whose teaching style was characterized by parables. It seems wisest to assume that at least *some* of the rabbis who taught during the time of Jesus made use of parables as well.

An interesting statement in the Mishnah lends support to such an assumption. According to *Mishnah Sotah* 9:15, "When Rabbi Meir [a fourth-generation Tannaitic rabbi, who taught about 150 CE] died, makers of parables ceased." It may be inferred from this statement, as well as from the context of gloom and doom in which it is found, that rabbis who lived earlier than Rabbi Meir composed and told parables — and that Rabbi Meir was particularly well known for his parables (just as Rabbi Hanina ben Dosa, for example, who is cited shortly afterwards in the same passage, was well known for his deeds of power and whose death saw a decline in the "men of deeds").

The more pressing concern, however, is not the identification of other parable-telling rabbis from the time of Jesus, but an understanding of the origins, forms, and functions of parables in Judaism. If Jesus did not invent the parable, where did it come from? An answer to our question suggests itself immediately: Jesus derived the parable form of teaching, whether directly or indirectly, from the Scriptures of Israel. This observation provides us a good start in our study of parables, though other factors for a fuller understanding will need to be taken into consideration as well.

1. The Linguistic Data

The noun *parabolē* ("parable") occurs forty-five times in the Greek Old Testament, the LXX. In every instance it translates the Hebrew noun *mashal* (with the verb *mashal* being rendered by *parabolēn eipein*, i.e., "to speak a parable"). Both *mashal* and *parabolē* are words that have a broad range of meaning.

The first occurrence of *mashal* in the Hebrew Bible (excepting, of course, those occurrences where the meaning is "to rule over") is found in Num 21:27: "For this reason they that speak in *meshalim* say, 'Come to Heshbon; Let the city of Sihon be built and established.'" Here *meshalim* may be rendered "proverbs," "parables," or even "riddles." Indeed, the LXX translator seems to have understood it in this latter sense, for he renders the passage: "For this reason *the enigmatists* will say (*dia touto erousin hoi ainigmatistai*). . . ." The next occurrence of *mashal* is in Num 23:7: "And he took up his parable, and said, 'From Aram has Balak brought me, the king of Moab from the mountains of the East: "Come, curse Jacob for me; and come, defy Israel".'" Several times we are told that the prophet-for-hire Balaam "took up his parable and said" such-and-such (cf. Num 23:18; 24:3, 15, 20, 21, 23). In all of these occurrences *mashal* is rendered by *parabolē*. Yet though the prophet's oracles are poetic, they do not constitute "parables," at least as we tend to understand them.

Warning the second generation of Israelites, on the eve of their entry into the promised land, Moses predicts dire consequences for sin and disobedience: "And you shall become an astonishment, a proverb, and a byword, among all the peoples to whom the Lord shall lead you away" (Deut 28:37). Here again *mashal* is rendered by *parabolē*. But what is interesting is that *parabolē* is here juxtaposed with other words that were evidently considered to be roughly synonymous. In the LXX it reads: "as an enigma and a parable and a story" *(en ainigmati kai parabolę kai diēgēmati;* see also LXX 2 Chr 7:20). So *parabolē* can mean a "byword" or "taunt-song," which is a meaning it has elsewhere in the Greek Scriptures (cf. Ps 43:15; 68:12; Jer 24:9; Mic 2:4; Hab 2:6; Tobit 3:4; Wisdom 5:4). But *parabolē* can also mean an enigma or riddle, as seen in Ps 49:4 (= LXX 48:5): "I will incline my ear to a parable; I will open my dark saying upon the harp"; or Ps 78:2 (= LXX 77:2): "I will open my mouth in a parable; I will utter dark sayings of old" (cf. Prov 1:6; Sirach 39:1-3; 47:15, 17). In Ezekiel, as well, *parabolē* connotes the idea of a riddle (cf. Ezek 12:22, 23; 16:44; 17:2; 18:2, 3). The prophet says that the Lord is a speaker of parables (Ezek 21:5 = LXX 20:49), but these parables appear to be oracles of judgment (24:3; cf. LXX Dan 12:8).

According to the Preacher of Ecclesiastes, to know wisdom approximates the knowledge of parables (Eccl 1:17). Jesus ben Sira held a similar view, saying, "In the treasuries of wisdom are parables of knowledge" (Sirach 1:25); and again, "A heart of discernment will appreciate a parable, and an ear of attentiveness is the desire of a wise person" (Sirach 3:29).

Mashal and its Greek equivalent *parabolē* sometime mean no more than a saying, as seen for example in 1 Sam 10:12: "Is Saul also among the prophets?" In this case there is nothing metaphorical about the saying. Indeed, there is nothing especially enigmatic about it, though it may have been meant as a taunt. Later in 1 Samuel we encounter an obvious example of a proverb: "As the proverb of the ancients says, 'Out of the wicked comes forth wickedness'" (1 Sam 24:13). In Hebrew it is appropriately designated a *mashal* (cf. the book of Proverbs, i.e., the book of *meshalim*), but the Greek translator curiously chooses *parabolē* instead of *paroimia* (i.e., "proverb"), as one might have expected. Likewise in 1 Kgs 4:32 (= LXX 5:12), where we are told that Solomon "spoke three thousand proverbs," in the Greek we have *parabolai,* not the expected *paroimiai.*

From this brief survey it seems that *parabolē, paroimia,* and *ainigma* can have overlapping meanings and that their usage is no certain indication of genre (cf. F. Hauck, *parabolē, TDNT* 5.744-61; *idem, paroimia,*

TDNT 5.854-56; G. Kittel, *ainigma, TDNT* 1.178-80). One thing they have in common is that they are the opposite of plain speech. This is seen, for example, in Num 12:6-8a: "When there are prophets among you, I the Lord make myself known to them in visions; I speak to them in dreams. Not so with my servant Moses; he is entrusted with all my house. With him I speak face to face — clearly, not in riddles (MT: *behidoth;* LXX: *di' ainigmatōn*); and he beholds the form of the Lord."

2. Old Testament Parables

There are approximately ten parables in the Old Testament that loosely resemble those spoken by Jesus (cf. Manson, *Teaching of Jesus,* 59-66; Gerhardsson, "Narrative Meshalim in the Synoptic Gospels," 339-63). The first parable that appears in Scripture, and possibly the oldest, is found in Judg 9:8-15 and has been called the Parable of the Trees. It reads:

> The trees once went forth to anoint a king over them; and they said to the olive tree, "Reign over us." But the olive tree said to them. "Should I leave my fatness, by which God and man are honored, and go to wave to and fro over the trees?" And the trees said to the fig tree, "Come, and reign over us." But the fig tree said to them, "Should I leave my sweetness and my good fruit, and go to wave to and fro over the trees?" And the trees said to the vine, "Come, and reign over us." And the vine said to them, "Should I leave my new wine, which cheers God and man, and go to wave to and fro over the trees?" Then said all the trees to the bramble, "Come, and reign over us." And the bramble said to the trees, "If in truth you anoint me king over you, then come and take refuge in my shade; and if not, let fire come out of the bramble, and devour the cedars of Lebanon."

Because trees, vines, and brambles are portrayed as speaking, this material is probably more of the nature of a fable than a parable, as T. W. Manson has rightly observed (cf. *Teaching of Jesus,* 62-63). Nevertheless, it is interesting to observe that the fable is explained in verses 16-21 that follow. This form may parallel those instances in the Gospels where parables are followed by explanations (e.g., Matt 13:24-30 + 13:36-43; Mark 4:2-9 + 4:13-20; 7:14-15 + 7:17-23).

The Fable of the Trees is supposed to interpret the slaughter of the seventy sons of Gideon at the hands of his son Abimelech and the men of Schechem. Whatever its original meaning — and interpreters dispute it, along with questions of sources, editing, and compilation in Judges 9 — Jotham's interpretation anticipates that judgment will befall Abimelech. For Abimelech had put to death the sons of Gideon "on one stone" (9:5), and so he will be consumed by fire (9:20). But whereas the fable speaks of being devoured by fire, the narrative itself draws an even closer parallel between what Abimelech did to the sons of Gideon and what would befall him, saying that Abimelech suffered a mortal injury when a woman crushed his skull with a millstone (9:53-54).

Two parables appear in 2 Samuel. The first is the Parable of the Ewe Lamb in 2 Sam 12:1b-4, which Nathan the prophet told against King David, after he had committed adultery with Bathsheba and then arranged the death of her husband Uriah. The parable reads as follows:

> There were two men in one city; the one rich, and the other poor. The rich man had many, many flocks and herds; but the poor man had nothing, save one little ewe lamb, which he had bought. He brought it up, and it grew up with him, and with his children; it used to eat of his own food, and drink of his own cup, and lie in his bosom, and it was like a daughter to him. And a traveler came to the rich man, and he was reluctant to take of his own flock and of his own herd, to dress for the wayfaring man who had come to him. Instead, he took the poor man's lamb, and dressed it for the man who had come to him.

David is outraged when he hears this parable. "The man who has done this," he avers, "deserves to die!" (v 5). But then Nathan explains the parable: "You are the man!" The Lord had given David everything, including the daughters of Saul the king, his predecessor. Unsatisfied with all of that he struck down Uriah the Hittite and took his wife. Therefore trouble will overtake the king's house (vv 7-14). To his credit, David confesses: "I have sinned" (v 13).

The Parable of the Ewe Lamb is a juridical parable (cf. Simon, "Poor Man's Ewe-Lamb," 207-42). Like the Fable of the Trees considered above, this parable is interpreted as a portent of judgment. Although David confesses his sin and so avoids a judgment of death on himself, the prophet foretells bloodshed within the king's family. The deaths of David's sons

Amnon, Absalom, and Adonijah offer the most shocking tokens, among others, of this prophecy's fulfillment.

The second parable of 2 Samuel, the Parable of the Two Brothers of 2 Sam 14:4-7, is, in reality, a ruse meant to deceive David (cf. vv 1-3, 12-20). David assumes that the story is factual (as he initially did in response to Nathan's Parable of the Ewe Lamb). Later, however, he learns that it concerns his son Absalom. The situation and portrayal of the Parable of the Two Brothers reads (vv 4-7):

> And when the woman of Tekoa spoke to the king, she fell on her face to the ground, and did obeisance, and said, "Help, O king." And the king said to her, "What is your trouble?" And she answered, "Of a truth I am a widow, and my husband is dead. And your servant had two sons, and they two strove together in the field, and there was none to part them, but the one struck the other, and killed him. And, behold, the whole family is risen against your servant, and they say, 'Deliver him that struck his brother, that we may kill him for the life of his brother whom he slew, even if we destroy the heir as well.' Thus will they quench my one remaining ember, and will leave to my husband neither name nor remnant on the face of the earth."

In this instance the hearer of the parable did not know that it was a parable. David assumed that the widow's dilemma was a real one. Indeed, in the ensuing conversation, she begs the king not to allow the avenger of blood to do any more killing. David assures her that "not one hair of your son shall fall to the ground" (v 11). After this pronouncement, the woman reveals that the king has convicted himself, for his determination to put to death his son Absalom is inconsistent with his judgment. Only then did David realize that the story was fiction, designed to prompt him to reconsider his thinking. As such, this parable is another example of a juridical parable.

A parable and a fable are found in 1 Kgs 20:38-43, where we have the Parable of the Escaped Prisoner. After being wounded and bandaged, a prophet waits on the road for Ahab, king of Israel. The parable and its explanation read as follows:

> The prophet departed, and waited for the king along the road, disguising himself with a bandage over his eyes. As the king passed by, he cried to

the king and said, "Your servant went out into the midst of the battle; and, behold, a man turned aside, and brought a man to me, and said, 'Keep this man: if by any means he be missing, then shall your life be for his life, or else you shall pay a talent of silver.' And as your servant was busy here and there, he was gone." And the king of Israel said to him, "So shall your judgment be; you have decided it." And he quickly took the headband away from his eyes; and the king of Israel recognized that he was one of the prophets. And he said to him, "Thus says the Lord, 'Because you have let go out of your hand the man whom I had devoted to destruction, therefore your life shall go for his life, and your people for his people.'" And the king of Israel went to his house heavy and displeased, and came to Samaria.

This parable is similar to the one told to David by the woman of Tekoa. Ahab assumes that he is being told a factual story. As David before him, the king of Israel passes judgment, only to be told that he has passed judgment on himself.

The Fable of the Thistle and the Cedar given in 2 Kgs 14:8-10 is another instance of a fable in the Old Testament:

Then Amaziah sent messengers to Jehoash, the son of Jehoahaz son of Jehu, king of Israel, saying, "Come, let us look one another in the face." And Jehoash the king of Israel sent to Amaziah king of Judah, saying, "The thistle that was in Lebanon sent to the cedar that was in Lebanon, saying, 'Give your daughter to my son for marriage; and there passed by a wild beast that was in Lebanon, and trod down the thistle.' You have indeed struck Edom, and your heart has lifted you up: glory in it, and abide at home; for why should you meddle to your hurt, that you should fall, even you, and Judah with you?"

Amaziah, king of Judah and cocky over his recent success against Edom, wishes to meet with Jehoash, king of Israel, perhaps to negotiate payments to mercenary troops from Israel (see the explanation given in 2 Chr 25:6-16; the marriage proposal hinted at in the fable itself probably does not reflect an actual detail in the historical drama). Jehoash tells him to stay home and enjoy his recent victory. The point is driven home with the Fable of the Thistle and the Cedar. The thistle's presumption will get him trampled by the big players in the drama.

One of the classic biblical parables is Isaiah's Song of the Vineyard in Isa 5:1-7. Although it is a song, most commentators agree that it is a parable — and, like several already considered, a juridical parable (cf. J. T. Willis, "The Genre of Isaiah 5:1-7," *Journal of Biblical Literature* 96 [1977] 337-62; G. A. Yee, "The Form-Critical Study of Isaiah 5:1-7," *Catholic Biblical Quarterly* 43 [1981] 30-40). It reads:

> Let me sing for my beloved a song of my beloved concerning his vineyard. My beloved had a vineyard on a very fruitful hill; and he digged it, and gathered out the stones from it, and planted it with the choicest vine, and built a tower in its midst, and also hewed out a winepress in it. He looked for it to bring forth grapes, and it brought forth wild grapes. And now, O inhabitants of Jerusalem and men of Judah, judge, I pray you, between me and my vineyard. What could have been done more to my vineyard that I have not done in it? Why, when I looked that it should bring forth grapes, brought it forth wild grapes? And now I will tell you what I will do to my vineyard: I will take away its hedge, and it shall be devoured; I will break down its wall, and it shall be trodden down; and I will lay it waste. It shall not be pruned nor hoed, but there shall come up briers and thorns. I will also command the clouds that they rain no rain upon it. For the vineyard of the Lord is the house of Israel and the men of Judah his pleasant plant. And he looked for justice, but, behold, oppression; for righteousness, but, behold, a cry.

We have in this song an instance of the hermeneutics of prophetic criticism, whereby the prophet alludes to Israel's sacred tradition but finds in it grounds for judgment, not assurance (cf. Sanders, "Hermeneutics in True and False Prophecy," 22-41). Israel may very well be likened to a chosen vine that God has planted on a mountain and lovingly cared for. But if justice and righteousness are lacking, one should expect judgment.

The remainder of the Old Testament parables are found scattered among the oracles in the first half of the book of Ezekiel. The Riddle (or Parable) of the Eagles and the Vine in Ezek 17:2-10 reads:

> Son of man, put forth a riddle, and speak a parable to the house of Israel; and say, "Thus says the Lord God: A great eagle with great wings and long pinions, full of feathers, which had various colors, came to Lebanon, and took the top of the cedar; he cropped off the topmost of

the young twigs of it, and carried it to a land of commerce; he set it in a city of merchants. He took also of the seed of the land and planted it in a fruitful soil; he placed it beside many waters; he set it as a willow-tree. And it grew and became a spreading vine of low stature, whose branches turned toward him, and the roots of it were under him. So it became a vine and brought forth branches and shot forth sprigs. There was also another great eagle with great wings and many feathers. And, behold, this vine did bend its roots toward him and shot forth its branches toward him, from the beds of its plantation, that he might water it. It was planted in a good soil by many waters, that it might bring forth branches and bear fruit and be a goodly vine." Say, "Thus says the Lord God: Shall it flourish? Shall he not pull up its roots and cut off the fruit from it, that it may wither — that all its fresh springing leaves may wither? And not by a strong arm or many people can it be raised from its roots. Yea, behold, being planted, shall it flourish? Shall it not utterly wither when the east wind touches it? It shall wither in the beds where it grew."

Parts of this extended parable are reminiscent of Isaiah's Song of the Vineyard. For like the older song, Ezekiel's Riddle of the Eagles and the Vine envisions judgment. The rhetorical question of verse 9, "Shall it flourish?," recalls the rhetorical question of Isa 5:4: "What more was there to do for my vineyard that I have not done in it?"

Another parable in Ezek 19:1-9 reads:

Moreover, take up a lamentation for the princes of Israel, and say, "What was your mother? A lioness: she couched among lions, in the midst of the young lions she nourished her whelps. And she brought up one of her whelps; he became a young lion, and he learned to catch the prey; he devoured men. The nations also heard of him; he was taken in their pit; and they brought him with hooks to the land of Egypt. Now when she saw that she had waited, and her hope was lost, then she took another of her whelps and made him a young lion. And he went up and down among the lions; he became a young lion, and he learned to catch the prey; he devoured men. And he knew their palaces and laid waste their cities; and the land was desolate, and its fullness, because of the noise of his roaring. Then the nations set against him on every side from the provinces; and they spread their net over him; he was taken in their pit.

And they put him in a cage with hooks and brought him to the king of Babylon; they brought him into strongholds, that his voice should no more be heard upon the mountains of Israel."

This is a funeral lament that is presented as a parable. Although animals play a part, it is not a fable. Yet it is more of an allegory than a simple parable. Indeed, Ezekiel's parables are beginning to exhibit features as encountered in such later apocalyptic works as Daniel and 1 Enoch, where symbolism is employed.

The Parable of the Lionness is immediately followed by the Parable of the Vine in Ezek 19:10-14, which is a lament that takes up again the imagery of the vine:

> Your mother was like a vine, in your blood, planted by the waters: it was fruitful and full of branches by reason of many waters. And it had strong rods for the scepters of them that rule, and their stature was exalted among the thick boughs, and they were seen in their height with the multitude of their branches. But it was plucked up in fury; it was cast down to the ground. The east wind dried up its fruit; its strong rods were broken off and withered; the fire consumed them. And now it is planted in the wilderness, in a dry and thirsty land. And fire is gone out of the rods of its branches; it has devoured its fruit, so that there is in it no strong rod to be a scepter to rule. This is a lamentation and shall be for a lamentation.

Here we have another highly allegorical parable, this time with an obvious allusion to Isaiah's Song of the Vineyard. "Your mother was like a vine" is a reference to the Davidic dynasty. As in many of the parables reviewed above, the point of the Parable of the Vine conveys a message of judgment. Though "planted by waters" and "fruitful," it was "plucked up in fury" and "cast down to the ground" where the "east wind" (i.e., the Babylonian Empire) "dried its fruit." The dynasty has been uprooted and replanted in the desert. Its is fruit devoured. It no longer rules.

Ezekiel provides two more parables. One is the Parable of the Forest Fire in Ezek 21:1-5 (MT = 20:45-49):

> And the word of the Lord came to me, saying, "Son of man, set your face toward the south, and drop your word toward the south, and prophesy

against the forest of the field in the South. Say to the forest of the South, 'Hear the word of the Lord: Thus says the Lord God, Behold, I will kindle a fire in you, and it shall devour every green tree in you and every dry tree. The flaming flame shall not be quenched, and all faces from the south to the north shall be burnt by it. And all flesh shall see that I, the Lord, have kindled it. It shall not be quenched.'" Then said I, "Ah, Lord God! They say of me, 'Is he not a speaker of parables?'"

The last verse identifies the text, at least by inference, as a parable. It is, however, more of a metaphor, for it lacks a plot. A fire burns a forest, and that represents judgment. But there are no true characters, there is no plot, and there is no moral or lesson to the story. God's judgment is likened to a consuming fire, which will destroy the "south" (i.e., Judah, not the Negev; cf. v 8). This is metaphor, therefore, not a parable (or a fable) in the more technical sense. Nonetheless, the allegorical features that were observed in the previous parables of Ezekiel are still in evidence.

Ezekiel's final parable is the Parable of the Seething Pot, which is found in Ezek 24:2-5. The parable reads:

> Son of man, write the name of the day, even of this very day: "the king of Babylon drew close to Jerusalem this very day." And utter a parable to the rebellious house, and say to them, "Thus says the Lord God: Set on the caldron, set it on, and also pour water into it; gather its pieces into it, even every good piece, the thigh and the shoulder; fill it with the choice bones. Take the choice of the flock, and also a pile of wood for the bones under the caldron; make it boil well. Yea, let the bones of it be boiled in the midst of it."

Ezekiel's *mashal* here is more of an object lesson than a parable (cf. Ezek 4:1–5:17, where the prophet performs various symbolic actions that portend a coming siege and hardship), which through symbolism conveys a message of judgment. Nevertheless, there is no indication in this case that the prophet actually acted out what he describes in his parable. The prophet enjoins the Babylonian king to cook rebellious Jerusalem, taking care not to leave out the "choice" parts, that is, the ruling elite who have promoted rebellion.

3. Dreams and Dream-Interpretations

Before leaving the biblical data, there is one other genre of parabolic material that should be considered briefly. For there are approximately one dozen dreams that are somewhat parallel to the parables and fables that have already been reviewed. And like the prophetic *meshalim,* they are understood as media through which God reveals things to human beings. All of them are symbolic, requiring interpretation.

Joseph and Daniel are the best-known dreamers or dream-interpreters of the Bible. Joseph's dreams of first the sheaves bowing down to his sheaf and then of the sun, moon, and stars bowing down to him (Gen 37:5-7, 9-10) offended his parents and brothers, for the meaning of these dreams was quite plain to them. Both of these dreams are allegories, though in very brief form. The dreams of Pharaoh's baker and cupbearer, which Joseph interpreted (Gen 40:5-19), are similar. Though allegorical, they are relatively simple. So also Pharaoh's dream of the seven fat cows eaten by seven emaciated cows and the seven fat ears of corn eaten by seven withered ears of corn. It comes as no surprise that they represent seven years of plenty followed by seven years of famine (Gen 41:1-7).

Daniel's stature as an interpreter of dreams is as impressive as that of Joseph's. He successfully interprets Nebuchadnezzar's dream of the great statue (Daniel 2) and Nebuchadnezzar's dream of the great tree (Daniel 4; cf. Ezek 31:3-14). Likewise, Daniel himself dreams his "night visions" and sees the four beasts, the convening of the heavenly court, the presentation of the kingdom to "one like a son of man," and the great struggle between the holy ones and the fourth kingdom of the earth (Daniel 7). Although somewhat similar to the dreams of Joseph, Daniel's dreams are more involved, more highly charged with symbolism. Moreover, Daniel's dreams are not concerned with Daniel himself, unlike Joseph's dreams, which mostly concern Joseph's fate. Rather, Daniel's dreams are national and eschatological, looking for Israel's redemption and restoration.

The other dreams in the Bible that contain parabolic details include Jacob's dream of the staircase (Gen 28:12-15), Jacob's dream about the goats and the flock and its meaning relative to his father-in-law Laban (Gen 31:10-13), and the dream that Gideon overheard, in which the cake of barley tumbled into the camp of Midian and caused a tent to collapse, thereby signifying Midian's certain defeat (Judg 7:13-14).

4. Early Postbiblical Parables

In the early writings of postbiblical Judaism there appear also some other Jewish parables. Three of these early postbiblical parables are particularly significant here.

In the *Genesis Apocryphon,* which was written about 50 BCE–50 CE, Abram recounts his Dream of the Cedar and Date-Palm. *1QapGen* 20.13-16 reads as follows (cf. Wise, Abegg, and Cook, *Dead Sea Scrolls* 79):

> I, Abram, had a dream the night of my entry into the land of Egypt. In my dream, I saw a cedar tree and a date-palm growing from a single root. Then people came intending to cut down and uproot the cedar, thereby to leave the date-palm by itself. The date-palm, however, objected, and said, "Do not cut the cedar down, for the two of us grow from but a single root." So the cedar was spared because of the date-palm, and was not cut down.

Abram's dream is very similar to the dreams related in the Old Testament, particularly in Genesis and Daniel. Like fables, these dreams are surreal, for date-palms do not talk to woodcutters any more than emaciated cattle devour fat cattle. As in the biblical dreams, Abram's Dream of the Cedar and Date-Palm conveys a message from God, guiding the patriarch and his wife through the perils they will encounter in Egypt. The elements of Abram's dream are drawn from Ps 92:13, a passage that in rabbinic literature is sometimes associated with Abraham and Sarah (cf., e.g., *Genesis Rabbah* 41.1 [on Gen 12:17]).

One more parable from Qumran is attested in fragments from cave 4. For fragment 1, column 2 of the Parable of the Fruitful Tree, which is identified as 4Q302a or *4Qpap Parable*, reads as follows (cf. Wise, Abegg, and Cook, *ibid.*, 296):

> Please consider this, you who are wise: If a man has a fine tree, which grows high, all the way to heaven [. . .] of the soil, and it produces succulent fruit [every year] with autumn rains and the spring rains [. . .] and in thirst, will he not [. . .] and guard it [. . .] to multiply the boughs of [. . .] from its shoot, to increase [. . .] and its mass of branches [. . .].

Fragment 2, column 1 possibly constitutes the interpretation of this parable. It may even mention God's kingdom, though this word must be partially restored.

Finally, we may consider a postbiblical parable that is associated with Ezekiel. Epiphanius (c. 315-403), the bishop of Salamis in Cyprus and an early historian, cites the Parable of the Lame Man and the Blind Man (*Panarion* or *Against Heresies* 64.70.5-17) and says that he took it from the *Apocryphon of Ezekiel* (= frag. 1). The parable also appears in briefer form in rabbinic literature (cf. *b. Sanhedrin* 91a-b, where it is attributed to Judah ha-Nasi; also *Lev Rabbah* 4.5 and the *Mekilta* on Exod 15:1, where it is attributed to Ishmael). The longer, Epiphanian version of this parable reads (cf. Mueller and Robinson, "Apocryphon of Ezekiel," 492, 494):

A certain king had everyone in his kingdom drafted, and had no civilians except two only: one lame man and one blind man, and each one sat by himself and lived by himself. And when the king was preparing a wedding feast for his own son, he invited all those in his kingdom, but he snubbed the two civilians, the lame man and the blind man. And they were indignant within themselves and resolved to carry out a plot against the king.

Now the king had a garden and the blind man called out from a distance to the lame man, saying, "How much would our crumb of bread have been among the crowds who were invited to the party? So come on, just as he did to us, let us retaliate (against) him." But the other asked, "In what way?" And he said, "Let us go into his garden and there destroy the things of the garden." But he said, "But how can I, being lame and unable to crawl?" And the blind one spoke, "What am I able to do myself, unable to see where I am going? But let us use subterfuge."

Plucking the grass near him and braiding a rope, he threw [it] to the blind man and said, "Take hold and come along the rope to me." And he did as he [the lame man] had urged [and] when he approached, he said, "Come to me, be [my] feet and carry me, and I will be your eyes, guiding you from above to the right and left." And doing this they went down into the garden. Furthermore, whether they damaged or did not damage [anything], nevertheless the footprints were visible in the garden.

Now when the partygoers dispersed from the wedding feast, going down into the garden they were amazed to find the footprints in the garden. And they reported these things to the king, saying, "Everyone in your kingdom is a soldier and no one is a civilian. So how, then, are there footprints of civilians in the garden?" And he was astounded.

He summoned the lame man and the blind man, and he asked the blind man, "Did you not come down into the garden?" And he replied, "Who, me, lord? You see our inability, you know that I cannot see where I walk." Then approaching the lame man, he asked him also, "Did you come down into my garden?" And answering, he said, "O lord, do you wish to embitter my soul in the matter of my inability?" And finally the judgment was delayed.

What then does the just judge do? Realizing in what manner both had been joined, he places the lame man on the blind man and examines both under the lash. And they are unable to deny, they each convict the other. The lame man, on the one hand, saying to the blind man, "Did you not carry me and lead me away?" And the blind man to the lame, "Did you yourself not become my eyes?" In the same way the body is connected to the soul and the soul to the body, to convict [them] of [their] common deeds. And the judgment becomes final for both body and soul, for the works they have done whether good or evil.

In the briefer, simpler rabbinic version of this parable, the point is the same. The king judges the blind man and the lame man as one. From this, the moral is drawn: "So the Holy One, blessed be he, brings the spirit and placing it in the body, he also judges them as one" (Mueller and Robinson, *ibid.*, 493).

5. Features of the Biblical and Postbiblical Parables

All of the materials surveyed above — with the possible exception of the last parable cited from the *Apocryphon of Ezekiel*, which has been dated between 50 BCE and 50 CE (cf. Mueller and Robinson, *ibid.*, 488) — were in circulation in Jesus' day, and so may have provided him with the themes, forms, and content out of which he could have constructed his own parables. The features of the biblical and postbiblical parables may be summarized as follows:

1. Many parables are juridical, that is, the hearer pronounces judgment on himself. This is evident in 2 Sam 12:1-4; 14:1-20; 1 Kgs 20:35-43;

but particularly so in Isa 5:1-7. Furthermore, most of the parables, even if they do not expressly draw the hearer into passing judgment on himself, are judgmental in perspective.

2. Some parables are told as fact, thereby initially deceiving the hearer. This device may have been intended to prevent the hearer from putting himself on guard against the parable's principal point.

3. The parables are true to life, though this is not the case with fables or dreams.

4. Some parables contain allegorical elements, especially those in Ezekiel.

5. The fables appear to serve similar functions as the parables.

6. All of the parables and fables are addressed to monarchs or leaders of the people.

7. The dreams are viewed as messages from God, which are in need of decipherment. Unlike the parables and fables, however, dreams are not devised for pedagogical purposes.

How do the parables of Jesus compare to these features? Many of Jesus' parables are juridical, inviting the hearers to judge themselves — or, at least, to draw their own conclusions. Jesus' parables are true to life, but are never told to deceive anyone (that is, to make someone think an actual event is being described). Jesus tells no fables, and his parables contain a relatively small amount of allegorical features. Although some of Jesus' parables are addressed to the leaders of Israel, most are addressed to his followers. Jesus neither dreams (though he may have had visions) nor interprets dreams.

Certain stylistic features and themes common to Jesus' parables are not found in the biblical and early postbiblical parables. Closer approximations, however, are to be found in the early rabbinic parables. And so it is to those parables that we must now turn.

6. Comparisons with Early Rabbinic Parables

Our purpose here is not to treat in any detailed manner Jesus' parables. That is the task assigned to those writing chapters 4-13 of the present volume. Rather, what is intended in this section is to show how the parables of the rabbis of the Tannaitic period, which roughly parallels the first two centuries of Christianity, offer valid and instructive points of comparison to the parables of Jesus. For to understand the early rabbinic parables is to be able to understand better the parables of Jesus.

Four features, in particular, need here to be highlighted: (1) that the rabbinic parables frequently speak of a king, (2) that "kingdom" is usually defined as God's sovereign reign over his dominion, (3) that the characters in the parables often behave in illogical ways, and (4) that rabbinic parables use terminology and themes that are often to be found also in parables attributed to Jesus. The recognition of these four features serves, in fact, to clarify in various ways the parables of Jesus.

1. God as King in the Rabbinic Parables

There are some 325 extant Tannaitic parables, more than half of which feature a king, who almost always represents God (cf. R. Pautrel, "Les canons du Mashal rabbinique"). Among these we have the Parable of the Forgiving King (*b. Rosh ha-Shanah* 17b; attributed to Rabbi Yose the priest, c. 90-100 CE; cf. Matt 5:23-24; 18:21-35); the Parable of the King's Wise and Foolish Servants (*b. Shabbath* 153a; also *Eccl Rabbah* 9:8 §1; *Midrash Prov* 16:11; attributed to Rabbi Yohanan ben Zakkai, c. 70-80 CE; cf. Matt 24:45-51; Luke 17:7-10); the Parable of the King's Banquet Guests (*Semahot* 8:10; attributed to Rabbi Meir, c. 150 CE; cf. Matt 22:1-10: Luke 14:15-24); the Parable of the King's Steward (*Aboth de R. Nathan* 14.6; attributed to Rabbi Eleazar ben Arak, c. 90 CE; cf. Matt 25:14-30 // Luke 19:12-27); and the King's Two Administrators (*Mekilta* on Exod 20:2 [*Bahodesh* §5]; attributed to Rabbi Simon ben Eleazar, c. 170 CE; cf. Matt 25:21 // Luke 19:17). Other parables could be mentioned, but these are among the most illustrative.

More than half of Jesus' parables speak of the "kingdom of God," which Jesus seemed to have understood in terms of God's powerful presence. Although the rabbinic parables usually speak of God as king and Jesus' parables speak of the kingdom of God, these expressions are closely related and merit comparison. The next point should make this evident.

2. Kingdom as God's Sovereign Reign over His Dominion

Years ago T. W. Manson noted that in a few rabbinic passages the term "kingdom" sometimes means God's dominion (cf. Manson, *Teaching of Jesus* 130-32; see also C. L. Blomberg, "Parables of Jesus"; B. D. Chilton, "Regnum Dei Deus Est" and "Kingdom of God in Recent Discussion"), which is the meaning that the term probably has in Jesus' parables. A parable found in the *Mekilta* on Exod 20:2 (*Bahodesh* §5) is illustrative:

> Why were the Ten Commandments not said at the beginning of the Torah? They give a parable. To what may this be compared? To the following: A king who entered a province said to the people: "May I rule over you?" But the people said to him: "Have you done anything good for us that you should rule over us?" What did he do then? He built the city wall for them, he brought in the water supply for them, and he fought their battles. Then when he said to them: "May I rule over you?" They said to him: "Yes, yes." So it is with God. He brought the Israelites out of Egypt, divided the sea for them, sent down manna for them, brought up the well for them, brought the quails for them. He fought for them the battle with Amalek. Then he said to them: "May I rule over you?" And they said to him: "Yes, yes."

Another illustrative passage is found in *Sifra Lev* §194 (on Lev 18:1-30). It is not formally introduced as a parable, but its fictive conversation between God and the wilderness generation is parable-like. In all probability this material is related to the above parable.

> The Lord spoke to Moses saying, "Speak to the sons of Israel and say to them: 'I am the Lord your God'" [Lev 18:1-2]. Rabbi Simeon ben Yohai says, "This is in line with what is said elsewhere: 'I am the Lord your God (who brought you out of the land of Egypt, out of the house of bondage)'" [Exod 20:2]. "Am I the Lord, whose sovereignty [literally, 'kingdom'] you took upon yourself in Egypt?" They said to him, "Yes, yes." "Indeed you have accepted my dominion [literally, 'my kingdom']. They accepted my decrees: 'You will have no other gods before'" [Exod 20:3]. That is what is said here: "I am the Lord your God," meaning, "Am I the one whose dominion [literally, 'kingdom'] you accepted at Sinai?" They said to him, "Yes, yes." "Indeed you have accepted my dominion [liter-

ally, 'my kingdom']. They accepted my decrees: 'You shall not copy the practices of the land of Egypt where you dwelt, or of the land of Canaan to which I am taking you; nor shall you follow their laws'" [Lev 18:3].

The definition of "kingdom" as God's kingly rule in this passage is quite clear — as the use of "sovereignty" and "dominion" in Jacob Neusner's translation (quoted above), instead of the more literal "kingdom," points up. This second passage coheres with the first one cited in declaring that God rules over Israel as a king. Furthermore, this second passage understands the people's acceptance of Torah as their acceptance of God's royal sovereignty. And this idea of God as a king who reigns sovereignly over the dominion of his people approximates Jesus' proclamation of the kingdom of God.

3. Illogical Characters in the Rabbinic Parables

Tannaitic parables present their characters as sometimes acting in illogical ways. The parable found in *Seder Elijah Rabbah* §28, for example, describes a remarkably foolish and incautious king who, against the sensible advice of his friends, entrusted his city, palace, and young son to a guardian who was an utter rascal. The parable reads:

> The parable, as told by Rabbi Yose the Galilean, concerned a mortal king who had set out for a city far across the sea. As he was about to entrust his son to the care of a wicked guardian, his friends and servants said to him: "My lord king, do not entrust your son to this wicked guardian." Nevertheless the king, ignoring the counsel of his friends and servants, entrusted his son to the wicked guardian. What did the guardian do? He proceeded to destroy the king's city, have his house consumed by fire, and slay his son with the sword. After a while the king returned. When he saw his city destroyed and desolate, his house consumed by fire, his son slain with the sword, he pulled out the hair of his head and his beard and broke out into wild weeping, saying: "Woe is me! How [foolish] I have been, how senselessly I acted in this kingdom of mine in entrusting my son to a wicked guardian!"

In Rabbi Yose's parable we have a man who appears utterly to lack common sense. Against the advice of friends and counselors he entrusts his son to a man known to be a "wicked guardian." But the actions of the guardian are just as difficult to comprehend. We are not told that he stole anything or profited in any way by his actions. He destroys the king's city, burns down his house, and murders his son. What could he possibly have hoped to gain? Did he imagine that he could get away with these crimes? Would not every hearer of this parable suppose that the king would send troops after the guardian and have him executed?

These are the same kinds of questions that critics have raised, from time to time, against the authenticity of the Parable of the Wicked Tenants (Mark 12:1-12). How could the owner have been so foolish and so reckless with the lives of his servants? How could he have been so stupid as to send his son to the vineyard after his servants had been maltreated, even murdered? What could the tenants have hoped to gain? Did they not know that the owner had the power to come and destroy them? Did they really imagine that they could inherit the vineyard? And one may ask similar questions with respect to the rude behavior of the invited guests in the Parable of the Great Banquet (Luke 14:15-24) or the eccentric behavior of the vineyard owner in the Parable of the Laborers (Matt 20:1-15).

Questions such as these do not constitute valid objections against the authenticity of any particular parable. The incomprehensible folly of the king in Rabbi Yose's parable — particularly since Yose applies the parable to God's trusting Nebuchadnezzar! — need not cast doubt on the question of the parable's authenticity. Nor should the folly of the vineyard owner or its tenants cast doubt on the authenticity of Jesus' parable. Indeed, such details provoke these kinds of questions — both for ancient hearers and for modern readers. But these shocking details, together with the questions they raise, are there to lead hearers and readers alike to a better grasp of the story-line of the parable, a better appreciation of its issues, and a better application of its intended lesson or lessons.

Sometimes objections are raised against the authenticity of certain parables of Jesus — most notably, again, the Parable of the Wicked Tenants — because they appear to be allegories based on the fate of Jesus or, it is alleged, on the experience of the early church. But rabbinic parables are also sometimes allegorical. The presence of allegory should not alone decide the question of authenticity.

4. The Terminology and Themes of the Rabbinic Parables vis-à-vis Those of Jesus

The parables of the rabbis and those of Jesus frequently use common terminology. These include the Hebrew noun *mashal* (cf. the Greek *parabolē*), the Hebrew verb *mashal* (cf. the Greek *parabolēn paratithenai*), the Hebrew term *domah*, which sets up a comparison (cf. the Greek *hōmoioun* or *homoia einai*), the Hebrew interrogatory pronoun *lemah*, which calls for a comparison (cf. the Greek interrogatory pronoun *tini*), and the Hebrew adverb *cak*, which applies the parable (cf. the Greek *houtōs*). Some examples of introductory wording to the parables are as follows:

> "I will give you a parable. To what does this matter compare? To a man who lent his neighbor a mina . . ." (*b. Rosh ha-Shanah* 17b);
>
> "It compares to a king who summoned his servants to a banquet . . ." (*b. Shabbath* 153a);
>
> "He set before them another parable, saying, 'The kingdom of Heaven may be likened to a man who sowed good seed . . .'" (Matt 13:24);
>
> "What is the kingdom of God like and to what shall I compare it? It is like a mustard seed . . ." (Luke 13:18);
>
> "Thus it happened to the Egyptians . . ." (*Mekilta* on Exod 14:5 [*Beshallah* 2]);
>
> "Thus did Moses speak to Israel . . ." (*Sifre Deut* §53 [on Deut 11:26]);
>
> "Thus is the kingdom of God" (Mark 4:26); and,
>
> "Thus it will be also with this evil generation" (Matt 12:45).

Likewise, many of Jesus' parables contain within them certain vocabulary and themes that can be paralleled in rabbinic literature. For example, the Parable of the Prodigal Son in Luke 15:11-32 contains many of these features.

> "And he sent him into his fields to feed swine" (Luke 15:15b) — cf. "No Israelite may raise swine anywhere" (*Mishnah, Baba Kamma* 7:7); "Cursed is the man who raises swine" (*b. Baba Kamma* 82b).
>
> "And he longed to be filled with the pods which the swine were eat-

ing" (Luke 15:16a) — cf. "When Israelites are reduced to eating carob-pods, they repent" (*Lev Rabbah* 13.4 [on Lev 11:2]).

"'How many of my father's hired servants have bread enough and to spare, but I perish here with hunger! I will arise and go to my father' . . . 'put shoes on his feet!'" (Luke 15:17) — cf. "When a son [abroad] goes barefoot [through poverty], he remembers the comfort of his father's house" (*Lam Rabbah* 1:7 §34).

"I am no longer worthy to be called your son" (Luke 15:19) — cf. "I [the son] am ashamed to come before you [the father]" (*Deut Rabbah* 2.24 [on Deut 4:30]); "I am not worthy" (*Targum Neofiti* on Gen 32:11).

"This my son was dead, and is now alive again" (Luke 15:24) — cf. "Four are regarded as dead: the leper, the blind, he who is childless, and he who has become impoverished" (*Gen Rabbah* 71.6 [on Gen 30:1]).

Furthermore, the Parable of the Prodigal Son gives expression to several themes commonly found in rabbinic parables. One thinks, for example, of the Parable of the King's Errant Son (*Deut Rabbah* 2.24 [on Deut 4:30]; attributed to Rabbi Meir, c. 150 CE); the Parable of the King's Youngest Son (*Sifre Deut* §352 [on Deut 33:12]; anonymous); the Parable of the King's Twelve Sons, one of whom the king loved more than the others (*Gen Rabbah* 98.6 [on Gen 49:8]; anonymous); the Parable of the Repatriated Prince, who according to one version returned to his "inheritance" (*Sifre Deut* §345 [on Deut 33:4]; anonymous) and according to another version was met halfway by his father (*Pesikta Rabbati* 44.9; anonymous); and, finally, the Parable of the Father who divided his inheritance among his sons (*b. Kiddushin* 61b; attributed to Rabbi Hanina ben Gamaliel, c. 120 CE).

7. Conclusion

Our survey of early Jewish parables makes it clear that Jesus' parables are right at home in first-century Jewish Palestine. In most respects Jesus' parables are not unique. Their emphasis on the kingdom of God roughly parallels the rabbis' emphasis on God as king, though with important differences. Jesus' parables are similar in form, beginning with such introductory phrases as "to what may this be compared?" or "the kingdom of God is like." They are about the same length as the rabbinic parables. Sometimes allegorical features are present. Kings, banquets, travels, and business dealings are common themes. Parables are usually used to illustrate or defend an interpretation of Scripture or a point of doctrine. The logic behind this is akin to the idea that nature and everyday life teach us the ways of God.

The Old Testament parables and related materials probably supplied the basic forms and contents out of which Jesus and his contemporaries fashioned their parables. But comparison with the parables of the rabbinic literature makes it clear that a certain amount of formalization had taken place between the composition and circulation of Israel's Scriptures, on the one hand, and the later highly formulated parables of the rabbis, on the other. David Stern has rightly observed that "Jesus used the parable (insofar as the gospel narratives tell us) in essentially the same way as the Rabbis employed the *mashal*— in public contexts (sermons or preaching), and as an instrument for praise and blame, often directed at the persons present in the audience" (*Parables in Midrash,* 200). But that is not to say that there are no important differences in emphasis and theology between the parables of Jesus and those of the rabbis, particularly with regard to matters of purity, election, and the nature of the kingdom of God (cf. Blomberg, *Interpreting the Parables,* 65-68).

One further point should also be mentioned here. For there is in Jewish lore an interesting association of parables with Solomon and with the proper interpretation of Torah. A rabbinic midrash reads:

> You will find that until Solomon came there was no parable. . . . So until Solomon arose no one who could properly understand the words of the Torah, but when Solomon arose, all began to comprehend the Torah. . . . So proceeding from one thing to another, from one parable to another, Solomon penetrated to the innermost meaning of the Torah . . . through the parables of Solomon we master the words of the Torah. Our rabbis say: "Let not the parable be lightly esteemed in your eyes, since by means of the parable a man can master the words of the Torah." (*Song Rabbah* 1:1 §8)

How early this tradition may be is difficult to determine. Perhaps it is quite old, for surely the claim of Jesus, the teller of parables, that "one who is greater than Solomon is here" (Matt 12:42 = Luke 11:31) — indeed, one

73

who interprets Torah with greater authority (cf. Matt 5:21-48; Mark 2:27) — points to a similar tradition and association.

What at first blush, therefore, appear to be disparate traditions — that is, the identification of Jesus as the son of David (Mark 10:47-48) *and* as a Solomonic figure who speaks parables, interprets Torah, casts out demons, and proclaims the kingdom of God — may, in fact, be essential features of a first-century Jewish messianic expectation. The telling of parables may be more than merely another indication that Jesus understood himself as a rabbi. It is quite possible that Jesus developed a teaching style consistent with his message and with his mission: that the proclaimer of God's kingdom proclaimed the kingdom in the manner and style expected of the son of David.

Selected Bibliography

Blomberg, Craig L. *Interpreting the Parables.* Downers Grove: InterVarsity, 1990.

————. "The Parables of Jesus: Current Trends and Needs in Research," in *Studying the Historical Jesus: Evaluations of the State of Current Research* (NTTS 19), ed. B. D. Chilton and C. A. Evans. Leiden: Brill, 1994, 231-54.

Chilton, Bruce D. "Regnum Dei Deus Est," *Scottish Journal of Theology* 31 (1978) 261-70.

————. "The Kingdom of God in Recent Discussion," in *Studying the Historical Jesus: Evaluations of the State of Current Research* (NTTS 19), ed. B. D. Chilton and C. A. Evans. Leiden: Brill, 1994, 255-80.

Drury, John. *The Parables in the Gospels: History and Allegory.* London: SPCK; New York: Crossroad, 1985.

Evans, Craig A. *Jesus and His Contemporaries: Comparative Studies* (AGJU 25). Leiden: Brill, 1995, esp. 252-62.

Gerhardsson, Birger. "The Narrative Meshalim in the Synoptic Gospels. A Comparison with the Narrative Meshalim in the Old Testament," *New Testament Studies* 34 (1988) 339-63.

Manson, T. W. *The Teaching of Jesus: Studies of Its Form and Content.* Cambridge: Cambridge University Press, 1948.

Mueller, James R., and Stephen B. Robinson. "Apocryphon of Ezekiel," in

The Old Testament Pseudepigrapha, 2 vols., ed. J. H. Charlesworth. New York: Doubleday, 1983, 85, 1.487-95.

Oesterley, W. O. E. *The Gospel Parables in the Light of Their Jewish Background*. London: Macmillan, 1936.

Pautrel, Raymond. "Les canons du Mashal rabbinique," *Recherches de science religieuse* 26 (1936) 6-45 and 28 (1938) 264-81.

Sanders, James A. "Hermeneutics in True and False Prophecy," in *Canon and Authority* (W. Zimmerli *Festschrift*), ed. G. W. Coats and B. O. Long. Philadelphia: Fortress, 1971, 22-41.

Simon, Uriel. "The Poor Man's Ewe-Lamb: An Example of a Juridical Parable," *Biblica* 48 (1967) 207-42.

Stern, David. *Parables in Midrash: Narrative and Exegesis in Rabbinic Literature*. Cambridge, MA: Harvard University Press, 1991, esp. 188-206.

Wise, Michael O., Martin G. Abegg, Jr., and Edward M. Cook, *The Dead Sea Scrolls: A New Translation*. San Francisco: HarperCollins, 1996.

Young, Brad H. *Jesus and His Jewish Parables*. New York: Paulist, 1989.

PART II

Parables of the Kingdom

CHAPTER 4

Mark's Parables of the Kingdom
(Mark 4:1-34)

MORNA D. HOOKER

WERE I TO TAKE my brief to discuss Mark's parables of the kingdom literally, this article would be very short indeed, for the Gospel of Mark has only two "parables of the kingdom" — the Parable of the Growing Seed in 4:26-29 and the Parable of the Mustard Seed in 4:30-32. It is clear, however, from the interpretation that the evangelist inserts between the parable and its explanation in verses 10-12, that he understands the Parable of the Sower in 4:1-20 as also having something to do with the kingdom. And we will, I think, discover that the Parable of the Lamp in 4:21-23 has a close connection with the same theme.

One of the reasons why Mark's Gospel is shorter than the others is, of course, that he includes much less of Jesus' teaching. This is not because he regards that teaching as unimportant, for he tells us frequently that Jesus taught and presents him as teaching with authority. In fact, in his portrayals of Jesus Mark uses the noun "teaching" (didachē) five times and the corresponding verb "to teach" (didaskō) seventeen times. We do not know whether the parables included by Matthew and Luke were available to Mark or not. If they were, that might tell us something very significant about Mark's choice. But we do not know, and we would be in danger of getting the wrong answer if we were to guess. All we can properly do is see what picture is built up by the material that Mark included.

1. The Markan Context

In order to appreciate the significance of the parables in Mark 4:1-34, it is necessary, first of all, to set them in context by considering four more general matters. In what follows, therefore, I want to consider briefly (1) the impact of the other parables included by Mark, (2) references to the kingdom in Mark, (3) Mark's arrangement of the main blocks of Jesus' teaching, and (4) the parallel between parables and miracles in Mark.

The Other Markan Parables

The first of the Markan parables occurs in 2:19-20. In response to his critics, Jesus says: "Can the friends of the bridegroom fast while he is with them? As long as the bridegroom is with them, they cannot fast. But the time will come when the bridegroom is taken away from them; and when that day comes, then they will fast." The parable is clearly understood to refer to Jesus himself, for he is the "bridegroom" whose presence — or absence — makes all the difference to his disciples.

This parable is immediately followed by two parabolic sayings. The first, in 2:21, is about mending a garment: "No one sews a patch of unwashed cloth onto an old garment; otherwise, the patch tears away from it, the new from the old, and makes a bigger hole." The second, in 2:22, is about storing wine: "No one pours new wine into old wineskins; otherwise, the wine will burst the skins, and both the wine and the skins will be lost. New wine goes into fresh wineskins." Both of these sayings, as recounted by Mark, point to the significance of what is taking place in Jesus.

In 3:23-27 we have what is explicitly said to be a "parable":

Then he summoned them and spoke to them in parables *(en parabolais)*: "How can Satan drive out Satan? For if a kingdom is divided against itself, that kingdom cannot stand. And if a household is divided against itself, that household will not be able to stand. And if Satan has rebelled against himself and is divided, he cannot stand; that is the end of him. But no one can break into a strong man's house and plunder his property without first tying up the strong man; then indeed he can plunder his house."

The suggestion that the strong man (i.e., Satan) has been bound is a clear reference to the work of Jesus himself, who confronted Satan in the wilderness (cf. 1:12-13). This parable, like the earlier ones, is addressed to Jesus' opponents.

Leaving aside the parables in 4:1-34 (which we will be examining later), we come to the saying in 7:15: "There is nothing outside a person that by going in can defile, but the things that come out are what defile." We might well have failed to recognize this saying as a parable, were it not for the explicit reference to it as such in verse 17 ("When he had left the crowd and entered the house, his disciples asked him about this parable" [*tēn parabolēn*]). In fact, though it plays on the double meaning of "what comes out of a person," the saying seems to be a fairly straightforward one about what it is that defiles. And if it is described as a parable, that is perhaps because its radical meaning was difficult to accept. The comment at the end of verse 19 ("Thus he declared all foods clean!") makes it plain that it is the word and authority of Jesus that are crucial in "making all foods clean."

The final parables of Mark's Gospel are presented as having been given in Jerusalem. In 12:1-12 we have the Parable of the Vineyard and the Wicked Tenants, which Jesus' opponents recognized as an attack on them (see the discussion of this parable in Chapter 7 of this book). The parable is, in effect, an allegory. Most important for our purposes here, however, is the fact that once again Mark's comments make it clear that he understands the parable to be about Jesus himself.

Then at the end of chapter 13, which consists of private teachings to four of the disciples, we have two parables about the End. In the first, that of the Fig Tree in 13:28-29, the point is that the End — or, is it Jesus himself? — will soon be at the door: "Learn a lesson from the fig tree: when its branch becomes tender and puts out leaves, you know that summer is near. In the same way, when you see these things happening, you will know that he is near, at the very door." In the second, that of a Householder Returning from a Journey in 13:33-37 (see the discussion of this parable in Chapter 8 of this book), the master of the house who is expected to return is clearly understood to be Jesus himself.

We see, then, that such other parables as Mark has included, in addition to the so-called "parables of the kingdom," focus our attention on the person of Jesus. We will discover, in due course, that the same is true of the parables in 4:1-34.

The Kingdom of God

The kingdom of God is first referred to in Mark's Gospel in 1:15, where Jesus announces its imminent arrival: "The time is fulfilled, and the kingdom of God is at hand; repent and believe the good news." His subsequent words and actions demonstrate that its effects are already being felt. In 9:1 he makes another announcement: "Truly I tell you, there are some standing here who will not taste death before they see the kingdom of God come with power." Mark's positioning of this saying is significant, for it is preceded by the first clear prediction of Jesus' death and resurrection in 8:31, and immediately following it we have the story of the Transfiguration in 9:2-13 in which Jesus is acknowledged by a heavenly voice to be God's Son — a scene reminiscent of the story of Jesus' baptism at the very beginning of Mark's Gospel. The close conjunction of both these announcements of the kingdom's coming with the heavenly revelations of Jesus' identity suggests that Mark saw a close link between these two ideas.

Jesus' third declaration that the kingdom is coming occurs in 14:25: "Truly I tell you, I will never again drink of the fruit of the vine until that day when I drink it new in the kingdom of God." The implication seems to be that his death is necessary before the kingdom can arrive. This time we have to read on to the end of the Passion Narrative to find the declaration that Jesus is God's Son. For it is only after Jesus has died that the centurion remarks in 15:39: "Truly this man was a son of God."

It has often been pointed out that these three declarations of Jesus as "Son of God" occur at three strategic points in the narrative — that is, at the very beginning (1:1), at the turning-point of the Gospel (9:7), and at the moment of Jesus' death (15:39). I am intrigued to discover that the three references to the future coming of the kingdom should also occur in very similar places: as Jesus' first words in the Gospel (1:15), at its turning-point (9:1), and as his final words at the Last Supper (14:25). I suggest, therefore, that for the evangelist Mark there was a very close connection between the coming of the kingdom and Jesus' identity as Son of God. And like the parables, these crucial references to the kingdom focus our attention on the person of Jesus, who proclaims and embodies its coming.

Other references to the kingdom in Mark's Gospel are found in chapter 4 (vv 11, 26, 30) and in various later chapters, where they all refer to entering or receiving the kingdom, or to being either far from it or near to it (so 9:47; 10:14-15, 23-25; 12:34; 15:43). In every case in the later chapters of Mark's Gospel, the kingdom is linked in some way with the authority of Jesus. The reference to the kingdom in 9:47 ("If your eye causes you to stumble, pluck it out! It is better for you to enter the kingdom of God with one eye than to have two eyes and be thrown into Gehenna") occurs in the context of teaching about what it means to be Jesus' disciple. The saying in 10:14-15 ("Let the children come to me; do not stop them. For it is to such as these that the kingdom of God belongs. Truly I tell you, whoever does not receive the kingdom of God as a little child will never enter it") is found in the context of children being brought to Jesus to be blessed by him. The sayings in 10:23-25 ("How hard it will be for those who have wealth to enter the kingdom of God! . . . Children, how hard it is to enter the kingdom of God! It is easier for a camel to go through the eye of a needle than for someone who is rich to enter the kingdom of God") are linked with Peter's remarks about leaving everything to follow Jesus in verses 28-31. The comment in 12:34 ("You are not far from the kingdom of God") is addressed to a scribe who gives wholehearted endorsement to Jesus' teaching. In 15:43 it is the fact that Joseph of Arimathea "was himself waiting expectantly for the kingdom of God" that leads him to pay honor to Jesus. And this same linkage of the kingdom with the authority of Jesus will be seen in the sayings of Mark 4, as we will observe in our examination of this chapter below.

The Teaching of Jesus

Although the Gospel of Mark does not contain a great deal of sustained teaching by Jesus, it does set out two main blocks of teaching material: the first, the parable chapter of 4:1-32, occurs toward the beginning of the Gospel; the other, chapter 13, consisting of eschatological teaching delivered on the Mount of Olives, is found toward the end. Similarities between these two passages suggest that Mark may have thought of them as balancing each other in some way. To be sure, the overall audience is different, for the Parable of the Sower in 4:1-10 is addressed to the crowd, while the teaching in chapter 13 is addressed to only four disciples. Nevertheless, in chapter 4 the explanation in verses 11-20 is taught privately to the disciples, while the audience for verses 21-32 is uncertain. Moreover, the effect of Jesus' teaching throughout chapter 4 is to narrow down the real hearers of his message to those who are committed disciples.

83

It is, however, in the settings of the two passages where we see parallels. Chapter 4 follows a series of confrontations between Jesus and the religious authorities in the previous two chapters. The healing of the paralytic (2:1-12), the meal with tax collectors and sinners (2:15-17), the dispute about fasting (2:18-22), the plucking of grain in the field (2:23-28), the healing of the man with a withered hand (3:1-6), and finally the accusation that he is possessed by Satan (3:20-35) — all of these episodes present the challenge of Jesus' authority and the refusal of his opponents to recognize it. Only two passages in these chapters give a different picture: 2:13-14, which recounts the call of Levi, and 3:7-19, which describes the response of the crowds to Jesus and his appointment of twelve disciples. These two passages contrast vividly with the rest of the material in chapters 2–3, showing the positive response made by those who recognize the authority of Jesus, over against the negative reaction of those who reject it.

A similar picture is found in the context of chapter 13, where we again find the religious leaders rejecting Jesus' authority. This time, however, Jesus is shown in several of the incidents as on the offensive: in (1) the cleansing of the temple (11:11, 15-19), which, however it is interpreted, is a condemnation of the nation's insincere worship; (2) the cursing of the fig tree that fails to produce fruit at the proper time (11:12-14, 20-25) — and that means, for Mark, not during the usual season for figs, but at the moment when the Messiah comes looking for fruit to eat (cf. W. R. Telford, *The Barren Temple and the Withered Tree*); (3) the Parable of the Vineyard and Wicked Tenants (12:1-12), where the leaders are condemned for their failure to hand over the produce of the vineyard; (4) the question about the Messiah being son of David and his Lord (12:35-37); and (5) the condemnation of the scribes (12:38-40), who are contrasted with the poor widow who gave everything she had to the treasury (12:41-44).

Parallel to the accusation regarding his exorcisms in 3:20-35 we have the question about Jesus' authority in 11:27-33: "By what authority are you doing these things? Who gave you this authority to do them?" (v 28). Both incidents focus on the vital question of the basis of Jesus' authority: Is it from Satan or from the Holy Spirit? From God or man? His opponents are unable to reply, but Mark's readers will by now be in no doubt regarding the correct answer! In this section there are also deliberate attempts to trip him up in the questions about tribute to Caesar (12:13-17) and the resurrection (12:18-27). In contrast, once again, we have those who respond positively to Jesus: the crowd that greets him as he enters Jerusalem on the back of a colt (11:1-10) and the scribe who approves his teaching (12:28-34).

As Mark's readers, therefore, turn from these incidents to the material in chapters 4 and 13, they hear in those chapters teaching that is given with authority. Furthermore, in both cases that teaching is closely related to the context in which it appears. For the incidents leading up to chapter 4 have focused on Jesus' ability to heal the sick and to exorcise demons: Jesus has attacked the kingdom of Satan, and the truth of his initial proclamation that the kingdom of God is at hand has been demonstrated in the crumbling of Satan's power. We expect in Jesus' teaching to learn more about this kingdom, but we now know that its coming is firmly linked with the authority of the one who proclaims it. We are not surprised, therefore, when the parables of chapter 4 seem to tell us as much about our response to Jesus as about the nature of the kingdom itself — that is, that those who respond positively to his message will produce a bumper harvest.

In chapters 11 and 12, on the other hand, Jesus' attack has been launched against those who have failed to produce a harvest. It is launched against the leaders of the nation, who are condemned for their failure to hand over fruit to God, and against the people in general, who have failed to worship God with sincerity or to produce ripe figs for the Messiah to eat. It is hardly surprising, therefore, that Jesus' teaching in chapter 13 concentrates on the coming judgment. Nor is it surprising that this teaching, too, is linked with his own authority. His rejection will inevitably bring suffering for his followers. But it will also bring final vindication, when the Son of Man gathers his elect from the far corners of the earth.

Parables and Miracles

The final matter we need to consider regarding the context of the kingdom parables in 4:1-34 concerns the parallel that exists between parables and miracles in Mark's Gospel. As we have seen, the parables in chapter 4 are preceded by various healing miracles, many of them exorcisms. Immediately following, we have a series of miracles: the stilling of the storm (4:35-41), the healing of the Gerasene demoniac (5:1-20), and the healing of the woman with a hemorrhage (5:25-34), which is intercalated into the account of the raising of Jairus's daughter (5:21-24 and 35-43). After the stories of Jesus' rejection in his hometown and the beheading of John the

Baptist, which both offer inadequate attempts to answer the question of Jesus' identity, we have the feeding of the five thousand (6:3-44), the walking on the water (6:45-52), and a summary of healings (6:53-56). And following those incidents, we have Jesus' teaching about what is clean and unclean (7:1-23, including the "parable" of v 15) and the miracle of the healing of the Syro-Phoenician woman's daughter (7:24-30). The connection between the teaching of verses 1-23 and the miracle of verses 24-30 is clear — indeed, if this passage had occurred in the Fourth Gospel, we should have labeled it "discourse + sign."

There then follows the healing of a man who was deaf and dumb (7:31-37), the feeding of the four thousand (8:1-10), and the request of the Pharisees for a sign, which is refused (8:11-13). The discussion between Jesus and his followers in the boat (8:14-21) indicates that for those with eyes to see and ears to hear, a "sign" has, in fact, been given in the two feeding miracles. Finally in this section we have the healing of the blind man at Bethsaida (8:22-26), which is closely followed by the account of the opening (or semi-opening!) of the disciples' eyes to the truth about who Jesus is at Caesarea Philippi (8:27-33). Once again, we have here the equivalent of a Johannine "discourse," which spells out the significance of a preceding miraculous "sign" (cf. the very similar pattern of a miracle and a subsequent discussion in John 9).

These miracles of 4:35–8:26 appear to have been carefully arranged by Mark to carry on the theme of the parable chapter, and, in particular, to pick up the key sayings in 4:10-12 about ears and eyes that are deaf and blind to the truth. Several of them hint at the true identity of Jesus — the issue that was openly raised at the beginning of this section in the disciples' cry, "Who can this be?" (4:41), and that was picked up in the hopelessly inept question posed by his former neighbors, "Is not this the carpenter, the son of Mary and brother of James and Joses and Judas and Simon, and are not his sisters here with us?" (6:3). And this same issue is reiterated in the story of the Baptist's death, with questions about whether he was "John the Baptist" raised from the dead, "Elijah" returned, or "a prophet, like one of the prophets of old" (6:14-16) — questions that are finally answered (though inadequately!) at Caesarea Philippi: "You are the Messiah" (8:29b).

In these miracles Jesus is revealed as the one who has power over wind and waves, power to give life to the dead, and power to provide food for his people. In these miracles, too, there are echoes of the Old Testament narratives about Moses and Elijah. Yet Jesus emerges in them as greater than both. Furthermore, the last four miracles suggest symbolic meanings: first, the healing of the Syro-Phoenician woman's daughter, the meaning of which is spelt out (7:24-30); then the opening of deaf ears (7:31-37) and blind eyes (8:22-26); while in between these latter two stories there is a repetition of the miracle of the feeding of the crowd (8:1-13), which, as the subsequent discussions make clear, emphasizes the refusal of Jesus' enemies to see the truth and the obtuseness of his own disciples (8:14-21).

In the rest of Mark's Gospel there are few miracles. The healing of a child in 9:14-19 is used as a lesson on the meaning of faith, while the healing of blind Bartimaeus in 10:46-52 is, like the account of the blind man at Bethsaida, a story with a double meaning — for although he is blind, Bartimaeus recognizes Jesus as Son of David; but when he receives his sight, he follows Jesus "on the way." Finally, the story of the cursing of the fig tree is, as we have already seen, a "sign" of the failure of Israel and her consequent fate.

Unlike the Fourth Evangelist, Mark rarely spells out the meaning of Jesus' miracles. He prefers to set incidents side by side and to leave it to his readers to make the necessary connections. But it is clear that for him miracles not only confront us with the significance of Jesus' teaching, but also serve the same purpose as the parables. For both parables and miracles, in their own way, present the message of Jesus in a dramatic form (cf. M. D. Hooker, *The Signs of a Prophet;* also W. D. Stacey, *Prophetic Drama in the Old Testament*). The parables are stories told *by* Jesus; the miracles are stories told *about* Jesus. Both parables and miracles, however, are dramatic presentations of the gospel, which for the evangelist is about Jesus himself. In his arrangement of his materials, therefore, Mark uses both parables and miracles — like his references to the kingdom — to focus his readers' attention on the figure of Jesus.

2. The Parable of the Sower (Mark 4:1-20)

This first block of teaching in Mark's Gospel begins with the Parable of the Sower, which is understood by the evangelist to be a parable about parables. This is made clear in the explanation of the parable in verses 13-20, which begins with the words: "Don't you understand this parable? Then how will you understand any of the parables?" Clearly, Mark regards this introductory parable as the key to understanding the rest.

Mark's Use of the Parable

The clue to Mark's own use of the parable is found in verses 10-12, which are intercalated between the parable itself and its explanation — though because of their difficulty, the significance of these verses for Mark's understanding of Jesus' ministry is often overlooked. In his teaching Jesus confronts men and women with an all-important decision, which is a matter of life and death. Those who do not respond are those whose hearts are hardened, whom Satan has in his power. Those who respond, who hear and follow Jesus, are those to whom the secret of the kingdom is given. Although Jesus does not announce or proclaim himself as the Christ, the effect of this parable, as presented to us by Mark, is to do precisely that. Jesus confronts the reader as the one who brings salvation. Thus to accept or reject his teaching about the kingdom is to accept or reject both the kingdom itself and the one who brings it.

For Mark, the parables of Jesus both reveal and conceal. For those who have ears to hear, they convey the good news of God's kingdom; for those who refuse to listen, their message is obscure. The parables are in some ways similar to crossword clues, making sense to those who are prepared to accept their challenge. The Hebrew word *mashal*, which is translated into Greek as *parabolē*, means "proverb" or "riddle" as well as "parable," and Mark may not be wrong in believing that Jesus' parables contained a certain enigmatic quality.

By the time that Mark was writing, however, the enigma seemed much greater. For one thing, it is clear that he saw in the parables some explanation for Israel's rejection of Jesus — that is, that the people of Israel had failed to respond to him because they had not understood his teaching, and they had not understood his teaching because they had not been able to decipher the parables. A second reason why Mark would be conscious of the parables' obscurity was the shift in the situation from Jesus' time to his own. Parables spoken by a wandering teacher in Galilee sounded very different when recited as words of the Master whom the community acknowledged as risen Lord. Inevitably, therefore, parables took on new meanings in new situations — and inevitably, in the process, their relevance sometimes seemed obscure.

It was natural, once the parables seemed unduly puzzling, to add explanatory comments. Applications to new situations would necessarily involve some form of allegorization. In the explanation of 4:14-20, in fact, we find an allegorical interpretation that sounds very much like an early preacher's exposition of the parable, warning Christians of the dangers that might overcome their faith.

Mark seems to have understood the Parable of the Sower as fundamental, providing not simply the key to understanding the teaching of Jesus' parabolic teaching (cf. v 13) but also the explanation of his whole ministry. This is brought out in the exposition of the parable in verses 14-20: the seed represents the word proclaimed by Jesus; the crop, the response of men and women to him. For the end of the story we have to turn to the Parable of the Vineyard and the Wicked Tenants in 12:1-12, where we find the Lord demanding grapes from his vineyard, just as he had once looked for a harvest in his field. In chapter 12, the tenants' failure to respond to the messengers leads ultimately to the death (and resurrection!) of the son of the owner of the vineyard. The fact that each of these parables is placed immediately after a direct challenge by the Jerusalem religious authorities concerning the nature of Jesus' authority — the Parable of the Sower after the challenges recounted in 3:20-35; the Parable of the Vineyard and Wicked Tenants after that of 11:27-33 — suggests that Mark regarded both of them as allegories of Israel's response to and rejection of Jesus. Taken together, they encapsulate the whole story of his ministry.

Jesus' first word of the parable in verse 3, "Listen!" *(akouete)*, is echoed in his final exhortation in verse 9, "Those who have ears to hear, let them hear!" *(akouetō)* — and then commented on in verse 12 in words quoted from Isa 6:10 to the effect that the people "listen and listen, yet understand nothing" *(akouontes akouōsin kai mē suniōsin)*. Birger Gerhardsson has argued that we have here echoes of the *Shema*, the traditional Jewish confession drawn from Deut 6:4-5 that begins "Hear, O Israel" (cf. his "The Parable of the Sower and Its Interpretation"). His evidence is much stronger for Matthew's version of the parable than it is for Mark's. Nonetheless, this language does, at the very least, indicate the authority with which Jesus is said to have spoken. Furthermore, it might well have evoked in the minds of Mark's readers the command to hear — and therefore to obey — the demands of the speaker. But whereas Deut 6:4-5 required its hearers to love God with heart and soul and strength, the parable of Jesus calls for wholehearted response to Jesus himself. The "word" that he sows is the word about himself. And it will take only one short step for the evangelist John to identify that word with Jesus (cf. John 1:1).

The symbolism of bearing fruit is common in both the Old Testament and the teaching of Jesus, and so it is possible that Jesus himself used the parable to confront the people with God's demand for obedience to his will. The contrast between fruitful and barren soils represents the contrast between those who are responsive to God's commands, and therefore true members of his people, and those who fail to obey his will. It is those who are responsive and obedient to God's will who belong to his Kingdom. However, insofar as Jesus' teaching represents a final challenge to Israel to respond to God's demands, Mark has correctly interpreted the parable in terms of the response made to Jesus himself. The opening command to "listen" in verse 3, together with the closing words "Those who have ears to hear, let them hear" in verse 9, remind us of the need to pay careful attention to Jesus.

The Purpose of the Parables

Verses 10-12 are perhaps the most difficult and most discussed verses in the whole of Mark's Gospel. Their meaning for the evangelist, however, is clear enough. Mark shares the fundamental Jewish conviction that God is at work both in historical events and in people, whose actions are ultimately the result of his decree. For the Christian community, therefore, looking back on the ministry of Jesus, the rejection by Israel of her Messiah, as well as the continued obduracy of the Jewish nation when confronted by the Christian gospel, could only be explained as part of God's mysterious purpose. If men and women had refused to accept Jesus, then it must have been the will of God that this should happen. In spite of attempts to soften the harshness of Mark's words, there can be no doubt that this was his meaning.

It must be noted, however, that there is for Mark another aspect to this picture. Those outside, to whom everything comes in parables, stand in contrast to those who were about him with the Twelve. To those who refuse to accept the challenge of the teaching of Jesus, his parables inevitably remain nothing more than parables. Though they see and hear him, they are totally without comprehension — and so without the salvation he brings. But to those who respond, the meaning of the parables is explained. To them the secret of God's kingdom is given (cf. Matt 11:25-27 // Luke 10:21-22 for a similar saying regarding hiddenness and revelation).

Yet though the choice between being a disciple or an outsider is such a

90

vital one, there is no rigid line between the two groups. The invitation of Jesus to listen in verses 3 and 9 is addressed to everyone, and the secret of God's kingdom is given to anyone who is prepared to receive it. As for the Twelve, they are rebuked in verse 13 for their failure to understand! Mark will later show them behaving with no greater understanding than the crowds. Indeed, their obtuseness stands in contrast to the remarkable faith of others.

As the story unfolds it becomes clear that the secret of the kingdom of God is inextricably linked with the person of Jesus himself. The disciples fail to understand the power of Jesus (cf. 4:40-41; 6:37, 49-52; 8:4, 14-21); they are mystified by his teaching (cf. 7:18) — especially on the need for suffering (cf. 8:32-4; 9:32-34; 10:32, 35-41) — and they fail him at the crucial hour (cf. 14:32-42, 47, 50, 66-72). But to those outside, faith is given: to the woman with a hemorrhage (5:34), the Syro-Phoenician woman (7:29), the father of the epileptic boy (9:24), the children who are brought for blessing (10:13-16), the woman who anoints Jesus (14:3-9) and — most remarkable of all — the centurion at the cross (15:39). How is it that those to whom the secret of the kingdom is revealed fail to comprehend, while those from whom it is hidden grasp it? This is the enigma of Mark's Gospel. The statement in 4:12 ("they listen and listen, yet understand nothing") proves to be true, but the identity of those to whom the secret is given provides some surprises — though Mark has, perhaps, prepared us for this by including a reference in verse 10 to others besides the Twelve who are with Jesus.

In their present form and context, these verses seem to reflect a time when the parables had become somewhat puzzling to the early church, probably because their original context had been lost. Although it is customary to contrast the self-evident character of Jesus' original parables with the attempts of the early community to extract meaning from what had become obscure, it is possible to exaggerate the difference. It seems likely that Jesus' intention in teaching in parables was to challenge his listeners and make them think for themselves. Whether or not it was necessary for Jesus to spell out their meaning to his disciples, as Mark suggests, we do not know. But Mark is certainly right in picturing the disciples as representing those for whom — through their response to Jesus — the parables had become meaningful, while for those outside the Christian community their significance was lost because their challenge was rejected.

The quotation in verse 12 comes from Isa 6:9-10. Although the words occur in the account of Isaiah's call, it seems probable that they represent the prophet's understanding of his ministry to Israel at the end of his life rather than at the beginning — that is, as he looked back on what seemed to him a complete failure to convert his people. But even this failure he saw as part of God's purpose. So his words would have seemed highly appropriate to early Christians wrestling with the problem of Israel's rejection of Jesus as its Messiah. The fact that the version of Isa 6:9-10 given here is closer to the Targum than to the LXX suggests that it may go back to an Aramaic source. It is possible, therefore, that Jesus himself commented on his failure to convert Israel (with so few exceptions) in words reminiscent of Isaiah. Certainly Mark understood Isaiah's words to have been fulfilled in Jesus' ministry (see M. A. Beavis, *Mark's Audience*, on the importance of this saying for Mark).

It was suggested by Joachim Jeremias (*Parables of Jesus*, 14-18) that the original Aramaic of the words "all things are in parables" of verse 11 meant "everything is obscure," and that Mark misunderstood the Greek phrase *en parabolais*, meaning "in riddles," as a reference to Jesus' parables. If Jeremias was correct, then it was this misunderstanding that led to verses 11 and 12, which originally made up a separate saying, being linked to the theme of parables. But as we have already seen, Jesus' words and actions are for Mark a unity. Therefore, whether these verses were originally a general saying about the effect of Jesus' ministry as a whole, or referred, as Mark believed, to his parabolic teaching in particular, this saying sums up Mark's understanding of the events that he describes: in Jesus, the power of God's kingdom is breaking into the world, and the signs of its coming are present for all to see; but only his followers grasp the true significance of what is happening.

For Mark there is no doubt that the paradoxical result of Jesus' ministry — and so its purpose — was that many failed to comprehend the truth even when they saw and heard it. Jewish thought tended to blur the distinction between purpose and result, for if God was sovereign, then, of course, what happened must be his will, however strange this appeared. It is less easy to see, however, what place these words could have had in the ministry of Jesus himself, for we may confidently assume that the purpose of his teaching was to stimulate response, not prevent it. Commentators have made innumerable attempts to tone down the meaning of the expression "in order that" *(hina)* at the beginning of verse 12, suggesting, for example, that it is a mistranslation of the Aramaic (see, e.g., T. W. Manson, *Teaching of Jesus*, 76-80). If Jesus used the quotation, the most likely explanation is that he felt Isaiah's words were being fulfilled in his own ministry — that is, that the people were as unresponsive to his mission as they had been to that of the prophet Isaiah.

The Explanation of the Parable

Most commentators believe that the explanation of the parable in verses 13-20 originated in the early Christian community and represents an early "exegesis" of it. The interpretation seems to presuppose a fairly long period during which the faith of Christians was tested in various ways, and to reflect the harsh experience of Christian preachers and communities. The elaboration of the misfortunes of the unfruitful seed in verses 15-19 has shifted the balance of the parable, so that there is now far more emphasis on the failures than there was in the original story in verses 1-9. The triple failure in production, though recounted there in some detail, was balanced by the triple success; but in the explanation, the various difficulties seem overwhelming. The setbacks encountered by the seed are allegorized, and, though there is no reason to deny (as some have done) that Jesus ever used allegory, the allegorization of details is often a sign of later attempts to expound the parables. This seems especially likely here, since the explanations suit the period of Christian mission better than the lifetime of Jesus. Yet though the interpretation may come from the church, rather than from Jesus, it has perhaps not distorted the original parable as much as is sometimes suggested. Rather, as with the account of Nathan's parable in 2 Samuel 12, we detect at each point the warning of an early preacher: "This could mean you!"

Why does Mark ascribe such importance to this parable and see it as the key to understanding all of the parables? The answer lies in verse 14. For the parable is about the proclamation of the gospel and how it is received — that is, about the response that is made to Jesus himself. The parable conveys the same message as the saying in verse 11, "To you has been given the secret of God's kingdom, but to those outside, everything comes in parables." Thus, although the story describes four different kinds of soils, its ending shows that the essential division is between that which produces fruit and that which does not. The proclamation of Jesus divides those who hear him into two camps, and the number of those who are "outside" is large by comparison with the circle of those who accept him.

The authorities whose hearts are hardened and who reject Jesus' teaching, the crowds who hear Jesus gladly but are not prepared to accept the way of discipleship, those men and women whose concerns are centered on themselves to the exclusion of thoughts about God's kingdom — all these groups stand in opposition to the small band of disciples who hear the word and accept it. The challenge to the members of Mark's community, who have gathered together to listen to the parable and to its explanation, is clear: they must ensure that they are found in the last group. Those who bear fruit are those to whom the kingdom is given. It is because it expresses the same truth as that found in verse 11 that the parable is primary for Mark. And if the disciples cannot understand this parable about their own response, they are numbering themselves with the outsiders (cf. Matt 7:24-27, at the close of the Sermon on the Mount, for another parable about the two possible responses to Jesus).

3. The Parable of the Lamp and
Associated Sayings (Mark 4:21-25)

Mark brings together four sayings in 4:21-25 that seem originally to have been separate. In Luke's Gospel, three of these sayings appear in their Markan context (cf. Luke 8:16-18); but the four sayings are also found scattered throughout Matthew and Luke (cf. Matt 5:15; 10:26; 7:2; 13:12, repeated at 25:29; and Luke 11:33; 12:2; 6:38; 19:26). The Parable of the Lamp appears also in the *Gospel of Thomas* (Logion 33), as well as sayings similar to those in Mark 4:22, 23, and 25. The evangelist Mark — or, perhaps, someone before him — has arranged these four sayings into two pairs, in each of which the second saying is linked to the first by the explanatory conjunction "for" (*gar*).

It is not clear whether Mark understands Jesus to be addressing the disciples or the crowd. The theme of this section — the contrast between what is hidden and what is revealed — suggests that the audience consists still of the disciples, though the injunctions to listen in verses 23-24 remind us of earlier commands that are addressed to the crowd. Probably their appearance in this context is meant to suggest that even the disciples were in danger of failure. The form of the question in Greek indicates that the answer expected is "No": "Of course, a lamp is not meant to be concealed, but to be put on a lampstand. It would be absurd to hide it, for a lamp is meant to give light, and cannot do so if it is hidden."

However, by linking the Parable of the Lamp in verse 21 with the saying of verse 22 ("For nothing is hidden, except to be revealed; and nothing is concealed, except to be brought into the open"), Mark shows that he believes that the light was, in fact, hidden during the ministry of Jesus. Nevertheless, this was an anomaly and of only a temporary nature. The true purpose of the light will finally be achieved. The notion that things are deliberately hidden in order to be revealed, or concealed in order to be brought into the open, is, on the face of it, absurd. But it is in keeping with Mark's understanding of the Messianic Secret — for the concealment of Jesus' true identity was a necessary part of God's purpose, which embraces both his crucifixion and his resurrection.

The image of the lamp reminds us of the contrast set out in verses 11-12 between the secret given to some and the truth hidden from many. For just as the seed is intended to grow, so the lamp is meant to give light. Neither the Parable of the Sower in verses 1-9 nor the Parable of the Lamp in verse 21 is specifically said to be about the kingdom. Yet the fact that the ideas in verses 21-25 are so similar to those in verses 11-12 suggests that Mark understood the Parable of the Lamp, like the Parable of the Sower, to be a "parable of the kingdom." Nevertheless, it is clear that for Mark the lamp is none other than Jesus himself ! He and the kingdom are, in effect, identified. And once again Mark's presentation is close to a Johannine declaration about Jesus, as expressed this time in the identification of "the Lamp" with "the Lamb" (cf. Rev 21:23).

The two pairs of sayings in verses 21-23 and 24-25 are linked together with two more injunctions to listen. The first in verse 23 repeats the command in verse 9 almost verbatim: "Those who have ears to hear, let them hear!" The second in verse 24 (literally: "Look what you hear") echoes the comment in verse 12 about looking and listening. The responsibility of men and women to respond to the word of Jesus remains. The sayings in verses 24-25 themselves, however, seem to have little connection with the Markan context — verse 24 ("the measure by which you give will be the measure by which you receive, and more besides"), for example, seems much more at home in the context given it by Matthew (7:1-2) and Luke (6:37-38), where the theme is that of judging others — but were presumably intended in Mark's context to mean that those who listen to Jesus will receive according to their response.

The final verse of this section, that of verse 25 ("For to those who have, more will be given; and from those who have nothing, even what they have will be taken away!"), is, perhaps, intended to sum up the ideas in verses 1-20. Those who accept the word — that is, the word *of* Jesus and *about* Jesus — and to whom the secret of the kingdom is therefore given, will receive all the joys of the kingdom; but those who do not have this secret will lose even what they had — that is, the word that was offered and rejected.

In its non-Markan contexts — that is, in Matt 5:15, Luke 11:33, and the *Gospel of Thomas* 33 — the Parable of the Lamp appears to have been understood in terms of the light that Jesus urged his hearers to spread, and not to conceal. Paradoxically, its meaning in those contexts is closer than in Mark to that of the Parable of the Sower, for the messages of the two parables are then remarkably similar: "Bear fruit! Shed light!" This may well have been the original meaning of the parable.

Or perhaps Jesus thought of the light as the equivalent of the seed, which represents "the word," for the lamp was a recognized image for "the word" (cf. Ps 119:105; Prov 6:23, specifically the word of the law). The word is spoken by God himself — the seed is sown; the light is set on a stand for all to see. Men and women, however, must respond by allowing the seed to grow and the light to shine. Within the setting of the ministry of Jesus, therefore, the sayings in verses 24-25 perhaps refer to those who, on the one hand, respond to God's call and possess the kingdom, and those who, on the other, imagine that they are within the community of Israel, but find out too late that they have lost that privilege.

4. The Parables of the Growing Seed and the Mustard Seed (Mark 4:26-32)

And so at last we come to the two parables in Mark's Gospel that are specifically about the kingdom of God: the Parable of the Growing Seed in verses 26-29 and the Parable of the Mustard Seed in verses 30-32. The first, the Parable of the Growing Seed, has no parallel in the other Gospels (though Matthew's Parable of the Tares in 13:24-30 may be an elaboration of it). Mark makes no mention at all of Jesus' audience in his original telling of these parables. Nonetheless, it seems clear from verses 33-34 that he thought of these parables as being once again addressed to the crowd and then explained in private to the disciples.

Many different interpretations have been given to these two parables. One suggestion is that they teach that there is to be a long period between sowing and maturity. This point, however, is not stressed in the first parable; and in the second it is quite inappropriate, since mustard is a fast-growing plant that springs up at a great pace. Others emphasize the harvest as a symbol of the Eschaton — either as a still future event or as dawning in the ministry of Jesus. On this reading, the parables are assurances of the coming of God's kingdom. The early Christian communities may well have taken comfort from the belief that, though response to the gospel was often indiscernible, God was, in fact, still in control. Therefore, even though they did not understand what was taking place, they could be confident that the harvest would eventually appear.

Since the Parable of the Growing Seed in verses 26-29 stresses that the growth of the seed is due to God, not man, it could have been used by Jesus to teach that the kingdom will come when God's purpose is complete, and cannot be hastened by violence (cf. Matt 11:12 // Luke 16:16). The Parable of the Mustard Seed in verses 30-32 lays emphasis on the power of God and the scale of the final outcome. Mustard seed was apparently proverbial for its smallness (cf. Matt 17:20 // Luke 17:6), but when it is sown, it springs up and grows bigger than any other plant (though Matthew and Luke exaggerate in describing it as a tree). It grows so large, in fact, that the birds of the air can build nests in its shade (or, perhaps, "roost" in its branches). These words echo Old Testament imagery of a tree in whose shade birds take shelter, as found in Ezek 17:23 and 31:6, or nest in its branches, as in Dan 4:12, 14, and 21 (cf. Matt 13:32 // Luke 13:19), with the tree symbolizing a great kingdom that gives protection to subject nations. If the Markan parable is interpreted allegorically, the birds may represent the Gentiles, who will one day have a place in God's kingdom — and, indeed, in Mark's day were perhaps already flocking in. But for Mark, the important point seems to be the contrast between the almost invisible seed and the enormous bush.

The fact that Mark has placed these two parables together as a pair suggests that he understood them both to be conveying the same message. Both of them end in language reminiscent of Old Testament references to the final unfolding of God's purpose — a final reaping and harvest in verse 29; the greatness of the plant and the birds that nest in its shade in verse 32. One would expect that the kingdom would be spoken of in terms of future judgment and of setting things right. Instead, we have here parables that imply that the kingdom is present and yet not present — and that continue the theme of the previous paragraph of the contrast between what is now hidden and what will assuredly be revealed.

For Mark, the kingdom of God is displayed already in the life of Jesus, but it is displayed like seed thrown onto the earth: you do not know that it is there unless you are let into the secret. But what the kingdom will finally be is a very different matter. Its greatness comes about by the power of God, as silent and mysterious and inevitable as the power of growth. Just as the harvest comes from grain sown in the earth, and the mustard bush springs from almost invisible seed, so the kingdom will follow from the ministry of Jesus. Unlike the Parable of the Sower, there is no hint here of even partial failure. Thus by means of these two parables, Mark seems to be delivering a message of hope to his community, which lives in the period between the initiation of the kingdom and its final consummation.

The question as to what these two parables might have meant in the mouth of Jesus is enormously complicated because of the uncertainty regarding his understanding of the nature of the kingdom of God. The emphasis in them both, however, is on the final result — that is, on the resultant harvest and the mature mustard plant. To those in Jesus' time wondering what had happened to God's promises, these parables would have conveyed the assurance that his kingdom would come.

In verses 33-34, Mark tells us that Jesus regularly taught in parables, implying that there were many more. Presumably the evangelist has selected those parables that were most appropriate for his purpose in the composition of his Gospel. Jesus taught, Mark tells us, "as they were able to hear." These words have seemed to some to be inconsistent with verses 11-12. In fact, however, they show us clearly Mark's understanding of that section: the parables are a challenge, but response to them lies within the power of those who hear (cf. vv 9, 23, and 24). Nevertheless, Jesus explained their full significance to his disciples (cf. v 34). Mark's readers would presumably identify themselves with this smaller group, since they were among those who had responded to Jesus' challenge. So Mark's readers would be able to comprehend everything, because to them the secret of the kingdom had been given.

5. Later Interpretations

Later expositors used allegory constantly as a method of exegesis, and the parables of Jesus provided ample scope for this method. It was hardly surprising, in view of Mark's handling of the Parable of the Sower, if commentators assumed the parables to be allegories that required a special understanding in order to unravel their hidden meanings. Preachers were able to extract innumerable meanings — and sermons — from one parable in this way. A book by Thomas Taylor, published in 1621, for example, consists of a discourse of some 450 pages on the Parable of the Sower! It was this approach that Adolf Jülicher challenged at the end of the nineteenth century, maintaining that the parables of Jesus were not allegories at all and should not be interpreted as such.

But Jülicher's basic assumption that the parables of Jesus were not intended to be allegories, and that each one contains only one point, has proved to be too rigid. While it is easy to see the difference between extremes — as between a simple parable and an artificial allegory (e.g., a fable in which animals or plants are substituted for people) — the line between parable and allegory is not always so simple to draw. When Jesus told a story about a vineyard, for example, his hearers would immediately assume that he was telling a story about Israel, for they would all have been familiar with the allegory about a fruitless vineyard in Isaiah 5. Similarly, well-known images like those of harvest and light may well have struck instant chords with their first hearers, and certainly would not have been as obscure as Mark suggests.

Mark's parables were a call to action in the particular situation of the evangelist's ministry — a call made to men and women of a particular religious and cultural background, and with presuppositions quite different from ours. Already, when retold in Mark's community, they took on a different meaning, for now they were being heard by those who had a commitment to Jesus as Lord and who accepted his authority to speak in God's name.

Retold in our modern world, however, they suffer from the problem of over-familiarity. We know them too well to be puzzled by the confused explanation of the different kinds of soil, or to be surprised by the notion of hiding a lamp under a bed. At the same time, the imagery of the stories belongs to a world very different from our own. Three of the four parables in Mark 4 are about sowing seeds — something very few of us now do — and the fourth is about a wick floating in oil, which is a far cry from an electric light bulb. Those who originally heard Jesus would have been challenged by his message every time they sowed or harvested their crops, or whenever they saw their crops growing in the field, and every time they lit a lamp and set it on a lampstand. But we are no longer reminded in this way of his words.

What, then, is the message of Jesus' parables for today?

First, they confront us with the demand to respond and to bear fruit. The kingdom of God is not about sitting around waiting for God to act, but about doing his will and acknowledging his kingship over our daily lives. Those who belong to his kingdom must accept his authority and obey him. This is why the parables are interspersed with the warnings "Listen!" and "Those who have ears to hear, let them hear!"

Second, they remind us that God confronts us with his demands and his salvation in the person of Jesus himself. If the word spoken *by* Jesus has become for the believing community the word *about* Jesus, this is because that community has recognized in what he said and did the voice and activity of God.

Third, since Christians today may well find themselves wondering, like first-century Jews, whether the kingdom of God will ever come in its fullness, these parables assure us that the harvest is certain, that the hidden will be revealed, and that God will ultimately be acknowledged as King. And since the lamp is not totally hidden but is already shedding light, these parables suggest also that for those with eyes to see, the harvest is already being gathered and the kingdom is already present in the hearts and lives of those who respond to God's call.

Selected Bibliography

Beavis, Mary Ann. *Mark's Audience: The Literary and Social Setting of Mark 4.11-12.* Sheffield: Sheffield Academic Press, 1989.

Boucher, Madeleine. *The Mysterious Parable.* Washington: Catholic Biblical Association of America, 1977.

Derrett, J. Duncan M. *Law in the New Testament.* London: Darton, Longman and Todd, 1970.

Dodd, C. H. *The Parables of the Kingdom.* London: Nisbet, 1935.

Drury, John. *The Parables in the Gospels: History and Allegory.* London: SPCK, 1980.

Gerhardsson, Birger. "The Parable of the Sower and Its Interpretation," *New Testament Studies* 14 (1968) 165-93.

Hooker, Morna D. *The Message of Mark.* London: Epworth, 1983.

————. *The Gospel according to St. Mark.* London: Black, 1991; Peabody: Hendrickson, 1992.

————. *The Signs of a Prophet.* London: SCM, 1997; Harrisburg: Trinity Press International, 1997.

Jeremias, Joachim. *The Parables of Jesus,* trans. S. H. Hooke. London: SCM; New York: Scribner's, 1963 (from 6th German edition).

Manson, T. W. *The Teaching of Jesus.* Cambridge: Cambridge University Press, 1935.

Marcus, Joel. *The Mystery of the Kingdom of God.* Atlanta: Scholars, 1986.

Stacey, W. D. *Prophetic Drama in the Old Testament.* London: Epworth, 1990.

Telford, William R. *The Barren Temple and the Withered Tree.* Sheffield: JSOT, 1989.

CHAPTER 5

Matthew's Parables of the Kingdom
(Matthew 13:1-52)

DONALD A. HAGNER

IN CHAPTER 13 of his Gospel, the evangelist Matthew devotes the third and central discourse of his five discourses to a series of seven parables that concern "the mysteries of the kingdom of heaven" *(ta mystēria tēs basileias tōn ouranōn,* v 11). When the disciples ask Jesus why he teaches the crowds using parables, he indicates that it is because of their unreceptive hearts. The disciples — that is, those who have received the kingdom — have, by implication, understood the mysteries of the kingdom more directly. Yet even they are unclear about the meaning of the parables, and so must ask about the Parable of the Weeds and the Grain (v 36). Nevertheless, they are the ones who have "the knowledge of the mysteries of the kingdom of heaven," to whom more understanding is given, and to whom the promise is made that they will in the future have even greater understanding — in fact, will have understanding "in abundance" (vv 11-12a).

Matthew builds the first part of his discourse on Mark 4, from which he borrows his introductory material (vv 1-2; cf. Mark 4:1), the story of the sower and seed (vv 3-9; cf. Mark 4:2-9), a statement on the purpose of the parables (vv 10-13; cf. Mark 4:10-12), and the interpretation of the Parable of the Sower and the Seed (vv 18-23; cf. Mark 4:13-20). Somewhat surprisingly, he omits Mark's second parable, the Parable of the Growing Seed, inserting instead the Parable of the Weeds and the Grain (vv 24-30). But he does include Mark's third parable, the Parable of the Mustard Seed (vv 31-32; cf. Mark 4:30-32). Apart from the fulfillment quotation in verse 35 applied to the purpose of Jesus teaching in parables, the remainder of the material in Matthew 13 is from the evangelist's own oral tradition source, which is commonly designated by the letter "M."

It is clear that the first part of Matthew 13 depends on the order of the material in Mark 4. The structure of this central Matthean discourse has been much discussed and need not detain us here. The lack of symmetry in its structure prevents any satisfying analysis of the whole. What is significant, however, is the clear transition that is caused by the narrative insertion at verse 36, where Jesus turns from the crowds to teach his disciples. This transition divides the discourse of chapter 13 into two main sections: that found in verses 3-35 and that of verses 36-52. In that division the Parable of the Weeds and the Grain is separated into two parts, with the story being given openly to the people (vv 24-30) and the interpretation given privately to the disciples (vv 36-43). But that division is part of the narrative strategy of the text, as we will observe again later. (On the narrative progression of this Matthean discourse, see J. P. Heil in Carter and Heil, *Matthew's Parables*, 64-95.)

We turn now to an analysis of each of the seven Matthean parables of the kingdom in turn.

1. The Parable of the Sower and the Seed (13:3-23)

The Story (vv 3-9)

Matthew follows Mark very closely in setting out the story of the sower and the seed. The changes in wording are minor, with many of them being simply the result of Matthew's characteristic abbreviation of Mark's Gospel. The only significant changes are (1) Matthew's use of the plural in referring to "seeds," rather than Mark's singular (except for the plural in Mark 4:8), and (2) Matthew's reversing of the order of the yield from Mark's "thirtyfold and sixtyfold and a hundredfold" to an enumeration that begins with the largest yield first: "some a hundredfold, some sixtyfold, some thirtyfold" (v 8).

The story speaks of sowing seed in four different circumstances: (1) along the path; (2) on rocky ground; (3) among thorn bushes; and (4) on good ground. Each of these is given a corresponding secondary element: (1) birds come and eat the seed; (2) the sun rises and withers the seedling; (3) thorns choke the seed; and (4) the seed bears fruit in varying amounts. The question arises whether the parable requires us to imagine a situation where the seeds were actually sown in such places. Or does the imagery of the parable merely refer to what may be conceived of as happening, unusual though it might be?

Some evidence can be cited from ancient agricultural practice to suggest that a field was ploughed *after* it was sown. Such a practice could possibly explain the instances of sowing seed "along the path" or "on rocky ground." But such an explanation is hardly necessary. Nor is it pertinent to the point of the parable. For the heart of the parable concerns the fact that seeds that are sown sometime become unfruitful and sometime are fruitful. The issue is success or lack of success. And the point is that under certain circumstances, seeds that are sown in a field are subject to hostile realities such as birds, scorching sun, and thorns.

Since the parable follows accounts of unbelief in Jesus and his message in Matthew 11 and 12, with the accounts set out in an escalating fashion in those two chapters, it is most natural to conclude that the parable alludes to the mixed success of Jesus' ministry. In that case, Jesus becomes the sower and the seed represents his message of the kingdom. For a variety of reasons, the seed does not bear fruit. Yet some seed falls on good soil and it "kept producing" (*edidou*, an imperfect tense) fruit, with spectacular to very good results. The high yield may also be an allusion to eschatological fulfillment, though in that case one might have expected even more fantastic numbers than these. At least the numbers point to the high success of the kingdom.

The concluding words of verse 9, "Let the person who has ears hear!", alert the reader to the fact that the parable points beyond itself to a matter of deep concern. The story has to do with receptivity. It amounts to an appeal to hear positively and to respond appropriately (cf. v 43). And this application is made unmistakable in the interpretation of the parable given in verses 18-23.

On the Purpose of the Parables (vv 10-17)

Between the story and its interpretation, we encounter in verses 10-17, as paralleled partially in Mark 4:10-12, a passage that deals with the purpose of the parables. This intervening material is important because of its references to positive and negative responses to the message of Jesus, which is the very concern of the Parable of the Sower and the Seed. Belief and receptivity, on the one hand, are attributed to the grace of God. For the words of verse 11, "to know the mysteries of the kingdom has been given to you" — which occur in the form of a divine passive — indicate that God is the source of the disciples' knowledge, as well as their receptivity to that knowledge (cf. 11:25-27). Unbelief and unreceptivity, on the other hand, are attributed to the hardheartedness of those who do not respond (hence the full quotation of Isa 6:9-10).

In this obvious lack of symmetry, which is so characteristic of the biblical writers on the subject, we encounter the mysterious sovereignty of God, who accomplishes his will without at any time violating a person's freedom of choice or the responsibility that goes with it. And parables function similarly in such a dual manner. For those who have responded positively to Jesus' proclamation of the kingdom, the parables convey further insight and knowledge. But for those who have rejected Jesus and his message, the parables have the effect of only darkening the subject further. Therefore belief and commitment lead to further knowledge, while unbelief leads to further ignorance.

The Interpretation (vv 18-23)

The interpretation of the Parable of the Sower and the Seed is thought by many New Testament scholars to be an allegorized addition of the early church to a simple story of Jesus. But while later meanings can be read into the story, it is not necessary to do so. The interpretation as it is, even with its slightly unusual vocabulary, makes quite good sense in the mouth of Jesus (cf. B. Gerhardsson, "Parable of the Sower," 192; see also W. D. Davies and D. C. Allison, *Matthew*, 397-99). It is simply unjustifiable prejudice to conclude that Jesus never allegorized a parable.

In the interpretation, Matthew replaces Mark's introductory words, which imply criticism of the disciples ("Do you not understand this parable? Then how will you understand all the parables?"), with the simple exhortation: "You, therefore, listen to the parable of the sower" (v 18). This is perhaps the counterpart to Matthew's omission of the verb "listen" (*akouete*) at the beginning of the story in Mark 4:3. Also to be noted is the oddity that whereas in the story Matthew consistently refers in the plural to "seeds" and Mark usually uses the singular (except in 4:8), here in the interpretation the reverse is the case, with Matthew using the singular and Mark the plural. This state of affairs may be due to cross-fertilization in the oral transmission of the materials.

The explanation of the last three instances of sowing is given in parallelism using the following elements: (1) the introductory formula "what was sown on . . ."; (2) the description formula "this is the one hearing the word"; (3) further description of the circumstances; and (4) the outcome. In the first instance, however, the first of these elements ("this is what was sown on the path") is placed last, enabling Matthew in verse 19 to put emphasis on hearing "the word of the kingdom." This also immediately identifies the sowing as a matter of hearing the word. And precisely for this reason the seed metaphor can refer both to the message itself and to the person receiving or not receiving the message (cf. vv 19, 20, 22, and 23). The person is like the particular instance of sowing seed in the described soil. Also, the carefully formed parallelism of the passage is noteworthy and suggests that it was designed for cate-chesis and easy memorization.

As in Mark, what is sown is identified as "the word." Matthew's ex-pression "the word of the kingdom" *(ton logon tēs basileias)* makes it clear that it is the word of Jesus that is in view. The word of the kingdom is the equivalent of Matthew's favorite phrase "the gospel of the kingdom" (cf. 4:23; 9:35; 24:14) — that is, the announcement of the dawning of "the kingdom of heaven," an expression synonymous with "the kingdom of God." This places the parable squarely within the life setting of the Jesus of history, where it would have been used to depict the varied responses of people to Jesus and his preaching (cf. G. E. Ladd, "*Sitz im Leben* of the Par-ables of Matthew 13"). Matthew's community, however, could easily have applied the parable to their own failures and successes in preaching the gospel.

In the first instance, where the seed was sown "along the path" (cf. v 4), the problem is described in verse 19 as a failure to understand. This is not the result of an inadequate presentation of the message, but rather of the hardheartedness of the hearer and his or her refusal to receive (cf. vv 13-15; see also 11:21, 23; 12:41-42). Those who will not receive the mes-sage do not understand it. The birds that eat up the seed are identified as "the evil one" *(ho ponēros)* who "snatches away what is sown in the heart."

In Jewish literature birds are sometimes identified with the devil (cf. *Jubilees* 11:11-12; *Apocalypse of Abraham* 13:3-7). Here, reference to the activity of the evil one in no way lessens the culpability of those who reject the message. Rather, it is because they have rejected the message that the evil one is enabled to snatch away the seed.

In the second instance, the seed fell on stony ground and immediately produced shoots (cf. v 5). This is explained in verse 20 as the one who, on hearing the word, receives it "immediately" and "with joy." At first this response seems to be an example of success ("receiving," *lambanōn*) rather than failure. The story, however, refers to a burning hot sun that withered the shoots in the shallow soil (v 6), and the interpretive counterpart in verse 21 speaks of the experience of "trouble or persecution on account of the word" — that is, of suffering for the message of the kingdom. That the disciples were to expect persecution has already been emphasized in Matthew's Gospel (cf. 5:11-12; 10:16-25). The follower of Jesus must be prepared for this eventuality and be ready to endure to the end (cf. 23:34-36; 24:9-13). In the present case, the eagerness of the new disciple is not matched with endurance under trial. This shows that the initial response of the hearer is not deep, and so the result is that the seed does not bear fruit that lasts.

The third instance refers to seed that falls among thorn bushes, which eventually choke the seedling (v 7). Here, too, there has been a hearing and a receiving that produce a measure of growth before the thorns do their destructive work. The interpretation in verse 22 identifies the thorns as "the anxiety of the world and the seduction of riches." Both anxiety and wealth are subjects dealt with in the Sermon on the Mount (cf. 6:19-34; on riches, see 19:23-24). It is not difficult, to see how these things can become obstacles to genuine discipleship and so thwart an appropriate response to the message of the kingdom.

Only in the fourth instance, where the seed falls on good soil, is the seed truly productive (v 8). In this case the word is heard and, in direct contradiction to the first instance, the hearer "understands." Here in verse 23, as in verse 19, the word "understand" *(sunieis)* implies receptivity. Furthermore, understanding results in a response of proper conduct. So the good soil represents the hearer who receives the seed of the word, nurtures that seed in discipleship, and bears fruit *(karpophorei)* in spectacularly abundant measure. "Fruit" here is probably to be understood as the pattern of conduct described in the Sermon on the Mount: the living out of the kingdom of God here and now. And thus, though the parable addresses particularly the problem of unbelief (cf. vv 10-15), it also contains a strong element of ethical exhortation.

It is important to understand this shift of focus in the Parable of the Sower and the Seed — a shift where the nature of the soil is highlighted — in its context (where both sower and seed play principal parts) and with the original purpose of the parable in mind (where the problem of unbelief is addressed). The key issue of the parable is responsiveness or non-responsiveness to the message of the kingdom. It is in this sense that one either understands (v 23) or does not understand (v 19). But there is also the possibility of an initial positive response that proves to be less than adequate. Two instances are given, though it would not be difficult to think of others.

In the first instance we encounter a fair-weather disciple who, under the pressure of adverse circumstances, abandons his or her faith and commitment. This person has thought only of the blessings of the kingdom, having made a simple equation between the enjoyment of them and being a disciple, and so is unable to cope with the reality of continuing evil in the world. The shallowness of such discipleship underlines the appropriateness of the metaphor of shallow soil. In the second instance, the response of discipleship is cut short by the ordinary cares of life (cf. 8:21) and the seduction of wealth (cf. 6:24; see also 1 Tim 6:9-10). The pull of the latter, of course, remains a dominant factor in the modern world with its rampant materialism.

We are, therefore, reminded in this passage of the absolute claim of discipleship. The word of the kingdom when received fully and without reservation results in an unqualified, constant, and abundantly fruitful discipleship (cf. John 15:8, 16; Gal 5:22f.). The parable contained a challenge to Matthew's church (cf. J. Lambrecht, *Out of the Treasure,* 176). It also contains an ongoing challenge to Christians and the church today.

2. The Parable of the Weeds and the Grain
(13:24-30, 36-43)

Matthew's second parable, the Parable of the Weeds and the Grain, addresses a major concern of the whole discourse — that is, the concern about God's delay in judgment. Here is one of the most innovative and difficult aspects of Jesus' doctrine of the kingdom. Indeed, it is truly one of the mysteries of the kingdom!

The immediate and natural reaction of the people to Jesus' announcement of the presence of God's kingdom was to wonder about the continuing presence of evil in the world, particularly as manifested in Roman rule over the people of God. The remaining parables of Matthew 13 deal with one aspect or another of the paradoxical nature of the presently dawning kingdom of God. This second parable is put alongside the preceding parable because of their common agricultural motifs, despite the fact that the two parables have entirely different purposes. For as in the first, here too is a story of one who sows seed with the end result being mixed.

The Story (vv 24-30)

The parable begins with the formula "the kingdom of heaven may be compared to *(hōmoiōthē)* . . ." (v 24). This reflects an underlying Aramaic construction that is to be understood as "it is the case with . . . as with. . . ." A similar formula introduces each of the remaining five parables ("the kingdom of heaven is like [*homoia*] . . ."). The first part of the story of this parable consists of a narrative in verses 24-26; the second part, a dialogue in verses 27-30 wherein the main point of the parable is made.

In the narrative section we learn of two sowings: the first by a man who sowed good seed in his field; the second by his enemy, who came by night to sow weeds (*zizania,* a common weed) among the good grain. When the plants came up, both the grain and the weeds appeared. There is some similarity here with Mark's Parable of the Growing Seed (cf. Mark 4:26-29), which is not repeated by Matthew. Yet despite some common features, the point in Matthew's Parable of the Grain and the Weeds is not the miraculous growth of the seed, but rather the growing of the grain and the weeds together.

The dialogue section brings out the point of the narrative section. The man who sowed good seed is identified as "the master of the house" *(ho oikodespotēs),* who, it may be inferred, represents Jesus — a point that is furthered by the address *Kyrie,* "Sir," which Matthew's readers would have understood as "Lord." When the servants *(hoi douloi)* ask how the weeds appeared, they are informed that "an enemy has done this" (v 28).

To the servants' question about whether they should pull up the weeds, a negative answer is given on the grounds that the grain might accidentally be pulled up with the weeds. This could well happen not because of any difficulty in distinguishing between the two, but rather because of the proximity of the two and the stronger roots of the weeds. Both are to be allowed to grow together until the harvest time when the two will be separated — the weeds to be burned and the grain to be put into the granary.

The key point here, which will be developed further in the remaining parables of Matthew 13, is that it is not yet the time of harvest, and so not yet the time for separating the grain from the weeds. The judgment motif of this imagery is clear. It is a motif that is found frequently in Jewish literature. And it will receive considerable elaboration in the interpretation of the parable given in verses 36-43: The kingdom of God has indeed come, but it involves a surprising delay in the coming of the eschatological judgment.

The Interpretation (vv 36-43)

Like the first parable, the story of the grain and the weeds also receives an allegorizing interpretation. Again, there is no compelling reason to conclude that this interpretation is the product of the church and not something that Jesus himself could have given. And as in the previous parable, the interpretation is separated from the story rather than placed immediately after it.

In this second parable, however, there is a shift in the audience, with Jesus in verse 36 portrayed as leaving the crowd and going into a house where he can address his disciples privately. Furthermore, between the story and its interpretation two other parables of the kingdom are presented, that of the Mustard Seed (vv 31-32) and that of the Leaven (v 33), as well as a summarizing comment that brings the first section to an end (vv 34-35). In the latter passage it is said that Jesus spoke to the crowd only in parables— a comment drawn from Mark 4:33-34. And to that remark Matthew appends a quotation of Ps 78:2, which he introduces by a fulfillment formula:

> This was to fulfill what had been spoken through the prophet: "I will open my mouth to speak in parables; I will proclaim what has been hidden from the foundation of the world."

This quotation becomes at once the *raison d'être* of the Matthean parables discourse (cf. the revealing of "the mysteries of the kingdom of heaven" in v 11) as well as a further confirmation of Jesus as the fulfiller of the Old Testament Scriptures.

Verses 37-39 contain a one-to-one identification in parallel form of seven key features in the story: the sower = the Son of Man (i.e., Jesus); the field = the world; the good seed = those who belong to the kingdom; the weeds = those of the evil one; the enemy = the Devil; the harvest = the end of the age; and the harvesters = the angels. Not every element of the parable, however, is explicitly allegorized. For example, "the master" could be identified with Jesus, "the servants" with the disciples, and "the bearing of fruit" with righteousness. It is, furthermore, unclear whether the reference to "everyone sleeping" in verse 25 is merely an incidental introductory statement or was intended to reflect a failure to be watchful. And what would a premature "rooting out" refer to? Possibly church discipline? Not every detail can or should be pressed for meaning. And while the extent of the explicit allegorical identifications is impressive, it should also be noted that two of the items identified (i.e., the world and the Devil) are not mentioned again in the continuation of the interpretation.

The field, which is explicitly identified as "the world" *(ho kosmos)*, cannot have been understood as the church by either the evangelist or his readers (*contra* R. K. McIver, "Parable of the Weeds among the Wheat"). Such an identification of the field as the world, however, does cohere with Matthew's understanding of the worldwide mission of the church in the spread of the gospel (cf. 24:14; 28:19). "The evil one" *(ho poneros)* of verse 38, who is referred to also in verse 19 as the one who snatches away the seed of the word that was sown on the path, is in verse 39a equated with "the Devil" *(ho diabolos)*, who sowed the weeds in the field. "The harvest" *(ho therismos)* in verse 39b is a common metaphor for the time of eschatological judgment (cf. Joel 3:13; Jer. 51:33; *2 Apocalypse of Baruch* 70:2). Likewise, "the angels" were commonly believed in Jewish tradition to be administrators of the will of God in accomplishing the eschatological judgment (cf. *1 Enoch* 46:5; 63:1).

Verses 40-43, which were called by Joachim Jeremias a "little apocalypse" (cf. his *The Parables of Jesus*, trans. S. H. Hooke [London: SCM; New York: Scribner, 1972 rev. ed.]), explain the central point of the parable. The gathering and burning of the weeds refer to the eschatological judgment (cf. 3:10). At "the close of the age" the wicked will be judged. This will be accomplished by the Son of Man, who is the sower of the good seed in the parable, and by his angels (cf. 16:27; 25:31-33; and 24:30-31). Here the angels are sent to gather "everything that causes stumbling" and "those guilty of lawlessness" — which are two of the most grievous offenses depicted in Matthew's Gospel (on "causing to stumble" [*skandalizō*], see 18:6-7; on "lawlessness" [*anomia*], see 7:23; 23:28; 24:12). People guilty of these offenses will be collected "out of his kingdom," that is, from the kingdom of the Son of Man. This probably refers to where the seed had been sown, and so, ideally, has in mind the whole world.

The wicked are gathered "out of" or "from" the kingdom not in the sense that they were actually a part of the church. Nor does the kingdom exactly equal the field/world. But the wicked are gathered from the kingdom in the sense that they were in the world and had existed alongside the righteous (cf. v 30). So they were even in the visible church, but are to be finally distinguished and separated from the righteous. The imagery of a furnace of fire is drawn from Dan 3:6. It occurs again in verse 50, as does also the formulaic language about the weeping and grinding of teeth (cf. 8:12; 22:13; 24:51; 25:30).

As the lawless will receive punishment, so "the righteous" *(hoi dikaioi),* which is a favorite term of Matthew for those who respond positively to Jesus, will be rewarded. "They will glimmer like the sun in the kingdom of their Father." This language is almost exactly the same as that used in describing the transfiguration of Jesus in 17:2, and so suggests the experiencing of the glory of God. The same imagery is used also in Dan 12:3, which says that those raised to everlasting life "will shine like the brightness of the firmament." And while verse 41 speaks of "the kingdom of the Son of Man" and verse 43 "the kingdom of their Father," these two phrases refer to the same reality and are not to be distinguished. The dramatic contrast of the fate of "the lawless" and that of "the righteous," therefore, concludes with the pointed exhortation: "Let the person who has ears, hear!" — an exhortation that is also found verbatim in verse 9 and 11:15.

In this world, even after the announcement of Jesus that the eschatological kingdom has already begun, those guilty of lawlessness — that is, people who belong to the evil one — continue to coexist with the righteous, who are the people of God's kingdom. There has not been, nor will there be, a dramatic separation of the lawless from the righteous until the harvest at the end of the age. The present age is therefore one in which human society — and so even the church — is a mixture of those of the evil one and those of the kingdom. This can result in a confusing situation, especially when the wicked seem to prosper and the righteous suffer. But the ambiguity of the present situation is a temporary one, and with the end of the age it, too, will be brought to an end. Then, and only then, will there be a clear demarcation between these two classes of people, with each receiving their eschatological due: for the lawless, a dreadful punishment; for the righteous, extravagant blessedness. Evil people will be shown for what they are. But the righteous, too, will become conspicuous. To this future expectation Matthew returns again and again in his Gospel, thereby setting before his readers both warning and encouragement.

3. The Parable of the Mustard Seed (13:31-32)

The third parable of Matthew 13, the Parable of the Mustard Seed in verses 31-32, continues the portrayal of the kingdom of God using the imagery of seed that is sown. The catchwords "sowing," "seed," and "field" provide continuity between the first three parables. In this third parable the kingdom is again portrayed as a present reality. But here its presence is in secret form — that is, its presence, though real, can be easily overlooked. The kingdom has come, but not in the spectacular, unmistakable fashion in which it was expected. That same point will be made in the Parable of the Leaven, which follows in verse 33. Indeed, this is one of the "mysteries of the kingdom" given to disciples of Jesus (cf. v 11).

This is the first parable in the discourse of Matthew 13 that does not receive an interpretation. None of the remaining parables, in fact, receives one. So the hearers (and readers) are left on their own to work out the implied interpretation. Furthermore, this is the last parable that Matthew draws from Mark, though the amount of agreement between the evangelists in their wording is small. Several verbal agreements between Matthew and Luke against Mark suggest the possibility of the influence of Q, which may have contained the parable as well — though those agreements may also be due to the influence of oral tradition on both Matthew and Luke.

In the Parable of the Mustard Seed, the kingdom is likened to the situation of a man who planted a mustard seed in his field. In the ancient world the mustard seed was known for its smallness. From this "smallest" of seeds (it matters not that we know of smaller seeds) an amazingly large bush-like plant emerged, which at maturity was eight to ten feet in height (cf. *Babylonian Talmud, Ketuboth* 111b, which refers to timber from a mustard tree sufficient in quantity to cover the roof of a potter's hut) and large enough to accommodate the nests of birds. This fact was so remarkable that it seems to have taken on a proverbial character.

Matthew's final clause, "the birds of the sky dwell in its branches," agrees nearly verbatim with Dan 4:21 (LXX, Theodotion version) and Ps 103:12 (LXX, which in English translations is 104:12), with these two passages alluding to the great tree of Belshazzar's dream and the cedars of Lebanon, respectively. It is the contrast between a tiny mustard seed and the large size of a mustard plant at maturity that is determinative in the parable of verses 31-32. But Matthew's use of the word "tree" *(dendron)* to describe the mustard plant probably involves hyperbole, with that hyperbole suggesting a symbolism that points beyond agriculture to a greater reality or kingdom (as is often the case in the OT; cf. Ezek 17:22-24; 31:2-13; Dan 4:20-21).

Although not impossible, the usual interpretation of the birds in the branches as referring to Gentiles (with OT support) introduces an allegory that is not intrinsic to the parable itself, but one both foreign to the context and unnecessary for a straightforward reading of the text. For the birds are mentioned only to indicate the remarkable size of the plant. The point of the parable is simply the miracle of nature symbolized by a mustard seed, which develops from the smallest of beginnings to an astonishing fullness. In the same way, the kingdom has begun inconspicuously. Yet *it has begun!* And in the end its greatness, when compared to its size at its beginning, will provide as amazing a contrast as that between a mustard seed and a full-grown mustard plant.

It is impossible to rule out an allusion in this parable also to growth, even though its main point is about contrast rather than growth. For though the kingdom of God has humble beginnings, did not overwhelm the world in its coming, and can be easily overlooked, it is destined to become an impressive entity. This parable, indeed, takes the place in Matthew 13 of the parable of Mark 4:26-29, which speaks of the miracle of the growth of seed as a metaphor for the growth of the kingdom. The point is the same: The kingdom's mysterious growth is the work of God. If we restrict the analogy only to size, then the contrast between Jesus with the Twelve, at the beginning, and the church universal, as it now is, has remarkably fulfilled the parable.

4. The Parable of the Yeast (13:33)

The fourth parable of Matthew 13, the Parable of the Yeast in verse 33, is the last of Jesus' public parables in the Matthean parabolic discourse. For the three remaining parables are addressed to the disciples. Furthermore, this parable, despite its change of imagery, is closely related to the preceding parable. For it, too, speaks of the initial unimpressiveness of the kingdom compared to what it will eventually become.

The Parable of the Yeast is drawn from Q (cf. Luke 13:20-21). Matthew, however, introduces it with his own formula, "he spoke another parable to them" (cf. vv 24, 31), and turns what was probably a question in Q to an indicative statement (cf. the same change in v 31). Likewise, Matthew changes "kingdom of God" (cf. Luke 13:20) to "kingdom of heaven." But beyond these changes, the agreements with Luke are quite close.

There are a number of formal similarities between this parable and the preceding one — most obviously, the initial reference to "another parable," the opening words "the kingdom of heaven is similar to," and the parallelism in the clauses "yeast, which a woman took and mixed" and "a seed (of mustard) which someone took and sowed." Yeast, or leaven, was a common and important ingredient in Palestinian households. Its special character of gradual fermentation made it a particularly suggestive metaphor for describing similar processes in the moral sphere, giving rise to the proverb "a little leaven leavens the whole lump" (cf. 1 Cor 5:6; Gal 5:9). Beyond its appearance here in chapter 13, Matthew again uses yeast metaphorically in 16:6, 11-12 to refer to the teaching of the Pharisees and Sadducees.

Although leaven in the Old Testament usually symbolizes the corrupting influence of evil (though not always; cf. Lev 23:17), and so was to be purged entirely from Israelite households at Passover (Exod 12:15, 19), there is no indication that it is to be viewed in this parable as something evil. What is portrayed here is the dynamic power of leaven whereby a small amount, which is imperceptible when first mixed into dough (note the verb "hid"), has an eventual, inevitable, and astonishing effect on the whole batch of dough. In this sense, this parable is parallel to the immediately preceding Parable of the Mustard Seed. Both speak of that which appears initially to be insignificant and of no consequence, but which in time produces an astonishing and dramatic effect. The kingdom of God is like yeast in this way. For although at its beginning it may look unimpressive, it will have an effect that is out of all proportion with that beginning.

The dynamic power of the kingdom of God — which, though it may express itself in seemingly hidden ways in the beginning, will eventually permeate everything — is the main point of the Parable of the Leaven. It is unlikely that the growth in view points to the work or influence of the disciples. Nor is there need to allegorize such details as the woman, the three measures, or the whole batch of dough itself. It is, however, worth noting that an exceptionally large amount of dough is indicated by the expression "three measures" (sata tria), which amounts to nearly 40 liters or 50 kilograms of bread and would be enough to feed about 150 people. Such an inflated figure may suggest eschatological fulfillment, though probably not the messianic banquet.

When a batch of dough is first leavened, it does not look altered. With the passing of time, however, the yeast takes its effect and the dough rises. Similarly, the parable suggests, though the initial coming of the kingdom of God does not look as though it has had any effect, the effect will become visible and dominant — just as surely as yeast has its effect.

5. The Parable of the Hidden Treasure (13:44)

The fifth of the parables of Matthew 13, that of the Parable of the Hidden Treasure in verse 44 — together with the sixth, that of the Parable of the Pearl in verses 45-46 — has as its focus the glorious character of the kingdom instituted by Jesus, which justifies the cost of absolute discipleship. These two parables, however, are linked with the preceding parables by the continuing motif of hiddenness and smallness. So, in effect, the hidden treasure (v 44) corresponds to the hidden leaven (v 33) and the smallness of the pearl (vv 45-46) to the smallness of the mustard seed (vv 31-32).

In addition to the same opening formula, "the kingdom of heaven is like," these two parables have the same five elements in the same order: (1) a reference to something very valuable; (2) finding it; (3) going; (4) selling everything; and (5) buying it (in the first parable, the field; in the second, the pearl of great value). The first parable has the additional features of hiding a treasure in a field and the mention of joy at its discovery. Although the syntax is not altogether parallel, certainly the content of the parables is quite parallel — which suggests an early linking of these two parables, at least in the oral tradition and perhaps even from the beginning.

116

It was not at all unusual in the ancient world to hide treasure in the ground. The background of this phrase, however, is probably to be found in Israel's Wisdom literature (cf. Prov 2:4; Sirach 20:30), although many folk tales also deal with this theme. The analogy here, like the re-hiding of a treasure by a person who finds it, suggests that something of tremendous worth can be present and yet not known to others who may have frequently traversed the same field. Similarly, the kingdom can be present and yet not perceived, because its present form does not overwhelm the world or overcome resistance to it. But the person who does discover the treasure goes with joy to sell everything in order to obtain that field and its hidden treasure.

The question of the ethical propriety of buying a field with hidden treasure is not addressed in the parable. The sole point being made is that the kingdom of God is worth everything. Furthermore, though no explanation of the parable is provided, it is obvious that a rigorous, self-denying and costly discipleship is in view (cf. 19:21, 29; see also Luke 14:33; Phil 3:7). This is the basic message of the parable. Other features, such as the re-hiding of the treasure and the buying of the field, are merely supportive details and need not be allegorized. The parable, like its companion parable following, is about the reality of the kingdom and its absolute worth in terms of personal sacrifice.

6. The Parable of the Pearl (13:45-46)

The Parable of the Pearl in verses 45-46, as we have seen, is parallel to the preceding parable, both in form and basic message. In this parable the kingdom is likened to the circumstance of a pearl merchant in search of fine pearls. This merchant finds one supremely precious pearl and sells everything he has in order to buy it (cf. the Wisdom texts of Job 28:18 and Prov 3:15; 8:11 for background). The pearl in the story clearly represents the kingdom. Pearls were very highly valued in the ancient world, even more than gold.

There is deliberate hyperbole in verse 46, for it is rather unlikely that any merchant would sell everything that he or she had in order to acquire any single pearl. But in the case of the kingdom, which is wonderful beyond price, such an analogous action of a disciple in full and unreserved commitment is more than justified!

117

As in the Parable of the Hidden Treasure, the supportive imagery of "buying" is not to be allegorized. Selling and buying together point to the response of the disciple. Rather, what is highlighted in the parable is that the kingdom of God, though like a small, inconspicuous pearl, is of incalculable value, and so, once discovered, calls for unrestrained response in the form of absolute discipleship. The kingdom of God is the greatest of treasures. Though its worth is immeasurable by any standard (cf. Wisdom of Solomon 7:7-9, 14 concerning wisdom), it is now present only in veiled form and can be possessed by some without the knowledge of those near them. Like a pearl that can be held in one's hand, the kingdom is known only to its joyful possessors.

Yet those who find the kingdom — that is, those who receive Jesus' message and respond in discipleship — have begun to experience the wonder of the kingdom's presence. They know that the kingdom is a reality worth everything, and so they joyfully make it their one priority in life (cf. 4:18-22; 10:39). They seek first the kingdom, sacrificing all to it; but at the same time, paradoxically, they find in the kingdom all they need (6:33).

7. The Parable of the Net (13:47-50)

The seventh and last parable of Matthew 13, the Parable of the Net in verses 47-50, returns to the motif of the eschatological separation of the righteous and the evil, proclaiming the judgment of the latter. The parable is reminiscent of the second parable, the Parable of the Weeds and the Grain in verses 24-30 and 36-43. We may, in fact, have to reckon with reciprocal influence between these two parables — perhaps even in the pre-Matthean tradition. For verse 50 of this parable is a verbatim repetition of verse 42 of that earlier parable: "and throw them into the furnace of fire; there people will weep and gnash their teeth." Furthermore, in rounding out his collection of parables in chapter 13, Matthew returns to one of his favorite themes: the judgment of the unrighteous. And the stress here, as it was earlier, is on the occurrence of judgment only "at the end of the age" (v 49; cf. v 40). Yet for all the similarities between this parable and the preceding parables, there is one striking difference. Here in verses 49-50 an interpretation is provided alongside the narrative imagery of verses 47-48.

The appropriateness of this parable for the several disciples who had been fishermen is obvious. The net in question, which in Greek is called a *sagēnē*, was a seine-net with floats at the top edge and weights at the bottom. When the net was thrown into the water it encircled the fish and then was dragged up on the shore. The net naturally gathered fish indiscriminately, hence "of every kind" *(ek pantos genous)*. The exaggerated inclusiveness of this phrase may be an intentional reflection on the universality of the invitation to accept the good news of the kingdom (cf. 22:9-10: "both bad and good," *ponērous te kai agathous)*. So while the Parable of the Weeds and the Grain may only have implied a mixture of the unrighteous and the righteous in the church, the Parable of the Net makes that point quite clearly.

In their proclamation of the kingdom, the disciples had become "fishers of men and women" (cf. 4:19: *halieis anthrōpōn)*. Among those who respond are many who will not persevere in their initial commitment (cf. 13:3-8, 18-23); there will be those who do not live up to the standards of the church (cf. 7:21-23; 18:17). The clause "when it was full" *(hote eplērōthē)* of verse 48 corresponds to "at the end of the age" *(en tē synteleia tou aiōnos)* of verse 49, and therefore hints at eschatological fulfillment. It would have been a very common experience at Capernaum, for example, to see fishermen sitting on the beach, going through the day's catch, keeping the good fish and throwing away the bad ones. The expression *ta sapra*, "the bad ones," of verse 48 is used also to describe bad trees or bad fruit in 7:17-18 and 12:33. And "to throw out" or "away" in verses 48 and 50 echoes the language of 8:12.

The determinative clause is at the beginning of verse 49: "So it will be at the end of the age." The separation of the evil from the righteous will occur only then. Here it is again the angels who are the agents of eschatological judgment (cf. v 41). They will separate the evil ones "from the midst of the righteous" *(ek mesou tōn dikaiōn)*. This last phrase highlights the present mixture of good and evil in the kingdom, and so points to the church as it now exists being a *corpus permixtum*. The evil ones, or false disciples within the church, will experience eschatological judgment. After the reference to that separation, the judgment of the wicked is described in terms of the standardized fire imagery (cf. 25:41), thereby departing from the imagery of the parable itself.

This final parable focuses again on the reality of eschatological judgment at the end of the age. In the present era, evil persons are allowed to live together with the righteous — in fact, in their midst — even within that manifestation of the kingdom known as the church. The net of the kingdom includes a mixture of both good and evil. That such circumstances could exist in the era of the kingdom of God is nothing less than astonishing — something, indeed, worth calling one of "the mysteries of the kingdom." That good and evil could be located within the net of the kingdom seemed equally strange, no doubt. Yet at the time of eschatological judgment, only the righteous — that is, those who have received the kingdom with an appropriate response in the form of discipleship — will survive. Those who are evil will experience their punishment.

A focus on judgment within the church, of course, presupposes the wider context of the judgment of the world. The evangelist Matthew never tires in warning his readers of the reality of judgment, and hence of the importance of a genuine discipleship. It is a warning that both the world and the church need today.

8. A Scribe Trained for the Kingdom:
The End of the Discourse (13:51-52)

The end of Matthew's parables discourse in chapter 13 is formed by a question concerning the disciples' understanding in verse 51 and a comment regarding those who teach this doctrine of the kingdom in verse 52, with that final comment being given in the form of yet another parabolic analogy. This concluding analogy throws light on the seven parables of the discourse by focusing on one of the basic tensions inherent in their message: the continuity and discontinuity of old and new.

Jesus asks the disciples if they have understood "all these things" — that is, about the preceding parables of the kingdom, but also the content of the entire discourse as Matthew has constructed it. The reference to understanding the parables recalls the discussion on the purpose of the parables in verses 10-17. For only if the disciples have understood these things will they be in a position to be fruitful for the kingdom (cf. v 23). And though there is still much ahead of them to learn, and though they will still stumble in ignorance on more than one occasion, they are able — at least with regard to these parables — to answer with a somewhat deceptively confident "Yes."

A "scribe" (grammateus) in Judaism was a scholar-teacher who was trained in the interpretation of the Torah. Such a scribe is described in Sirach 39:2-3 as one who will not only "seek out the wisdom of all the ancients," but also one who will "penetrate the subtleties of parables" and "be at home with the obscurities of parables." Jesus here, however, refers to a new kind of scribe: one who is instructed (*mathēteutheis*, literally: "having been made a disciple") in the kingdom of heaven — that is, instructed as a disciple concerning the nature of God's kingdom as elucidated by Jesus through his parables. So, it seems evident, Jesus had here in mind the disciples whom he has been teaching. (Later in 23:34 Matthew again refers to Christian scribes, but there the reference is probably to Christian scholars of the Torah.)

This new type of scribe, who is trained in the knowledge of the kingdom, is likened to a "master of a household" (*oikodespotēs;* cf. 20:1; 21:33), who brings out of his storeroom "new things and old things" *(kaina kai palaia).* The key here — as, indeed, the key to the parables themselves — is the combination of new and old. For the parables, like Jesus' other teachings about the kingdom, involve old and familiar things juxtaposed with new elements.

In view here are not merely new hermeneutical applications of the Torah in new situations — something the Jewish scribes were always concerned with. Nor is it simply new applications of old sayings of Jesus. Rather, what is in view is the relation of the Torah to the genuinely new reality of the kingdom of God (cf. Mark 1:27) — that is, the "mysteries" concerning the purposes of God, which were hidden from the beginning but now are being made known (cf. v 35). The Christian scribe, who is trained and prepared to teach others, must be able to use the old and the new together to bring clarity and understanding to the message of the kingdom in its application to the present. The old things and the new things of the Christian scribe are both indispensable to the gospel.

The gospel of the kingdom as announced by Jesus, believed in by the disciples, and established as the foundation of the church, is by its very nature a blend of continuity and discontinuity with the old (i.e., the OT as ordinarily understood). At its heart the gospel consists of "new things," and that newness must never be underestimated. But for Matthew, these "new things" presuppose and are fundamentally loyal to the "old things" (cf. 5:17-19). The Christian scholar or "scribe," therefore, is one trained in the mysteries of the kingdom, and so is able to maintain a balance between the continuity and discontinuity that exists between the era inaugurated by Jesus and that of the past.

It is remarkable the extent to which New Testament theology is characterized by this tension between the old and the new. And for Matthew, in particular, who wrote for a Jewish Christian congregation that probably had its own Christian scribes (the counterpart of the Jewish rabbis), it is no wonder that this was an especially important theme. Some have even taken the description of the scribe in verse 52 as a self-description of the evangelist. But whatever the exact referent of the passage, certainly Matthew would have thought of himself as included among those scribes who had been trained in the mysteries of the kingdom of heaven.

If the church today is to carry on the work of the disciples, there is a sense in which not only biblical scholars but also every Christian must bring out of his or her storeroom both new things and old things. To be true to the teaching of the parables of Jesus and to the presentation of those parables by the evangelist Matthew, Christians today must represent a Christianity that encompasses both Testaments, with a loyalty to both.

9. Conclusion

The evangelist Matthew has placed his discourse of collected parables in the middle of his Gospel — in particular, at a major turning point in the ministry of Jesus. Following the people's widespread rejection of his message, Jesus here in chapter 13 begins to articulate the Gospel of the Kingdom through the medium of parables. In so doing, he makes use of teaching devices that could both conceal and reveal the mysteries of that kingdom.

But the parables of Matthew 13 are not just to be understood as teachings pertinent for disciples of that day, for all of the issues treated remain current today. The first parable is concerned with receptivity and non-receptivity; the second and seventh parables with the problem of the delay of the expected judgment; the third and fourth parables with the present apparent insignificance of the kingdom; and the fifth and sixth with the incalculable value of the kingdom, unknown to those who do not possess it. In an increasingly secular day, when the success of the gospel seems questionable, the kingdom a doubtful reality, and final judgment an idea of the past, these parables retain their significance. Faced with the mystery of a kingdom that is both present and future, Christians living between the times need these truths.

The parables of Matthew 13, in short, address realities that continue to be of great importance for the church today. They confirm to us the reality of God's kingdom and motivate us in our discipleship. But they do so only if we have ears to hear!

Selected Bibliography

Blomberg, Craig L. *Interpreting the Parables*. Downers Grove: InterVarsity, 1990.

Carter, Warren, and Heil, John Paul. *Matthew's Parables: Audience-oriented Perspectives*. (CBQMS 30). Washington: Catholic Biblical Association of America, 1998.

Dahl, Nils A. "The Parables of Growth," *Studia Theologica* 5 (1952) 132-66.

Davies, W. D., and Allison, Dale C., Jr. *A Critical and Exegetical Commentary on the Gospel According to Saint Matthew* (ICC), vol. 2. Edinburgh: T & T Clark, 1991.

Gerhardsson, Birger. "The Parable of the Sower and Its Interpretation," *New Testament Studies* 14 (1968) 165-93 (a translation and revision of an article in *Svensk Exegetisk Årsbok* 31 [1966] 80-113).

———. "The Seven Parables of Matthew XIII," *New Testament Studies* 19 (1972) 16-37.

———. "If We Do Not Cut the Parables Out of Their Frames," *New Testament Studies* 37 (1991) 321-35.

Hagner, Donald A. *Matthew 1–13* (Word Biblical Commentary 33A). Dallas: Word, 1993.

———. "New Things from the Scribe's Treasure Box (Mt. 13:52)," *Expository Times* 109 (1998) 329-34.

Jones, Ivor H. *The Matthean Parables: A Literary and Historical Commentary*. Leiden: Brill, 1995.

Kingsbury, Jack D. *The Parables of Jesus in Matthew 13*. St. Louis: Clayton, 1969.

Ladd, George Eldon. "The *Sitz im Leben* of the Parables of Matthew 13: The Soils," *Studia Evangelica* 2 (1964) 203-10.

Lambrecht, Jan. *Out of the Treasure: The Parables in the Gospel of Matthew*. Louvain: Peeters; Grand Rapids: Eerdmans, 1992.

Marshall, I. Howard. *Eschatology and the Parables*. London: Tyndale, 1963.

McIver, Robert K. "The Parable of the Weeds among the Wheat (Matt 13:24-30, 36-43) and the Relationship between the Kingdom and the

Church as Portrayed in the Gospel of Matthew," *Journal of Biblical Literature* 114 (1995) 643-59.

Wenham, David. *The Parables of Jesus.* Downers Grove: InterVarsity, 1989.

CHAPTER 6

Luke's Parables of the Kingdom
(Luke 8:4-15; 13:18-21)

RICHARD N. LONGENECKER

THREE PARABLES IN Luke's Gospel parallel the kingdom parables of Mark 4 and Matthew 13: The Parable of the Sower (8:4-15); the Parable of the Mustard Seed (13:18-19); and the Parable of the Leaven (13:20-21). All three contain the same stories as found in Mark and/or Matthew; all three include the phrase "the kingdom of God" (8:10 [see also v 1]; 13:18 and 20); and all three apply the metaphors contained in the stories in a manner relevant for the audience being addressed. In form and content, therefore, these three parables may rightly be called "kingdom parables." In the way Luke uses them in the development of his Gospel, however, they function differently and serve other purposes than they do in Mark and Matthew.

Consideration of these three Lukan parables is particularly rewarding for a study of how the parables of Jesus were used in the early church, for it highlights a somewhat different use by one evangelist (i.e., Luke) vis-à-vis that of the other two evangelists (i.e., Mark and Matthew). Such a difference is not always apparent when dealing with parables that appear in only one Gospel or in the "double tradition" of two Gospels. But in "triple tradition" parables, diverse redactional features stand out rather clearly. And such redactional features not only aid us in identifying the various levels of understanding in the early church, but also alert us to possible ways of contextualizing the parables of Jesus today.

1. The Kingdom Parables in the Structure of Luke's Gospel

Luke's two volumes, which make up about thirty percent of our New Testament, are distinctive in many ways. One important way is the prominence given to symmetry or "the principle of balance" in their structuring, which seems to be primarily "due to deliberate editorial activity by the author of Luke-Acts" (Talbert, *Literary Patterns*, 5, 23, *passim*). For not only are there significant structural parallels *between* Luke's Gospel and his Acts (cf. *ibid.*, 15-23, 58-65), there are also striking parallels both *within* his Gospel and *within* his Acts (cf. *ibid.*, 23-58) — with such parallels evident not only in the architecture of each of his two volumes, but also in the evangelist's repeated paralleling of significant words, narratives, miracle stories, and (most significant for our purposes here) the parables of Jesus.

This phenomenon of symmetry in Luke's writings may be explained, to some extent, by an appeal to the Jewish rubric that testimony, to be accepted, must be validated by at least two witnesses (cf. Deut 19:15), as Robert Morgenthaler has argued (*Die lukanische Geschichtsschreibung als Zeugnis: Gestalt und Gehalt der Kunst des Lukas,* 2 vols. [Zurich: Zwingli, 1949]). In most cases, however, it should probably be viewed as simply reflecting a "principle of balance" (or, "law of duality") that not only pervaded Greek classical literature and Greco-Roman art and architecture, but also is to be found in various Near Eastern artistic traditions and Jewish writings, as Charles Talbert has pointed out (*Literary Patterns*, 67-88). It may, therefore, be rooted, at least to some extent, in the traditions used by the evangelist in writing his two volumes — though its extensive use throughout Luke-Acts should probably be understood more as signalling Luke's own literary proclivities, as coupled, of course, with his perception of the interests and appreciation of his audience.

This "facet of Luke's artistry," which Talbert defines as "his tendency to balance some feature of his work with another which corresponds or is analogous to it in some way" (*ibid.*, 1), comes most obviously into view in the Third Gospel in the parallels set up between the Galilee Ministry of 4:14–9:50 and the Travel Narrative of 9:51–19:27. Two prominent examples of symmetrical paralleling in these sections are (1) the presentations of certain of Jesus' teachings, which are brought together as the Sermon on the Mount in Matthew 5–7, but appear in the first section of Luke's Gospel in chapter 6 and in the second section in chapters 11, 12, 14, and 16, and

(2) the setting out of the three Passion Predictions of Jesus, which are closely related in Mark 8:31-38, 9:31-37, and 10:32-34, but widely separated in Luke: the first two in 9:22-26 and 9:43-48; the third in 18:31-34. Also important, particularly for our purpose here, is the fact that when Luke treats the kingdom parables of Jesus, which appear as unified bodies of material in Mark 4 and Matthew 13, he does so by including the Parable of the Sower in the first section of his narrative at 8:4-15 — pairing it with "A Lamp on a Stand" and other exhortations in 8:16-18 — and then presenting the Parable of the Mustard Seed and the Parable of the Leaven in the second section, at 13:18-19 and 13:20-21 respectively.

Before any detailed study of the Lukan kingdom parables, it is important to note how they appear within the structure of Luke's Gospel. For redactional analysis and exegesis, as Talbert reminds us, "cannot be done in a satisfactory way without attention to the formal patterns that make up the architecture of a writing" (*Literary Patterns*, 5). In what follows, therefore, we will need constantly to keep in mind the contexts into which Luke has placed these three kingdom parables and the ways he has paired them, allowing such considerations to inform both our redaction-critical analyses and our exegesis.

2. The Parable of the Sower (8:4-15): On Hearing and Responding to the Word of God

The context of the Parable of the Sower in Luke's Gospel is set by the statement of 8:1: "After this, Jesus traveled about from one city and village to another, *proclaiming the good news of the kingdom of God*" (*kērussōn kai euaggelizomenos tēn basileian tou theou*). The two units that follow this statement — that is, the Parable of the Sower in 8:4-15 and the pericope about putting a lamp on a stand (with its associated exhortations) in 8:16-18 — are given as examples of that preaching. The focus in these two units of material is on Jesus' proclamation of "the word of God" (cf. 8:11, 15), with the emphasis being on *hearing* and *responding* to that word (cf. 8:8b; 15; 18). The concluding episode in 8:19-21, which depicts the reactions of Jesus' mother and brothers to his preaching, brings to a climax all that is presented in the section with the statement of verse 21: "My mother and brothers are those *who hear and put into practice God's word*" (*hoi ton logon tou theou akouontes kai poiountes*).

Literary Relations

Assuming a two-source theory of synoptic relationships, Mark 4:1-20 is probably the source for the parable in Luke 8:4-15. There are, of course, a number of omissions in Luke's version when compared with that of Mark. For example, Luke omits details about the shallowness of the soil and the scorching sun (8:6; cf. Mark 4:5b-6), the failure of the seed among the thorns to "bear fruit" (8:7; cf. Mark 4:7c), and the redundant expression "growing up and increasing" (8:8; Mark 4:8b). None of these matters, however, are of any major importance. More significant differences between Luke and Mark are (1) the greater emphasis that Luke gives to the seed (8:5: "A sower went out to sow *his seed*," *ton sporon autou*), with that "sown seed" then being the focus of the explanation given in 8:11-15 (cf. 8:11: "The seed is the word of God"), (2) Luke's dropping of Mark's "thirtyfold, sixtyfold, and a hundredfold" language to read simply "it yielded grain a hundredfold" (8:8a), thereby driving home the main point, in Luke's view, of the parable, and (3) the stress laid by Luke on the motif of "hearing and responding" to the word of God by the addition of the introductory phrase "he [Jesus] *called out*" (8:8b). But these are matters most easily explained in terms of Luke's redactional purposes, and so probably not to be credited to another source other than Mark.

There are, admittedly, a few verbal agreements of Luke and Matthew against Mark in the parable, which some scholars have taken as evidence of some sort of literary dependence between Luke and Matthew: the articular infinite "to sow" (*tou speirai*) in 8:5a (cf. Matt 13:3b); the use of the personal pronoun "he" (*auton*) as the subject of the second articular infinitive in 8:5b (cf. Matt 13:4); the omissions of "did not bear fruit" in 8:7 (cf. Matt 13:7) and "growing up and increasing" in 8:8 (cf. Matt 13:8); and the participial form "the one who has" (*ho exōn*) in 8:8 (cf. Matt 13:9). But these are such minor and rather standard ameliorations of wording that it may be postulated that both Matthew and Luke, in separate attempts to improve the style of Mark's Greek, made such changes quite independently.

On the other hand, Luke is exactly in line with Mark in the wording of the main, climactic statement of the parable — which statement Luke seems to have wanted to highlight, as witness his addition of "he called out" (*ephōnei*) in introducing it: "The one who has ears *to hear*, let that person hear!" (8:8b; cf. Mark 4:9). The fact that the infinitive "to hear" (*akouein*) is omitted in the better manuscripts of Matt 13:9 (i.e., the fourth-century codicies Sinaiticus [uncorrected] and Vaticanus), but included in Mark 4:9, suggests that Luke — despite his omissions, stylistic revisions, and redactional alterations — was basically dependent on Mark for his version of the Parable of the Sower. And the fact that Luke pairs Jesus' teaching about a Lamp on a Stand (and its associated exhortations) in 8:16-18 with the parable of the Sower in 8:1-15 also suggests his literary dependence on Mark. For these units are similarly paired in Mark's Gospel (cf. 4:1-20 and 4:21-25, respectively), but not in Matthew's Gospel (cf. 13:1-23 and 5:15, respectively).

Redactional Features

Source criticism gives rise to redaction criticism, for it is always necessary to propose explanations for the differences as well as for the agreements that appear in the various Gospels. And Luke's version of the Parable of the Sower offers fertile ground for such a redactional treatment, both with respect to data observable between the Gospels (i.e., "horizontal redaction criticism") and to data of significance within the Gospel itself (i.e., "vertical redaction criticism").

Luke's placement and structuring of the parable are somewhat different from Mark's. For whereas Mark set the parable first in the setting of a large crowd gathered by the sea, whom Jesus addressed while sitting in a boat (vv 1-9; cf. Matt 13:1-9), and then in the context of the Twelve and a few other followers, to whom Jesus explained the parable when he was *alone (kata monas)* with them (vv 10-20; see the principle stated in vv 33-34; cf. Matt 13:10-23), Luke states that Jesus addressed a large crowd from various cities and villages — with that crowd including not only the Twelve, but also some named women and "many others" (Luke 8:1-4). Such an inclusion of women in the purposes and program of God is prominent throughout Luke's two volumes (cf. his focus on Mary, Elizabeth, and Anna in Luke 1–2; see also Luke 10:38-41; 11:27-28; 13:10-17; 15:8-10; 18:1-8; 23:49, 55-56; 24:1-11; and Acts 1:14; 2:17-18; 9:36-42; 16:14-15; 17:34b; 18:2, 18-19a, 26).

Furthermore, whereas Mark distinguishes between an open declaration to the crowd and a private explanation to the disciples — a distinction that was, it seems, a feature of Jewish rhetoric (cf. D. Daube, "Public Retort and Private Explanation," *The New Testament and Rabbinic Judaism* [London: Athlone, 1965], 141-50), and therefore carried on by both Mark and Matthew — Luke lessens that distinction, thereby making his portrayal more cohesive and understandable for a Gentile audience. And whereas in Mark 4 the Parable of the Sower appears in the context of Jesus attempting to withdraw from the crowd to prepare his disciples for what they will face in the future (cf. Matthew 13), in Luke 8 it is presented as a prominent example of Jesus' preaching to a large crowd of people gathered from various cities and villages around and of his proclamation to them to "hear the word of God and put it into practice" (cf. esp. vv 1, 4, 8b, 15, 18, and 21).

Of greatest significance in evaluating Luke's redactional treatment of the Parable of the Sower, however, are those matters that the evangelist himself emphasizes by his rather subtle additions and that he tones down by his omissions. Chief among his additions are (1) his insertion of "he [Jesus] *called out*" *(ephōnei)* in the introductory words of 8:8b, which calls on the reader to take with great seriousness the statement that follows, and (2) his characterization of "good soil" as being "people with a noble and good heart" *(hoitines en kardią kalē, kai agathē)* in the explanation of 8:15 — neither of which additions appears in Mark (or in Matthew). For by introducing Jesus' words with the emphatic "he called out," Luke signals that his main interest in setting out the parable for his readers is to trumpet the challenge of Jesus: "The one who has ears to hear, let that person hear!" And by speaking of "good soil" as being "people with a noble and good heart," he implies that these are the type of people he wants to address.

On the other hand, the omissions of Luke are also significant. For Luke (1) omits the possibility of a varied response on the part of those who represent the good soil, condensing Mark's "thirtyfold, sixtyfold and a hundredfold" (Mark 4:8; cf. Matt 13:8: "some a hundredfold, some sixty, and some thirty") to simply "a hundredfold," (2) deletes the quotation of Isa 6:10b, "otherwise they might turn and be forgiven" (Mark 4:12; cf. Matt 13:15), and (3) says nothing about the disciples' lack of understanding (Mark 4:13; as also omitted in Matt 13:18). Evidently Luke excised these matters because he did not consider them to be appropriate for either his own purpose or his audience's edification.

The Parable of the Sower in Luke 8:4-15 is, therefore, addressed principally to people at large — including, of course, the Twelve and a number of women who "were helping to support them out of their own means" (vv 2-3), but not with the Twelve or those women being primarily in view. Its focus is on Jesus' proclamation of the word of God. Its appeal is for people to hear and respond positively to Jesus' preaching. But it is not, as in Mark 4 and Matthew 13, the first in a series of parables given to explicate certain enigmatic features regarding the reign or "kingdom" of God — though it carries on, in large measure, the discussion between Jesus and his disciples found in Mark 4:10-20. Nor is it concerned with the identity of the sower or the intrinsic quality of the seed.

Furthermore, Luke has no interest in such a varied response as suggested by the "thirtyfold, sixtyfold and a hundredfold" wording of Mark 4:8 (or, conversely, "some a hundredfold, some sixty, and some thirty" of Matt 13:8). Rather, what Luke is pleading for in his reproduction of the Parable of the Sower — which in his handling should probably more accurately be called "The Parable of Those Who Hear the Word," as Eduard Schweizer titles it (*The Good News according to Luke,* trans. D. E. Green [Atlanta: John Knox, 1984], 143) — is that "people with a noble and good heart" *hear* "the word of God" and *respond* to it positively in a "hundredfold" fashion, and so "hold it fast" (8:8, 15).

Pairing with Additional Gospel Material

Understanding Luke's use of the Parable of the Sower in this manner, it becomes clear why he paired this parable in 8:4-15 with Jesus' teaching about a Lamp on a Stand (and its associated exhortations) in 8:16-18. Evidently he viewed these two units of material as having already been paired by Mark because of their common emphases on "hearing" and "responding": "The one who has ears to hear, let that person hear!," as in Mark 4:9; and, "If anyone has ears to hear, let that person hear!," as in Mark 4:23 — which is, of course, what Luke highlighted by inserting "he called out" *(ephōnei)* into his introduction to the statement in Luke 8:8b.

It may be, of course, that Luke (perhaps also Mark) considered the teachings and exhortations of Mark 4:21-25 to constitute a further parable. Certainly the imagery of a lamp on a stand is parabolic in nature; and the words of Mark 4:25 ("Whoever has will be given more; whoever does not have, even what he has will be taken from him") appear in Matt 13:12 (in expanded fashion) in connection with Matthew's version of the parable of the Sower. Yet the four rather discrete elements of Mark 4:21-25 — the imagery of a lamp on a stand (v 21); the aphorism about what is hidden being disclosed (v 22); exhortations to "hear" and "hear carefully" (vv

23-24a); and statements about being measured, with more given to those who have and less to those who have not (vv 24b-25) — also appear as individual sayings scattered throughout Matthew and Luke (cf. Matt 5:15; 10:26; 7:2; 25:29; Luke 11:33; 12:2; 6:38; 19:26; see also *Gospel of Thomas,* Logia 33, 5-6, 41). This fact makes it seem likely that these four somewhat different elements were originally separate proverbial or wisdom sayings of Jesus. It may also suggest that Luke, at least, viewed the evangelist Mark as the one who first brought them together into a pairing relationship with the Parable of the Sower. But whatever these sayings might have meant in their original contexts, and however they were brought together, Luke treated them as a unified body of teaching material that served to buttress his main point: "Consider carefully how you listen" (8:18).

Likewise, it needs to be noted that Luke has taken material from Mark 3:31-35 (cf. Matt 12:46-50) about the reactions of Jesus' mother and brothers and used it for his own purpose in 8:19-21 to close off this section regarding Jesus' preaching. Given what he said about Mary in the Infancy Narrative of his Gospel (cf. 1:26-56; 2:5-7, 19, 22, 33-35, 39, 41-51) and about Jesus' mother and brothers being among the first Christians in Acts (1:14), Luke evidently had no desire to reproduce Mark 3:20-21 about Jesus' family (*hoi par autou,* "those who were his own") coming to take him away because they thought he was "out of his mind." But Luke does reach back to that same narrative in Mark 3, where it speaks again of the reactions of Jesus' family to his ministry, and he reproduces that second account in 8:19-21. And he does this, it seems, simply because Mark 3:31-35 enunciates quite clearly the point he has been making throughout his recitals of the Parable of the Sower in 8:4-15 and Jesus' teachings in 8:16-18: that "those with a noble and good heart" (v 15) are to "hear God's word [as proclaimed by Jesus] and put it into practice" (v 21).

Dominical Status and Intent

That the Parable of the Sower was originally given by Jesus is fairly easy to establish. It has more than enough conceptual and stylistic features to justify confidence in its dominical status. It reflects a Palestinian agricultural practice of sowing seed in a field — whether the field was left unploughed after the previous year's harvest or given a first rough ploughing — and then turning in the seed by a final ploughing or disking (cf. *Jubilees* 11:11).

Furthermore, it evidences marks of oral composition in its tight, lean and compressed style, its unadorned and uncomplicated plot, and its concrete, vivid images.

Probably more telling in support of the parable's authenticity, however, is the shocking nature of the metaphor used. For to compare the coming kingdom of God to something great or imposing was what was expected by most Jews during the period of Second Temple Judaism (cf. Ezek 17:1-24, which compares the eschatological kingdom to the top of a noble cedar of Lebanon that is transplanted onto a high and lofty mountain in Israel). But to compare the kingdom of God to seed that is devoured by birds (along the path), withered by the sun (on rocky places), or choked by weeds (among thorns) — and even when falling on good soil produces variously a crop that yields "thirtyfold, sixtyfold, or a hundredfold" more (Mark 4:8; cf. Matt 13:8) — would, undoubtedly, have been jarring to the sensibilities of the majority of Jesus' hearers.

But while the authenticity of the parable on Jesus' lips can be defended, many believe that any attempt to determine Jesus' own intent in giving the parable to be pure speculation. Admittedly, its setting in Luke's Gospel provides no clue as to its original intent. But in that both Mark and Matthew place the parable in the context of Jesus clarifying for his disciples the nature of his ministry and how they should understand the kingdom of God — being, in fact, the first of the explicit kingdom parables in both of these Gospels, with the first parable evidently meant as the key for their understanding of the rest — it may be proposed that Jesus intended this parable to signal something of great importance about his ministry and about the reign or "kingdom" of God in his disciples' lives and in the world. And in that the focus of the parable in all three Gospels is on the seed that is sown (Mark 4:3-8; Matt 13:3b-8; Luke 8:5-8a; see also *Gospel of Thomas* 9), it should probably be concluded that Jesus' intent was to use the metaphor of "sown seed" to reveal something of importance regarding his own ministry and the nature of the reign of God in people's lives.

It seems evident on any reading of the parable that a large part of Jesus' intent was to assure his disciples that the reign or "kingdom" of God would come about, despite the seeming insignificance of its beginning. Likewise, though the sower in the parable is never identified, it is difficult to imagine that Jesus in giving the parable did not also imply that he himself, as God's agent, was to be seen by his disciples as that sower; and though the seed is spoken of simply as "the word" (Mark 4:14; or "the word of the kingdom," as in Matt 13:19, or "the word of God," as in Luke 8:11), it is difficult to think that Jesus had in mind anything other than his teaching and ministry. Furthermore, it seems evident that in giving the parable Jesus was calling for a positive response to his teaching and ministry, and that his disciples understood his words in that way. Jesus' Parable of the Sower, therefore, seems, on the face of it, to have been intended for a number of reasons: (1) to offer words of hope and assurance regarding the future (the kingdom of God would come), (2) to assert the importance of his person and ministry (he is the sower and his teaching and ministry the seed), and (3) to issue a call to respond positively (to bear fruit).

Yet underlying these more obvious features, there seems also to be a challenge given by Jesus in the parable for his disciples to revise in quite a radical fashion their views about the work of the Messiah and their understanding of the reign or "kingdom" of God. In contradistinction to the dominant Jewish views of the day that the Messiah would be all-glorious and the Messianic Age would come about victoriously and with overwhelming power, Jesus, it appears, taught his disciples that his ministry and the reign of God should be compared to seed sown in a field — which, for various reasons, can be rejected; and even when accepted, will manifest various degrees of response. The enigma or "mystery/mysteries" of the gospel proclamation (Mark 4:11; Matt 13:11; Luke 8:10) is evidently this: that God's reign in people's lives and in the world does not come about with overwhelming power and majestic glory, but is more like seed that is sown, which experiences various responses — in many cases, rejected; in other cases, however, accepted, though in varying degrees.

Such a teaching would, indeed, have been shocking to Jesus' disciples. For they expected "the kingdom of God" to come in glory and power, with Israel being its chief beneficiary (cf. Acts 1:6). It was necessary, therefore, for Jesus to clarify for them the nature of his ministry — and, derivatively, also of their ministries — and how they should understand the reign or "kingdom" of God, particularly vis-à-vis the understanding of contemporary Judaism regarding Messiahship and the Messianic Age.

Varied Uses

The Parable of the Sower appears to have been used variously in the early church. Like a diamond cut with numerous facets, it was seen, it seems, to cast reflections of truth in many directions. Jesus, we have postulated, used the parable generally as a message of hope for the future realization of the reign or "kingdom" of God, as a means of self-identification, and as a call for response. More particularly, however, he seems to have focused on the "sown seed" in the parable, and used that metaphor to define the nature of his ministry and the character of the reign of God. His intent was principally to clarify for his disciples how they should understand his ministry — and, derivatively, also their ministries — and how they should conceptualize the reign or "kingdom" of God in people's lives and in the world, in contradistinction to their inherited views. It was certainly a radical understanding of ministry and God's reign that he set before them. And he did this, as Mark's Gospel suggests, at the very beginning of his time with them (cf. the near juxtaposition of the call of the Twelve in 3:13-19 and the Parable of the Sower in 4:1-20).

Among the earliest Jewish believers in Jesus, questions regarding Israel's rejection of Jesus and the minority status of believers in Jesus became dominant: Why did the nation reject its Messiah? Why are believers in Jesus in the minority in the Messianic Age? The evangelists Mark and Matthew, as Jewish followers of Jesus, undoubtedly felt the force of these questions. So while carrying on the imagery of the Parable of the Sower and reflecting something of how Jesus himself used it in teaching his disciples, they highlighted, it appears, the implicit rationale for Israel's rejection that they found in the parable: (1) that Isa 6:9-10 foretold such a rejection (Mark 4:12: "Ever seeing, but never perceiving, and ever hearing but never understanding; otherwise they might turn and be forgiven!"; which is expanded in Matt 13:13-15); (2) that a lack of spiritual understanding brought it about (Mark 4:13); and (3) that rejecting Jesus is the work of Satan, stems from people's desire to avoid trouble or persecution, and/or arises from "worries of this life, the deceitfulness of wealth and the desires for other things" (Mark 4:15-19; cf. Matt 13:19-22).

Furthermore, by bringing closely into association with this parable many other parables of the kingdom spoken by Jesus, the evangelists Mark and Matthew were able to suggest additional nuances or overtones of meaning that, evidently, would have resonated well within early Jewish Christianity. Thus Mark includes with this parable the Parable of the Growing Seed (4:26-29) and the Parable of the Mustard Seed (4:30-32), thereby allowing the Parable of the Sower to be read with an understanding of the instrinsic quality of the seed ("the seed sprouts and grows" on its

135

own) and the growth of the seed from a state of insignificance to one of great importance ("the smallest of seeds" to "the greatest of plants"). And thus Matthew adds the Parable of the Weeds (13:24-30), the Parable of the Mustard Seed (13:31-32), the Parable of the Leaven (13:33), the Parable of the Hidden Treasure (13:44), the Parable of the Pearl of Greatest Value (13:45-46), and the Parable of the Dragnet (13:47-50) — with these parables supplying their own harmonic overtones to what was heard originally in the first of these parables, the Parable of the Sower (13:1-23).

Luke's Gospel, however, does not have the same concerns as the Gospels of Mark or Matthew. Luke seems to have had little interest in assuring his readers of the coming of God's promised kingdom. Neither was he concerned with Jesus' instruction to his disciples about the nature of his or their ministries, nor about how they should understand the reign or kingdom of God (cf., e.g., the separation in Luke between Jesus' call of his disciples in 6:12-16 and the Parable of the Sower in 8:4-15). Nor was he driven by questions regarding Israel's rejection of its Messiah or about the minority status of believers in Jesus among Jews.

Rather, what Luke wants to present to his Gentile audience is (1) that Jesus' ministry was a prophetic ministry (cf. Luke 4:24; 7:16, 39; *passim*), as is also that of the Christian church (cf. Acts *passim*); (2) that in carrying out that prophetic ministry, Jesus proclaimed "the good news of the kingdom of God" (cf. Luke 4:43; 11:32; 16:16; *passim*), as do also prophets within the church (cf. Acts *passim*); and (3) that such preaching calls for a wholehearted response on the part of those to whom it is directed. Thus Luke sets the Parable of the Sower in the context of Jesus traveling about in various cities and villages "proclaiming the good news of the kingdom" (8:1), and he uses it as the prime example of such preaching. His principal concern is not to spell out details regarding how or why the "seed" was rejected — or to suggest by association with other kingdom parables how Jesus' teaching in this parable can be nuanced further — but simply to call for his readers to "hear" the proclamation of Jesus (8:8b; cf. also vv 18 and 21) and to respond to it as "those with a noble and good heart" in a "hundredfold" fashion (8:8, 15; cf. also vv 18 and 21).

3. The Parables of the Mustard Seed and the Leaven (13:18-21): On the Growth and Development of the Gospel

Luke finishes off the first part of his Travel Narrative (9:51–19:27) with two kingdom parables of Jesus, both of them aphoristically brief: the first about a mustard seed (13:18-19); the second about leaven (13:20-21). These two tersely worded parables are paired parables. For not only do they both use rather surprising metaphors in their highlighting of something of significance regarding "the kingdom of God," they also present a balance between a man planting a mustard seed in his garden and a woman mixing leaven into a batch of flour. Furthermore, both parables in Luke's handling speak about the reign or "kingdom" of God in terms of its growth and development.

There then follows in 13:22 the second mention of Jesus traveling to Jerusalem in Luke's Travel Narrative (the first being in 9:51), which is often seen to signal the start of the second section of a three-part narrative (i.e., 9:51–13:21; 13:22–17:10; 17:11–19:27) — with references to Jesus on his way to Jerusalem serving to introduce each part.

Literary Relations

The wording of the Parable of the Mustard Seed in Luke 13:18-19 is closer to Matt 13:31-32 than to Mark 4:30-32. It is similar to Mark in its use of "he said" *(elegen)* and "the kingdom of God" *(hē basileia tou theou),* rather than Matthew's "another parable he put before them" and "the kingdom of heaven." But otherwise its similarity to the longer and fuller form in Mark is rather minimal. It is closer to Matthew, however, in its wording "which a man took *(ho labōn anthrōpos)* . . . it became a tree *(egeneto eis dendron, ginetai dendron)*" and "[the birds] built their nests in its branches *(kateskēnōnsen en tois kladois autou),*" rather than Mark's "which when sown . . . it grows up and becomes the greatest of all shrubs and puts forth large branches, so that the birds of the air can make nests in its shade." Yet Luke's version is dissimilar to both Mark and Matthew in its omission of the comparative phrases "the smallest of all the seeds [on earth]" and "the greatest of [all] shrubs."

It appears, therefore, that the principal source for Luke's Parable of the Mustard Seed — assuming, again, a two-source theory of synoptic re-

137

lationships — was Q. Both Matthew and Luke may be assumed to have known Mark's version, and possibly they had it before them when writing. Matthew's version, in particular, seems to reflect Mark's influence in its contrast between "the smallest of all the seeds" and "the greatest of shrubs." Nonetheless, both Matthew and Luke were probably primarily dependent on the wording found in Q, with Luke's version being the most concise of the three evangelists and therefore probably the closest to Q.

And this primary dependence of Luke on Q for the Parable of the Mustard Seed seems to be confirmed when taking into consideration the literary relations of Luke's Parable of the Leaven in 13:20-21. For this second of these paired parables has nothing to do with Mark's Gospel, since it is absent in Mark. Rather, its only synoptic parallel is Matt 13:33. And apart from the introductory narrative formulas and the opening words, the wording of the parable in Matthew and Luke is almost identical.

So it may be postulated that Luke has drawn these two parables principally from an early collection of Jesus' "Sayings," which is identified by scholars today as "Q." It may be that the Parable of the Mustard Seed and the Parable of the Leaven existed as separate sayings in Q, not being paired together in that collection. Their appearance in the *Gospel of Thomas* as Logion 20 ("Mustard Seed") and Logion 96 ("Leaven") may suggest such a separation. Yet the fact that they are paired in both Matt 13:31-33 and Luke 13:18-21 makes it more likely that Luke found them already paired in his Q source and that he simply accepted that pairing as fitting nicely into his own interests and purpose.

Redactional Features

In evaluating Luke's treatment of the Parable of the Mustard Seed in 13:18-19, it is important to observe not only those matters that the evangelist has retained from his sources but also those features that he appears to have altered — whether by omission, addition, or intensification. And in comparing Luke's version of the parable with that of Matthew, assuming both were written with an awareness of Mark but are primarily dependent on the wording in Q, two differences stand out. The most obvious is Luke's omission of the contrast in Matt 13:32 between "the smallest of all seeds" and "the greatest of shrubs" (cf. Mark 4:31b-32a). But also to be noted is the intensification of the rather oblique wording "when it should be grown" (*hotan auxēthē*, which is an aorist subjunctive passive construction) in Matt 13:32 to "it grew and became" (*euxēsen kai egeneto*, which are aorist indicative active verbs) in Luke 13:19. For Luke's wording focuses attention in a more direct and straightforward manner than does Matthew's on the seed's growth and development.

Such differences may, at first glance, seem somewhat insignificant. On closer examination, however, they suggest matters of real importance for an understanding of Luke's purpose in setting out this parable for his readers. For whereas in Matt 13:32 there is an emphasis on contrast in the growth of the kingdom of God, from "the smallest of all seeds" to "the greatest of shrubs" (cf. also Mark 4:31b-32 and *Gospel of Thomas*, Logion 20:2), in Luke 13:19 there is no reference to the size of the seed when planted and no contrast made between when it is planted and when grown. Rather, Luke's emphasis is simply on the growth and development of the seed: "it grew and became a tree" (13:19b) — that is, on the reign or "kingdom" of God as proclaimed by Jesus as growing and developing into something significant, whatever might be said about its start.

Likewise in the Parable of the Leaven in 13:20-21, Luke's emphasis seems to be simply on the growth and development of the gospel in Jesus' preaching. The wording of the parable in Luke 13:21 corresponds exactly to that of Matt 13:33b, and so may be postulated to have been drawn from Q. Furthermore, the fact that the Parable of the Mustard Seed and the Parable of the Leaven appear in the context of Luke's Travel Narrative — and, in particular, at the end of the first section of that narrative — suggests that the evangelist's main point in giving his readers these two parables was to highlight his theme throughout this section: that in Jesus' proclamation of the reign (or "kingdom") of God on his journey (or "way") to Jersualem, the good news of the gospel was growing and developing.

Such an emphasis on growth and development generally, as well as on the growth and development of the gospel proclamation in particular, is a feature often found in Luke's two volumes. For example, in his Gospel, at the close of his Infancy Narrative of 1:5–2:52, the evangelist makes the comment that "Jesus increased in wisdom and in stature, and favor with God and people" (2:52). And at many places in his Travel Narrative of 9:51–19:27 he highlights not only Jesus' travel "on the way" but also the advances in his preaching as "he set his face to go to Jerusalem" (9:51). Similarly, features of growth and development are prominent throughout Luke's Acts. For example, Acts starts off with the suggestion that the author's second volume will continue the story "about all that Jesus *began* to do and to teach," which was set out in the first volume (1:1); it then recounts in its twenty-eight chapters numerous episodes in the ministries of Peter and Paul that depict both advances of the gospel and heroic exploits by the apostles; and it concludes with the triumphal statement that for two whole years at Rome, even while under house arrest, Paul "proclaimed the kingdom of God and taught about the Lord Jesus Christ . . . boldly and without hindrance" (28:31).

Perhaps by comparing the grown plant to "a tree" and saying that "the birds of heaven made nests in its branches" (13:19c), Luke also wanted to highlight something about the kingdom's universality. For a great tree that supplies a home for birds is a common representation in the Old Testament for a great empire that provides security for the people and nations of the world (cf. Ezek 17:23; 31:6 and Dan 4:12; see also *1 Enoch* 90:30, 33, and 37). But this is wording that Luke found in both Q and Mark, and he seems to have given it no greater emphasis than he found in his sources.

Dominical Status and Intent

It is probably easier to argue for the dominical status of the Parable of the Mustard Seed and the Parable of the Leaven than for any other of Jesus' recorded parables. Matthew Black has pointed out that the Parable of the Mustard Seed, when translated back into Aramaic, exhibits semitic alliteration and a typically Jewish play on words (cf. *An Aramaic Approach to the Gospels and Acts*, Oxford: 1967³, 165-66), and Joachim Jeremias makes the point that the word "measure" *(saton)* used in the expression "three measures *(sata)* of flour" is a Palestinian measure that equals 13.13 litres (cf. *Parables*, 146-47). Yet even more significant than these semitic features in establishing the authenticity of these parables on the lips of Jesus are the metaphors used in the parables. For to compare the kingdom of God to a mustard seed or to leaven would have been shockingly incongruous to most Jews of the day, and therefore, most likely, should be seen as stemming from Jesus himself.

While the Jesus Seminar may be viewed as being excessively radical in its use of the tools of contemporary critical scholarship, its conclusions regarding the dominical status of these two parables are commonly accepted: (1) "The Mustard Seed originated with Jesus because the proverbially small mustard seed is a surprising metaphor for the kingdom. In everyday usage, the proper figure for the kingdom of God is greatness, not smallness" (Funk, Scott, and Butts, *Parables of Jesus: Red Letter Edition*, 34); and (2) "The parable of the Leaven transmits the voice of Jesus as clearly as any ancient written record can, . . . Jesus employs the image of the leaven in a highly provocative way. In Passover observance, Judaism regarded leaven as a symbol of corruption, while unleaven stood for what was holy. . . . The Leaven provides a suprising reversal of expectations" (*ibid.*, 29). In modern critical theory, such incongruities provide a high degree of critical certainty for authenticity.

But while the authenticity of these parables can be critically defended, many believe it impossible to speak about Jesus' purpose in giving them. There are, however, a number of features in these parables that seem to reflect something of Jesus' own intent and what he wanted to teach his disciples about his ministry (and, derivatively, *their* ministries) and about the reign of God in people's lives and in the world.

First, it needs to be noted that implicit in both the Parable of the Mustard Seed and the Parable of the Leaven — whether in all three Synoptic Gospels, as with the former, or only in Matthew and Luke, as with the latter — are suggestions that the growth of the reign or "kingdom" of God takes place through the mysterious operation of divine power (whether represented as being in the seed itself or in the leaven) and that such divine power is already at work in Jesus' preaching. As Joseph Fitzmyer notes regarding the Parable of the Mustard Seed: "The parable implies the same divine operation of which Ezek 17:22-24 spoke explicitly, in connection, however, with a cedar (cf. Ezek 31:2-9)" (*Luke* 2.1016).

Second, the wording of Matt 13:32 and Luke 13:19 — which, we may believe, represents more adequately the words of Jesus, being derived from Q — that (1) the mustard seed becomes "a tree" *(dendron)*, that (2) "the birds of heaven" found refuge in it, and that (3) they made "nests in its branches," suggests an "eschatological character" for the parable in its original setting. For, as Joachim Jeremias pointed out, (1) the metaphor of a mustard seed becoming a tree transcends "the bounds of actuality" (since no mustard seed ever becomes a tree), (2) the picture of birds nesting in a tree's branches was a rather common symbol in Second Temple Judaism for Gentiles seeking refuge with Israel (cf. Ezek 17:23; 31:6; Dan 4:12; *1 Enoch* 90:30, 33, and 37), and (3) the verb "to nest" *(kataskēnoun)* is probably to be taken as "an eschatological technical term for the incorporation of the Gentiles into the people of God" (cf. *Parables,* 147). Also, the fact that in Matt 13:33b and Luke 13:21, which wording also stems from Q, the leaven is worked "into three measures of meal" *(eis aleurou sata tria)* is probably to be seen as reminiscent of Abraham's action in Gen 18:6, where the patriarch prepared an "overflowing mass" of bread for his three angelic guests at Mamre — and so to suggest something of an eschatological banquet (cf. *ibid.*).

It may be postulated, therefore, that Jesus' intent in giving the Parable of the Mustard Seed and the Parable of the Leaven to his disciples was not only to assure his disciples that the kingdom of God would surely come, but also to reveal something of importance to them about his ministry, their ministries, and the nature of the reign or "kingdom" of God vis-à-vis their inherited understandings of ministry and the kingdom of God. In these two paired parables, therefore, it may be postulated that he wanted his disciples to be assured that the kingdom of God would certainly come, whatever might be thought about its beginnings in his or their ministries. But also, it seems, he wanted them to realize (1) that the kingdom would come about only through the mysterious operation of divine power, not by human authority, expertise, or ingenuity (using the metaphors of a mustard seed and leaven, which have power in themselves), (2) that it has to do with eschatological realities, not with mundane actualities (using the eschatological figures of a tree and a great amount of dough), and (3) that the eschatological kingdom has universal dimensions, and is not to be confined to the national interests of Israel (using the imagery of "the birds of heaven" making "nests" in the tree's branches). And these are matters that he wanted his disciples to know as he began his ministry with them.

Varied Uses

As with the Parable of the Sower, what appears to have taken place in the telling, re-telling, recording, and then re-recording of the Parable of the Mustard Seed and the Parable of the Leaven was a constant reshaping of original stories so as to make them more applicable for the various audiences being addressed. This is not to imply that the spin given to the parables by the canonical evangelists was opposed to their original telling. Rather, it is to suggest that what the evangelists did with Jesus' parables was to give them a *sensus plenior* or "fuller sense," which they saw as being inherent in the stories themselves and which they believed to be particularly important for their readers. At least three levels of usage, it seems, can be seen in the New Testament itself.

Jesus, we have postulated, originally told the Parable of the Mustard Seed and the Parable of the Leaven for both general and particular purposes. Generally, he wanted to assure his disciples of the certainty of the coming kingdom of God. In particular, he wanted to teach them about the mysterious operation of God's working in people's lives and in the world, about the eschatological nature of the kingdom of God, and about the universal implications of his ministry and the reign of God. On this level, these two parables function as important pedagogical devices, with which Jesus instructed his disciples at the start of their association together.

Among the earliest Jewish believers in Jesus, confronted as they were with their compatriots' rejection of Jesus and their own minority status within the nation, questions undoubtedly arose regarding the significance of Jesus' earthly ministry and their continued allegiance to him. As Jeremias characterizes their queries: "How differently the beginnings of the Messianic Age announced by Jesus appeared than was commonly expected! Could this wretched band, comprising so many disreputable characters, be the wedding-guests of God's redeemed community?" (*Parables*, 149).

Mark certainly felt the force of these questions. So, as with the Parable of the Sower, while carrying on the message of assurance and hope regarding the coming kingdom of God — and while reflecting, to some extent, how Jesus himself must have used the parable in teaching his disciples — the evangelist highlighted, it appears, the aspect of contrast inherent in that parable. Thus he laid stress on the following words in his reproduction of the parable: "It is the smallest of all the seeds on earth, yet when it is sown it grows up and becomes the greatest of all shrubs, and puts forth large branches" (4:31b-32).

Likewise Matthew, working from both Mark and Q, highlights the same contrast in speaking about the kingdom of God as being "the smallest of all seeds, but when it has grown it is the greatest of shrubs and becomes a tree" (Matt 13:32; cf. *Gospel of Thomas* 20:2: "the smallest of all seeds" but "produces a great plant"). In addition, Matthew, now working only from Q, brought into consideration the Parable of the Leaven (Matt 13:33). For evidently he saw in the smallness of the leaven and the climactic wording of the story ("until it worked all through the dough") the same contrast in this parable as well — that is, an inherent contrast between present insignificance and future greatness.

Luke, however, completely omits the contrast highlighted by both Mark and Matthew. His and his readers' concerns were not those of the evangelists Mark and Matthew or their readers. Rather, Luke's emphasis in the giving of these two parables seems to be simply on the fact that in Jesus' proclamation of the reign or "kingdom" of God the good news of the gospel was growing and developing.

4. Contextualizing Jesus' Kingdom Parables Today

That Jesus' Parable of the Sower, Parable of the Mustard Seed, and Parable of the Leaven are set in somewhat different contexts and used for differing purposes in the Synoptic Gospels, and therefore can be read with multiple meanings, seem to be truisms that few would debate. The multifaceted or polyvalent nature of these parables can hardly be denied. But viewing Jesus' parables in such a fashion, a number of questions regarding our use of them arise. First, of course, is the question: How, then, are these three parables to be contextualized today? And if these parables are taken as something of test cases, the broader question arises: How are any of Jesus' parables to be used today?

Furthermore, we need to ask: To what extent can the polyvalence of these parables be appealed to and expressed in our own contextualizing of them? Are we held to the plots, metaphors, perspectives, and applications that Jesus and the evangelists made in telling and recording these stories? Or are we free — perhaps even encouraged by the genre "parable" itself — to play with the plots and metaphors and to apply them in almost unlimited ways to contemporary issues, events, and situations? Or to restate the question in a slightly different manner: In our use of Jesus' parables, are we committed to what can be found *within* the parables themselves, or are we free to develop new plots and metaphors, discover new perspectives, and make new applications that go *beyond* the Gospel texts?

Widely diverse answers are given to these questions. For my part, I feel myself constrained to hold to the stories and contextualizations found in the Synoptic Gospels. For in the parables of Jesus as set out in the Gospels we are presented with a number of ways of contextualizing the stories told — a variety, I believe, that provides us with more than enough stimulus for theological contemplation and more than enough challenge for ethical action. The three parables we have dealt with might not tell us everything about God, the ministry of Jesus, the nature of redemption, or a believer's response and resultant actions. Other parables and other biblical teachings need also to be taken into account for a fuller understanding of such matters. Nonetheless, dealing separately or in concert with the truths presented in these three multifaceted parables alone, followers of Jesus are challenged anew in both their thought and their action.

The task for Christians today, both in our proclamation and in our living, is to apply the individual features found in these parables to the needs and circumstances that we encounter *and* to incorporate into our lives and ministries something of the fullness of that parabolic teaching as given in the Gospel portrayals. That means that in various situations we will need to highlight one or more of the features that were central (as we have postulated) in Jesus' own use of the parables, such as: (1) the conviction that the reign or "kingdom" of God will assuredly come about in abundance (as in all three parables); (2) that God's kingdom has uniquely entered our human existence in the person and ministry of Jesus (as implicitly represented by the sower); (3) that people are called to respond positively to "the word of God," as expressed in the ministry of Jesus (the seed sown); (4) that Jesus' followers are to revise quite radically their views about the ministry of the Messiah and the reign or "kingdom" of God (the smallness of the seed and the differing responses to it); (5) that the kingdom will come about only through the operation of divine power (the mustard seed and the leaven); (6) that the kingdom has to do with eschatological reality (the tree and the dough); and (7) that the eschatological kingdom has universal dimensions (the birds nesting in the tree's branches).

It could mean, of course, that in certain circumstances the redactional emphases of Mark and Matthew — though without confining those emphases to the nation Israel, but understanding them in the broader context of all people — should be highlighted as well, such as: (1) a rationale for people's rejection of Jesus, and (2) a contrast between the present smallness and future greatness of the kingdom. Probably more pertinent today, however, are Luke's redactional treatments of these parables, which presents them (1) as understood in the context of a prophetic ministry, (2) as examples of the proclamation of the good news of the kingdom of God, (3) as highlighting the growth and development of that kingdom, and (4) as calling on those who hear to respond positively in a wholehearted fashion.

This is not to suggest some new allegorical method in the study of the parables. Rather, it is to note that the Lukan kingdom parables express a wide range of significant teachings — with these teachings, while varied, possessing a certain "sense of center" — and to argue that it is the task of contemporary interpreters to explicate and contextualize those teachings today, both individually and collectively. To go *beyond* the texts in the Gospels may be considered an existential exercise in the literary genre "parable." But it is no longer a study of Jesus' parables. And being no longer an explication of his parables, it lacks the authority of his teaching and turns our thoughts in other directions. To stay *within* the texts, however, attempting to contextualize for our day the multifaceted nature of the explicit and implicit teachings of the parables of Jesus, is, as Luke's Gospel has it, to proclaim "the good news" to "those with a noble and good heart, who, hearing the word, hold it fast and bring forth fruit" (8:15).

Selected Bibliography

Albright, William F., and C. S. Mann. *Matthew*. Garden City: Doubleday, 1971, esp. "XI. Parables in Matthew," CXXXII-CL.

Barclay, William. *And Jesus Said*. Edinburgh: Saint Andrew Press, 1970.

Carlston, Charles E. *The Parables of the Triple Tradition*. Philadelphia: Fortress, 1975.

Dodd, C. H. *The Parables of the Kingdom*. New York: Scribner's, 1961 rev. ed.

Fitzmyer, Joseph A. *The Gospel According to Luke*, 2 vols. New York-London-Toronto: Doubleday, 1981, 1985.

France, Richard T. *The Gospel according to Matthew*. Leicester: InterVarsity, 1985.

Funk, Robert W., Bernard Brandon Scott, and James R. Butts. *The Parables of Jesus. Red Letter Edition*. Sonoma, CA: Polebridge, 1988.

Hagner, Donald A. *Matthew*, 2 vols. Dallas: Word, 1993, 1995.

Hooker, Morna D. *The Gospel according to St. Mark*. London: Black, 1991; Peabody: Hendrickson, 1992.

Jeremias, Joachim. *The Parables of Jesus,* trans. S. H. Hooke. Rev. ed. London: SCM; New York: Scribner's, 1972.

Lane, William L. *The Gospel according to Mark.* Grand Rapids: Eerdmans, 1974.

Marshall, I. Howard. *The Gospel of Luke. A Commentary on the Greek Text.* Grand Rapids: Eerdmans; Exeter: Paternoster, 1978.

Moule, C. F. D. *The Gospel according to Mark.* Cambridge: Cambridge University Press, 1965.

Schweizer, Eduard. *The Good News according to Luke,* trans. D. E. Green. Atlanta: John Knox, 1984.

Stein, Robert H. *An Introduction to the Parables of Jesus.* Philadelphia: Westminster, 1981.

Talbert, Charles H. *Literary Patterns, Theological Themes, and the Genre of Luke-Acts.* Missoula: Scholars, 1974.

Parables of Warning and Preparedness

CHAPTER 7

"Produce Fruit Worthy of Repentance": Parables of Judgment against the Jewish Religious Leaders and the Nation
(Matt 21:28–22:14, par.; Luke 13:6-9)

ALLAN W. MARTENS

SOME OF JESUS' most pointed words were directed against the Jewish religious leaders of his time. In one episode in Matthew's Gospel, for example, Jesus is reported to have rebuked the scribes and Pharisees as follows:

> You hypocrites! Isaiah rightly prophesied about you when he said, "This people honors me with their lips, but their hearts are far from me. In vain do they worship me, teaching human precepts as doctrines." (15:7-9)

The narrative then goes on to say that Jesus' disciples informed their teacher: "Do you know that the Pharisees took offense when they heard what you said?" (15:12). It is hardly surprising that the Pharisees were offended, for Jesus had marshaled Isaiah's words against *them*, the most pious people of Israel! Yet in the next verse of this passage, rather than modifying his rebuke of these religious leaders, we read that Jesus continued his condemnation of them by pointing to an impending divine judgment:

Every plant that my heavenly Father has not planted will be uprooted. Let them alone; they are blind guides of the blind! And if one blind person guides another, both will fall into a pit." (15:13)

A similar judgment is directed against the religious leaders of Jesus' day in the three highly polemical parables of Matt 21:28–22:14 — with that judgment including, at least by extension, the Jewish nation as well. The major part of this article, therefore, will examine these three Matthean parables, which are commonly identified as the Parable of the Two Sons (21:28-32), the Parable of the Wicked Tenants (21:33-46), and the Parable of the Wedding Banquet (22:1-14). Luke's Gospel also includes the Parable of the Unproductive Fig Tree (13:6-9), which is similar in its judgment theme to those of Matt 21:28–22:14. So we will analyze these four parables with reference to (1) the literary and theological contexts in which they appear, (2) the evangelists' editorial purposes in presenting each parable, (3) the meaning that Jesus gave to these parables, and (4) why the early Christians preserved them in their collective memory. In addition, we will highlight (5) some applications for today.

1. The Context of Matthew's Parables of Judgment

The Literary Context

Matthew's three parables of judgment in 21:28–22:14 are positioned immediately after three narratives that speak of judgment and feature the Jerusalem temple in one way or another. The first narrative in 21:12-17 depicts Jesus cursing the Jerusalem temple, wherein is acted out a symbolic judgment on the temple. The second in 21:18-22 presents Jesus cursing the fig tree, which probably is to be understood not only as a symbolic act of judgment on the Jewish leaders but also as an act of judgment on the Jewish nation and its religion. And the third in 21:23-27 sets out a question about Jesus' authority as he teaches in the temple precincts, where he is portrayed as demonstrating his dialectical mastery over the Jewish leaders.

After these three narratives of judgment, Matthew goes on to recount the three parables of "the Two Sons," "the Wicked Tenants," and "the Wedding Banquet," which speak of further judgment. Up to this point in his Gospel, Matthew seems to have been following Mark's basic order (assuming that Matthew used Mark as his primary narrative source). His procedure now, however, changes. For though Mark 12:1 declares that Jesus "began to speak to them in *parables,*" Mark records only *one* parable, the Parable of the Wicked Tenants. Matthew, on the other hand, seems to have taken his cue from Mark's reference to "parables" to record a trilogy of parables — the first drawn from his special material, or so-called "M" material (i.e., "the Two Sons"), the second from Mark's Gospel (i.e., "the Wicked Tenants"), and the third from the Sayings material that he seems to have used in common with Luke, or "Q" (i.e., "the Wedding Banquet"). And following these three parables there then appear three controversy dialogues in 22:15-40.

Thus Matthew's literary artistry becomes evident in both his use of various sources and his predilection for arranging material into groups of three (for further examples of Matthew's preference for a threefold arrangement, see Davies and Allison, *Matthew* 1.62-72, 86-87). And throughout the context of these three parables, Matthew has effected a number of other literary parallels, some of which will be noted in what follows (for further discussions of the redactional, literary, and thematic features in the context of these parables, see my dissertation on "The Compositional Unity of Matthew 21:12–24:2").

The Theological Context

In addition to their literary context, however, we need also be aware of the theme of judgment that reverberates throughout the theological context of these three parables. Many scholars hold that these parables were directed — either by Jesus himself or by the evangelist Matthew — *only* against the hypocrisy of the Jewish religious leaders of the day, and so should *not* be viewed as having any anti-Judaistic or contra-national sense at all. Yet several features appear in these parables, both in their context and in the parables themselves, that have relevance for the nation as well.

A first feature that needs to be noted is the fact that the whole controversy section of 21:23–22:46 presents the Jewish leaders as representatives of the nation. Matthew specifically mentions almost all of the categories of the Jewish leaders of that day: chief priests, elders, Pharisees, Sadducees, scribes, and even Herodians (see 21:23, 45; and 22:15, 23, 34, 41). Furthermore, he introduces the chief priests and elders in 21:23 as being the leaders "of the people." All of this is significant, for it gives the reader the sense that the judgment articulated by Jesus is directed more broadly than just against the Jewish leaders. There is here, in fact, a clear national implication.

Second, the episodes of the cursing of the temple and the cursing of the fig tree in 21:12-20 have national significance. For the temple was viewed as being at the very heart of the national cultus and the nation's consciousness. And the fig tree was a well-known symbol of the nation (see Hos 9:10, 16; cf. Isa 28:4; Jer 8:13; 24:1-8; Mic 7:1).

And third, near the end of the unit in which Matthew's parables are located — that is, at the end of the woes pronounced in chapter 23 — Jesus' seventh woe in 23:29-36 modulates from denunciations of the scribes and Pharisees (cf. vv 29-33, which begin: "Woe to you, scribes and Pharisees, you hypocrites!") to a statement of doom directed against the whole nation (cf. vv 35-36, which speak of judgment on "this generation"). In particular, witness the supra-historical role that Jesus takes on in the following words: "I am sending you prophets and wise men and scribes. Some of them you will kill and crucify; others you will flog in your synagogues and pursue from town to town" (v 34). This language depicts Jesus as an extra-terrestrial figure, like Sophia in Israel's Wisdom literature, who sends envoys to the nation in order to rebuke, judge, and correct the people and their leaders.

Furthermore, in the parables themselves there are two very clear indications that the nation of Israel is also included in Jesus' words of judgment. The first is in the Parable of the Wicked Tenants, where the concluding words of Jesus render a sharp judgment against Israel: "Therefore I tell you that the kingdom of God will be taken away from you and given to *a people* [*ethnei*, "to *a nation*"] who will produce its fruits" (21:43). The second is in the Parable of the Wedding Banquet, where there is reference to a king who burned the city of those who had murdered his servants (22:7) — which is probably a post–AD 70 reflection on the burning of Jerusalem, the nation's capital.

In dealing with these three Matthean parables, therefore, it needs first of all to be appreciated that the theological context of judgment in which they are set — a judgment that is directed against both the religious leaders of the day and the nation itself — is of crucial importance for their interpretation. The question, however, naturally arises: To whom is this strong anti-Judaistic and contra-national tone to be attributed — to Jesus, or to Matthew's interpretation of Jesus' words? To answer this question we must analyze more carefully these three parables from both redaction-critical and historical perspectives.

Matthew's Redactional Activity

Redaction criticism is an analytical method that attempts to determine an evangelist's theological motivations as evidenced by his editorial use of sources. It seeks to understand *how* and *why* a Gospel writer collected, selected, adapted, arranged, linked, expanded, and/or interpreted the early traditions about Jesus, believing that by a better understanding of his methods one can gain a better sense of his theological purposes. What follows, therefore, is a redaction-critical analysis of each of Matthew's three parables of judgment in 21:28–22:14. In concert with most interpreters, the analysis assumes that Matthew made use of (1) Mark's Gospel, (2) a Sayings source, which is commonly designated "Q," and (3) disparate "M" materials, which were either oral or written.

2. The Parable of the Two Sons (Matt 21:28-32)

The Parable of the Two Sons appears only in Matthew's Gospel, and so is usually judged to have come from the evangelist's special "M" material. As a result, tradition-historical questions are difficult to answer. Helmut Merkel, who represents the view of some scholars, has argued — based on Matthean linguistic peculiarities in the parable and thematic similarities with other traditions — that Matthew himself composed this parable (cf. "Das Gleichnis"). But the general view among scholars is that the parable stems from Jesus, though there is little doubt that it has been subjected to Matthew's redaction.

Evidence for Matthean redaction is threefold. First, it is clear that Matthew has assimilated the three parables of 21:28–22:14 by using similar vocabulary and themes throughout. Without doing a complete linguistic analysis, we may simply point to three expressions that appear in all three parables: "man," "son," and "kingdom."

All three parables include a major character, a "man" (*anthrōpos*, 21:28, 33; 22:2) who represents God — though he appears, respectively, as

155

a father, a vineyard owner, and a king. The significant point about this figure is that in each case he has a "will" that is both obeyed and disobeyed. The emphasis in each of the three parables, however, falls on those who reject this will. Furthermore, in all three parables there is a "son" (or sons), though the term is not uniform (*teknon* in 21:28; *huios* in 21:37; 22:2). And in each case the son or sons represent unique characters.

Another similarity in these three parables is the appearance of the expression "kingdom of God/heaven" (*basileia tou theou/tōn ouranōn*, 21:31, 43; 22:2). And in each case the kingdom is associated with a displacement of people. In the first parable, the outcasts of society enter the kingdom "ahead of" the Jewish religious leaders (21:31); in the second, the kingdom "will be given to a people that will produce its fruits" (21:43); and in the third, where the kingdom is symbolized by the messianic banquet or feast of salvation, the original guests — that is, Jews — are replaced by outsiders — that is, Gentiles (22:8-10). Even if these three terms are not seen as indicating Matthew's redactional treatment of Jesus' parabolic teaching, but viewed as being traditional, at least the fact that the evangelist collected similar parables together shows evidence of his editorial activity.

A second evidence of Matthean redaction is to be seen in the introduction to the Parable of the Two Sons, for the question "What do you think?" (*Ti humin dokei*) of 21:28 is characteristically Matthean (cf. 18:12; 22:42; 26:66; also 17:25; 22:17): it appears elsewhere only in John 11:56.

And a third evidence of Matthew's redaction comes to the fore in 21:32, the parable's final verse, which is probably to be seen as an independent saying that Matthew has added as an application to the original parable. One reason for viewing verse 32 as an independent saying is that Jesus' judgment expressed in verse 31c — "I tell you the truth, the tax collectors and the prostitutes are entering the kingdom of God ahead of you") forms a fitting conclusion to the parable, whereas the statement about John the Baptist is somewhat inconsistent with the thrust of the parable. For the parable itself concerns obedience to the father's (i.e., God's) will, and it sets out a contrast between words and deeds. And while Jesus' pronouncement in verse 31c does not pick up on this contrast of words and deeds, it does portray society's outcasts as being obedient to God's will in contrast to the disobedience of the Jewish leaders. Verse 32, however, takes up a new topic, one that focuses on *believing* the message of John the Baptist — as evidenced by the threefold use of the Greek verb *pisteuō* ("believe") in the three parts of the verse: "For John came to you in the way of righteousness, and you did not *believe* him" (v 32a); "but the tax collectors and prostitutes *believed* him" (v 32b); "and even after you saw this, you did not repent later and *believe* him" (v 32c).

Another reason for thinking that verse 32 is a later Matthean addition stems from the opening formula of verse 31c: "Truly I say to you" *(amēn legō soi)*. For this formula marks the end of Jesus' teaching in other instances in the Gospel tradition (cf. Matt 5:26; also Luke 15:24; 15:7, 10; 18:14).

And a third reason for viewing verse 32 as an independent "saying" or logion is the fact that there is a somewhat parallel logion in Luke 7:29-30:

> And all the people who heard this, even the tax collectors, acknowledged the justice of God, because they had been baptized with John's baptism. But the Pharisees and the lawyers rejected the will of God for themselves, because they had not been baptized by him.

The broad similarities between the "sayings" of Matt 21:32 and Luke 7:29-30 probably point to a common tradition underlying these verses. Yet in Luke the saying is expressed as part of the narrative about John, whereas in Matthew the saying is now placed on the lips of Jesus as the punchline to a parable.

As for Matthew's reason for adding verse 32, it is likely that the reference in verse 31 to "tax collectors and prostitutes" provided the "catchword" for the addition of this logion about the tax collectors.

The basic message of Jesus' Parable of the Two Sons, therefore, is that what counts in relation to the kingdom of God, or salvation, is obedience to God's will. Words by themselves do not matter. It is deeds that count before God. And so, based on the criterion of obedience, society's outcasts, like the tax collectors and prostitutes, will enjoy God's salvation "ahead of" — or, instead of — the Jewish leaders.

By the addition of verse 32, Matthew, it seems, has intensified the polemic of verse 31. For not only is Jesus now presented as condemning the Jewish leaders more harshly ("You did not believe John!"; "You did not repent and believe John!"), but the message of John the Baptist, which was a proclamation of "the way of righteousness," now becomes the focal point for salvation. And by linking this saying of verse 32 with the earlier pericope in verses 23-27 (which material immediately precedes the parable itself in verses 28-31) about Jesus' authority in relation to John's baptism, the reader of Matthew's Gospel is led to understand that belief in John the Baptist's message compels belief in Jesus as well. Therefore by his redactional treatment of Jesus' Parable of the Two Sons, Matthew has highlighted the call given by Jesus to Israel's leaders to respond in obedience to God — that is, to respond positively to a "righteousness" that centers in the message of both John the Baptist and Jesus.

3. The Parable of the Wicked Tenants (Matt 21:33-46, par.)

Matthew's second parable in his trilogy of judgment parables, that of the Parable of the Wicked Tenants, is drawn from Mark 12:1-12 and paralleled by Luke 20:9-19, which makes it relatively easy to note the evangelist's editorial changes. Matthew makes the owner of the vineyard an authority figure (an *oikodespotēs* or "landowner," in contrast Mark's simple *anthrōpos*), who justifiably demands "*his* fruit" (contrast Mark's "the fruit of the vineyard") from the tenants to whom he has rented the vineyard. The parable is obviously an allegory based on the Song of the Vineyard in Isa 5:1-7 where the vineyard represents Israel.

Once the identification of the vineyard with Israel is made, the other features of the story are easily identifiable. Thus the owner is God; the tenants are Israel's leaders; the envoys are the prophets sent to Israel; the son and heir is Jesus the Son of God; the killing of the son represents the crucifixion; the punishment of the tenants represents the ruin of Israel; the "other tenants" represent the (Gentile) church; the proper "rendering of fruits to the owner" (21:34, 41, 43) is doing the will of the Father (cf. 21:31; 7:21); the "rejection of the stone by the builders" and its "elevation to the head of the corner by God" allude to the death and resurrection of Jesus; and the final stone saying, "The one who falls on this stone will be broken to pieces, and the one on whom it falls will be crushed!" (21:44), serves as a warning that rejection of Jesus will result in condemnation (cf. 10:32-33). In general, Matthew follows closely what has been termed Mark's "christological allegory." The changes that Matthew makes, however, strengthen the christological, ecclesiological, and anti-Judaistic features of the parable.

Matthew effects some transitional changes in the story, which cause the telling of the story to unfold more naturally: "When the time of fruit approached" in verse 34a; "When the owner of the vineyard comes" in verse 40a; and "Have you never read in the Scriptures?" in verse 42a. The first of these transitional changes in verse 34a also introduces the theme of fruitfulness, which is a central theme not only in the parable but also throughout Matthew's Gospel. "Producing fruit" and similar expressions in Matthew signify such actions as repentance, doing the will of God, and doing righteousness — all of which can be summed up in terms of a proper response to God. Ultimately, however, the fruit required of Israel is the acceptance of Jesus, the Son of God, whom the Father has sent.

Moreover, particularly for the nation Israel, it is always the "season for fruit." This lesson was implicit in the Cursing of the Fig Tree pericope of 21:18-22, which portrayed Jesus in symbolic fashion as looking for righteousness in Israel but unable to find it. And the same lesson is implicit here in the Parable of the Wicked Tenants, where the repeated sending of servants to receive "his fruit" suggests that God has continually sought righteousness from Israel.

Matthew also reconstructs Mark's description of the sending of servants to receive the landowner's fruit (vv 34-36). According to Mark, the owner sent three servants individually and successively, and then "many others." Matthew, however, has it that the owner sent two *delegations* of servants, the first composed, presumably, of three men, one of whom was beaten, another killed, and another stoned (cf. 23:37). The second delegation consisted of a larger number of servants ("more than the first"), who were treated "in the same way." Luke's version of the parable, it should be noted, has an even different scenario (cf. Luke 20:10-12), which suggests that the three evangelists felt considerable freedom to allegorize the parable in their own ways — with the part about the sending of envoys particularly susceptible to allegorization.

The two delegations of servants in Matthew have been variously interpreted, with commentators usually viewing them as representing the preexilic prophets and the postexilic prophets. More likely, however, they represent for Matthew "the prophets and righteous men," which is a coupling of classifications that is uniquely Matthean (cf. 10:41; 13:17; 23:29, 34-35). "Prophets" and "righteous men," of course, could be thought of as distinct categories of redemptive figures. But Matthew apparently views them together as God's servants and as opponents of the "unrighteous," who throughout Israel's history have rejected God's ways.

Both Matthew and Mark describe the sending of the son and his rejection in similar terms. For some reason, however, Matthew omits Mark's christologically significant adjective "beloved" from the description of the son (v 37). Furthermore, Matthew reverses Mark's order regarding the treatment of the son, presenting him as being first thrown out of the vineyard and then killed (v 39). It may be impossible to speculate as to why Matthew omitted the word "beloved." But this latter change of first being thrown out of the vineyard and then killed, which also appears in Luke's presentation, almost certainly was made to conform the parable to the circumstances of Jesus' crucifixion outside the city walls (cf. John 19:17; Heb 13:12).

Matthew follows Mark in recording Jesus' question, "Therefore, what will the lord of the vineyard do?" (v 40). But whereas Mark has Jesus answer his own question, "He will come and kill the tenants and give the vineyard to others" (Mark 12:9), Matthew has the hearers — that is, the Jewish religious leaders — answer the question and thereby inadvertently judge themselves (v 41). Matthew adds a Greek legal idiom to their answer, "He will bring those wretches to a wretched end," thereby intensifying the expression of judgment. Furthermore, the leaders' answer is expressed once more in terms of the fruit theme, for they add that the vineyard will be given to other tenants "who will give him the fruit in its season." This addition clearly alludes to Ps 1:3 ("it will give its fruit in its season") and strengthens Matthew's polemic, for now the Jewish leaders are compared to the godless men of Psalm 1.

Matthew also follows Mark in setting out the stone saying of verse 42 ("The stone the builders rejected has become the capstone; the Lord has done this, and it is marvelous in our eyes!"), which follows the saying of judgment in verse 41. The stone saying is a quotation of Ps 118:22-23, which, as it appears in conjunction with the Parable of the Wicked Tenants, presents Jesus as the rejected but now exalted Son of God. Much has been written about the possible authenticity of this quotation on the lips of Jesus — particularly since it refers to the vindication of the Messiah, which is a topic that does not appear in the parable itself. One feature of note is the Aramaic pun on "son" (ben) and "stone" (eben) that appears in comparing the parable and the saying, which may suggest that Jesus himself (or, perhaps, the early church) joined the parable and the stone quotation on this basis. Here, however, we are more interested in the later stages of the use of the parable. And with respect to these later stages, it is evident that Matthew has taken over the saying from Mark, with the result that the quotation of Ps 118:22-23 serves to reinforce the theme of judgment already in the parable and to highlight the new theme of exaltation that is not intrinsic to the parable itself. So the presence of the quotation in both Mark and Matthew provides another bit of "christological coloring."

In verse 43 Matthew adds a very significant concluding saying to Mark's parable: "Therefore [i.e., because of Israel's rejection of the son/stone] I tell you, the kingdom of God will be taken away from you [i.e., the nation Israel] and given to a people *(ethnei)* who will produce its fruits *(tous karpous autēs)*." Here we have the salvation-historical scheme carried one step further, for not only is the son/stone exalted but also the kingdom is transferred from Israel to the church. The saying shifts imagery so that the vineyard no longer represents Israel but now the kingdom. Verse 41 had already made an implicit connection of the vineyard and the kingdom by referring to the transfer of the vineyard (cf. also Mark 12:9). Verse 43, however, makes that identification explicit.

As for the origin of this concluding saying in verse 43, the matter is hotly debated. Some scholars hold that Matthew himself composed it and added it here. Others believe that the evangelist found the saying as an independent logion of Jesus and added it here. And still others posit that the saying was already attached to the parable in a pre-Matthean stage of the Jesus tradition. The most plausible solution, it seems, is that Matthew used such traditional elements as the "producing fruit" theme, which is common in the synoptic tradition, and the contrasting formula "it will be taken away . . . it will be given" (cf. Mark 4:25 par.; Luke 19:26//Matt 25:29). And on such a view, verse 43 should probably be attributed primarily to Matthew and seen as carrying on in quite consistent fashion the evangelist's distinctive theological emphases of "kingdom," "fruit-bearing," "church," and "anti-Judaism."

The second stone saying of verse 44 ("The one who falls on this stone will be broken to pieces, and anyone on whom it falls will be crushed!") is absent in Mark. But it appears in nearly identical language in Luke 20:18, where it follows the first stone saying (cf. verse 17, quoting Ps 118:22). Despite some scholars' arguments for an original association of Matt 21:43 and 44, verse 44 seems so awkwardly placed after verse 43 that it should probably be considered an interpolation from Luke 20:18 by some early copyist. And the absence of verse 44 in several manuscripts (D 33 et *al.*) supports this view.

Also to be noted in comparing Matthew's version of the Parable of the Wicked Tenants with that of Mark is the fact that, while the narrative aftermath of the parable is related by both evangelists in similar terms, Matt 21:45-46 intensifies the Jewish leaders' guilt by reversing the sequence found in Mark 12:12. For in Matthew's version the leaders' perception of the point of the parable is highlighted by being placed first, with their attempt to arrest Jesus then placed second. Furthermore, Matthew adds to Mark's version a note that the crowds "held Jesus to be a prophet." This additional clause recalls a similar one in the pericope about Jesus' authority in 21:23-27, where John the Baptist is said to have been held by the people to be a prophet (v 26). These references, therefore, draw another parallel between John the Baptist and Jesus, who as God's messengers form a united front against the Jewish religious leaders. Hence, John and Jesus are associated in the last three pericopes of this chapter — that is, in the narrative that deals with the Question about Authority in 21:23-27, in the Parable of the Two Sons in 21:28-32, and in the Parable of the Wicked Tenants in 21:33-46.

Undoubtedly the Parable of the Wicked Tenants has undergone a number of secondary changes and additions in its retelling by the synoptic evangelists, which have brought about a shift of meaning at certain points. Its main emphasis, however, lies in the following analogy: that as the wicked tenants rejected the landowner's son, and therefore were punished and lost the vineyard to other tenants, so also Israel has rejected Jesus, the Son of God, and will be judged and will forfeit the kingdom to another people who will produce righteousness for God. This parable, therefore, continues the theme of Israel's rejection of God's messengers that appeared in the immediately previous Parable of the Two Sons. In that previous parable, Israel's rejection of John the Baptist was explicit (cf. 21:32), while her rejection of Jesus was only implied. In this parable, however, the rejection of the Baptist is only implied in Israel's rejection of the many servants sent to her, while the rejection of Jesus as the Son of God and the "capstone" of the divine history of salvation is explicit.

4. The Parable of the Wedding Banquet
(Matt 22:1-14//Luke 14:15-24)

Matthew inserts the Parable of the Wedding Banquet, which is the third of his trilogy of judgment parables, between narrative material taken from

Mark 12:12 and Mark 12:13. There is general agreement that this parable derives from Q, for a similar version is in Luke 14:15-24. Both Matthew and Luke, however, have placed the parable within their own respective contexts, with the opening statements of Matt 22:1-2a and Luke 14:15-16a being separately composed redactional transitions.

This parable begins with the notice that a man prepared a great meal to which he invited many guests (cf. Luke 14:16). In Matthew's version, however, the man is a king and the occasion is a wedding banquet for his son (22:2). And this setting is used in Matthew's Gospel not only for the parable itself in 22:3-10, but also for the additional story about the man without a wedding garment in 22:11-13 and the application made of that story in 22:14.

Both accounts relate three missions of servants sent out to call people to the feast. But they are not parallel. For Matthew has restyled the first mission, as found in Luke, into two missions, with the second corresponding to Luke's first (cf. Matt 22:3-6; Luke 14:17-21a). And Matthew's third mission corresponds to Luke's second mission (cf. Matt 22:8-10; Luke 14:21b-22). In Luke's Gospel, however, there is a third mission that seems to be the evangelist's own addition (Luke 14:23).

Matthew's account of the initial mission in 22:3 has the plural "servants," in contrast to Luke's singular "servant." This alteration begins Matthew's assimilation of this parable to his earlier presentation of the Parable of the Wicked Tenants, where in 21:34 "servants" also appeared in contrast to Mark's "servant." Also to be noted is the fact that the first mission, in Matthew's handling, ends abruptly with the notice that those invited "were not willing to come," which is a phrase that recalls the response in 21:19 of the first son in Matthew's Parable of the Two Sons.

Matthew's second mission in 22:4 corresponds more closely to Luke's first mission in 14:17. But Matthew introduces it with the words "Again, he sent other servants" — which words are identical to those that were used in 21:36 for the second delegation of servants in the Matthean version of the Parable of the Wicked Tenants. But whereas the two delegations in that previous parable represented "the prophets and righteous men," here they represent the New Testament apostles and Christian missionaries who are sent to invite Israel to the royal "messianic banquet." For the second mission ends in the destruction of the city, which surely has in mind the fall of Jerusalem in AD 70.

Also to be noted in Matthew's version of the Parable of the Wedding

Banquet is the fact that the king's son is not sent or killed, as in the previous Parable of the Wicked Tenants. So Jesus the Messiah is presented in this parable in his postresurrection state, with his Father inviting Jews to a "messianic banquet." An eschatological scenario is evident, as well, in the king's instructions to his servants to announce to the invited guests: "Everything is ready. Come to the wedding banquet!" (22:4).

Matthew heightens the fact that the banquet was ready by his reference to the king having already slaughtered his oxen and fattened cattle (v 4). The rejection of the king's invitation, however, comes in the remark: "But they took no notice and went away — one to his farm, another to his business" (v 5). Luke has the invitees making excuses why they could not come (14:18-20). And Luke's version is probably more original, even though more detailed. For Matthew seems to have wanted only to highlight the absolute refusal of the invitees, who represent Israel, and so to have narrowed the focus of the parable to that point.

In focusing on the refusal of the invitees, Matthew has created a dramatic intrusion into the Parable of the Wedding Banquet by his addition of verses 6-7. Verse 6 says that some of those invited to the banquet "seized his servants, mistreated them, and killed them." Here again there occurs an assimilation to the previous Parable of the Wicked Tenants, where the owner's servants were "seized . . . beaten . . . killed . . . and stoned" (21:35). And verse 7 tells the reader that the king, because of the ill treatment afforded his servants, becomes angry, and so sends his armies to destroy "those murderers" and burn "their city." On the "image" level, this latter verse is incredible, for it pictures a king destroying murderers and burning their city while his banquet meal remains hot for the next set of invited guests. On the "reality" level, however, it can only refer to the destruction of Jerusalem, which was viewed as having been caused by Israel's rejection of God's messengers — particularly the nation's rejection of Jesus. Two expressions in verse 7 recall earlier expressions in the previous parable: "those murderers" recalls "those tenants" of 21:40, with both expressions being used in the context of judgment; and "destroy" points back to the leaders' self-condemnation in 21:41, "He will destroy the evil men evilly."

The third mission in Matthew's version of the parable (22:8-10) resumes the narrative after the intrusion of verses 6-7. This mission corresponds to Luke's second (14:21b-22). The motive for this mission is given by Matthew himself — namely, that "those who were invited [were] not worthy" (v 8). Here, once more, Matthew's polemic against the nation of

Israel for rejecting God's salvation comes to the fore. For he views "the ones invited" as being "not worthy," which is a particularly Matthean concept (cf. 3:8; 10:10, 11, 13, 37, 38). At the same time, however, the banquet remains ready — that is, the feast of salvation is open to all those who will come. So the servants, who now represent the post-destruction apostles and Christian missionaries, are sent out a third time. But this time they are to go out into the environs of the Gentiles (*diexodous tōn hodōn*, which suggests roads going out of the city into the pagan world) in order to find as many as they can for the wedding banquet prepared by the king for his son (v 9).

This third mission is finally successful, for "the servants went out into the streets and gathered all the people they could find, both good and bad, and the banquet hall was filled with guests" (v 10). Here is Matthew's portrayal of the church as an *ethnically* mixed body, for Gentiles are now included. Israel as a nation has refused the invitation to the feast, yet the banquet hall is eventually filled with both Jews and Gentiles. And here also is Matthew's portrayal of the church as an *ethically* mixed body, which will continue mixed until the end of the age when evil people will be separated from the good (cf. 13:24-30, 36-43, 47-50; 25:31-33).

There is, however, always a danger that Christians will think they have been included in the eschatological wedding feast simply because they were invited or "called." So Matthew adds the Parable of the Man without a Wedding Garment (22:11-13). This parable is probably a traditional one, though some scholars think that Matthew composed it. Some also believe that a pre-Matthean editor added this parable to the previous one. But it seems more probable that it was Matthew himself who joined these two parables together.

The joining of these two parables reflects another feature in Matthew's concern for the church. For the appended parable functions as a warning for Christians to be properly "attired" — that is, to produce the fruit of righteousness. Like the nation Israel, the church is also subject to judgment. Some members may, in fact, be found lacking at the eschaton. The combining of these parables, therefore, serves to set out another allegorical scenario regarding the history of salvation, albeit this time a scenario that extends from the call of Israel by the apostles and Christian missionaries up to the final judgment of Christians.

The statement in 22:14, that "many are called, but few are chosen," is not only the evangelist's final saying in concluding this parable, but also serves as his final, climactic conclusion to all three of his judgment parables in 21:28–22:13. It applies to both the Parable of the Wedding Banquet and the Parable of the Wedding Garment, since the first deals with those who have been "called" while the second concerns those who in the final judgment will be "chosen." In effect, the saying in its immediate context serves as a warning to Christians against a false sense of security. But it also functions as the conclusion to Matthew's trilogy of judgment parables, for it sums up the evangelist's more general view of judgment vis-à-vis Israel — namely, that Israel's calling cannot guarantee her election to salvation. What is also required are such things as (1) doing the Father's will (the Parable of the Two Sons), (2) producing fruit (the Parable of the Wicked Tenants), (3) heeding the call to salvation, with its attendant requirements (the Parables of the Wedding Banquet and the Wedding Garment), and, above all, (4) accepting Jesus, the Son of God. In these matters Israel as a nation has failed, and so has been rejected.

5. Jesus' Meaning and Early Christian Memory

Given the editorial shaping that we have seen in Matthew's presentation of these parables of judgment, it is understandable why it is not always easy to determine Jesus' original words and meaning. Most interpreters, therefore, take a stance somewhere between the extremes of saying either that Jesus spoke these parables exactly as we have them in our Gospels or that the early church or the evangelist was responsible for creating them. In any case, determining Jesus' meaning must be carried out for each parable on an individual basis.

With regard to the Parable of the Two Sons, the material contained in Matt 21:28b-31 — that is, the story of the parable as we have it, minus Matthew's introduction (v 28a) and conclusion (v 32) — is very much like what we would expect from Jesus. It is a simple story about a family and a work situation, with the point being that obedience is more important than mere words. The punchline in verse 31 about tax collectors and prostitutes entering the kingdom of God ahead of the Jewish leaders — presumably because the former people have repented and obeyed, whereas the latter group has not — gives us no reason to think that Jesus did not apply the call to obedience and to the kingdom in this way.

The Parable of the Wicked Tenants is much more complex. In its present form it is a full-blown allegory and highly christological in its application. If one were to attempt to remove later allegorical features, where would one stop? For the whole parable is imbued with a Christian salvation-historical point of view. The sending of servants, with that sending culminating in the sending of the landowner's son, is essential to the parable. The main question, then, revolves around whether Jesus would have told a parable that featured his own person, especially as the Son of God, as the main focus of the story. And the root of the issue concerns the messianic consciousness of Jesus.

Opinions, of course, differ widely. Yet if Jesus did understand his role in salvation history as being God's Son and humanity's Savior, there is no *a priori* reason that he could not have told a parable that pointed to God's sending Old Testament prophets and finally his own son to call Israel to repent — with a threat of punishment included! Such an image of Israel's recalcitrance, despite having messengers repeatedly sent to her by God, was part of a widespread tradition that scholars today term the "deuteronomistic view of Israel's history."

Furthermore, the proclamation of judgment was not something new to Jesus. The proclaiming of judgment was, in fact, a standard feature in the prophetic message. And as to whether Jesus himself added the rejected stone saying of 21:42 to the image of the rejected son — which is a matter still hotly debated — there is no question that Jesus could have employed the pun on *son (ben)* and *stone (eben)* by using the quotation from Ps 118:22-23. Yet since the quotation seems to have been a favorite Old Testament text used by Christians to explain the meaning of Jesus' rejection and crucifixion by means of his consequent vindication (see Acts 4:11; 1 Pet 2:7), the use of this text here should probably be viewed as a later interpretation.

The Parable of the Wedding Banquet is also colored christologically and strongly allegorized, especially in Matthew's version where we are dealing with the "wedding banquet" of the "son" of a "king." Luke's version is likely closer to the version that was in Q, though Luke has also allegorized the story — particularly with regard to the second and third missions of the slave, who is sent to invite Jewish outcasts (the poor, crippled, blind, and lame) and then Gentiles to the feast. The original Q wording of the parable is extremely difficult to reconstruct, let alone what words Jesus himself might have said. Nevertheless, it is very possible that Jesus told a parable about someone who invited guests to a feast, only to be rejected — despite the cultural taboo that such a situation depicts. And it is not out of the question that Jesus told of the anger of the rejected host and his action of inviting others to his feast, with a consequent judgment of the first rejecters. This scenario is akin to what we might call a "use it or lose it" situation, though with an added threat. Moreover, it is entirely possible that Jesus applied this situation to the realm of the kingdom, with the point being that one must respond to God's gracious offer to join the "feast of salvation," or else lose the opportunity and face punishment.

The disciples of Jesus no doubt remembered these parables from the lips of their Lord, especially in their arguments with other Jews regarding the significance of Jesus, whom they confessed to be Israel's Messiah. Thus they would have appealed to Jesus' own words of judgment on those who refused to obey the divine will, to produce the fruit of righteousness, or to believe the message of John the Baptist and Jesus. But with the benefit of hindsight and a developing theology about the person and meaning of Jesus, these early Christians obviously felt a measure of freedom to extrapolate on Jesus' words, especially as those words could be made to focus on the Jewish rejection of Jesus himself. And so in Matthew we see that the evangelist has — sometimes subtly and sometimes blatantly — interpreted Jesus' words to highlight the Jewish repudiation of their Messiah.

6. The Parable of the Unproductive Fig Tree (Luke 13:6-9)

Literary and Theological Context

Unlike the context of the parables in Matt 21:28–22:14, where there is a distinctive literary structure and unified theme, the context of the Parable of the Unproductive Fig Tree in Luke 13:6-9 is relatively unstructured and made up of rather disparate materials. The parable appears only in Luke's Gospel, and so source-critical questions are difficult to answer. Moreover, the parable is found in Luke's so-called Travel Narrative of 9:51–19:27, which focuses on Jesus' goal of getting to Jerusalem, the city of destiny. And while the reader gets the impression that Jesus is going on a journey (cf. 9:51-56, 57; 10:1, 38; 11:53; 13:22, 33; 17:11; 18:31, 35; 19:1, 11, 28) — and while there is a great deal of teaching given by Jesus in this section, whether to his disciples, to the crowd, or to his opponents — "the general themes of this section," as Howard Marshall has noted, "are hard to define, and it is even more difficult to find any kind of thread running through it" (*The Gospel of Luke* [Grand Rapids: Eerdmans, 1978], 401-2).

There are, of course, judgment statements that surround the parable of 13:6-9, as can be found in 12:49-59; 13:22-30, 34-35. But this material does not really shed light on the parable's interpretation. Rather, we need to look at the immediate context in 13:1-5 for an understanding as to how to interpret the parable.

Luke's Redactional Activity

It is clear that the discussion about "the Galileans whose blood Pilate had mixed with their sacrifices" of 13:1-5 is meant to be interpreted with the parable of 13:6-9. Yet the exact nature of the relationship between these two units is somewhat ambiguous. Do Jesus' words in verses 2-5 interpret the parable? Or, does the parable in verses 6-9 illustrate Jesus' earlier words? An analogous situation prevails in other Lukan texts where Jesus' teaching is expanded in parabolic form (cf., e.g., 10:27-29 and 30-37; 11:9-10 and 11-13; 12:14-15 and 16-21; 12:54-57 and 58-59; see also 11:1-4; 12:35; 15:1-2; 18:1; 19:11). The specific problem here, however, is that while both units of material warn about the urgent necessity for repentance, the first speaks merely about the need for a universal repentance whereas the parable itself suggests that grace and mercy are available for those who repent in time.

It is impossible to determine whether it was Jesus himself who originally linked these two units together or the evangelist Luke who first made the connection. Yet given the facts (1) that Luke has assembled together a great deal of disparate material in this section and (2) that the two units have somewhat differing lessons, it may be surmised that it was Luke who was mainly responsible for their being so placed in tandem. Verse 6 makes the connection between the two units only very loosely by the transitional statement: "Now he was saying this parable *(elegen de tautēn tēn parabolēn)*."

The setting for both Jesus' teaching and his parable in 13:1-9 is stated in verse 1: Some people came to Jesus, who was probably still in Galilee, to tell him about an incident that took place in Jerusalem, where the Roman governor Pilate had massacred certain Galilean Jews as their sacrificial animals were being slaughtered at the temple. Pilate's brutality is well-docu-

169

mented by Josephus (cf. *Antiq* 18:60-62, 85-87; *War* 2:175-77), though this incident is not attested by any other source. Judging by Jesus' response, what motivated the report was the view that calamity is always a punishment for sin (cf. Job 4:7; 8:20; 22:4-5; John 9:1-2). Jesus' reply in verses 2-5a, however, emphatically repudiates such a notion. Those who suffered this gruesome catastrophe, Jesus asserts, were not worse sinners than others. Then Jesus turns the question into a solemn warning: "Unless you repent, you too will all perish!" (v 5b).

The parable in verses 6-9 then takes up the ideas of repentance and perishing, though under a different guise. The threat of judgment is to be seen in the owner's command to cut down the unproductive fig tree. For just as an unfruitful tree is sooner or later cut down, so the judgment of God will come on people who never produce the fruit of repentance. The situation presented is reminiscent of the Baptist's message: "The ax is already at the root of the trees, and every tree that does not produce good fruit will be cut down and thrown into the fire" (Luke 3:9).

The word "repent," of course, does not appear in the parable. Nonetheless, the idea of repentance is implied by the fact that judgment is stayed, thereby giving the fig tree (figuratively) time to repent and produce good fruit. The new feature of the parable, however, is the emphasis on God's patience and mercy, for the owner lets the gardener talk him into allowing the fig tree to remain for one more year in the hope that the tree will bear fruit the next year. And so the twin aspects of God's judgment and mercy become evident, with repentance being the criterion that determines what God will mete out.

But the question naturally arises: In what sense can the Parable of the Unproductive Fig Tree be viewed as directed against the nation? Some interpreters, of course, do not see national implications in the parable at all. Yet there are several hints that point in that direction, and so most commentators have understood Israel in some sense to be the target of Jesus' warning. One hint can be found in the teaching material that precedes the parable, where calamitous incidents are related about some Galileans being slaughtered at the temple (v 2) and certain residents of Jerusalem being killed when the Tower of Siloam fell on them (v 4) — which calamities involve people from both Galilee and Judea, and so may suggest something of a national perspective. More particularly, however, the point is made that those victims were not worse than all the other Galileans or Jerusalemites, which suggests that everyone in Israel is a sinner and needs to repent. Furthermore, Jesus reinforces these suggestions of "all" in his concluding statement of verse 5: "Unless you repent, *all of you* likewise will perish." It is even possible, as J. M. Creed has observed, that Jesus had here in mind not the destruction in the world to come, but the destruction of Jerusalem and the nation as a whole (*The Gospel according to St. Luke* [London: Macmillan, 1930], 181).

A second hint of national judgment appears in the parable itself. For the fig tree was a rather standard symbol for Israel (cf. Isa 28:4; Jer 8:13; 24:1-8; Hos 9:10; Mic 7:1), as was also the vineyard (cf. Isa 5:1-7; Hos 9:10; Mic 7:1). Some commentators have gone too far in interpreting the parable's details by positing that the vineyard = Israel, the fig tree = Jerusalem, the gardener = Jesus, and the three years = Jesus' ministry. There is need, therefore, to take seriously Earle Ellis's words when interpreting this parable: "Some allegorical elements appear in Jesus' parables but, like the subtle features of a painting, they are more in the nature of hints than of precise equations, more susceptible to feeling than analysis" (*The Gospel of Luke,* rev. ed. [London: Marshall, Morgan & Scott, 1974], 185). The main point of the parable, however, is clear: the need for timely repentance. And this point is equally applicable to individuals today as it was for the nation of Israel.

Jesus' Meaning and Early Christian Memory

Both the teaching of verses 1-5 and the parable of verses 6-9 were probably recorded essentially as Jesus spoke them. That the parable is traditional is evidenced by the use of the historic present "he says" *(legei)* in verse 8 (cf. Jeremias, *Parables,* 182-83). Furthermore, that the story stems from the religious folklore of the Jews is suggested by its parallel to the *Story of Ahikar* 8:35, which dates from at least the fifth century BCE — though Jesus' emphasis on God's grace and mercy, as well as his judgment, differs from Ahikar's harsh reply to his son Nadan's plea for patience in that earlier story:

> I [Ahikar] answered and said to him [Nadan], 'My son, thou hast been to me like that palm-tree that stood by a river, and cast all its fruit into the river, and when its lord came to cut it down, it said to him, "Let me alone this year, and I will bring thee forth carobs." And its lord said unto

it, "Thou hast not been industrious in what is thine own, and how wilt thou be industrious in what is not thine own?"' (8:35)

Jesus' Parable of the Unproductive Fig Tree as a lesson to the nation, as well as to all who would hear, regarding the urgent need for repentance, certainly fits in with Jesus' teaching elsewhere — as witness, for example, his announcement at the very beginning of his ministry: "The time has come! The kingdom of God is near! Repent and believe the good news" in Mark 1:15; or his Parable of the Two Sons (discussed earlier) in Matt 21:28-32; or his condemnation of Bethsaida in Luke 10:13, whose residents had seen Jesus' miracles but did not repent. And since the parable is not christologically colored, it poses no problem to critics as to having been composed later.

Yet early Christians probably saw places in the parable where later interpretations could be made. For example, if the barren fig tree is to be cut down because it uses up the soil, is there not also here a hint that another vine will be planted in its place? And if that point is made — even though not implied in the story itself — the parable could be seen to approach the sense of Matt 21:43: "Therefore I tell you, the kingdom of God will be taken away from you and given to a people who will produce its fruits" (cf. also the imagery of "natural branches" and "engrafted branches" in Rom 11:17). Likewise, it is possible that the early Christians saw in the parable an allusion to the role of Jesus, as represented by the gardener, who pleads for a reprieve from the judgment pronounced against the nation, as represented by the fig tree.

7. The Parables of Judgment Today

Two matters need to be recognized and dealt with when interpreting these parables of judgment today. The first concerns the harsh polemic, or anti-Judaism, that appears in them. How are we to respond to this? For if these parables not only condemn the Jewish religious leaders of the day, but also extend that judgment to the nation of Israel itself, does that then give Christians the right to condemn Jewish people *en masse*? Our answer to this is unequivocal: Certainly not! "Anti-Judaism," which is a polemic against the *religion* of Judaism, must never be used as an occasion or excuse for "anti-Semitism," which is a racial hatred of Jews (and/or other

Semites). But we must then try to understand why Matthew, in particular, used such harsh tones against his own people.

Perhaps the best way of understanding the harsh and judgmental language of these parables — which is present in all of their appearances, but is especially prominent in their Matthean redactions — is to see it as rooted in a particular sociological and theological context. For the earliest Jewish believers in Jesus were facing ostracism and persecution by their Jewish compatriots for subordinating the major symbols of Jewish identity — that is, Torah, temple, circumcision, Sabbath, and dietary laws — to a position below the crucified and risen Christ. To an extent, therefore, the harsh language of these parables can be explained by the social situation that the early Christians faced as they sought to maintain their own identity as a rejected people. More importantly, however, Matthew's rhetoric against the nation should be seen as grounded in the theological conviction that if Jesus is truly Israel's Messiah, then those who reject Israel's God-given hope for fulfillment will necessarily be judged. Thus the central issue in the anti-Judaism polemic of these parables of judgment — just as it is throughout all of the New Testament, whatever the specific topic being treated — is christological in nature.

Christians today need to be extremely sensitive to issues regarding anti-Semitism and careful not to repeat the sins of their forbears, many of whom were anti-Semites in blaming the death of Jesus on the Jewish race. We need to develop a hermeneutic that allows the writers of the New Testament to speak to issues in their own contexts and in their own ways, but also one that does not permit us to move from "anti-Judaism" to "anti-Semitism." Indeed, Matthew may report that certain Jewish people once said, "Let his blood be on us and on our children" (27:25). But that statement must not be taken as equivalent to a decree of God! For God is not only a God of judgment, but also a God of grace and mercy. Nor should it be used as a pretext for a Christian attitude toward others, whoever he or she might be!

A second matter that needs to be highlighted when considering these parables of judgment is how they define the concept of righteousness, particularly when they define righteousness in terms of doing the will of God. If the Jewish religious leaders — and, indeed, the whole nation — were disobedient to the will of God, what, then, does it mean to be righteous? What did Jesus want to see in the Jewish leaders and the Jewish people that he also wants to see in us? The parables themselves are rather brief on this matter. What they do, in the main, is to set out the primary response desired — that is, the acceptance of Jesus as the Messiah. And they urge God's people to do God's will, which is defined as a positive response to God's Messiah.

Other passages in Matthew's Gospel, however, should also be considered when seeking to understand further how the will of God can be accomplished in our lives today. One such passage has to do with John the Baptist, as found in 3:1-12. There we learn that we may begin in our understanding of righteousness by heeding his message, which was: "Produce fruit worthy of repentance" (v 8). A second passage that should be considered is the so-called Sermon on the Mount in 5:1–7:29, where the teaching of Jesus regarding righteousness is collated for us by the evangelist Matthew. In fact, of Matthew's seven references to "righteousness," five appear in the Sermon on the Mount. And in that sermon Jesus is presented as saying: "Unless your righteousness surpasses that of the Pharisees and scribes, you will certainly not enter the kingdom of heaven" (5:20).

A third passage in Matthew's Gospel where the meaning of doing God's will is made explicit is the story of the rich young man in 19:16-22, who is told that to receive eternal life he must obey the commandments, be willing to sell his possessions and give to the poor, and follow Jesus. And for a fourth such passage we may point to the teaching in 23:23 as a model of what it means to do God's will. For though set in a negative context of woes against the scribes and Pharisees, Jesus says to his hearers: "You give a tenth of your spices — mint, dill, and cummin. But you have neglected the more important matters of the law — justice, mercy, and faithfulness. You ought to have practiced the latter, without neglecting the former."

The dominant issue that comes to the fore in all of Jesus' parables of judgment — whether as presented by Matthew alone, by all three synoptic evangelists together, by Matthew and Luke in concert, or by Luke alone — is a christological issue. And that same issue faces us as squarely today when reading these parables as it did those who either heard or read them in the first century. We are challenged by the Parable of the Two Sons (Matt 21:28-32) to follow the "way of righteousness" by believing in the message of John the Baptist and Jesus. The Parable of the Wicked Tenants (Matt 21:33-46, par.) urges us to produce the fruits of righteousness by accepting Jesus, the Son of God. The Parable of the Wedding Banquet (Matt 22:1-14//Luke 14:15-24) calls on us to make sure that we have actually responded to the invitation to the feast of salvation and are producing the fruit of righteousness. Finally, the Parable of the Unproductive Fig Tree (Luke 13:6-9) warns us to produce the fruit of repentance before it is too late.

As in the days when these parables were originally given, so today God is giving people another chance. It is foolhardy to fly in the face of divine judgment! And it is foolish to flout God's grace, patience, and mercy!

Selected Bibliography

Blinzler, Josef. "Die Niedermetzelung von Galiläer durch Pilatus," *Novum Testamentum* 2 (1958) 24-49.

Davies, W. D., and Allison, Dale C. *A Critical and Exegetical Commentary on the Gospel according to Saint Matthew,* 3 vols. Edinburgh: T. & T. Clark, 1988, 1991, 1996.

Dillon, Richard J. "Towards a Tradition-History of the Parables of the True Israel (Matthew 21,33–22,14)," *Biblica* 47 (1966) 1-42.

Dodd, C. H. *The Parables of the Kingdom.* London: Nisbet, 1935.

Jeremias, Joachim. *The Parables of Jesus,* trans. S. H. Hooke. 2nd rev. ed. New York: Scribner's, 1972.

Linnemann, Eta. *Parables of Jesus. Introduction and Exposition,* trans. J. Sturdy. London: SPCK; New York: Harper & Row, 1966.

Manson, T. W. *The Sayings of Jesus.* London: SCM, 1949 (first published as Part II of *The Mission and Message of Jesus.* London: SCM, 1937).

Marguerat, Daniel. *Le Jugement dans l'Évangile de Matthieu.* Geneva: Editions Labor et Fides, 1981.

Martens, Allan W. "The Compositional Unity of Matthew 21:12–24:2: Redaction-Critical, Literary Rhetorical, and Thematic Analyses" (Th.D. dissertation, Wycliffe College, University of Toronto, 1995).

Merkel, Helmut. "Das Gleichnis von den 'ungleichen Söhnen' (Matt. xxi.28-32)," *New Testament Studies* 20 (1974) 254-61.

Ogawa, Akira. "Paraboles de l'Israël véritable? Reconsidération critique de Mt xxi 28–xxii 14," *Novum Testamentum* 21 (1979) 121-49.

Smiga, George M. *Pain and Polemic: Anti-Judaism in the Gospels.* New York: Paulist, 1992.

Snodgrass, Klyne R. *The Parable of the Wicked Tenants: An Inquiry into Parable Interpretation.* Tübingen: Mohr-Siebeck, 1983.

175

Stanton, Graham N. *A Gospel for a New People: Studies in Matthew.* Edinburgh: T & T Clark, 1992; Louisville: Westminster/John Knox, 1993.

Strecker, Georg. *Der Weg der Gerechtigkeit: Untersuchung zur Theologie des Matthaus.* Göttingen: Vandenhoeck & Ruprecht, 1962, 1966, 1971.

Trilling, Wolfgang. "Zur Überlieferungsgeschichte des Gleichnisses vom Hochzeitsmahl Mt 22,1-14," *Biblische Zeitschrift* 4 (1960) 251-65.

————. *Das Wahre Israel: Studien zur Theologie des Matthäusevangeliums,* 3 Aufl. Munich: Kosel, 1964.

CHAPTER 8

On Being Ready

(Matthew 25:1-46)

RICHARD T. FRANCE

MATTHEW'S GOSPEL is distinguished by a series of five discourses compiled from the sayings of Jesus. Each discourse concludes with the formula: "And it happened, when Jesus had finished [these words]" (7:28; 11:1; 13:53; 19:1; 26:1). It seems that the evangelist has set these five discourses into his narrative as something of the nature of five commentaries on the significance of the events of Jesus' ministry portrayed in his Gospel.

The fifth and last of these discourses, that contained in Matthew 24–25, is about the future. It takes its cue from Jesus' prediction of the destruction of the temple in 24:2, which provokes the disciples to ask when that destruction will happen. But their question associates with this imminent historical event the more far-reaching hope of Jesus' future "coming" *(parousia)* and the "end of the age" (24:3). And the discourse moves from the first of these events to the second.

Just where in the discourse that change of subject from an imminent historical occurrence to events in the future takes place is a matter of dispute. I myself believe it is not until after 24:35 (see my *Matthew* commentary). But commentators generally agree that from at least 24:36 onwards it is Jesus' future *parousia* that is in view. And just as the first part of the discourse in chapter 24 has focused on the judgment of Jerusalem and its temple, so also the second part in chapter 25 carries a dominant note of judgment which note reaches its climax in the great universal judgment scene of 25:31-46.

Most of Matthew 24 is roughly paralleled in the shorter discourse of Mark 13, though in Matthew's Gospel the theme of judgment is developed more extensively. None of Matthew 25, however, is paralleled in Mark. One of the component parables of the second half of Matthew's discourse, that found in 25:14-30, has a parallel of sorts in Luke 19:12-27, where it is recorded separately from the discourse about the fate of the temple (cf. Luke 21:5-36). But, as we will see, the differences between Matt 25:14-30 and Luke 19:12-27 are as striking as are their similarities. To all intents and purposes, therefore, Matthew 25 represents Matthew's unique contribution to our knowledge of Jesus' teaching about future judgment. And the evangelist does this by the inclusion of two parables and an appended tableau.

1. The Context

Jesus' parables on being ready for his coming do not begin in Matthew's Gospel only at 25:1. Already in 24:43-51 two short parables have underlined the call to be ready for the coming of the Lord at a time when he is not expected. In 24:43 the simple analogy of a burglar, whose success depends on the element of surprise, provides the basis for the call in 24:44 to "be ready." Then in 24:45-51 a rather more elaborate parable underlines the same point: A man goes away, leaving his slave in charge of his household, and everything depends on what the houseowner finds when he returns; if the house is in good order, the slave will be rewarded, but if he has taken advantage of his master's absence he will be caught out and severely punished.

The focus in these two mini-parables is on the unexpectedness of Jesus' future coming — that is, the burglar's surprise appearance and the master's unannounced return. The time of the Lord's coming is unknown (24:36). It can be prepared for not by attempting to calculate the date, but by behaving in such a way that one is ready *whenever* it may occur.

It is this theme that is taken up and developed in the first parable of chapter 25, that of the bridesmaids in 25:1-13. The parable of the talents that follows in 25:14-30 takes up the theme again in depicting a master going away and leaving his slaves with responsibilities during his absence, and the different ways in which they acquit themselves until the time of his return. There can be little doubt, therefore, of the intended application of these parables at the point where they occur in Matthew's Gospel. For Jesus — having "gone away" in his death, resurrection, and ascension to heaven — will one day come back. But no one knows when that will be. His disciples must therefore be ready at all times. If they are not, there is the prospect of judgment.

But the call to be ready raises the important question regarding what that readiness consists of. Just how is one supposed to prepare for the unexpected coming of the Lord? As we work our way through chapter 25, this question becomes more urgent. Throughout the chapter, in fact, it begins to receive an answer — though, admittedly, by the end of the chapter the answer may not be as specific as we might wish.

It has long been fashionable to assume that Jesus' parables have mostly been adapted by the first-century church to address their own concerns, which may have been quite different from the thoughts of Jesus himself or the reactions of his disciples at the time when the story was first told. Paul's letters leave us in no doubt that the return of Jesus was a prominent concern of Christian congregations in the middle of the first century, and that many believed it would be soon. The relevance of these parables to that concern is obvious. As years went by, however, such a feeling of urgency may well have faded, with the result that "parousia delay" came to loom larger in their consciousness than imminence. Features having to do with the delay of Jesus' *parousia* are prominent in these parables (cf. 24:48; 25:5; 25:19, "after a long time"). This may reflect a concern of church leaders that people should not become complacent, since in each story the delay is followed by a sudden arrival.

But the relevance of these stories to the concerns of the middle and latter part of the first century does not necessarily mean that they were coined then, even if they were later modified by the church to speak to issues regarding the delay of Christ's *parousia*. The question is: Can the focus of these stories on a future "coming" be also understood as appropriate to the setting in which Matthew has placed them — that is, immediately before the cross and resurrection of Jesus? Our answer to this question depends largely on whether we accept that Jesus did, in fact, teach his disciples, while he was still with them, that after his death and resurrection he would one day return. This belief is so firmly established in what is perhaps the earliest of Paul's letters, that is, in his letters to his Thessalonian converts (cf. esp. 1 Thess 4:13–5:11; 2 Thess 2:1-12), that it is hard to explain where else it could have come from so quickly.

In the Gospels we have sayings of Jesus that speak of such a future event — not only in the discourse of Matthew 24–25, but also in Luke 12:35-48; 17:20-37; and 18:8. On the basis of such teaching, therefore, it is not difficult to believe that the disciples had already grasped this *parousia* concept sufficiently to need to ask the question that Matthew attributes to them in 24:3: "Tell us, when will this happen, and what will be the sign of your coming and of the end of the age?" And if they were already concerned to know the time of Jesus' future coming, it is no surprise that, having told them that they could *not* know the time of it (24:36), he went on to warn them about the need to be always ready for it. Moreover, a prospect of judgment and themes regarding rewards and punishments occur frequently throughout the recorded sayings of Jesus. So these stories of Matthew 25 deal with matters with which the disciples would not have been unfamiliar.

Chapter 25 consists of three units. Two of them are parables in the normal sense of the term. The third contains a parabolic image — that of a shepherd separating sheep from goats. It is not itself, however, a story-parable, but rather a magnificent tableau of final judgment. In all three units the theme of judgment is central.

2. The Parable of the Bridesmaids (25:1-13)

The division of bridesmaids into two groups, the "wise" and the "foolish," picks up a contrast that is familiar from Jewish wisdom literature and has already been set out earlier in other parables in Matthew's Gospel — that of the "wise" and "foolish" builders in 7:24-27, and of the "wise" and "foolish" slaves in 24:45-51. In those parables, as here, the "wise" — or probably better the "prudent," which more accurately translates the Greek word *phonimos* — are those who recognize the need to take action in readiness for a coming crisis, so that they will not be caught unprepared.

Our knowledge of ancient Palestinian wedding customs is not sufficient for us to be sure just who the "virgins" *(parthenoi)* would be. They may have been attendants of the bride, or servants in the bridegroom's house, or just friends and neighbors. But their role in the ceremonies was to accompany the bridegroom in a torchlight procession into "the wedding," presumably the marriage feast. Their torches (*lampades,* which is not the same word used for standing "lamps" in 5:15; 6:22, and elsewhere) would probably be bundles of oil-soaked rags wrapped on a stick, so that it was necessary to carry jars of oil to dip them in before lighting. Those girls who had not brought oil with them could not relight their torches when they dried out while waiting for the bridegroom. When his arrival was announced, it was too late. And their futile attempts to get new supplies in time resulted in their missing the procession and being shut out of the feast.

So this is, in general terms, a story of readiness and unreadiness, with either inclusion or exclusion the result. Any more specific identifications drawn from the details of the story must be made with care, and only insofar as they can be justified from the context in which the story is set. Nonetheless, since the preceding verses have been about the *parousia* of Jesus, it seems clear that Jesus is the bridegroom (an image that he had used earlier of himself, as depicted not only in Matt 9:15 but also in Mark 2:20 and Luke 5:35). And if that is so, then the feast to which the girls were invited would naturally be seen in the light of the Jewish hope of the "messianic banquet," which would take place when the Messiah comes (cf. Matt 8:11-12; 22:1-14). So much seems required by the story's context. But the effect of the parable does not depend on our discerning a specific meaning in the oil; nor of identifying the girls, whether wise or foolish, as a particular group in the church. Still less do we need to explain the lack of any mention of the bride.

It may, however, be appropriate to notice certain details in the way the story is told that do not seem to be required by the main story line, since such details may hint at the way the story was meant to be understood. One such detail is the emphasis placed on the bridegroom's delay. The inclusion of this detail should probably be taken as an acknowledgment that time had passed since Jesus promised to return. More importantly, it probably should be seen as a recognition that the church needed guidance on how to live in what seemed to be an unlimited interim period.

During that delay all the girls go to sleep, not merely the foolish ones. So readiness does not consist in living in a constant state of "red alert." Life must go on in the interim; and provision for the *parousia* of Jesus depends rather on having made preparation beforehand so that one can safely go to sleep, secure in the knowledge that when the time comes everything will be in place. This tallies not so much with the Parable of the Burglar in 24:43,

181

which seems to require staying awake, as it does with the Parable of the Slave in 24:45-51 — whose "readiness" was not in constantly sitting by the door, but in getting on with the job he had been given to do. We will hear a similar note in the Parable of the Talents, where the fault of the third slave was in his doing nothing rather than being actively involved in everyday business.

The unsuccessful attempt of the foolish girls to borrow from the wise may be no more than dramatic storytelling. But the moral would be easily drawn that "readiness" is something for which each of us is responsible — that is, that we cannot be passengers on another person's readiness. The apparent selfishness of the wise is not the point of the story. Rather, as David Garland points out: "The parable is an allegory about spiritual preparedness, not a lesson on the golden rule" (*Reading Matthew*, 240).

The climax of the story comes at the end of verse 10 when the door is shut. There is a grim finality about this shutting of the banquet door that is unlikely to reflect the bonhomie, or general atmosphere of geniality, usually associated with a village wedding ceremony. No doubt in real life the pathetic appeal of the foolish girls in verse 11 would have met with a more sympathetic response. But the story is increasingly losing the contours of everyday life and taking on the dimensions of the final judgment. For the girls appeal to the bridegroom, rather than to the porter, with the cry: "Lord! Lord!" — thereby echoing the appeal of those who in 7:22 have claimed their right of entry to the kingdom of heaven on the basis of their charismatic achievements. Furthermore, the bridegroom answers them in almost the same words as directed to evildoers on the day of final judgment, as given in 7:23: "I never knew you!" Their unreadiness, the story suggests, consisted not in what they did or did not do, but in a failure of relationship. And so, as in Jesus' teaching in 7:21-23, what ultimately decides whether one is inside or outside the door is being known by the bridegroom.

To this already complex set of criteria for inclusion — that is, (1) oil, whatever it is; (2) being there when it counts; and (3) being known by the bridegroom — verse 13 adds another that seems entirely incongruous: that of remaining awake. This is just what neither the wise nor the foolish did in the story. It echoes, rather, the language of 24:42-44, and so should perhaps be understood as a coda to the whole section of 24:36–25:12 rather than a summary of the story of the bridesmaids specifically. It reverts to the Parable of the Burglar in order to reinforce the call to be ready by means of a complementary, though literally an incompatible, metaphor.

The effect of this story, then, is to stress the need to be ready for a "coming" that will be at an unexpected time. Furthermore, the story suggests that among those who to all outward appearances were all in the same category (i.e., ten girls sleeping together by the roadside) there is, in fact, a fundamental division between those who were ready and those who were unready, and that this division has eternal consequences for their contrasting destinies — that is, either sharing the feast with the bridegroom or wailing unavailingly outside the closed door.

But the question as to how that readiness is to be understood has not yet been clearly answered. The answer suggested by the words of the bridegroom in verse 12, "I don't know you," seems strangely out of keeping with the way the rest of the story is told. To carry a jar of oil looks more like some sort of provident preparation for a coming crisis. But what sort of preparation? The parable that follows goes at least part of the way in providing an answer.

3. The Parable of the Talents (25:14-30)

Before considering the Parable of the Talents as found in Matthew, we must note that in Luke 19:11-27 there appears a parable that is clearly a version of the same story — an absent master giving his slaves money to use in his absence; two of the slaves trading well and being rewarded; one slave, claiming to fear his master's known rapaciousness, keeping the money safe, but being punished because of his lack of enterprise — with some of the same dialogue (cf. Matt 25:21a, 24, 26-27, 28 and Luke 19:17a, 21, 22-23, 24) and the same interpretative comments (cf. Matt 25:29 and Luke 19:26). Luke's version, however, is very different in the details of the story itself — that is, a nobleman, ten slaves, much smaller sums of money, all receive the same amount, varying rates of return, proportionate governorship of cities as a reward, money wrapped in a cloth. Furthermore, it is expanded with the apparently unrelated themes of the nobleman seeking to have himself appointed a king, a delegation of his disaffected subjects voicing their opposition to his appointment, and their ultimate annihilation. Moreover, the setting of the story in Luke is not in the context of a discourse about the future (as found in Luke 21), but just before Jesus' arrival at Jerusalem and because "the people were thinking that the kingdom of God was about to appear immediately" (Luke 19:11).

Those words of introduction in Luke 19:11 suggest that the theme of "parousia delay" is important for Luke's version. The delay in Luke is related to the appearance of the kingdom of God rather than, as in Matthew's context, to the *parousia* hope — though it is not difficult to detect this latter motif in the Lukan symbolism of the nobleman's return as a king. In Luke, as in Matthew, however, the essential message seems to be that the period of waiting must be used responsibly, though the themes of kingship and rebellion introduce new dimensions to the parable that do not sit very comfortably with the story's main theme (somewhat similar, it appears, to the way that the king's military expedition intrudes into the Parable of the Great Supper in Matt 22:1-14).

Most commentators believe that Luke's version represents a later adaptation and expansion of Jesus' parable. But the differences between the two versions — even in the basic story line — are such that here, if anywhere, we should take seriously the possibility that Jesus himself may have retold the story with differences on another occasion, thereby giving rise to two separate parable traditions, and that these two separate tellings found their way ultimately into the accounts of Matthew and Luke respectively. It is remarkable how resistant some New Testament scholars are to the possibility that Jesus, in the course of several months or even years of public ministry, may have used and reused similar material a number of times with different audiences and for different purposes. Any preacher could have told them that this is the most natural scenario in the world!

Our focus here, however, must be on Matthew's version of the story, the Parable of the Talents, as it relates to the overall effect of the parables in the latter part of the discourse about the future. Like the preceding parables of the slave left in charge and of the bridesmaids, it speaks of a period of waiting before the master's return, and it calls on those who hear to be ready when he comes. But this time there is more emphasis on what the slaves have done, or should have done, during the master's absence. And it is this focus that takes us further than the previous parables toward an understanding of what it means to "be ready."

The story is of a wealthy man who during an absence from home leaves very large sums of money with his slaves. A talent was normally reckoned as 6,000 denarii. And since in Matt 20:2 a denarius is an acceptable day's pay for a laborer, a talent presumably represents something like twenty years' wages. So the man who receives five talents is handling more than he could have expected to earn in a lifetime! This is serious money! The purpose of this allocation of money to his slaves is not stated in Matthew, as it is in Luke 19:13 ("Trade with it until I come back"). But the sequel makes it clear that the master expected — and that the slaves knew he would expect — that they would find means of increasing it during his absence.

The focus of the story is on the contrasting achievements and fates of the first two slaves in comparison with the third. And since the third — like the bad slave of 24:48-51 and the foolish girls of 25:8-12 — is dealt with at greater length than those who succeeded, it seems clear that it is his example that we are particularly meant to notice and to heed as a warning. It is in the difference between his action (or lack of it) and the actions of the first two slaves that we will find the key to "being ready."

The first two slaves "traded with" (*ergazomai en,* literally "to work in") the money they had received and "gained" (*kerdainō,* "to gain, make a profit") a one hundred percent profit. The nature of their trading is not specified, and is not important. It was apparently something more productive — probably, as well, more risky — than merely placing it on deposit with a bank, since the master's comment in verse 27 suggests that depositing it with a bank would have resulted in only a minimal gain. But even that would have been better than nothing.

. The third slave, however, played it safe. Merely tying money up in a cloth (as in Luke 19:20) was regarded as inadequate security, rendering a trustee liable to make good whatever was lost or stolen (cf. *Mishnah, Baba Metzia* 3:10). But this slave went for maximum security, and so hid his master's money in the ground (25:25). A later Rabbi is reported to have declared that, since bankers could not be trusted: "Money can be guarded only by placing it in the earth" (*Babylonian Talmud, Baba Metzia* 42a; though see Jesus' parable in Matt 13:44 for what might happen even to money buried in the earth). In a period free of inflation, the slave apparently viewed his action as being prudent and as guaranteeing that his master would incur no loss.

Yet his prudence is condemned as timidity. The master requires profit, not just the return of his capital. The slave's portrayal of his master as grasping and unreasonable was meant to justify his caution, so as to avoid punishment for loss of the deposit. But it, in fact, is turned against him, for a grasping master is not going to be satisfied with a nil profit. As in other parables (notably Luke 11:5-8; 18:2-5), where an unattractive human trait is used to illustrate the character of God, we need not assume a simple allegorical equivalence. The message is not that God is a "rapacious capitalist" (F. W. Beare, *Matthew*, 486), but that he is not satisfied with inaction. To play it safe and keep one's slate clean is not enough. God looks for more than "a religion concerned only with not doing anything wrong" (E. Schweizer, *Matthew*, 473). Discipleship in the kingdom of heaven is not a matter of safety but of risk, of losing life in order to gain it (cf. Matt 10:39; 16:25-26).

What, then, do the talents represent? What sort of "trading" is required of disciples in the interim period before their Lord returns? Here we must put out of our minds the meaning of the English word "talent." For the Greek *talanton* means a large sum of money, and nothing more. It does not carry within it any necessary indication of what such a sum represents. The metaphorical use of "talent" in English for "innate ability, aptitude, or faculty" (Collins' *English Dictionary*) derives not from the meaning of the Greek word but from subsequent interpretations of this parable, on the assumption that that was what the sums of money were intended to represent. But the Greek term has no such meaning.

In the context of Jesus' ministry, and especially of the expectation of his return, it is unlikely that we are intended to think of what we now call "talents" — that is, the general aptitudes and abilities that people have as natural endowments or as a result of their various environments. Jesus' central message was about the kingdom of God (or, as Matthew's wording has it, "the kingdom of heaven"). Consequently, in Matthew's Gospel, particularly in the Sermon on the Mount of chapters 5–7, discipleship is portrayed as a style of life peculiarly appropriate to that divine regime — that is, as the distinctive values and commitments of those who have been called to follow Jesus and who have a Father in heaven. And in 13:11-17 Jesus is presented as making a ringing declaration of the special privilege enjoyed by his disciples, which is a privilege that has been denied to many prophets and righteous people before them. For to the disciples, but not to the crowds at large who came merely to hear Jesus' teaching, has been entrusted the "secrets of the kingdom of heaven." So having received such a privilege, they are expected to exploit it in the service of their master, for "much will be expected of those to whom much has been given" (Luke 12:48).

The primary meaning of the talents, therefore, has to do with the special privileges and opportunities entrusted to Jesus' disciples as subjects of the kingdom of heaven. When the master goes away, it is their responsibility not to wait in pious idleness but to get on with the job he has entrusted to them. He will leave behind great potential. But he expects that potential to be developed through the faithful discipleship of his people.

The different sums given to the three slaves may be no more than good storytelling. Still, perhaps we are intended to note that not everyone has the same opportunities and abilities to achieve results for the kingdom of heaven (cf. the different rates of yield of the good seed in 13:8), and that the results expected will be proportionate to the initial endowment (cf. the teaching on varied gifts in such passages as Rom 12:3-8; 1 Cor 12:4-11; and Eph 4:7-13). It is, therefore, an encouragement to find that the commendations given to each of the first two slaves in verses 21 and 23 are identical, even though the sums involved differed. After all, 100 percent *is* 100 percent, even if the initial capital sums varied!

While growth is a recurrent theme in the Parables of the Kingdom of Heaven in Matthew 13, an impression could easily be drawn from those parables that growth is automatic — that is, that the good seed will develop by its own power, and all that men and women have to do is to wait for the outcome. But the Parable of the Talents refines the idea of growth by changing the metaphor. For just as seed grows, so does money. Yet it does not grow by its own efforts, but only as people put it to use. For unlike seed, money buried in the ground will not grow. So if the tiny mustard seed is, indeed, to become a great bush, it will be because disciples have been making it grow. These two parabolic metaphors, of course, are not linked together in the same story, but by taking note of them side by side a creative fusion is achieved.

The interval between Jesus' initial sowing of the seed and his ultimate return to collect the harvest is, therefore, not to be seen as one of passive waiting (as the parable of Mark 4:26-29, taken on its own, might suggest). Rather, it is a time for enterprise and initiative on the part of those who have been called to follow Jesus, and he will expect results. Thus to be ready for his coming is to be active on behalf of the kingdom of heaven and to have results to show for it. It is to show initiative and to take risks in order to achieve something for God. Those who have cause to fear his coming are those who have not made use of the opportunities and privileges entrusted to them, who have buried their money in the ground, and so achieved nothing for the kingdom of heaven — or, to echo another parable, who have hidden their lamp under a meal-tub, with the result that no one has been able to see their light and so been drawn to give glory to their Father in heaven (5:15-16). For them there will be no "Well done!"

It is at the level of rewards and punishments that, as in the two preceding parables of the slave left in charge and the ten bridesmaids, the application invades the telling of the story. For "Enter into your master's joy!" (vv 21, 23) hardly rings true as a real-life businessman's response to his slaves' successes. This is not the language of commercial transactions, but of the kingdom of heaven — of the messianic banquet that is foreshadowed in 8:11 and symbolized in the wedding feast into which the five wise girls were welcomed in the previous parable at 25:10. Joachim Jeremias has suggested that "joy" represents an Aramaic word that can also mean "banquet" (*Parables*, 60). But this seems an unnecessarily prosaic way of reinforcing what is already a fairly obvious symbolism.

Likewise, the language of verse 30, "throw that worthless servant into outer darkness, where there will be weeping and gnashing of teeth," goes far beyond the dismissal of an unsatisfactory servant. The "outer darkness" and the "weeping and gnashing of teeth" echo the words of 8:12 and 22:13, which describe the fate of those who fail to qualify for the messianic banquet (cf. also 13:42, 50; 24:51, where "weeping and gnashing of teeth" is used in connection with parables about the fate of those rejected at the final judgment). Such language is not the language of human transactions and employment, but traditional Jewish language of the ultimate fate of the ungodly.

Another curious touch that sits uncomfortably within the framework of the story of this parable is the command in verse 28 to take the third slave's carefully preserved talent and give it to the slave who now has ten talents. The story was of slaves who were expected to trade for their master's benefit, not their own, and the reward promised in verses 21 and 23 is not personal gain but further responsibility. So it is surprising to find that the successful slave is now not only allowed to keep both the capital and the profit, rather than return them to his master, but also given a further personal bonus at the expense of his less successful colleague.

In Luke 19:24 the same command is given, and, understandably, it provokes a shocked protest: "Lord, he already has ten pounds!" (19:25). But, again, we need to remember that a parable is not meant to be a mirror of real life. When incongruous features occur, they usually appear in order to introduce additional points of application. And here in Matthew 25 this strange feature is explained by the saying to which it gives rise in verse 29: "To all those who have, more will be given so that they have more than enough; from those who do not have, even what they have will be taken away."

This epigram occurs in a number of places in the Gospels (cf. Matt 13:12; also, though in a different setting, Mark 4:25 and Luke 8:18). But it does not fit very neatly with the parable here. For the focus of the story up to verse 27 was not on the personal gain of the first two slaves. Furthermore, the third slave was not destitute, but still had one talent. It is the addition of verse 28, however, that has allowed the epigram to be introduced, thereby adding a related but separate moral based on a principle of capitalist economics — that is, that capital breeds income, but a lack of capital spells ruin. So also, the parable teaches, there is reward for the spiritually successful, but disaster for the spiritually bankrupt. The kingdom of heaven is, it seems, an enterprise culture, with no place accorded for mere passengers.

The Parable of the Talents, therefore, develops the theme of "being ready" by spelling out a little more concerning what is expected of disciples in the period before their Lord returns. Just as the slave of 24:46 was commended and rewarded for being hard at work when his master returned, so this parable calls followers of Jesus to responsible activity — or, in the imagery of the parable itself, to maximize one's potential for the benefit of the kingdom of heaven. And just as the five wise bridesmaids were not caught out because they had already made sure of their oil supply, so followers of Jesus are expected not to sit and watch but to make preparations. Our "readiness" consists in having faithfully and boldly discharged our responsibilities as disciples, whether they have been small or great. It is the master who allocates the scale of responsibility; it is the slave's responsibility to carry out faithfully the role that has been entrusted. The vision that follows in 25:31-46 spells out more explicitly what at least part of that role is to be.

4. A Tableau of Final Judgment (25:31-46)

The final section of Jesus' discourse about the future in Matthew 25 has only a limited place in a discussion of parables. Its language is vivid and visionary. It is not, however, at least in any normal sense of the word, a parable, though commentators display a remarkably persistent tendency to describe it as such. Jeremias, for example, calls it "a masal" or "an apocalyptic revelation," like those of *1 Enoch* (*Parables*, 206). But few English readers would recognize this as a natural meaning of "parable." Others tend simply to cite Jeremias's authority for calling it a parable!

Admittedly, the passage *contains* a parabolic simile of a shepherd dividing sheep from goats in verses 32-33 (cf. Ezek 34:17). Nonetheless, the shepherd imagery is not developed and the dramatic judgment scene is presented in terms of a dialogue between the King and two groups of people, without further recourse to that shepherd imagery. We will, therefore, first comment briefly on the simile in verses 32-33, and then consider how the judgment scene as a whole rounds off the theme of readiness for the master's return, which the preceding parables have opened up.

Mixed flocks of sheep and goats are often seen in Palestine. While sheep (when clean!) are normally white and goats mainly brown or black, some sheep (more than in most Western flocks) have brown or black patches and some are generally dark. It can, therefore, take an experienced eye to separate them at the end of the day, when the goats need to be taken indoors while the hardier sheep remain in the open air. So at the last judgment, it may not be obvious to all observers — even to the participants themselves, as verses 37-39, 44 graphically illustrate — who belong to the "righteous" and who do not. It takes, in fact, the expert judgment of the King to tell them apart.

It is probably not helpful to speculate why the righteous are represented as sheep and the unrighteous as goats, since both animals were valuable in a society that (unlike ours) was not prejudiced against goat-meat, and in which goatskin was as much in demand as sheep's wool. It should be noted, however, that the Old Testament often describes God's people as his sheep, but never as his goats. The point here is not the identification of the animals, but the fact of their separation. And insofar as there is the possibility of visual confusion between the sheep and the goats, this little simile reinforces the message of the Parable of the Weeds (cf. Matt 13:24-30, 36-43): that it is only at the final judgment that we can know who is who.

As in the conclusion to the Parable of the Weeds (cf. 13:41), the judge in this tableau of final judgment in 25:31-46 is not, as we might have expected, God. Rather, it is "the Son of Man," who is described as "the King." The imagery of the great vision of Dan 7:9-28 is used to depict his ultimate enthronement as sovereign over "all peoples, nations and languages" (Dan 7:14), and so "all nations" are gathered before him for judgment. The setting at the end of a discourse that has increasingly focused on the *parousia* of Christ — and that climaxes in verse 46 with the unrighteous going off to "eternal punishment" and the righteous being led into "eternal life" — indicates that this is the final judgment, as a result of which people will find themselves either enjoying "the kingdom prepared for you from the foundation of the world" (v 34) or sharing "the eternal fire prepared for the devil and his angels" (v 41). This is the moment for which we have been insistently warned that we must be ready, with the choice between these two destinies depending on that readiness.

But how does this tableau of final judgment in 25:31-46 define that "readiness"? The answer is disarmingly but disturbingly simple — "disturbingly simple," that is, for those of us who believe with the apostle Paul that we cannot be saved by good works. For what is said here is that those who will find life are those who have performed acts of kindness to people in distress, whereas those destined for the fire are those who have ignored people's needs. The Greek conjunction *gar* ("because") at the beginning of both verse 35 and verse 42 makes a direct link between a person's ultimate destiny and the acts of kindness that he or she has performed or withheld. The least that this use of *gar* implies is that the performance or non-performance of such acts of kindness are the *evidence* of a person's blessed or cursed state. More probably, however, the Greek *gar* ("because") should be understood as signaling the actual *basis* — or, at least, part of the basis — for that judgment. Being ready for final judgment, then, would seem to consist in having acted kindly towards anyone in need.

This apparently "Pelagian" teaching has understandably met with stout exegetical resistance (cf., e.g., R. H. Stein, *Introduction to the Parables,* 135-40; see also the commentaries on Matthew by R. H. Gundry, D. A. Carson, and D. A. Hagner). It is probably true to say that the majority of recent commentators have opposed it, though there are those who continue to support it (cf., e.g., D. Wenham, *Parables,* 90-92; see also the Matthew commentary by W. D. Davies and D. C. Allison).

The obvious point of departure in attempting to restrict the apparently universal scope of the acts of kindness described is the fact that these acts are described by the King as having been done not to people in general, but to *him*. It is only in response to the incredulity of the righteous that the King explains that it was through kindness to "one of these smallest brothers and sisters of mine" that they showed it to him. Their kind deeds toward other people, therefore, were taken as evidence of a positive attitude toward Jesus, even if those who did them were not themselves conscious of their significance.

Moreover, the beneficiaries are not people in general, but "little brothers and sisters of Jesus." The crucial question, therefore, is whether Jesus, or the evangelist Matthew, would have used such a phrase to mean just anybody, however insignificant — or whether it must mean specifically the members of Jesus' true family ("my brother and sister and mother"), who have been defined in 12:50 as "those who do the will of my Father in heaven." In other words, is the basis of divine judgment an undiscriminating philanthropy; or is it, rather, kindness shown specifically to Christian disciples (cf. 28:10 for the disciples as Jesus' "brothers"), and through them to their Lord?

Some have gone further and argued that the reference in 25:31-46 is specifically to Christian missionaries (e.g., J. R. Michaels, "Apostolic Hardships and Righteous Gentiles: A Study of Matthew 25:31-46," *Journal of Biblical Literature* 84 [1965] 27-37; R. H. Gundry in his *Matthew* calls them "the persecuted messengers of Jesus"), so that people's basic allegiance is revealed by whether they receive or reject those who come to them in the name of Jesus. The comparison is made with statements in Matthew 10, where a judgment worse than what befell Sodom and Gomorrah is said to await those who reject Jesus' emissaries (vv 11-15) and Jesus is quoted as saying: "Anyone who receives you [the disciples] receives me" (v 40). But it may be doubted that Christian missionaries are specifically in view in 25:31-46. For while Matthew 10 goes on to commend the gift of a drink of water to "one of these little ones, because he is a disciple" and declares that such an act of kindness to such a "little one" will be rewarded (v 42), that chapter does not specifically speak of these "little ones" as missionaries.

The similarity of 25:35-40 to these statements in Matthew 10 is striking, and the reference here to Jesus' brothers and sisters as "little ones" suggests a deliberate echo. The same language about "little ones" occurs also in 18:6, 10 and 14, and there, too, it is specifically disciples of Jesus who are in view. Moreover, the cue for talk about "little ones" in Matthew 18 is Jesus' use of a child as a model of true discipleship (vv 2-5), and it is in that connection that he declares: "Whoever receives one such child in my name receives me" (v 5). So in Matthew's Gospel there appears a recurrent theme of disciples as "little ones" in whom Jesus himself is to be recognized, with how they are treated being an indication of people's attitude also to him. And 25:35-40 fits snugly within that developing motif, bringing it to a climax in the solemn context of the final judgment.

There is, then, a strong case to be made for understanding the kindness of the righteous and the hardness of the unrighteous as specifically directed toward Jesus in the person of his insignificant followers, rather than toward human needs in general. On that basis, it is possible to argue that the criterion of judgment is not so much good works *per se* as it is one's response to Jesus — and that is a much more comfortable conclusion for Protestant theology! Unfortunately, however, neither the righteous nor the unrighteous *knew* that they were responding to Jesus. If the acts of the righteous reveal them as Christians, it is apparently as "anonymous Christians," who are surprised to find themselves on the side of Jesus at the great divide. Thus the interpretation of this passage as locating the criterion of judgment in sheer undiscriminating good deeds to the needy — even when full weight has been given to the fact that Jesus describes the recipients as his brothers and sisters — refuses to evaporate completely.

The criterion of judgment, and therefore the basis of our "readiness," spelled out in this climactic judgment scene is a very practical one: one's works of kindness. These works are, Jesus declares, directed toward him in the person of his followers. But those being judged are apparently unaware of that fact. It is their kindness in itself, rather than any conscious targeting of such acts toward those known to be disciples, that marks them out as those "blessed by my Father." Here, then, is a more tangible spelling out of what was symbolized by the slave's care for the household (24:45-46), the girls' supply of oil (25:4), and the first two slaves' trading activities (25:16-17). It is how we behave toward other people that will be a key criterion of judgment.

It is possible, of course, to argue from other parts of Scripture — even from Matthew's Gospel — that this is not the only criterion, but rather a symptom of an underlying relationship with God of which works of kindness are a natural outworking. But that is not what this particular passage says. No other criterion, in fact, is mentioned. As Jesus is reported to have said on other challenging occasions, and so must be understood to have intended here as well: "If you have ears, hear!"

5. Conclusion — "Being Ready"

Jesus' great discourse on future events in Matthew 24–25 has come to a far-reaching climax. Having left behind the initial question of the fate of the Jerusalem temple, Jesus has turned the spotlight onto his own future return in glory. And it is this theme that has given rise to a powerful sequence of parables of judgment, leading up to a searching tableau of the final judgment of all nations executed by himself as King upon his throne.

Throughout the immediate context and the latter part of this eschatological discourse, the motif of an ultimate division has been predominant. The parables have centered on contrasting individuals or groups: the responsible and irresponsible slaves (24:42-51); the sensible and foolish bridesmaids (25:1-13); the successful and unsuccessful traders (25:14-30); and the sheep and the goats (25:31-46). Every reader is left to ponder where he or she stands within this radical separation. Am I a responsible or irresponsible slave? A sensible or foolish bridesmaid? A successful or unsuccessful trader? A sheep or a goat?

At the end of each story, just as in the earlier Parable of the Weeds and Parable of the Net in Matthew 13, there appears the moment of decision — when the master returns, the bridegroom arrives, or the shepherd separates the flock. At that time it will be too late to change sides, to go looking for oil, or to start trading. The door will be shut! And there will be some inside and some outside!

No one knows how soon that moment of decision may come. That is why the note that sounds throughout the latter part of the discourse is a call to "be ready" — so as not to be caught out in riotous irresponsibility, to discover too late that you have no oil, to have nothing to present to the returning master but bare capital, or to find oneself on the left side of the throne.

We have traced the gradual unfolding of the theme of "being ready" for the final judgment in these stories, highlighting the fact that in Jesus' teaching such preparation has to do with (1) a responsible fulfillment of duty (24:43-51), (2) making adequate provisions in the present for events in the future (25:1-13), (3) boldly and actively exploiting opportunities for advancing the growth of the kingdom of heaven (25:14-30), and, most searchingly of all, (4) giving food and drink, welcoming, clothing, caring for, and visiting the "little brothers and sisters of Jesus" (25:31-46). Here is an eminently practical agenda of preparation for the coming judgment. It has nothing to do with eschatological timetables or ascetic regimes. Rather, it is all about living to the full a life of responsible and joyful discipleship, and doing it now before it is too late.

Selected Bibliography

Beare, Francis W. *The Gospel according to Matthew.* Oxford: Blackwell, 1981.

Carson, Donald A. *Matthew,* in *The Expositor's Bible Commentary,* vol. 8, ed. F. E. Gaebelein. Grand Rapids: Zondervan, 1984, 1-599.

Davies, W. D. and Dale C. Allison, Jr. *The Gospel according to Saint Matthew,* 3 vols. Edinburgh: T. & T. Clark, 1988, 1991, 1996.

France, Richard T. *Matthew.* Leicester: Inter-Varsity; Grand Rapids: Eerdmans, 1985.

————. *Matthew: Evangelist and Teacher.* Exeter: Paternoster; Grand Rapids: Zondervan, 1989.

Garland, David E. *Reading Matthew: A Literary and Theological Commentary on the First Gospel.* New York: Crossroad, 1993.

Gundry, Robert H. *Matthew: A Commentary on his Literary and Theological Art.* Grand Rapids: Eerdmans, 1982.

Hagner, Donald A. *Matthew 14–28* (Word Commentary 33B). Dallas: Word, 1995.

Jeremias, Joachim. *The Parables of Jesus,* trans. S. H. Hooke. Rev. ed. London: SCM, 1963.

Ladd, George E. "The Parable of the Sheep and the Goats in Recent Interpretation," in *New Dimensions in New Testament Study,* ed. R. N. Longenecker and M. C. Tenney. Grand Rapids: Zondervan, 1974, 191-99.

Schweizer, Eduard. *The Good News according to Matthew,* trans. D. E. Green. London: SPCK; Atlanta: John Knox, 1975.

Stein, Robert H. *An Introduction to the Parables of Jesus.* Philadelphia: Westminster, 1981.

Wenham, David. *The Parables of Jesus: Pictures of Revolution.* London: Hodder & Stoughton, 1989.

PART IV

Parables of the Christian Life

CHAPTER 9

Parables on God's Love and Forgiveness
(Luke 15:1-32)

STEPHEN C. BARTON

1. Introduction: Cheap Grace

Dietrich Bonhoeffer, the German theologian and martyr, began his memorable book on *The Cost of Discipleship* (ET, 1948) as follows:

> Cheap grace is the deadly enemy of our Church. We are fighting today for costly grace.
>
> Cheap grace means grace sold on the market like cheapjack's wares. The sacraments, the forgiveness of sin, and the consolations of religion are thrown away at cut prices. Grace is represented as the Church's inexhaustible treasury, from which she showers blessings with generous hands, without asking questions or fixing limits. Grace without price; grace without cost!
>
> Cheap grace means grace as a doctrine, a principle, a system. It means forgiveness of sins proclaimed as a general truth, the love of God taught as the Christian "conception" of God. An intellectual assent to that idea is held to be of itself sufficient to secure remission of sins. The Church which holds the correct doctrine of grace has, it is supposed, *ipso facto* a part in that grace. In such a Church the world finds a cheap covering for its sins; no contrition is required, still less any real desire to be delivered

from sin. Cheap grace therefore amounts to a denial of the living Word of God, in fact, a denial of the Incarnation of the Word of God. (35)

These prophetic words provide an apt starting point for a study of the parables about God's love and forgiveness in Luke 15:1-32. For they help us toward an understanding of what the question — or, at least, one of the questions — is to which these parables might be an answer.

Admittedly, these words of Bonhoeffer come from the mid-twentieth century, not the first century, and they talk about the church and the incarnation, not about the Pharisees, the scribes, or Jesus of Nazareth. But that is the point! For we read the parables of the Gospels in the light of our resurrection faith as words of Christian Scripture within the ongoing life and witness of the church in the world. It is, in fact, a fallacy rooted in Enlightenment rationalism and the hermeneutics of Romanticism to think that we can start with the parables "then" and, as a final afterthought, say something Christian about their meaning "today." This is to abdicate our responsibility as interpreters who stand in a long line of parable interpretation, a line that goes back into Scripture itself (cf. 2 Sam 12:1-15). It is also to misconstrue our relationship to the communities of faith whose vocation is the ongoing performance of the parables — and, of course, of Scripture as a whole — for the glory of God and the life of the world (cf. Lash, *Theology*, 37-46).

Our reading of the parables should not be to try to strip away their "inessentials" in order to get to their "real message" — whether of Jesus, or the early church, or the evangelist. This strategy of historical criticism, though sometimes of value as a corrective to uncontrolled over-interpretation, is always in danger of being rationalistic and reductionist. In the end, the parables themselves become dispensable. Once we have worked out what they meant, we need not concern ourselves further with them, except perhaps to find appropriate platitudes with which to replace them. Rather, reading the parables as they were meant to be read is to be "once more astonished" by the gospel — to so *engage with the text* in all of its detail, contingency, and after-life in the tradition, that, like Jacob after his struggle with God at the Jabbok, we come away marked for life.

Returning to the point made by Bonhoeffer, I want, therefore, to suggest that one way — though not the only way — of engaging fruitfully with the Lukan parables about God's love and forgiveness is to consider them as explorations of divine grace and, in particular, as providing answers to the problem of "cheap grace."

2. The Parables of Luke 15 in Context

The three parables of Luke 15 are among the most famous parables of Jesus and have been transmitted by Luke with consummate literary skill. As John Drury puts it, "The parables of Luke 15 and 16:1-8 are Luke's *pièce de résistance*" (*Parables*, 139). Following an introduction, which sets out a scene of controversy with the Pharisees and scribes over his table-fellowship with "sinners" (vv 1-3), Jesus is depicted as responding with a powerful verbal defense in the form of a sequence of four parables, the first three of which are the Lost Sheep (vv 4-7), the Lost Coin (vv 8-10), and the Lost (or, as commonly known, the Prodigal) Son (vv 11-32).

There are a number of indications that these three parables of Luke 15:1-32 (perhaps also the Parable of the Unjust Steward of Luke 16:1-8, though that parable will be treated later by Stephen Wright in chapter 10) were intended by Luke to be read as a literary unit, which, in turn, is part of the evangelist's larger narrative regarding Jesus' journey to Jerusalem in 9:51–19:44. At least three features in the parables highlight their essential unity. First, and most obviously, they share a common theme: God's delight in a sinner's repentance (vv 7, 10, 24, 32). Second, there are certain words and phrases that recur and serve to bind the parables together — as, for example, "repentance" (vv 7, 10, 18), "joy"/"rejoice"/"make merry" (vv 5-7, 9-10, 23-24, 32), and "because the lost is found" (vv 6, 9, 24, 32). Third, the first two, shorter parables share a common structure: a man/a woman; one lost sheep/one lost coin; the sheep/coin is sought and found; a summoning of friends and neighbors for celebration; and a concluding lesson (cf. Bailey, *Poet and Peasant*, 144-58).

The structure of the longer Parable of the Prodigal Son, even if more elaborate and complex, is also recognizably similar, with features of loss, recovery, restoration, and celebration present. Furthermore, the beginning and end of the material in Luke 15 constitute an *inclusio*, with the elder son's complaint about his father's hospitality to the prodigal (vv 28-30) echoing the opening complaint of the Pharisees and scribes about the hospitality of Jesus to "sinners" (vv 1-2). In passing, it could be noted, as well, that there are significant parallels linking the Parable of the Prodigal Son in 15:11-32 and the Parable of the Unjust Steward in 16:1-8 (cf. Donahue, *Gospel in Parable*, 162-69), but that is another story.

Now let us consider this tightly knit sequence of parables in more detail. The redactional introduction of verses 1-3 is important. A rather ironic contrast is drawn between two paired groups: on the one hand, there are present "all the tax collectors and sinners," who draw near to hear Jesus teaching God's word; whereas, on the other, the Pharisees and scribes are also there, though not to hear but to "murmur" (*diagogguzō*, which is reminiscent of the Israelites in the wilderness as depicted in Exodus 15–17). In relation to the immediately preceding blocks of tradition, the former are like "the poor" invited to the banquet (14:15-24); while the latter are reminiscent of those who made their excuses (14:18) — or, even more, like the salt that had lost its taste (14:34-35).

Their complaint, "This man receives sinners and eats with them" (15:2), is a repetition of the complaint made by the Pharisees and scribes against Jesus at the outset of his ministry, when he called the tax collector Levi to follow (cf. 5:27-32, noting the verb *gogguzō*, "grumble" or "murmur," in v 30). And it is a complaint that is voiced against Jesus elsewhere in Luke's Gospel (cf. 7:39; 19:7). As Charles Talbert points out (*Reading Luke*, 148), the complaint reflects at a general level the scriptural, prudential warning against association with evildoers (cf. Prov 1:15; 2:11-15; 4:14-19). It reflects also the symbolic weight accorded table fellowship in Early Judaism and in antiquity generally, where the sharing of a common table was a basic mechanism for initiating or maintaining sociability and the bonds of a common identity, as well as for marking one group or society off from another (cf. Dan 1:3-17; *Judith* 12; 2 Macc 7; *Joseph and Asenath* 7; see Moxnes, "Meals and the New Community," for a discussion of table fellowship and identity in antiquity).

For the Pharisees, in particular, setting boundaries around the household and the common table were primary ways of setting themselves apart as God's chosen ones, who were called to be holy in a world that was constantly threatened by defiling impurity (cf. Neusner, "Two Pictures of the Pharisees"). One source of impurity was contact with people labeled "sinners" — a label that extends *inter alios* to "tax collectors" (15:1-2; cf. 5:30; 18:9-14). The identity of the people so labeled "sinners" is a matter of ongoing debate. As a label it was a term for *outsiders*, and James Dunn has shown that such a usage had wide currency in the factional context of first-century Judaism (see his *Jesus, Paul and the Law*, 61-88). Used by the Pharisees, it likely connoted people who for one reason or another — whether occupation, racial identity, physical incapacity, or moral weakness — failed to conform to the holiness code derived from the temple cult.

The way of Jesus, however, was different. For him, holiness is a matter not so much of separation from "sinners" as of separation from anything that inhibits full commitment to *the God who is drawing near* (cf. 14:25-33). It is not a status to be possessed and hedged around for self-protection, but a relationship to be celebrated and shared. Jesus' proclamation was: "I have not come to call the righteous, but sinners to repentance" (5:32).

Jesus' coming in the power of the Spirit inaugurates the time of eschatological salvation when God's covenant mercy is offered to all — particularly to those on the margins of Israel and beyond. This offer is made tangible in prophetic acts of open hospitality and unrestricted table fellowship that represent a transformation of the conventional patterns of sociability. Not surprisingly, such a challenge to the piety of the day generates resistance. So Jesus offers a defense in the form of parables.

But, we might ask, why did Jesus give his defense in the form of parables? One answer is that this was one of Jesus' usual ways of defending his practice, as the accounts in Luke 13:10-21 and 14:1-11 suggest. But if we press the question further, the possibility arises that Jesus spoke in parables because parables are a form of discourse that have the potential both to image God differently and to open up a wider range of imaginative and volitional responses among listeners and readers than the discourse of law and purity. In other words, Jesus did not respond to his Pharisaic critics *on their own terms* — perhaps because holiness defined in terms of law and cult forecloses prematurely or restricts too narrowly the boundaries of God's mercy and love as embodied in Jesus himself.

Related is the idea that extended parables such as we find in Luke 15 have the potential, by virtue of their very mundane, human, realistic, and subtle character, for revealing "God in the ordinary." Such parables are an invitation to see God and the world differently — that is, to be converted by a divine grace mediated through everyday stories, whose content, on the surface, is quite mundane, but which, for that very reason, paradoxically, brings God near. On this view, and against the historical-critical trend in parable interpretation inaugurated by Jülicher, the details of the parables are not to be discounted in the quest for the supposed "simple truth" that a parable conveys. Rather, as Donald MacKinnon has helped us to see (cf. R. White,

"MacKinnon and the Parables," in *Christ, Ethics and Tragedy*, ed. K. Surin [Cambridge: Cambridge University Press, 1989], 49-70), they are the imaginative stuff of an exploration that has the potential for opening the eyes and redirecting the wills of both hearers and readers alike.

3. The Parable of the Lost Sheep (Luke 15:1-7)

The first parable in the series is the Parable of the Lost Sheep. That this parable comes first is probably not coincidental. For its message is hardly an incidental one, but concerns matters of real importance.

The parable contains strong echoes of scriptural texts like Ezekiel 34, where God's prophet speaks vehemently against the leaders of Israel on account of their failure as "shepherds" of the people to seek out the lost and scattered sheep and feed them (cf. Green, *Luke*, 574-75). According to the prophet, so great is the failure of Israel's leaders that God himself will take their place in seeking for his lost sheep:

> For thus says the Lord God: Behold, I, I myself will search for my sheep, and will seek them out. As a shepherd seeks out his flock when some of his sheep have been scattered abroad, so will I seek out my sheep; and I will rescue them from all places where they have been scattered. . . . I will seek out the lost, and I will bring back the strayed." (Ezek 34:11-16a)

The resonances of this passage in Ezekiel 34 with the parable of Luke 15:1-7 are strong. Against such a backdrop, the Pharisees and legal experts who murmur against Jesus find that they themselves are under God's indictment for their failure as leaders to seek the lost in Israel. Jesus, on the other hand, acts in accordance with Scripture and the will of God. He is the one who seeks out the lost and feeds them.

Also worth noting is the fact that of these three Lukan parables, the Parable of the Lost Sheep is the only one with a synoptic parallel, appearing also in Matt 18:12-14. A comparison with its Matthean counterpart is instructive for bringing out the distinctive emphases of Luke's version. In Matthew the parable occurs in the context of the fourth of five discourses of Jesus, which — because of its attention to matters of intramural discipline and by analogy with a similar text from Qumran identified as 1QS (with the "S" of the designation signaling *serek* or "rule") — has become known as Matthew's "community rule." Here Jesus' teaching is directed not to outsiders but to insiders, and the parable is part of an extended instruction on how to live together as fellow-members of the kingdom of heaven. More precisely, in Matthew's version the parable speaks to the problem of what to do if, as the result of moral "stumbling blocks" *(ta skandala)* being thrown in the path of a low-status member of the brotherhood (i.e., a "little one"), he or she "goes astray" (cf. 18:6-11). It is an encouragement to seek out the errant brother or sister, even if success is not guaranteed.

The value of the parable for Matthew, therefore, is its pastoral relevance in an ecclesial context. In Luke, however, the thrust of the parable is its pastoral relevance in relation to those *outside* the community of the faithful. To risk an anachronism, the thrust of Luke's version may be said to be not so much ecclesial as evangelical. For where in Matthew the sheep has "gone astray," in Luke it is "lost"; and where in Matthew the rejoicing is over the retrieval of "one of these little ones," in Luke it is rejoicing (in a much more convivial style) over the repentance of a "sinner."

Taking now the parable as it stands in Luke, there are several other observations to be made that deepen our appreciation of it. First, there is the apparent recklessness of the shepherd in leaving the ninety-nine other sheep "in the wilderness" (of all places!) to go in search of just one lost sheep (15:4). There is a lack of a sense of proportion here that is surprising and almost shocking (cf. 1 Sam 17:28). But God's grace is like that. It does not fit into our ordinary patterns of accounting. Each sheep is so valuable that the shepherd risks the well-being of the entire flock in order to find it. The concern for the "lost" is emphatic. And that is a feature that highlights a profound point about divine accounting — that is, that *God counts by ones.*

Then there is the shepherd's perseverance, for he searches "*until* he finds it" (v 4; cf. Matt 18:13: "*if* he finds it"). Such is the value of each sheep! There is also the shepherd's demonstration of his care for the sheep, for, rejoicing, he carries the sheep home on his shoulders (v 5). Then, finally, there is the public testimony that the lost sheep has been found, along with an invitation to share in the shepherd's joy (v 6) — presumably, by sharing his table. The shepherd does not keep his joy to himself. It spills over to others and becomes an occasion for joyful sociability.

All of this, it should be added, comes in the form of one long question, beginning "Which one of you . . . ?" (vv 3-6). The question is addressed to Jesus' interlocutors, the Pharisees and scribes. They are being challenged to rethink their understanding of the divine economy and to respond accordingly. For God's grace cannot be fenced in. It is not limited to "the righteous." On the contrary, in Jesus' open hospitality it is extended first and foremost to "sinners" — that is, *to those who need it most.*

The redactional conclusion to this first parable of Luke 15 makes the parable an analogy of the life of God: "Just so, I tell you, there will be more joy in heaven over one sinner who repents than over ninety-nine righteous persons who need no repentance" (v 7). The emphasis on repentance both here and at the end of the Parable of the Lost Coin (v 10) is demonstrably Lukan (cf. Barton, *Spirituality of the Gospels,* 77-83). But it is also traditional (cf. Mark 1:15). Clearly, the parable is being interpreted by being amplified in a particular direction, for, after all, neither lost sheep nor lost coins "repent"! Nonetheless, the interpretation is appropriate in the context and anticipates what is to become much more central in the climactic third parable of the Lost/Prodigal Son (cf. Drury, *Parables,* 141). If Jesus' meal table solidarity with "sinners" is a tangible expression of God's grace and the joy of the kingdom of God, then repentance is the obvious and appropriate response — and that goes for the "righteous" as well as for the "sinner."

What Jesus offers in parabolic mode, therefore, is not cheap grace — the concern (we may surmise) of the Pharisees and scribes — but an altogether different *economy of grace.* The mood of this new economy is joy and welcome, not separation and self-justification (cf. 16:15; 18:9). Furthermore, the repentance that it calls for is not cheap. It is not something narrowly bound to the preservation of the elect and the holy. Rather, it is something much *more* costly — not separation from "sinners," but being "found" by Jesus, God's Son and Servant, becoming part of his company, and (as 14:33 makes clear) leaving everything behind for his sake.

The Pharisees of Luke 15 failed to understand the teaching, which was also given in parables to the Pharisees of Luke 14 (see esp. vv 1-14, 25-35). Like the guests of 14:15-24, who were invited to the banquet and made their seemingly legitimate excuses, the Pharisees in 15:2 are offering one more such excuse. But what Jesus offers is not cheap grace but "grace abounding" and grace demanding.

206

4. The Parable of the Lost Coin (Luke 15:8-10)

The Parable of the Lost Coin can be dealt with more briefly. In structure, theme, and interrogative mode, it fits closely with the Parable of the Lost Sheep, as indicated above. In fact, there is a sense in which this whole sequence of three parables is really just one — as suggested by the evangelist's introduction statement: "He told them *this* parable *(tēn parabolēn tautēn*, not *tas parabolas tautas)*" (15:3; cf. 5:36). The repetition has an intensifying effect. Like repetition in good liturgy, these three parables seem designed to deepen engagement with the fundamental matters of faith and life.

But repetition does not mean sameness, for there are also subtle differences which are significant. Most noticeable is the fact that the first is a story about a man out in the open spaces, who pursues his occupation as a shepherd, which is paired with a story about a woman pursuing her work in the more secluded space of the home. Such a balancing of men and women is characteristic of Luke in his writings, as Mary Rose D'Angelo has pointed out in her study of "Women in Luke-Acts" (*Journal of Biblical Literature*, 109 [1990] 441-61). In this particular case, Luke appears to have added the parable about a woman from his special source (so-called "L" material) to the parable about the shepherd from the tradition he shares with Matthew (i.e., "Q"). And taking Luke's Gospel as a whole, such a pairing is reminiscent of the balancing or pairing of the Parable of the Good Samaritan and the story of Martha and Mary earlier on (in 10:25-37 and 38-42), or of the Parable of the Widow and the Judge and the Parable of the Pharisee and the Tax Collector subsequently (in 18:1-8 and 9-14) — as well, of course, the pairing of the prophecies of Simeon and Anna at the beginning of Luke's Gospel (in 2:25-35 and 36-38) and of the resurrection appearances to women and men at the end (in 24:1-11 and 12-43).

This is not just a compositional technique. It expresses Luke's conviction that the "good news to the poor" that Jesus announces (4:18-19) and that his practice embodies is good news for people of all kinds — for "sinners" as well as those who are "righteous," women as well as men, workers in the household and workers in the city or country, Gentiles as well as Jews, and so on. To put it otherwise, God's grace is not a "limited good" (cf. Malina, *New Testament World*, 71-93). It is available freely to all who will receive it.

In the Parable of the Lost Coin, instead of one lost sheep out of one hundred, it is one lost coin out of ten. This increases further in the Parable of the Prodigal Son, where it is a case of one lost son out of two — with, of course, an even greater difference being that it is not an animal or a coin that is lost, but a human being, who is a much loved son. So the dramatic intensity increases from one parable to the next. And in this second parable, the tension is related also to the value of the coin lost, which was probably the equivalent of a full day's wages — the loss of which would be a cause of great hardship for a household in a village economy where cash is a rare commodity (cf. Bailey, *Poet and Peasant*, 157).

The woman's actions parallel the shepherd's, but are appropriate to the domestic setting. There is a threefold movement conveying urgent action: she lights a lamp, sweeps the house, and searches "diligently" *(epimelōs)*. Furthermore, like the shepherd, she searches "*until* she finds" her coin (v 8; cf. v 4). The coin is valuable, worth searching for — so much so, that the joy of finding it has to be shared with her female friends *(tas philas)* and neighbors. As with the shepherd, her only reported speech is the all-important invitation, "Rejoice with me, for I have found [that] . . . which was lost" (v 9b; cf. v 6b). Then follows the authoritative commentary of the Lukan Jesus, which is addressed to the Pharisees and scribes (and also to the reader), that the joy of the angels in heaven over the repentance of a "sinner" is like the joy of the woman and her friends over the recovered coin (v 10). And here, subversively once more, is "God in the ordinary." For the parable is an invitation to Jesus' interlocutors to be (to use an expression coined by C. S. Lewis) "surprised by joy."

Significantly, the last word in the Greek text of both of these first two parables of Luke 15 is the verb *metanoeō*, "repent," or the noun *metanoia*, "repentance" (vv 7 [twice] and 10). We are, therefore, being prepared for the parable to follow (see esp. vv 17-20a and 21). But what is important here to stress is that this redactional theme does not distort the parables by narrowing their focus in a "moralizing" direction, as if Jesus himself did not seek by the formulation of parables such as these to evoke repentance. Against E. P. Sanders (cf. his *Jesus and Judaism* [London: SCM, 1985], 174-211), it needs to be insisted that the summons to repentance was not a minor feature in the teaching and mission of Jesus, nor was it confined only to a few individuals (cf. Chilton, "Jesus and the Repentance of E. P. Sanders").

Jesus was not some kind of antinomian libertarian just "hanging out" with the people on the boundaries of Judaism. That would have meant leaving everything as it was, for antinomianism is often intensely conservative. But that is not what Jesus was about (cf. Luke 4:16-30). Rather, Jesus was seeking to shift the focus from concerns about boundaries — that is, regarding "who's in" and "who's out" — to concerns about *ethos and action* — that is, regarding what kind of people Israel and the nations needed to be (and to become) in the light of God's coming in mercy and judgment. If the accent of these first two parables falls most heavily on an active search for the lost, that does not mean that response (i.e., "repentance") is not the obvious corollary. It means only that what the Pharisees needed most to hear was a challenge to be the kind of leaders whose priority was to engage in such a search.

5. The Parable of the Prodigal Son (Luke 15:11-32)

The third and longest in the sequence of parables in Luke 15 is the famous Parable of the Prodigal Son. Now we move from the realm of animals and property as ways of talking about right priorities in the life of the kingdom to talk about people.

The Parable of the Prodigal Son has two parallel parts: the first speaks about the lost younger son (vv 11-24); the second, about the elder brother, who was, it seems, equally lost (vv 25-32). In each part the focus is on the son first and then on the father. It is the father in both parts of the story, however, who has the last, authoritative word (vv 23-24, 31-32). It is noteworthy that this word in both cases is directed to the issue of how to respond appropriately to the recovery of the prodigal. That is what ties the parable so closely to the concerns of the Pharisees and scribes at the outset of the chapter, when they muttered about Jesus' table companions (vv 1-2). So we are still in the realm of Luke's exploration of divine grace as it has been revealed in Jesus.

That helps to explain why this parable has such strong echoes of the stories of the Old Testament. For biblical stories about younger brothers were a classic source of reflection on the unpredictability of God's ways — in particular, of *God's refusal to limit the measure of his grace* to human ways of seeing and doing things. The story of Joseph, who goes down to a far country where there is a famine and is later reunited with his father, is a case in point (cf. Genesis 37, 39–50). Speaking of such stories, John Drury puts it well:

209

There is a sneaking distrust of older brothers and fondness for the younger, even when less meritorious. It gave the excitement of reversal to many tales — and more scope to God. Of Cain and Abel, God preferred the younger. Younger Jacob/Israel supplanted senior Esau. There is an echo of that classic tale of sibling rivalry in the *prodigal son*. The elder son was "in the field" when he heard of his younger brother's return . . .
(*Parables in the Gospels*, 145)

To say that such tales give "more scope to God" is exactly right. The Parable of the Prodigal fits the bill with stunning effect.

After the briefest of introductions to the three protagonists, a man and his two sons, the story focuses on the younger of the two. He is cast in a negative light from the start, and his actions precipitate a tight downward spiral in his fortunes. First, he acts presumptuously and covetously (cf. the parallel situation and parable of 12:13-21) in initiating a division of the family inheritance — not least while his father was still alive (cf. Sirach 33:20-24), but also without prior consultation with his older brother (v 12). Second, having converted his share of the inheritance into transportable capital, he turns his back on his family, departs into "a far country" (presumably Gentile territory) and squanders his resources, living beyond the pale of the law (v 13). Next, when famine strikes — which presents us with a kind of natural justice — he attaches himself to "a citizen of that country" (presumably a Gentile) and submits to the shame (both for himself and for his family) of becoming a swineherd, something abhorrent to Jewish sensibilities (cf. 8:32-33; see also Lev 11:17; 14:8; 1 Macc 1:47; 2 Macc 6:18; 7:1). His lonely, pitiable plight is summed up in the clause at the end of verse 16: "and no one gave to him" (*oudeis edidou autō*). Having been given everything by his father at the beginning, he is now alone and left with nothing. He is as good as dead, having experienced a moral and social death (vv 24, 32) that would function as a prelude, in due course, to his physical death as well.

But now there is a turning point: the young man "came to himself" (v 17a). In a characteristically Lukan soliloquy marking a change in fortune (cf. 16:3-4; 18:4-5), he articulates for the first time the peril of his situation and a strategy for his rescue. He is, of course, at last being prudent, having realized the catastrophe he has brought on himself and his kinsfolk. But that prudence need not be interpreted as mere self-serving cunning (*contra* Bailey, *Poet and Peasant*, 173-80).

The words that the young man uses, "Father, I have sinned against heaven and before you; I am no longer worthy to be called your son" (v 18, and repeated at v 21), are grave words of humble repentance that invoke the presence of God (cf. vv 7, 10) as well as a response from his father. Also to be noted is that the repeated use of the participle *anastas*, "rising," in verses 18 and 20 is suggestive of coming back to life — that is, of resurrection. In the overall context of these three parables, where the theme of repentance is so strong, Luke can hardly have meant the son's words to be taken otherwise. It is unnecessary, therefore, to polarize "repentance" and "prudence." On the contrary, for Luke (and for Jesus) salvation is about the restoration of people's *full humanity* — both body and soul; both individual and corporate (cf. Green, "Good News to Whom?").

Attention now turns to the extraordinary actions of the father. That he saw his son "while he was yet at a distance" implies that, like the shepherd of the first parable, his looking out for his lost son has been ongoing. Seeing his son provokes compassion (v 20: *esplagchnisthē*, "he was filled with compassion") — a response to need that reminds us of the response of Jesus to the plight of the widow of Nain (7:13) and the response of the Samaritan to the "half-dead" traveler (10:33). What these various episodes have in common is the fundamental moral-theological point that it is *compassion for the lost* that brings about life out of death and that makes restoration — even transformation — possible in people's lives.

The father's compassion leads to action. At the risk of his honor, and in a rhetorically powerful threefold movement, he runs to meet his son, embraces him, and kisses him (v 20). The son speaks his words of confession. But he is prevented from completing the lines he has rehearsed, for the father will not hear of him being accepted back as a hired servant (v 21; cf. vv 18-19). Instead, in actions that speak of forgiveness and full reconciliation, he orders for his son the "best" robe to clothe him, a ring for his finger, sandals for his feet, and a magnificent feast to celebrate his return and mark his reincorporation into the family and society (v 22). As in the two previous parables, the return of that which was lost is marked by joyful feasting, with that feasting having strong eschatological overtones (cf. 19:9; 22:16, 18) and serving as the climax of the episode. In this case, however, the joy is even more emphatic. For as befits the recovery of a *son*, there is a fatted calf, an invitation to an unspecified number to "eat and make merry," and an elaborate justification for this astonishing munificence — all concluded by the narrator's report that "they began to make merry" (vv

23-24). As a parable of divine grace and forgiveness, what Luke gives us here is unsurpassed.

But the parable does not stop there, as we might have expected. There is a second, contrasting part, this time involving the father and the *elder* son. The narrative characterization is deft and subversive. We expect the older son to compare well with his younger brother, but instead he is in some ways a mirror image, as selfish and preoccupied with his own interests as his sibling. First, we may surmise that he has not been with his father on the lookout for the prodigal, for he was "in the field" (v 25). Second, the sound of music and dancing arouses in him suspicion, not excitement. Third, he keeps his distance and makes inquiry via a servant about what is going on. Next, at the news of his brother's safe return, and in contrast with his father's compassion and hospitality, he gets angry. In fact, he refuses (shamefully, in a Mediterranean context) to go in to share in the festivities at the common table (v 28).

So the father comes out and entreats him. Like the shepherd in the Parable of the Lost Sheep, the father is the one who is *always going out* to bring in the lost. But the elder son, in the one piece of direct speech attributed to him, responds only with words of bitter complaint and self-justification: "Listen! For all these years I have been working like a slave for you, and I have never disobeyed your command. Yet you have never given me even a young goat so that I might celebrate with my friends. But when this son of yours came back, who has devoured your property with prostitutes, you killed the fatted calf for him" (vv 29-30; cf. 16:15). What the words reveal is a son so insecure in himself, and therefore rigid in his relations with his father and his brother, that he can only rage against the apparent unfairness of his father's *largesse*. What he might have seen as a natural expression of joy and reconciliation he interprets, instead, as threatening the usurpation of his position in the household. In so doing, he reflects the insecurities, not of a son, but of a slave: "For all these years I have been working like a slave for you, and I have never disobeyed your command" (v 29a). Ironically, it is as if by not disobeying his father's commands he has become as much a slave as his brother became by a life of lawlessness.

Thus, at the moment the younger brother is being embraced back into the family, the older brother is separating himself from it. He refrains from addressing his father as "father" (in contrast to his brother's attitude and address in vv 17, 18, 21), refers to his brother as "this son *of yours*," and, by ungraciously characterizing him as the one "who has devoured your property with prostitutes" (v 30, though not explicit in v 13b), shows no sign of reconciliation. All he can think of is his own sense of the unfairness done to him. The disproportion between "even a young goat," which was never provided for him and his friends, and the "fatted calf" that his father prepared for his brother, becomes for him not a measure of his father's love and happiness, but a sign of paternal unpredictability smacking of favoritism.

Yet even in such a situation, the father's love persists. He does not repay evil for evil (cf. 6:27-36). The elder brother is still his son and he addresses him as such, trying also to reassure him that his position in the family is assured: "Son, you are always with me, and all that is mine is yours" (v 31; cf. v 12b). At the same time, however, he remains firm. There is a larger economy within which the economy of inheritance and primogeniture, as well as matters of personal honor, must be set if it is to be of true worth. Thus the father says: "It was *necessary* [*edei*, "fitting" in NRSV is too weak] to make merry and be glad, for this your brother was dead and is alive; he was lost and is found" (v 32).

In Lukan perspective, it is the *economy of divine love* that is reflected in the father's joy at the prodigal's return. And that economy of love is highlighted in the use of the imperfect verb *edei* ("it was necessary"), which is a common expression in Luke (cf. 2:49; 4:43; 9:22; 13:16, 33; 17:25; etc.). For just as rejoicing over the recovery of a sheep and a coin is made a window into the joy in heaven over a sinner who repents (vv 7, 10), so the rejoicing and banqueting of a father over the repentance and return of his son is a window into the divine love and forgiveness that was being made manifest at Jesus' table fellowship with tax collectors and "sinners."

That this third parable (unlike the first two) remains open-ended, at least with respect to the response of the elder son, is significant. This allows the parable to speak directly to its context (cf. vv 1-2) and to pose a question to those who themselves questioned Jesus. Joel Green puts it well:

> Scribes and Pharisees are invited to find themselves represented in the parable as the elder son — responsible and obedient, it would seem, but failing in their solidarity with the redemptive purpose of God. Will they identify with God's will and, having done so, join repentant sinners at the table? Putting aside their own concerns with status and recognition (cf. 14:7-14), will they accept as members of the family of God those whom God accepts? Or, refusing to embrace God's gracious calculus,

213

which works to include those who (re)turn to him, will they exclude themselves from the family of God? The parable is open-ended and so is the invitation. (*Luke*, 586)

6. Conclusion

There is no good reason to doubt that Luke is a reliable guide to the *Sitz im Leben Jesu* to which the parables of chapter 15 of his Gospel were a response. Attacked by Pharisees and scribes for eating with "sinners," Jesus responds not in terms of Torah and halakic statements but in parables. The parables he tells are a way of changing the terms of reference of an influential pattern of thought. They are Jesus' characteristic way of inviting his critics to recognize that in his ministry a new order of things is breaking in. At the heart of this new order or economy is a truly radical insistence on divine compassion — a compassion that overflows in the forgiveness of sinners, hospitality to the poor, the healing of the sick, and the proclamation of the "good news" of the kingdom of God.

This new economy is eschatological — that is, it has to do with the reordering of one's priorities and practices in a way appropriate to the coming of God in mercy and justice. It brings heaven to earth, at least in anticipatory ways. It reflects the divine communion that is mediated by Jesus and present among those who commit themselves to him. This is a time not for a separation of *withdrawal* in the interests of purity (since the temple is no longer at the heart of things), but of separation for a *mission with Jesus* for the sake of the "lost." It is a time not for dividing into parties antagonistic to one another, but for uniting in a new kind of solidarity that is grounded on the grace of God and sustained by ongoing practices of repentance, forgiveness, and reconciliation.

Table fellowship with tax collectors and "sinners" is one such practice. This new economy is not a matter of "cheap grace," which is how we have characterized the criticism voiced by the Pharisees. What the parables show, and what Jesus' life shows as well, is that separation for mission is costly and demanding because it requires risk and sacrifice. For it requires going to the lost in love, offering forgiveness to those who are penitent (cf. 7:36-50; 18:9-14; 23:39-43), and welcoming them into a people being renewed by God's Son in the power of the Spirit.

As we listen again to these parables we find that they speak powerfully still. Their challenge is not in spite of their historical and literary particularities, but because of them — that is, because also of the communities of faith that have nurtured and been nurtured by their ongoing interpretative performance. Accepting the parables as constituent parts of Christian Scripture, it is vital that we not allow questions of *method* in parable interpretation to distract us from questions of *content and truth.* As Dietrich Bonhoeffer has helped us to see, making method central encourages us to read the Bible *for* ourselves, in terms of our own interests, whereas making content central allows us to hear the Spirit speaking through Scripture *over against* ourselves (cf. also Fowl and Jones, *Reading in Communion,* 135-64). That is not to say that questions of content and truth can be separated from questions of method in any straightforward way. But it is an important reminder of our fundamental obligation to hear the parables on their own (scriptural) terms: as testimonies to the transforming reality of the kingdom of God manifest in Jesus and his followers, *and* as testimonies to the same transforming reality at work in the world today through the Spirit.

It is, therefore, quite legitimate — indeed essential — to ask: *Do we believe* it to be true that "there is joy in heaven before the angels of God over one sinner who repents"? Do we believe it to be true that God is like that shepherd, that woman, and that forgiving father? Do we believe it to be true that Jesus embodied such an understanding of God in his practice of eating with "sinners," and that to be a follower of Jesus means to engage in practices that are in creative fidelity with his teaching and example? No amount of agreement *in principle* will show in any convincing way that what is affirmed is true. In Bonhoeffer's terms, what is necessary is the step beyond "agreement in principle." What is necessary is the step (as he provocatively put it) from being a theologian to being a Christian. In other words, what will show it to be true is whether or not the testimony of the parables to the overflowing grace and forgiveness of God, which leads to repentance, becomes embodied in our own lives and practices.

Selected Bibliography

Bailey, Kenneth E. *Poet and Peasant: A Literary Cultural Approach to the Parables in Luke.* Grand Rapids: Eerdmans, 1976.

————. *Through Peasant Eyes: More Lucan Parables, Their Culture and Style.* Grand Rapids: Eerdmans, 1980.

Barton, Stephen C. *The Spirituality of the Gospels*. London: SPCK, 1992.

Chilton, Bruce D. "Jesus and the Repentance of E. P. Sanders," *Tyndale Bulletin* 39 (1988) 1-18.

Donahue, John R. *The Gospel in Parable*. Philadelphia: Fortress, 1988.

Drury, John. *The Parables in the Gospels: History and Allegory*. London: SPCK; New York: Crossroad, 1985.

Dunn, James D. G. *Jesus, Paul and the Law: Studies in Mark and Galatians*. Louisville: Westminster/John Knox, 1990.

Fowl, Stephen E. and Jones, L. Gregory. *Reading in Communion. Scripture and Ethics in Christian Life*. London: SPCK, 1991.

Green, Joel B. "Good News to Whom? Jesus and the 'Poor' in the Gospel of Luke," in *Jesus of Nazareth: Lord and Christ*, ed. J. B. Green and M. Turner. Grand Rapids: Eerdmans, 1994, 59-74.

————. *The Gospel of Luke*. Grand Rapids: Eerdmans, 1997.

Jones, L. Gregory. *Embodying Forgiveness: A Theological Analysis*. Grand Rapids: Eerdmans, 1995.

Lash, Nicholas. *Theology on the Way to Emmaus*. London: SCM, 1986.

Malina, Bruce J. *The New Testament World*. London: SCM, 1983.

Moxnes, Halvor. "Meals and the New Community in Luke," *Svensk Exegetisk Årsbok* 51 (1986) 158-67.

Neusner, Jacob. "Two Pictures of the Pharisees: Philosophical Circle or Eating Club," *Anglican Theological Review* 64 (1982) 525-38.

Talbert, Charles H. *Reading Luke: A Literary and Theological Commentary on the Third Gospel*. New York: Crossroad, 1982.

CHAPTER 10

Parables on Poverty and Riches
(Luke 12:13-21; 16:1-13; 16:19-31)

STEPHEN I. WRIGHT

JESUS' PARABLES of the Rich Fool (Luke 12:13-21), the Shrewd Manager (Luke 16:1-13), and the Rich Man and Lazarus (Luke 16:19-31) focus on issues having to do with poverty and riches. They warn against the allure of wealth. They point the poor to a way of liberation by forsaking the illusion of ownership, by making friends through the just remission of debts, and by trusting God for justice. At the same time, however, they summon the rich to repentance. They hold in tension a prophetic and a practical vision. Their message is rooted in the law, prophecy, and wisdom of Israel's Scriptures. But it is also couched in a fresh and subversive style.

1. Social and Literary Questions

Each of these three parables begins with the phrase "a rich man," which invites modern interpreters to locate these words in their first-century social world. Furthermore, these words bring immediately into play the question of how character emerges in a story. Thus social and literary questions are intertwined in these parables. For the way a storyteller gives character to a figure in a story — particularly in short parables drawn with such terse brush-strokes as these — and the way an audience understands that teller's

217

characterization depend heavily on a general perception of the figure's role in society.

Along with other ancient agrarian societies, the Near East of the first century was marked by stark disparity between a small, wealthy ruling class and a large number of peasants who barely eked out a living from their tiny plots of land. The rich maintained and enhanced their status and wealth by exacting tribute from the poor. A layer of bureaucracy, of course, developed in tandem with the expansion of an exploitive, oppressive economy. For agents were needed to collect tribute; merchants were required to sell produce and import goods. But though some of these intermediaries may have accumulated a rather comfortable nest egg for themselves, it is important that we clear our minds of any anachronistic notions of a prosperous middle class in antiquity, such as might have been influenced by something comparable to our Protestant work ethic. Life in first-century Palestine was lived out in a basically two-tier society. And in such a society the retainers of the rich did not rise much above the insecurity of the poor (cf. Herzog, *Parables as Subversive Speech*, 53-66).

Do these three parables of Jesus represent characters and occurrences that were, within such a social setting, either typical or extraordinary — or, perhaps, are what they represent somewhere in between? Here literary as well as historical judgment comes into play. For while the stories of these parables seem realistically grounded in the world of first-century Palestine, they are, nonetheless, presented in ways that are striking in their developments and strange in their outcomes. Indeed, the story-form itself leads one to expect the unexpected. Thus while the characters are typical, the plots are unusual.

The rhetoric of the stories is also fragile and understated. The parables of the Rich Fool (Luke 12:13-21) and the Rich Man and Lazarus (Luke 16:19-31) present scenes that are hidden from normal human perception: the voice of God in the night (cf. 12:20); the destinies of two men beyond death and a conversation with deceased Abraham (cf. 16:23-31). Here there is no knockdown argument; no appeal to some universally obvious principle. Rather, what reverberates throughout these two parables is a provocative summons to thought and imagination: "What if it were so?"

Likewise, the conclusions of these parables are quite terse and restrained. We do not read of the foolish farmer's response to God's voice, or of his death, or of anything that may have taken place beyond it. We do not know whether the five brothers eventually repented. Even the chasm between the rich man and Lazarus may be "fixed" in a *functional* rather than *eternal* sense (cf. Herzog, *ibid.*, 124), reflecting a rabbinic belief that even the wicked in Hades may be able to repent (cf. Oesterley, *Gospel Parables*, 208). The true "end of the story" in both cases remains untold.

The fact that two of these tales unfold in private, invisible ways lends weight to the belief that the third, the Parable of the Shrewd Manager (Luke 16:1-13), was also intended to represent an imaginary rather than an actual incident, though the latter possibility cannot be ruled out. That parable, too, ends abruptly, with the master praising the steward (v 8). But much is left for the hearer or reader — particularly someone familiar with the social scene — to ponder.

Since Adolf Jülicher's treatment of Jesus' parables at the end of the nineteenth century, the Parable of the Rich Fool and the Parable of the Rich Man and Lazarus have usually been classed with the Parable of the Good Samaritan and the Parable of the Pharisee and the Tax Collector as "example stories" — being, thereby, distinguished from "parables proper," which category would include the Parable of the Shrewd Manager. Yet all three of the stories with which we are here concerned seem to have been given for exemplary purposes, and our treatment of them in what follows will attempt to demonstrate the validity of such an understanding.

In particular, interpreters have often been embarrassed by the idea of an exemplary purpose for the Parable of the Shrewd Manager. But this coyness is due, we believe, to a failure to appreciate the social and literary questions of characterization in the parable. For every reading of a parable, whatever its nature, requires a "reading between the lines," which is entirely proper. And tales of "the rich" and "the poor" would have evoked for their first hearers a sense of the whole web of ancient society, which modern readers must try to imagine. So our task as present-day interpreters is to re-visualize the features of ancient society that are contained within both this parable and the other two of our present concern — and having positioned ourselves back into the society depicted in these parables, to make sense of them as examples.

2. The Parables in Their Immediate Context

All three of these Lukan parables are set in contexts that imply that they were addressed to both private and public audiences. These audiences were composed of the rich and the poor, the crowds, the disciples, and the Pharisees.

The Parable of the Rich Fool in 12:13-21 is set broadly in a discourse directed to a crowd of thousands of people who had gathered about Jesus (cf. 12:1), but it is explicitly told in response to one person who asks for a specific decision from him (v 13). It is unlikely that this "person in the crowd" was one of "the rich" (see the discussion of the parable below), yet the story has to do with a rich man. The opening words of the discourse stand as a rubric over everything that is said: "Beware of the leaven of the Pharisees" (12:1) — with much of what is said in the discourse being directed not just to the crowd but also to Jesus' disciples, who are identified as his "friends" (12:4) and his "little flock" (12:32).

The Parable of the Shrewd Manager in 16:1-13 is addressed by Jesus explicitly to "his disciples" (v 1). But it follows immediately on the heels of three other parables in 15:3-32 that were directed toward grumbling "Pharisees and scribes" (cf. 15:2) and given in the presence of a number of "customs-officers and sinners" (cf. 15:1). And the parable concerns both a landowner and his retainer.

The Parable of the Rich Man and Lazarus in 16:19-31 continues a response of Jesus to the Pharisees, who had scoffed at his warnings about money (cf. 16:14). But since the Pharisees in this verse are said to "hear" what Jesus had been saying to the disciples (i.e., the contents of 16:1-13), the implication is that these same "disciples" continue to hear what Jesus says to the Pharisees. Nor does the narrative give us any reason to assume that the customs officers and sinners of 15:1 had departed. Furthermore, the parable contains in roughly equal measure both warning to the rich — including those who, like the Pharisees, while perhaps not overly wealthy, are said to have been "lovers of money" (16:14) — and encouragement to the poor.

Luke, therefore, has set these three parables in literary nexuses that highlight their applicability to different groups of people, with these diverse groups evidently serving to represent the whole of society in Jesus' day. Jesus warns the crowds — particularly those he speaks of as his "little flock," his disciples — not to fear their poverty or to imitate those who aspire to be rich. Such a warning of itself, however, does not imply a blanket rejection of the rich or the greedy. For in these parables Jesus appeals to them as well as to the poor.

3. The Parable of the Rich Fool (Luke 12:13-21)

The Parable of the Rich Fool in Luke 12:13-21 appears as part of Jesus' answer to a man calling on him to settle an inheritance dispute between himself and his brother (v 13). The man was probably from a peasant family. Wealthy families would have had their own means to get what they wanted, and probably would not have resorted to seeking advice from a wandering teacher.

The poor in an Israelite agrarian culture had their precious little patrimonies, and inheritance laws were designed so that each member of a large family would receive a share — with, of course, the largest share being reserved for the eldest. But the harsh reality was that sometimes a plot of land became too small to divide any further. In such a situation, one or more members of the family might be driven off the land to a life of insecurity, where one could only seek casual labor or sink to crime or beggary (cf. Herzog, *Parables as Subversive Speech,* 65).

Jesus' refusal to act as "a judge or divider" in the dispute (v 14) is the more striking when this social background is appreciated. In so doing, he not only renounces the role that Moses was accused of having arrogated to himself (cf. Exod 2:14), he also refuses the task given by God to Joshua to be the divider of the land (cf. Joshua 13–22). Jesus proposes no instant solution. Rather, he points out to both parties (cf. "them" in v 15) the heart of the problem — that is, the matter of "greed" or "covetousness."

If Jesus' answer to the man here seems a somewhat harsh response to a potentially desperate situation, we should note that it fits well with his other sayings in the same chapter that warn against anxiety (cf. 12:6-7, 22-31) and that encourage generosity (cf. 12:32-34) — with 12:22 carrying a specific reminder that Jesus was addressing his disciples in all of these statements. The disciples are identified as "the poor" *(hoi ptōchoi)* in Luke 6:20; and since the poor have special reasons to be anxious, these other sayings have the same shocking quality as the warning against covetousness in 12:15. But while Jesus' warning is shocking, it is also realistic and practical. For if both disputants would abjure greed — even if the situation was perilous — the sting would be drawn and a way forward could be discerned.

A reason is added to the warning: "because one's life does not consist in the abundance *(en tǭ perisseuein)* of possessions" (12:15b). "Abundance" suggests the surpluses that sustained the wealth and status of the elite members of society. Though frequently taken as pitting *material* life against *spiritual* life, it is probably better to read this saying as contrasting *luxury* with *necessity*. Thus peasants are not to be deluded by the harshness of their poverty into thinking that "life" means having more than one needs — that is, not to be deceived into thinking that the solution to poverty is to be found in imitating the delight of the elite in their excesses.

The larger context of this parable makes it natural that a story about a rich man should be given in answer to a problem posed by a poor man. Jesus' largely peasant audience had been told to beware of the attitude of the rich, just as they were told to beware of the leaven of the Pharisees (12:1). So now they are told of a rich man who had a bumper harvest, which gave him an ample surplus (12:16). Though technically the land might not have been "his," for legally the peasants were allowed their patrimony, the system of exploitation was such that he had *de facto* ownership of the lands, both his and theirs.

In Jesus' telling of the story his hearers are given a glimpse into the rich man's thinking, which would have been readily recognizable to them in that day. The man's plans were in line with ancient recommendations to farmers to maximize their productive land area. So he decided not to add further barns to his existing ones, but to tear down his old barns and build more spacious and efficient ones on the same site (vv 17-18). Grain could be kept for a number of years. Perhaps he thought that one day he would get a better price for it. But whether or not he was an astute speculator, he foresees that this great surplus could finance a life of comfort, luxury, and ease (v 19). The saying "relax, eat, drink, and be merry" represents the typical outlook of a hedonist (cf. Hedrick, *Parables as Poetic Fictions*, 154-56).

The rich man's thought-process, however, is dramatically interrupted by God (v 20). God calls him "a fool" *(aphrōn)* — that is, one who "has said in his heart: 'there is no God'" (cf. Ps 14:1, where *aphrōn* is also used in the LXX). He is a fool because his own life is about to be "demanded" of him, and all his goods will then pass into other hands. The illusion of ownership he has maintained will be shattered. The things he has regarded as "his" will be "his" no more. Even his "soul" or "life" *(psuchē,* v 19), which he had called "mine" and planned to pamper indefinitely, is the selfsame "soul" or "life" *(psuchē)* that is suddenly revealed as a loan, not a possession, and required from him (v 20).

The comment with which the story is rounded off in verse 21, "So it is with those who store up treasures for themselves but are not rich toward

God," crystallizes its message by pointing to the contrast between "storing up treasures" for oneself, as this man did, and being "rich toward God." The latter phrase is best taken as referring to acts of generosity expressed to others, with sharing one's bounty with the poor being the equivalent of giving to God (cf. Prov 19:17). The man in the story is made a warning example — not so much on account of his sudden death or anything that might lie beyond death, but because of the searing words that tear his dreams to shreds.

We miss the force of the story if we see the rich man as being especially wicked. Commentators sometimes describe the characters of the parables in very lurid colors, and so they become figures that the pious love to hate. But the point here, as in many another tale, is not that this man was a monster, but that he is typical — that is, typical of a class of people and typical of a whole social system. His thought-processes are normal. They encapsulate the whole basis of an exploitative, agrarian society that seeks control over land and wants to use surpluses to finance luxury. They are thought-processes that exclude God and other people — who both, alike, inevitably reassert themselves at the end.

The story is all the more powerful for being so restrained. Jesus does not launch into a tirade about the wickedness of the system. He proposes no manifesto about the redistribution of wealth. The tactic is actually more subversive and more radical than that. For what Jesus does is to prick the bubble of a self-satisfied sense of ownership. In effect, he says to the peasants: "The rich will find out soon enough that they don't control even their own lives. Don't be fooled into aspiring to be like them."

Two things need to be noticed about Jesus' teaching in this parable, particularly as that teaching is expressed in the context of the Israelite culture of that day. First, his words are prophetic words. The thoughtful would see in them a challenge to the whole system. For with God's rebuke of the rich man, everything that he represented in the society of that time was called to account. At the same time, however, his words are very practical words. Jesus was steeped in the Wisdom tradition of the Scriptures, which exalted common-sense instruction as something God-given and portrayed obedience as not only right but also the best and safest course of action. Indeed, as Wisdom teaches, disobedience is folly.

Jesus' refusal to adjudicate in an inheritance dispute entailed neither a dismissal of the rich as irretrievably wicked nor a detachment from the problems of the poor. On the contrary, his words called for a response that was immediately possible for both rich and poor. They must awaken to the illusory nature of ownership. Even the poor will find their security only in God, not in clothing, food, or drink (cf. 12:27-31).

This message was not new. The parable can be read as a transmutation into story form of the poetry of Psalm 49 (see esp. vv 11-14, 16-17) or the teaching of Sirach 11:18-21, with their emphases on the inevitability of death and the folly of trusting in wealth or envying the wealthy. Another interesting precursor is *1 Enoch* 97:8-10, which speaks of the injustice that accompanies great wealth. But Jesus' story brings the message into sharper focus. Something striking happened in Jesus' story to a typical rich man: God spoke to him!

4. The Parable of the Shrewd Manager (Luke 16:1-13)

In Luke's Gospel, Jesus' telling of the Parable of the Shrewd Manager to his disciples in 16:1-13 follows immediately on the heels of the Parable of the Prodigal Son, which he told to his detractors in 15:11-32. Furthermore, there is an interweaving of common themes in these two parables (cf. Bailey, *Poet and Peasant*, 109; Donahue, *Gospel in Parable*, 167). So we may assume from its connection with what goes before in chapter 15 that Luke intended his readers to understand this parable of the Shrewd Manager as part of Jesus' defense concerning the company he keeps (cf. 15:1-2), which he sets out in 15:3–16:13. And having addressed the Pharisees and scribes directly in 15:3-32, Jesus is portrayed in 16:1-13 as turning to his disciples and warning them as to where to look and not to look for examples of right behavior.

In a sometimes desperate search for "spiritual" messages in the parables, the social situation embedded within this seemingly difficult parable has frequently been downplayed. The commentator who has done most to redress this imbalance is William Herzog (cf. his *Parables as Subversive Speech*), and much of what follows is indebted to his treatment.

The story of the parable is as follows: An estate manager is accused of squandering his rich employer's goods (v 1). Linguistically, the balance is slightly in favor of viewing the aorist passive verb *dieblēthē* ("he was accused") as signaling a false or slanderous accusation. Middlemen then, as now, were vulnerable, and especially so given the cutthroat nature of the oppressive system within which they worked. They were unpopular with the peasants because they collected the landlord's tribute, which included a cut for themselves. But they could also arouse the suspicions and resentment of their masters if they began to look too powerful or wealthy. Furthermore, peasants struggling to survive might well make trouble between a manager and a landlord as a ruse to improve things a bit for themselves. No party would have operated in a world of moral ideals. Rather, what is reflected in the story told by Jesus is simply brute oppression, on the one hand, and a battle for survival, on the other.

In such a world there is nothing surprising about the "justice" with which the accused manager is treated: he must hand over his account books and is summarily fired (v 2). The manager's response shows the harshness of the choice with which he is faced — a harshness to which most modern readers of the parable have generally been rather insensitive. For digging and begging were the activities of day laborers who had been driven off the family parcel of land. As a bureaucrat he would not have been able to compete for work with those who had labored all their lives on the land. And his reluctance to beg should not be seen as sinful pride, but, rather, an apprehension of the loss of all human dignity — which could herald only a beggar's fate of impoverishment, disease, and death (cf. 16:20-22). For once out of his job he would all too easily sink "into the class of expendables" (Herzog, *ibid.*, 242). So his lament "What shall I do?" (*ti poiēsō* of v 3) carries with it a clear tone of near despair.

His plan of action is probably to be understood against the background of wealthy estate owners using merchants to sell their goods. The fact that his master's debtors could write, together with the size of their debts, suggests that they were more likely merchants than peasants (cf. Herzog, *ibid.*, 249-50). Such salesmen would receive the surpluses of the big estates and promise the landowners a monetary return on what was sold. The return promised, however, was not only the price of the commodity at the time of its sale but included also a hidden interest rate, which was kept hidden because of the Jewish prohibition of usury. The debt would then be stated simply in terms of a quantity of produce (cf. vv 6-7).

The manager, whose job it was to negotiate these contracts with the merchants on behalf of his wealthy employer, is pictured as secretly changing the contracts with them in such a way as to cancel the hidden interest due his employer. This would give the merchants with whom he dealt more opportunity to profit from the transaction, for they could retain the "interest" portion themselves — or, at least, could have greater scope to take their own cut. This interpretation is supported by the difference in the proportion of debt that is canceled in the case of the two merchants mentioned, where the interest is higher for goods with more risk attached to them. Thus for the debt of oil, which could have been adulterated, fifty percent is canceled (v 6); while for the debt of wheat, it is only twenty percent (v 7; cf. Herzog, *ibid.*, 255).

What was the manager's logic in this? It is probably only a somewhat sentimental idea, as Herzog rightly observes, to think that he hoped to live off the gratitude of the merchants he had thus benefited. Would sharp businessmen, operating on low profit margins, have had much time or inclination to show such generosity — especially when they would soon realize that the manager with whom they had dealt had just been sacked for maladministration? Rather, the clue seems to lie in the fact that this manager, like the manager referred to in 12:44, had been given considerable authority. His remission of the interest owed would, therefore, reflect well on his employer. For the merchants would be put in a relationship of further indebtedness to the landowner, and the landowner would be lauded for his generosity — positions the landowner would not wish to renounce. The result? Either the landowner would reinstate the manager, who had proven himself to be a skilled public-relations man, or, at the very least, he would recommend him to others. And the "homes" into which the manager hoped to be welcomed (v 4) should, therefore, be seen not as places where he might receive endless hospitality in exchange for doing nothing, but as the large households of the rich where he might get a job he could do well.

The manager's plan, it seems, paid off. His master "commends" him for his "shrewdness" (v 8). He recognizes in his employee's actions the skill of simultaneously benefiting his employer, his clients, and himself. The manager has won popularity from others for his master and, more importantly for his own situation, has reminded his master of his own usefulness, for he has regularly accumulated the hidden interest on his master's behalf (cf. Herzog, *ibid.*, 257). And though he has been tricked by his employee, the estate owner cannot help but admire such quick-wittedness.

In the master's praise of the manager, the narrative implicitly commends the master and explicitly sets forth the shrewd manager as an example. Caught in the midst of an oppressive system, the manager finds his own way out of a crisis by means of an act of justice that benefits the far-from-wealthy merchants (cf. Herzog, *ibid.*, 258, see also Daube, "Neglected Nuances of Exposition," 2335, and Bindemann, "Ungerechte als Vorbilder?,"

963ff.). For the cancellation of illegal interest, so far from being an act of "unfaithfulness" to his master, actually turns out to be an act of faithfulness to God that challenges the inherent abuse of an exploitative economy.

Many readers of this parable have been unable to see the manager in any way as being exemplary, simply because, notwithstanding his shrewdness, he is so clearly a sharp operator. But other parable characters, too, are portrayed as being at the same time both self-interested and right — as, for example, the prodigal son in his decision to return (cf. Luke 15:18-19), the judge in his verdict delivered under pressure (cf. Luke 18:4-5), and the customs officer in his plea for mercy (cf. Luke 18:13). The teaching of Jesus generally presupposes not an ethic of selfless motivation, but the conjunction of righteousness and one's own best interests — as highlighted also in Israel's Wisdom tradition. So there is no need to resort to tortuous arguments about irony in the words of 16:8b, "the children of this age are more shrewd in dealing with their own generation than are the children of light," or in the exhortation of 16:9, "Make friends for yourselves by means of dishonest wealth, so that when it is gone, they may welcome you into the eternal homes" — as if Jesus meant the opposite of what he seems to have said. Nor need we evacuate the story of its details or its social resonances by saying, with Joachim Jeremias, that the parable's sole point has to do with the man's shrewdness in a time of crisis, which is the only proper response of every person to the urgent message of the kingdom (cf. *Parables of Jesus*, 182).

It remains, however, to comment briefly on some of the difficulties that the text of 16:1-13 appears to raise against our reading of the parable. For if the manager is meant to be exemplary not only in his skillfulness but also in the substance of his action, why is he then called a manager "of unrighteousness" *(tēs adikias)* in verse 8? First we should note that this phrase denotes an ordinary "man of the world," not a person of special wickedness (cf. Ellis, *Luke*, 199). But particularly we must see the connection between this description and the judge "of unrighteousness" *(tēs adikias)* in 18:6 (cf. Bindemann, "Ungerechte als Vorbilder?"). The judge is presented as a man of few scruples, but one who nevertheless, under pressure, reaches a just verdict. The designation "unrighteous," therefore, refers not to the action that brings each story to a climax, but to the general character of the judge and the manager at the outset — or, perhaps more accurately, to a general perception of their characters.

Indeed, this is a point where it is possible to detect a touch of irony in the story of the shrewd manager. Like the tax collectors of 15:1, he —

along, of course, with his master — is up to his eyes in shady financial dealings, the likes of which the Pharisees viewed with disapproval. He regularly handles "the mammon of unrighteousness" (16:9; cf. "the unrighteous mammon" of 16:11, which Jeremias translates "tainted money" [*Parables of Jesus*, 46]). Yet surprisingly such a person, even though caught up in the midst of "unrighteousness," can act rightly and even be imitated. It is exactly this kind of irony that hovers over Jesus' words of Luke 5:32, "I did not come to call the righteous, but sinners to repentance" — that is, the irony of how certain groups identified themselves over against others.

So the disciples are exhorted to look to "the sons of this world" as examples, rather than to "the sons of light" (16:8). Christians, of course, have regularly shrunk back from the force of this exhortation. But it makes good sense within our reading of the parable suggested above. Self-styled "sons of light" — like the sectaries at Qumran, who used the phrase "sons of light" of themselves (cf. 1QM 1); or the Pharisees, who seem to have taken over for themselves the prophetic designation "a light for the nations" (cf. Isa 42:6) — are not to be trusted. Instances of wisdom and obedience can be found closer to hand, even among those very types who were despised by the so-called "sons of light."

But what of Jesus' injunction in 16:9: "Make friends for yourselves by means of dishonest wealth [literally, 'the mammon of unrighteousness'], so that when it is gone, they may welcome you into the eternal homes"? Again, idealist readings have tended to miss the thrust of this exhortation, with many modern readers being suspicious about the idea that money can buy friends. But though, indeed, the structures of this world are unjust, there remains still the possibility of a creative and proper use of the world's unrighteous mammon. Bonaventure (1221-74), the Franciscan philosopher, educator, and commentator of the Middle Ages, recognized such a positive motivation in the shrewd manager's actions, and so proposed that the manager sought by his actions to make friends among his fellow underlings rather than to gain money for himself by whatever means (cf. his *In sacrosanctum Jesu Christi Evangelium secundum Lucam Elaborata Ennaratio, ad loc.*). Like the "faithful and shrewd" manager of 12:42-46, he benefited — not bullied — his fellow servants. Money will, of course, one day be "gone"; it will "fail" (in contrast to "the treasure that does not fail" of 12:33). The transaction that opened the door will be forgotten. But human friendship, the manager knew, is more permanent.

The horizon here is not otherworldly. An early textual variant in 16:9

replaced "when *it* is gone *(eklipḗ)*" with "when *you* are gone *(eklipēte)*," thereby usurping a reference to the impermanence of money by a reference to people's deaths — which is the sense that became enshrined in the Latin Vulgate. This is, however, an erroneous shift of meaning, which has been compounded by viewing the adjective "eternal" *(aiōnious)* in an exclusively other-worldly sense. But the "eternal homes" mentioned at the end of this verse likely signify "the tabernacles *(tas skēnas)* of the Age to Come." They probably allude to the ancient feast of tabernacles that was associated with the remission of debts every seven years (cf. Deut 31:10). So Jesus should be understood at the end of verse 9 to be referring to the hospitality of those who respond here and now to gestures of forgiveness.

The sayings on being "trusted with very little," "dishonest with very little," and "serving two masters" in 16:10-13, though able to stand on their own, are, therefore, not so ill-fitted to the preceding parable as has often been thought. The manager is, indeed, an example of one who was "faithful" in a "very little" thing, an everyday dealing (v 10), in handling "unrighteous mammon" (v 11), and in caring for the possessions of someone else (v 12). In his canceling of hidden interest he not only found a way of escape from his own problems, but his action also resulted — however motivated by self-interest — in being faithful to God's covenant as it concerns usury and justice for the poor.

In Luke's portrayal, the manager contrasts with the Pharisees, who, despite their protestations to the contrary (16:15; 18:11), neglected in their actions the basic features of justice and the love of God (11:42). The rewards held out in 16:10-12 are privileges of the Age to Come, but they are not to be viewed as entirely otherworldly. The trust of a master referred to in verse 10, the "true riches" mentioned in verse 11, and the possession of property spoken of in verse 12 are not to be gained by one's neglect of the humdrum responsibilities of life — or, by some affected antagonism to "tainted money" — but are to be attained through creative faithfulness within the present, unjust socioeconomic system. The manager did not try to serve both God and mammon, as verse 13 warns against. He gained no profit for himself. He only secured his reinstatement to the only position in which he could possibly survive. And he did so courageously, with his action entailing putting God before his mammon-obsessed master.

Like the Parable of the Rich Fool, this story offers a provocative, though quite understated, moral challenge that is both prophetic and practical. It is prophetic because the character praised subverts an unjust system. But it is practical because it suggests not a grand blueprint for revolutionary action in the future, but something that an ordinary person under pressure can do here and now. For to remit debts — and, especially, to cancel interest — is not only just, but it opens up a future of new possibilities. Even a rich master can soften his approach, and so there is a message inherent in this parable for this type of person as well. What Jesus has given us in the Parable of the Shrewd Manager, therefore, are typical characters found in striking pose: a hard-pressed middle manager and a possessions-obsessed estate owner — with both being used, though in differing ways, as examples of wisdom and justice.

5. The Parable of the Rich Man and Lazarus (Luke 16:19-31)

The Parable of the Rich Man and Lazarus in Luke 16:19-31 is set as a warning to the Pharisees about the dangers of the love of money, which was a love they denied but secretly embraced (16:14). Like the Parable of the Shrewd Manager, which it follows in chapter 16, it presents a picture of the human cost of preoccupation with wealth. Whereas the story of the manager implied a happy conclusion of human reconciliation, with money fading into the background, this tale portrays bleak alienation both in this life and beyond.

The opening description of the rich man and Lazarus in verses 19-21 is not an exaggerated picture, but a stark portrayal of the kind of society that was familiar to Jesus and his hearers. On one side of the ornamental gateway lives the rich magnate in luxury and self-indulgence, with ostentatious attire brought by merchants from distant parts. On the other side lies the beggar, the unclean and "expendable" Lazarus, whose only covering is his sores, which are licked by the dogs; and who longs for, but fails to satisfy his hunger with, the pieces of bread used by the rich household as napkins (cf. Oesterley, *Gospel Parables*, 205).

The story tells of no action by either man. The first event is the death of Lazarus, who remains unburied, closely followed by that of the rich man, who is given a proper burial. The remainder of the narrative unfolds in another world. Similar tales from antiquity are extant today (cf. Bauckham, "The Rich Man and Lazarus: The Parable and the Parallels"). The parable, of course, assumes conventionally accepted details about the afterlife. Its main concern, however, is not with the next world, but with this one.

Lazarus is carried to the bosom of Abraham, while the rich man languishes in the torments of Hades (vv 22-23). The rich man then speaks (v 24). He calls Abraham "father," presuming on a family relationship — though before his death he had not recognized Lazarus as being equally Abraham's child. Now Abraham was a figure of legendary hospitality in Judaism. So there is an irony here, for the rich man was wealthy as Abraham had been, but lacked his generosity. He wants Lazarus to cross over a great gulf to alleviate his torture, even though he had never so much as opened his own gate to him in life. Abraham's response is not unkind: he returns "father" with "child" (v 25). But he points out the justice of the reversal in the two men's conditions — and, ominously, speaks of the great gulf that now lies between them (vv 25-26).

The rich man then appeals to Abraham on behalf of his five brothers, asking that Lazarus be sent to warn them (vv 27-28). He thus reveals his awareness of the justice of his own fate. Abraham's laconic response, however, is that they already have all the warning they need — that is, in the words of Moses and the prophets (v 29). But the rich man persists: Surely someone returning from the dead would convince them! (v 30). No, says Abraham: "If they do not listen to Moses and the prophets, neither will they be convinced even if someone rises from the dead" (v 31).

The story, therefore, stresses the freight of urgency with which human decisions in this life are invested. Death confirms those decisions. It does not overturn them. Nor will an apparition from beyond death change hearts and minds that are set in disobedience to the law of God. It was, in particular, the rich man's self-imposed separation from a fellow human, who was a poor child of Abraham, that became a fixed gulf between bliss and torment. So it is the Lazaruses of this life to whom his brothers must pay attention, not a Lazarus from another world.

The parable is all the more powerful for its restraint. The rich man and Lazarus, in life, are simply pictured. They do nothing. What might appear as an excessively harsh treatment beyond death — for, what had the rich man done? — turns out to be the righteous verdict of God on the way things are. Perhaps more than in any other parable, the characters here are types who represent the poles of an unequal society, a society that is under judgment. The striking feature in this story is not so much about something that one or the other of them had thought or done, but the portrayal of their diverse destinies — which portrayal is so unlike the conventional picture of riches as a token of divine blessing.

The Parable of the Rich Man and Lazarus is, therefore, like the two other parables we have considered, for it has both a prophetic and a practical message. Prophetically, obscene injustice is held up for all to behold and denounce. It is revealed to be temporary — though the yawning gulf between human beings in which that injustice had been expressed is shown to persist even beyond death. The rich man has put himself outside the family circle of "father" Abraham. And if his brothers continue in the same ways, they will do so too.

On the practical level, however, the way of wisdom, which is also the way of obedience, lies close at hand. The rich, like the poor, have Moses and the prophets. They should listen to them. The poor are encouraged to put their hope in God's justice. But the sober realism of the parable needs here also to be noted, for the reversal does not take place until after death. As in the Parable of the Rich Fool of 12:13-21, no quick solution is here proposed to the problem of poverty — though, of course, it is implied that if the rich man or his brothers would have taken heed, the situation could have been changed overnight. It is productive, in fact, to read this parable with Psalm 73 as a backdrop, where the temptation of the godly to envy the state of those who are wicked and luxuriantly rich is overcome through a glimpse — which was given to the psalmist when he entered the sanctuary of God (cf. v 17) — of their ultimate fate.

6. The Ancient Contexts of the Parables

Each of the three parables we have considered presents a suggestive incident as an example. They warn the poor against the allure of wealth. Yet they also summon the rich to repentance. They hold in tension a prophetic and a practical vision. No false hope of an immediate release from poverty is offered. Rather, they proclaim that if the rich as well as the poor were to obey God's word, ultimate liberation for all would be on its way. But more needs also to be said here with regard to the ancient contexts of these parables.

In the Narrative of Luke

A comparison of the language of these parables with the language of Luke-Acts as a whole highlights the presence of Luke's hand in the recounting of these stories. In particular, these three parables reflect the evangelist's intense concern with poverty and wealth. They demonstrate how, contrary to appearances, the poor can be blessed (6:20-21) and the rich are in danger (6:24-25). Because of the contexts in which they are found, these parables are permeated by a sense of divine purpose. And they offer not only examples for living, both negative and positive, but also encapsulate the good news itself — that is, they proclaim that a certain pattern of life is possible, as well as good, for all kinds of people, even for society as a whole.

Luke in his two volumes gives a prominent place to the sharing of goods by the earliest Christian community (cf. esp. Acts 2:44-45; 4:34–5:12). Luke T. Johnson has argued that an attitude toward riches functions in Luke-Acts as a metaphor for faith-commitment to Jesus, and that the portrayal of the Pharisees in Luke 16:14 as "lovers of money" owes something to such a stylized presentation (cf. his *Literary Function of Possessions in Luke-Acts*). But it should also be recognized that later generations of Christians have "spiritualized" much of Jesus' teaching concerning wealth, while Luke seems to have preserved in quite a literal fashion a truly genuine emphasis of Jesus on its right use.

There are other parables in Luke's Gospel where literal wealth is an often unnoticed sub-theme — such as the Good Samaritan (10:30-37), the Lost Sheep, the Lost Coin, and the Lost Son (15:1-32), the Widow and the Judge (18:1-8), and the Pharisee and the Tax Collector (18:9-14). Furthermore, Luke presents Jesus as announcing "the year of the Lord's favor," which is a time to let the oppressed go free (4:18-19). Thus, although indebtedness can be used as a metaphor for sin, we ought not thereby underplay Jesus' message regarding economic and social forgiveness as it is presented in Luke's Gospel. And this is the message that appears in the manager's discovery of a way out of oppressive practices in 16:1-8, which is analogous to the liberation of Zacchaeus in 19:1-10.

In the Earliest Christian Communities

Luke's presentations suggest that the parables of the Rich Fool in 12:16-21 and the Shrewd Manager in 16:1-8 were clarified for the early Christians by the admonitions of 12:15, 21 and 16:9-13 (possibly also 16:8b). It is, however, a false logic and bad literary criticism to claim that the hortatory material of these verses was foreign to the intention of Jesus. Indeed, all three parables in their entireties bear the marks of Luke's hand. Nonetheless, it is legitimate to assume that a real continuity exists between the exemplary force of the parables for Jesus' hearers and a similar force for Christians after Easter.

Warnings to poor believers against emulating the oppressive practices of the rich, as well as warnings to the rich not to oppress the poor, continued to be necessary among the early Christians, as we see particularly in the Letter of James (see esp. 1:9-11; 1:27–2:17; 4:13–5:11). The phrase "even if one should rise from the dead" *(oud' ean tis ek nekrōn anastę̄ peisthēsontai)* of 16:31 — which resonates with language used in connection with Jesus' own resurrection, whether that language comes from early Christian tradition or is a product of the evangelist's wording — provides a natural bridge from a story of hard-heartedness, which Jesus told to his hearers, to a story that reflects the continuing hard-heartedness and unbelief of many after he himself had been raised from the dead.

In the Ministry of Jesus

The readings I have offered for these three parables sit well with an understanding of Jesus as a social prophet, which is a perspective that is supported today by many historical studies. Though these parables would also fit the picture of Jesus as being Israel's final prophet, who heralds the nation's ultimate crisis, they do not themselves assert such a view. The presence of death in the first and third of these parables could, of course, be taken to hint at judgment in a wider sense, with the hope for hospitality in the second suggesting a new age feasting. At the same time, however, it should be noted that it is the death of an individual person or persons that is depicted in 12:13-21 and 16:19-31. Furthermore, the manager's hope in 16:1-8 is a very earthy one.

The one phrase that has unambiguous overtones of a final age expectation is "the tents of the Age to Come" in 16:9. This verse, however, could be a Lukan (or earlier) gloss — though even if that be so, the idea of an "age to come" should not be confused with notions of a somewhat immaterial "heaven." But however the phrase "the Age to Come" came about and is to be understood, the three parables with which we are here concerned can fittingly be read as three summons to repentance in Jesus' challenge to Israel — with this triad of parables setting out practical examples of what Jesus' message means for both the rich and the poor. In effect, it seems, the message of these parables is closely similar to John the Baptist's earthy responses to those who sought his counsel (cf. Luke 3:10-14).

Such an interpretation contrasts with two other interpretations that have been popular in recent decades. On the one hand, Joachim Jeremias has treated these parables, like all the other parables of Jesus, as simple illustrations of the kingdom, which was coming in judgment and grace — and of the response that it required. The significance of the specific details of these parables was so minimized that even Lazarus's poverty was regarded as being purely incidental (cf. Jeremias, *Parables of Jesus*, 186: "Jesus does not want to comment on a social problem"). On the other hand, Dominic Crossan has offered us a version of Jesus the existentialist (cf. Crossan, *In Parables*) and Bernard Scott has presented Jesus as a social radical (cf. Scott, *Hear Then the Parable*). Both of these constructions, however, underplay the practical, moral, and exemplary dimensions of Jesus' stories. The former, that proposed by Jeremias, does this by assimilating these stories to Jesus' proclamation of the kingdom as seen through a Pauline lens, and so, despite protestations to the contrary, inevitably allegorizes them. The latter, as argued by Crossan or Scott, underplays the practical, moral, and exemplary dimensions by preferring either a philosophical or sociopolitical framework for the parables rather than a theological framework.

The version of the Parable of the Rich Fool in the *Gospel of Thomas*, Logion 63, lacks a moral conclusion, and so many scholars, including Crossan, regard it as being more authentic than the version in Luke's Gospel (see the summary of opinions in Scott, *Hear Then the Parable*, 130). Introductions and conclusions to the parables are often dismissed today as being inauthentic by the use of the pejorative label "moralizing." But it is a strange sort of literary idealism or theological fastidiousness that shrinks from allowing Jesus to explain parables or make moral pronouncements. As Luke himself shows, heightening the moral impact of the parables is perfectly compatible with their being the bearers of good news. In particular, these three parables on poverty and riches proclaim that returning to God is possible for all kinds of people.

STEPHEN I. WRIGHT

7. Modern Contexts for the Parables

In Theological Discourse

The fondness for seeing figures in the parables as analogues for God (e.g., "the master" of 16:1), which existed within the Christian church from earliest times, has in our day been widely abandoned. But an appreciation of the realism of Jesus' stories must not cause us to overlook the presence of God as the guarantor of the order of life that they present. His speech to the foolish farmer in 12:20 ("You fool! This very night your life is being demanded of you. And the things you have prepared, whose will they be?") is no alien intrusion into the story. Likewise, God is the one who stands behind the rich employer of 16:1 — not, of course, as the subject of the story, for whom the employer is a mere code, but as the master of all masters, just as he is present in 18:1-8 as the judge of the judges (cf. Psalm 82). And he is the undoubted, though unmentioned, author of judgment in the story of the rich man and Lazarus in 16:19-31. These three parables, in fact, appeal not to a reality only lately sprung on the world through the arrival of Jesus, but to an unchanging order that is continually sustained by a Creator God.

These parables, however, should not be pressed into service as fodder for a doctrine of the afterlife. As we have seen, the climactic word of God spoken to the foolish farmer in 12:20 is spoken while the man is still alive. Likewise, the language used in commendation of the shrewd manager in 16:8-9 is this-worldly; while the story of the rich man and Lazarus in 16:19-31 adopts, rather than asserts, traditional views of the next world. Nonetheless, there is an urgency about each story that serves to point up the importance of right decisions here and now. It is an urgency that is reminiscent of the earthy, this-worldly stance of much of the Old Testament. The thrust of these stories is that people need not — in fact, *must not* — wait for death to find the way to true personal and communal well-being.

Our interpretation of these three parables has distanced itself from that of Joachim Jeremias, who found them to be simply expressions in vivid language of the call to respond to Christ in repentance and faith. Instead, we have highlighted their moral and social implications. Yet these parables do connect on a deeper level with Paul's teaching concerning justification, as well as with the roots of the concept of justification in the Old Testament. For they present to human beings who are immersed in this world's unjust structures — perhaps, it might seem, hopelessly compro-

236

mised either as victims of the system or as its operators, or, sometimes, simultaneously both — the possibility of action that is wise and right. Thus just as Paul was quite sure that people do not need to wait until they are perfectly uncompromised by the world before they can enjoy a relationship with God and express it in right action, so Jesus points us in these parables to the meaning of a working, earthy faith. The argument of both Jesus and Paul, in fact, as biblical scholarship has increasingly come to recognize, was not about faith versus action or action versus faith, but about the potential inclusion of all sorts and conditions of people within the one penitent people of God.

In Social Application to Contemporary Society

With respect to the applicability of these three parables of Jesus to contemporary society, perhaps that can best be shown by citing significant issues raised in two articles by two contemporary and respected journalists.

The first article is by Simon Jenkins, who writes in *The Times* (April 11, 1998) a penetrating review of a television documentary by Roger Graef, *Keeping It in the Family*. The documentary concerned a disturbed, hyperactive child of parents who were separated, unemployed, alcoholic, and sometimes violent. Jenkins uses the story as an illustration of the sheer misery that modern "family life" can be:

> The characters were desperate in every sense. . . . Lacking the diversion and self-esteem of a job, they endured the claustrophobia of nuclear families in council houses, and took it out on each other and their children. They were what middle-class viewers would call "awful people." . . . What went wrong was not an absence of values or policy. It was that two people found they could not live together or offer security to a child. . . . You may love your child and ache to be seen as a responsible parent, yet when you foul it up, all the hobgoblins of politics and religion descend on you and call you evil. These people are no help. They can resort to preaching, but they never tell you what to do when you are at your wits' end.

But that is precisely what Jesus did do in these parables! To those in hopeless situations he offered hope and practical advice. Not policies, patronizing, or empty promises, but the encouragement to trust in God and not lose a generous spirit. His followers should go and do likewise. And if they are rich, they should ask themselves about their complicity in a society that has nurtured such hopelessness, and how they can change it.

The other article suggests a global application. Jeremy Seabrook, in *The New Internationalist* (October 1997), writes of the rich North's export of consumerism to the South:

> Throughout recorded time a majority of the world's people have been tormented by poverty or by the fear of poverty, by want, hunger and insecurity. Consumerism promises not only that they will be released from this ancient bondage, but also that they can by-pass a bare sufficiency, a frugal security, and break through into the satisfaction of limitless desire. . . . Consumerism's greatest weakness is that it eliminates other fundamental needs — for example, the need to provide for ourselves and the need to create and to do things for each other. . . . Reclamation of our human powers has to be the objective of people both in the North and in the South.

A central thrust of Jesus' rhetoric, as we have seen, is precisely to warn the poor against being like the rich. Even a peasant family on the bread line should not get possessive about their patrimony. A manager discovers that doing something for others that is within his limited power will give him a "frugal security," which is all he requires. He has no need to imitate the tactics of a grasping superior. Most piercingly of all, even a beggar should not dream of being like the unseeing, uncaring potentate at whose gate he lies. Jesus urges us to see that all have enough. But he also warns us that having too much can destroy that humanity-in-relationship that is our greatest treasure. His words are as relevant for the global village as for the Palestinian one.

Selected Bibliography

Bailey, Kenneth E. *Poet and Peasant: A Literary Cultural Approach to the Parables in Luke.* Grand Rapids: Eerdmans, 1976.
————. *Through Peasant Eyes: More Lucan Parables, Their Culture and Style.* Grand Rapids: Eerdmans, 1980.

Bauckham, Richard J. "The Rich Man and Lazarus: The Parable and the Parallels," *New Testament Studies* 37 (1991) 225-46.

Bindemann, Walther. "Ungerechte als Vorbilder? Gottesreich und Gottesrecht in den Gleichnissen vom 'ungerechten Verwalter' und 'ungerechten Richter'," *Theologische Literaturzeitung* 11 (1995) 956-70.

Crossan, John Dominic. *In Parables: The Challenge of the Historical Jesus.* San Francisco: Harper & Row, 1973.

Daube, David. "Neglected Nuances of Exposition in Luke-Acts," in *Aufstieg und Niedergang der römischen Welt* II. 25.3 (1984), 2329-56.

Donahue, John R. *The Gospel in Parable: Metaphor, Narrative and Theology in the Synoptic Gospels.* Philadelphia: Fortress, 1988.

Ellis, E. Earle. *The Gospel of Luke* (New Century Bible Commentary). Rev. ed. London: Marshall, Morgan & Scott, 1974.

Hedrick, Charles W. *Parables as Poetic Fictions: The Creative Voice of Jesus.* Peabody: Hendrickson, 1994.

Herzog, William R., II. *Parables as Subversive Speech: Jesus as Pedagogue of the Oppressed.* Louisville: Westminster/John Knox, 1994.

Jeremias, Joachim. *The Parables of Jesus.* Rev. ed. London: SCM, 1963, trans. S. H. Hooke from *Die Gleichnisse Jesu,* 6th ed. (Göttingen: Vandenhoeck & Ruprecht, 1962). First published 1947.

Johnson, Luke T. *The Literary Function of Possessions in Luke-Acts* (Society of Biblical Literature Dissertation Series, ed. H. C. Kee and D. A. Knight, 39). Missoula: Scholars, 1977.

Oesterley, W. E. O. *The Gospel Parables in the Light of Their Jewish Background.* London: SPCK, 1936.

Scott, Bernard Brandon. *Hear Then the Parable: A Commentary on the Parables of Jesus.* Minneapolis: Fortress, 1989.

Sellew, Philip. "Interior Monologue as a Narrative Device in the Parables of Luke," *Journal of Biblical Literature* 111 (1992) 239-53.

CHAPTER 11

Parables on Prayer

(Luke 11:5-13; 18:1-14)

WALTER L. LIEFELD

THERE ARE THREE PARABLES of Jesus on prayer in the Synoptic Gospels, with all three of them appearing in Luke: the Parable of the Friend at Midnight (11:5-8), the Parable of the Persistent Widow (18:1-8), and the Parable of the Pharisee and the Tax Collector (18:9-14). Connected with the story of the friend at midnight are two short parabolic sayings about asking, seeking, and knocking (11:9-10) and about a son's requests of his father (11:11-13), which we will consider, as well, with that parable.

Luke's presentation of these three parables and two sayings is consistent with his interest on prayer, as seen throughout his Gospel and Acts. Indeed, these parables and sayings bear the evangelist's own stamp. But this fact should not preclude an acceptance of them as being genuinely from Jesus and faithfully interpreted by Luke. Parables cry out for a context. If we should denude them from their canonical wraps, we would then need to propose some other contexts and some other meanings.

The first parable will be given here the most attention, and the last one the least. This is partly because of the complexity of the lexical issues in 11:8 and partly because some of the discussion regarding the latter two parables will have already been anticipated in dealing with the first.

1. The Friend at Midnight (Luke 11:5-8)

⁵Then he said to them, "Who among you has a friend, and he goes to him at midnight and says, 'Friend, lend me three loaves of bread, ⁶because a friend of mine on a journey has come to me, and I have nothing to set before him.'

⁷"Then the one inside answers, 'Don't bother me. The door is already locked, and my children are with me in bed. I can't get up and give you anything.' ⁸I tell you, though he will not get up and give him the bread because he is his friend, yet because of the man's boldness he will get up and give him as much as he needs."

The Literary Context of the Parable

Luke has set the Parable of the Friend at Midnight in the context of an extended presentation on prayer in 11:1-13. The four parts of this section have in common an emphasis on *the nature of the God* to whom Christians pray. The first part in verses 1-4 contains the Lord's Prayer. Although Luke's placement and wording of the Lord's Prayer is different from Matthew's, a main point in common with Matthew's version is the use of the term "Father." This carries with it an assurance of the basis on which God will answer our prayers — that is, because he is *loving* and *caring*. The portrayal of God in the second part of this section, in verses 5-8, is in the parable itself, which is the focus of this study.

The third part of this section in verses 9-10 calls for action on the part of a petitioner: asking, seeking, and knocking. But still the focus is not on the petitioner; rather, it is on *the God who is faithful and consistent in his response*. The petitioner could not be guaranteed an answer if God were not faithful. The fourth part in verses 11-13 portrays the *wisdom* and *kindness* of a father who gives good gifts to his children.

The emphasis throughout this section, therefore, is on God who receives petitions in prayer and who will surely hear and answer. The first component, the Lord's Prayer, and the last, the wise father, are linked by references to a father. The second component, the parable, and the third, the invitation to ask, seek, and knock, have in common references to the petitioner taking the initiative — and doing so with the expectation of an answer.

241

The study of the Parable of the Friend at Midnight in the context of Luke's Gospel, however, also invites attention to the Parable of the Persistent Widow in 18:1-8. Several points of comparison have been noted between these two parables. The most obvious one is that the person to whom the petition is brought is at first reluctant, but that the petition is eventually granted. There is also a striking verbal similarity in the sayings of the man in bed, who replies "Don't bother me" (*mē moi kopous pareche*, 11:7), and the judge, who acts "because the widow keeps bothering me" (*dia ge to parechein moi kopon*, 18:5).

Such similarities invite the supposition that there was a connection between the two parables in the oral tradition and/or in Luke's redaction. This supposition, however, can lead to the wrong conclusion that the two parables were intended — either by Jesus or by Luke — to teach exactly the same lesson. The context of the parable in 11:5-8 probably stems from the petition for daily bread (v 3) in the Lord's Prayer, which immediately precedes it, while the context of the parable in 18:1-8 is the need for vindication during a long period of waiting. But if the interpretations we will offer of these two parables are correct, the need for continued prayer in the circumstance that prompted the parable of 18:1-8 does *not* carry the implication that importunity is always a necessary element in prayer. Therefore, Luke's inclusion of these two parables in 11:5-8 and 18:1-8 — while, indeed, they may possess some similar features — does not mean that the one interprets the other, as is commonly assumed.

The Social Context of the Parable

The social context of the parable in 11:5-8 is, like that of the other two parables on prayer, clearly in view. It was in accord with the customs of the day that a visitor be heartily welcomed and be provided with food and lodging. Hospitality continued to be an important virtue in the early church and was a qualification for elders (cf. 1 Tim 3:2; Tit 1:8). A century later, the satirist Lucian of Samosata told of the Cynic preacher Peregrinus who professed Christianity for a while, benefited from the legendary hospitality of Christians, and then returned to Cynicism (Lucian, *The Passing of Peregrinus*). A major social context of the parable, therefore, is the culture of honor and shame, which is a matter to which we must return later.

The Form of the Parable

As to its form, the story of the parable has some of the characteristics typical of most parables. It is an extended metaphor with a narrative movement. The focus is on two main characters and their dialogue. The "law of end stress" is seen in the response of the man in bed, which is unexpected. The parable draws the hearer into the action with the words, "Who among you?" (NIV and NRSV: "Suppose one of you"). Because of its positive outcome, with the realization of hopes and potential, it could possibly be considered close to the category of a "comic" parable, as proposed by Dan O. Via (*The Parables* [Philadelphia: Fortress, 1967], 145-76).

But this is a narrative within a dialogue. The only action outside of the dialogue is the midnight walk of a man over to his friend's house. The rest of the action takes place within the dialogue: a recitation of the unexpected arrival of a guest, who is also described as a friend; a reference to the guest's journey leading up to this visit; and the consternation of his host at not being able to provide the meal required as part of one's customary hospitality. The dialogue continues with the rather abrupt, though not unreasonable, response of the sleepy man in bed describing his circumstances. The conclusion of the story is also not part of the parable narrative as such. Rather, it comes in the words attributed to Jesus (v 8): "I tell you, though he will not get up and give him the bread because he is his friend, yet because of the man's boldness (NIV; or 'importunity,' NRSV) he will get up and give him as much as he needs."

What is presented in this parable, therefore, is an extended metaphor — a graphic one, but one with the external framework of a narrative being minimal. There is also no character delineation, at least at the beginning. The desire of the host to provide for his guest is normal, as is also the reluctance of the man in bed to get up. All of this, however, is in contrast to the character descriptions of the "unjust" judge and the "persistent" widow in 18:1-8.

Dominical Status and Lukan Redaction

If this were not an authentic parable of Jesus, which was preserved essentially in its original form, it would be difficult to conceive how it arose in the early church (unless, of course, because of its similarities with the story about the persistent widow, it is to be viewed as only a spinoff from that parable). But while, indeed, such an act of hospitality as represented in the parable would not have been unusual, it is hard to conceive of this particular complex of circumstances as having been created by the early Christian community. The theme of honor and shame that underlies the story was not one of such concern to the early church that it would have motivated the development of a story like this. More likely, it may be assumed that there was a lively interest among the earliest believers in Jesus in the Lord's Prayer, and that any parables and sayings of Jesus that related to that prayer were treasured and included in their oral traditions. Furthermore, it may be assumed many such stories and sayings would have been customarily repeated together by the time Luke became aware of them.

It is easy to postulate that Luke found the Parable of the Friend at Midnight in what has sometimes been called "L" or his special source. The Travel Narrative of 9:51–19:27 and the Last Supper of 22:7-20 (esp. vv 15-20) give evidence of a source that was used by Luke but not by either Mark or Matthew, and which contained narrative material as well as sayings of Jesus. But another source, which was also used by Matthew and is commonly identified as "Q" (i.e., *Quelle* or "source"), is perhaps also supported by a comparison of Luke with Matthew.

On the basis of comparisons between the story of the Friend at Midnight of Luke 11:5-8 with that of the Persistent Widow of Luke 18:1-8, as well as the "answer to prayer" material of Luke 11:9-13 with Matt 7:7-11, David Catchpole has proposed a reconstruction of Q that would see many of the prayer passages of the Gospels having been earlier joined together — that is, not only the Lord's Prayer of Luke 11:1-4 (and its parallel in Matt 6:9-13) and the other prayer texts of Luke 11:5-13 (with postulated parallels in Luke 18:1-8 and Matt 7:7-11), but also such an extended passage as found in Matt 6:25-33 and Luke 12:22-31 (cf. his "Q and 'The Friend at Midnight'"). But while such a complex of prayer texts might very well have been brought together in early Christian tradition, the question must be asked as to *how* and *why* the evangelist Luke sorted out this material in his Gospel as he did. Furthermore, Catchpole's reconstruction involves an interpretation of the parables of Luke 11:5-8 and 18:1-8 that not only brings the two, in their canonical forms, into conflict with each other, but also interprets the use of the Greek noun *anaideia* differently from our understanding (as proposed below).

There is no treatment of Luke 11:5-8 in *The Parables of Jesus: Red Let-*

ter Edition, which was authored by Robert W. Funk, Bernard Brandon Scott, and James R. Butts (Sonoma, CA: Polebridge, 1988) and represents the work of the Jesus Seminar. Nor is there any explanation for that omission. Robert Funk and Roy W. Hoover, however, in their later book entitled *The Five Gospels* (New York: Macmillan, 1993), report on the attitude toward the Parable of the Friend at Midnight by the "Fellows" of that seminar as follows:

> The Fellows decided this anecdote probably originated with Jesus, although Luke has obscured its original meaning by adapting it to the context of prayer. He makes it cohere, in other words, with the Lord's prayer, which precedes, and with the complex of sayings that follows. The burden of the whole section is that if one is persistent in prayer, God will respond. (327)

Thus we are told that the Fellows of the Jesus Seminar assigned a high degree of authenticity to the parable itself, which they interpreted (rightly, I believe) in terms of "the honor/shame culture of first century Palestine," but that they decided (wrongly, I suggest) that "the original point of the anecdote and the Lukan context clash" (*ibid.*, 328).

Without entering into all of the issues involved in the decisions of the Jesus Seminar, we need here only note that the charge that Luke "obscured the original meaning" assumes that the evangelist's understanding is that "if one is persistent in prayer, God will respond." But the "whole section" of Luke 11:1-13 does not teach persistence. This could be read into the saying about knocking in verses 9-10, but the knocking is not said to be repeated. Furthermore, Luke is well aware of the honor/shame culture of his day (cf. B. J. Malina and J. H. Neyrey, "Honor and Shame in Luke-Acts," in *The Social World of Luke-Acts*, ed. J. H. Neyrey [Peabody: Hendrickson, 1991], 25-65). So one would expect that any redaction on the part of the evangelist would have featured this theme rather than clashed with it. In short, the assumption by the Fellows of the Jesus Seminar that the parable is to be accepted as an original parable is to be commended, but their negative judgment on Luke's framework is not.

The Story of the Parable

The story of the Friend at Midnight starts with an invitation for the hearer to identify with the person "in the middle," that is, with the host of a midnight guest who is his friend. The host must somehow procure bread for his guest, and so he makes his appeal to another "friend." The hearer is therefore placed in the role of a petitioner interceding for someone else. This would make the man in bed represent God, which immediately sets up static in the communication. The question then arises: Does the parable teach that an unresponsive God must be prodded and pressured ("importuned") into responding?

The host comes at midnight. It was, of course, customary to go to bed not long after dark, for oil lamps did not facilitate much late night activity. So being awakened at midnight would have been later in the sleep cycle than is the case today. There is, however, no reference to knocking. This is mentioned in the saying that follows the parable (v 9), but such loud knocking at midnight would have been inappropriate in the story. Furthermore, it is important to note that there is no reference to any repeated requests — a fact that reduces the possibility that the purpose of this parable is to encourage persistence in prayer. The host immediately begins his petition and the narration continues within the dialogue. The opening word "friend," with the same word being used for the guest, puts the request on the basis of friendship. But the man in bed refuses to respond on that basis. Three loaves are requested as a gesture of kindness to the guest. Villagers would know who had baked that day.

The narrative within the dialogue vividly portrays the inner scene of a sleeping family, who were probably together on a mat and with the door secured by a wooden bar thrust through two rings — all of which sets up the improbability of a response. The reason the man does provide the bread in spite of all this is surprising. It is expressed in the phrase "because of his *shamelessness*" (*tēn anaideian autou,* or "his boldness" or "his persistence"). There are two linguistic problems here in verse 8: (1) the meaning of the noun *anaideia,* which is a *hapax legomenon* in the New Testament, and (2) the referent of the pronoun *autou* ("his"), which is either (a) the host at the door or (b) the man in bed.

The Noun anaideia *and Pronoun* autou

It may seem, at first glance, rather curious that interpreters have traditionally translated the noun *anaideia* in two diametrically opposed ways —
one that renders the word positively, usually translating it as "importunity" or "persistence," and the other negatively, translating it as "shamelessness." The preponderance of linguistic evidence has favored the negative meaning, but it has seemed difficult to accommodate such an
understanding to a parable on prayer. Some option other than "shamelessness" has seemed almost necessary to most interpreters if the parable is to
have a meaning that can be easily grasped and applied. A more recent suggestion (discussed below) is *"avoidance* of shame," which acknowledges
the negative element of shame, but puts it in a positive light.

Readers of English and German Bibles have gotten used to the idea
of "importunity" or "persistence," as expressed in the following versions:

> *Douay Version:* "importunity" (which is probably dependent on the
> Latin phrase *propter inprobitatem,* variant *improbitatem*);
> Luther: "Zudringlichkeit";
> *King James Version:* "importunity";
> *Twentieth Century* (1900-1904): "persistence";
> *Weymouth* (1909, 1912): "persistency" (with the amazing footnote:
> "The primary sense of this word is 'impudence,' but it would be
> ridiculous always to translate words according to their original
> meaning");
> *New King James:* "persistence";
> *Revised English Bible:* "his very persistence"; and,
> *NRSV:* "persistence."

The Message, which is a paraphrase by Eugene Peterson, is worth noting for
its vivid presentation of the idea of persistence: "If you stand your ground,
knocking and waking all the neighbors, he'll finally get up and get you
whatever you need."

However, with lexicons such as *Liddell-Scott* and *Bauer* pointing toward a negative meaning, and with the several articles and commentaries
proposing "shamelessness," some recent translations (but not all) are evi-
dencing a change:

NIV: "boldness," with the alternate "persistence";
New American Standard: "persistence," with the marginal alternative reading "shamelessness";
New Living Translation: "so his reputation won't be damaged," with the alternatives "in order to avoid shame" and "because of [your] persistence."

Joachim Jeremias included the parables of "the Friend" and "the Widow" together in a chapter he happily entitled: "The Great Assurance" (*The Parables of Jesus,* trans. S. H. Hooke [London: SCM, 1963], 146-60). He considered 11:5-7 to be one rhetorical question, with verse 7 not "describing a refusal of the request, but rather the utter impossibility of such a refusal." So by separating verses 7 and 8 he was able to concentrate on the man in bed, rather than on the importunity of the visitor. However, he retained the idea of importunity even though he attempted to place this reading in the setting of "oriental hospitality." He allowed the option of the man in bed acting "that he may not lose face in the matter" (*ibid.,* 158).

Kenneth Bailey in *Poet and Peasant* (1976), building on his general cultural orientation and his supposition that the underlying Aramaic word meant "sense of shame," argued for *anaideia* as being formed from the noun *aideia,* which meant "shame," and the so-called "alpha privative," which functions to negate the word in question — thereby bringing about *an-aideia,* which would then mean "avoidance of shame." And he understood this characterization to apply to the man in bed.

As Bailey understood matters, in that culture *aideia,* "shame," was a virtue. It did not mean being ashamed for some wrongdoing. Rather, it suggested an appropriate modesty and conformity to social standards. *Anaideia,* therefore, meant a lack of this proper sense of shame, that is, "shamelessness." In this context Bailey thought that to do something on account of shamelessness meant that one was doing it to *avoid* that shamelessness. In contrast, Duncan Derrett, in an article on "The Friend at Midnight: Asian Ideas in the Gospel of St. Luke" (1978), argued that *anaideia* meant the shamelessness of the petitioner, who approached his neighbor with boldness, and thus with a sense of urgency.

Howard Marshall in his commentary on the Third Gospel suggested that there are "two possible lessons in the parable": one is the contrast between God and the reluctant householder; the other, "an encouragement to go on praying, despite the lack of an immediate answer" (*Luke* [1978],

462). Marshall's way of stating matters avoids making the parable teach that importunity is necessary for securing an answer to prayer. At the same time, however, it leaves space for the possibility of continued prayer when necessary, as is the case with the widow in Luke 18.

Everett Huffard in his article on "The Parable of the Friend at Midnight: God's Honor or Man's Persistence?" (1978) proposed that *anaideia* meant to remain blameless. Alan Johnson in an article entitled "Assurance for Man: The Fallacy of Translating *anaideia* by 'Persistence' in Luke 11:5-8" (1979) argued that it meant avoidance of shame — though he acknowledged the difficulty that those not familiar with ancient Near Eastern customs have with the concept of the avoidance of shame. Both Huffard and Johnson applied the characterization to the man in bed. Charles Talbert, like Marshall, observed two possible lessons in the parable: the first, that we should be persistent; the second, a "how much more" story showing the contrast between God and the reluctant neighbor, with God being far more eager to answer (cf. his *Reading Luke*, 132).

David Catchpole in "Q and 'The Friend at Midnight'" (cited above) objected to finding a double meaning in the parable, specifically rejecting Marshall's proposal. Two of his reasons are that such a procedure is wrong in principle and that "a decision must be made concerning whether the petitioner or the person petitioned is the focus of interest" (*ibid.*, 408). The first of his reasons calls for a review of principles for interpreting parables that goes beyond our scope here. As for Catchpole's second reason, certainly the work of exegesis is a continual decision-making process regarding matters having to do with grammar, language, cultural backgrounds, and so on. Nevertheless, some factors in the texts themselves lie beyond certain recovery. Furthermore, it is not always certain that we should rule out multiple foci in a passage. And to complicate matters further, listening to pronouns in any narration can be somewhat confusing when there are repeated references to "he," "she," "his," "her," "them," and "their."

Joseph Fitzmyer in his discussion of "The Parable of the Persistent Friend" in his Luke commentary illustrates the difficulty of assigning the pronouns in a text to their proper referents. He rejects the interpretation offered in 1934 by Anton Fridrichsen, which has been accepted by many recent scholars — that is, that *his* in verse 8 attributes the matter of shamelessness to the man in bed. "That interpretation fails," Fitzmyer notes, "because the *autou*, 'his,' that modifies *anaideia* has to be understood in the same sense as the *autou* with the preceding *philon*, 'his friend,' a reference to the begging neighbor" (*Luke* 912, citing K. E. Bailey, *Poet and Peasant*, 119-33 in support). Yet others have taken the opposite position. The effect of the various efforts to incorporate the idea of "shamelessness" along with the lingering idea of "persistence" is seen in the work of John Donahue, who speaks of "persistence" with "overtones of shameless boldness" (*Gospel in Parable*, 187).

Three former students of mine have worked extensively on this problem. Craig Blomberg in *Interpreting the Parables* (1990) concisely surveys the issues. He acknowledges the grammatical difficulty of determining whether the pronoun "his" of verse 8b refers to the man who asks for bread or the householder in bed. But he opts for the former, and so reads the text "because of the man's [i.e., the friend's] importunity [or, 'persistence']." Furthermore, he proposes two lessons in the parable: the lesson of "bold, unabashed forthrightness in prayer," but also that "God will provide for the needs of his people even more generously and willingly [than the man in bed]" (*ibid.*, 276).

Greg Spencer, another former student, has written "An Exegetical Study of the Lucan Concept of Perseverance in Prayer: Men's Persistence or God's Honor?" as a master's thesis at Trinity Evangelical Divinity School in 1993. One of his contributions is an exhaustive survey of *anaideia* using the IBYCUS search resource. He observes that "in all the references of the word *anaideia* from the 1st century AD to the 3rd century AD, 52 out of 60 occurrences are clearly negative, 8 are ambiguous and 0 are positive" (*ibid.*, 34). And Klyne Snodgrass's careful analysis of the linguistic evidence in his article "*Anaideia* and the Friend at Midnight" (1997) makes it now impossible to conclude anything other than that the term *anaideia* is to be understood in a thoroughly negative sense.

William R. Herzog II in *Parables as Subversive Speech: Jesus as Pedagogue of the Oppressed* (1994) took the discussion of *anaideia* further. He proposed an extension of the meaning of *anaideia*, suggesting that in "several instances the word seems to refer to greed." He cites 1 Sam 2:29 (LXX), Sirach 23:6, and Isa 56:11 in support of such an extended meaning. But he also sees "another cluster of meanings . . . [that] describes attitudes that challenge socially constructed boundaries or behaviors and that break these established barriers" (*ibid.*, 212-13). It is impossible to summarize, let alone evaluate, Herzog's work without describing his sociological theories. His approach, however, can be seen in the following two quotations:

The Torah was the source of boundary drawing, and in the interests of protecting Jerusalem elites and the Temple hierarchy, the retainers of the elites and the Temple recodified the Torah through the oral torah so that the boundaries would be drawn along "purity" lines.

Because "friendship" had become entangled in the web of patron-client loyalties, it could no longer be appealed to. But boundary-breaking hospitality was something else! (*ibid.*, 213, 214)

Unfortunately, the potential value of such a study loses sight of the Lukan context of the Parable of the Friend at Midnight, particularly its relevance to the Lord's Prayer — to say nothing of its possible earlier setting in Q. Nonetheless, as I understand him, Herzog's approach would accommodate my own conclusions (as in the following paragraph), but would take them in a different direction beyond and away from a contextual application.

Personally, I lean toward applying the noun *anaideia* and the pronoun *autou* to the petitioner, but see that only as a means of directing attention to the man in bed who will deal with his friend's "shamelessness" and vindicate it. The man in bed took the action he did as the right way of dealing with the *anaideia* of the petitioner. If he had refused, not only would the opprobrium of shamelessness have remained on the petitioner, but it would also have rested on the man in bed — and, indeed, on the whole village. The entire story has to do with honor and shame. It starts out with the host acting honorably to provide for the midnight guest, continues with the host then acting in a shameful manner toward the man in bed, and concludes with the latter dealing with that shame in an honorable way. This is consistent with the action of God who honors his own name when his people dishonor it (cf. Ezek 36:22-23).

The Teaching of the Parable

We conclude, therefore, that Jesus' disciples would have understood this story as teaching that they could approach God confidently, even brashly, in a way that might offend the sensibilities of others. In a culture of honor and shame, what is at issue is not necessarily what is morally right or morally wrong but what is acceptable or unacceptable among one's peers. The disciples can approach God in a shameless way, but they can do so only because God himself will "cover" for their shame when he acts in accordance with his own honor.

As we read the parable today in its Lukan context, matters become even more clear. The Lord's Prayer begins with the request that God's name be honored. The Lord's Prayer also deals with the provision of bread for the day. So we can approach God knowing that he has already invited prayer regarding his honor and regarding daily provisions. The basis is God's Fatherhood. Furthermore, following the parable, verses 9-10 assure us that God will be consistent and faithful in responding to our asking, seeking, and knocking. Then verses 11-13 show us that a father acts wisely and kindly as he responds to the requests of his children. The whole passage, therefore, is teaching us about God: He is (1) a loving Father, who (2) will uphold his own honor and will not let us be ashamed when we pray; he (3) will be consistent and faithful, and he is (4) a wise and kind Father in his response.

2. The Persistent Widow (Luke 18:1-8)

¹Then Jesus told his disciples a parable to show them that they should always pray and not give up. ²He said: "In a certain town there was a judge who neither feared God nor cared about people. ³And there was a widow in that town who kept coming to him with the plea, 'Grant me justice against my adversary.'

⁴"For some time he refused. But finally he said to himself, 'Even though I don't fear God or care about people, ⁵yet because this widow keeps bothering me, I will see that she gets justice, so that she won't eventually wear me out with her coming!'"

⁶And the Lord said, "Listen to what the unjust judge says. ⁷And will not God bring about justice for his chosen ones, who cry out to him day and night? Will he delay doing anything for a long time? ⁸I tell you, he will see that they get justice, and quickly. However, when the Son of Man comes, will he find faith on the earth?"

The Literary Context of the Parable

The context of the Parable of the Persistent Widow in Luke is quite different from that of the Parable of the Friend at Midnight. For whereas the former parable is preceded and followed by teachings on prayer, the theme of prayer does not appear in the context of the parable here. Instead, this parable is linked with Jesus' eschatological teachings in 17:22-37 — which teachings were a major concern of the evangelist Luke, as has been particularly recognized since the work of Hans Conzelmann.

Following a brief interchange between Jesus and the Pharisees about the nature of the kingdom in 17:20-21, Luke presents in 17:22–18:8 the first of Jesus' two eschatological discourses in his Gospel (the other being in 21:5-36, with parallels in Mark 13:1-37 and Matt 24:1-42). This first discourse is framed by references to the coming of the Son of Man in 17:22 ("The time is coming when you will long to see one of the days of the Son of Man, but you will not see it") and 18:8b ("When the Son of Man comes, will he find faith on the earth?"), which function rhetorically as an *inclusio*. The somber mood of the discourse — as seen in the mention of Jesus' sufferings and rejection (17:25), the detailing of people's evil behavior during the time of Noah (17:26-28), and frequent allusions to judgment (17:27, 29, 32, 33), which culminate in a gruesome depiction of vultures gathering over a dead body (17:37b) — is picked up in the need of both the widow and the elect for vindication (18:3, 7, 8a).

In addition to the prominence of prayer in Luke's theology, which was noted above in connection with the Lord's Prayer, the Parable of the Friend at Midnight, and the two additional prayer Sayings in 11:1-13, there are several other Lukan characteristics that appear prominently in Luke 18. One is the expression to "tell" a parable (cf. vv 1 and 9), which appears more frequently in Luke than in Mark or Matthew. Another is the appearance in verse 1 of the infinitive of the Greek particle *dei*, "it is necessary" (the translation "should" of NIV is weak), which Luke uses in the first passion prediction of 9:22 (cf. the equivalent expressions *mellei* in the second prediction of 9:44 and *telesthēsetai* in the third of 18:31b-33) and elsewhere throughout his Gospel in such texts as 2:49; 4:43; 12:12; 13:14, 33; 19:5; 21:9; 22:37; 24:44. The adjective *tēs adikias* with reference to "the unjust judge" in verse 6 — that is, to a judge characterized by injustice — appears in the same form in Luke's portrayal of "the shrewd manager" in 16:1-9 (see esp. v 8). Furthermore, the introduction to the parable of the persistent widow in verse 1 and the closing word of application in verse 8 both involve issues of the nearness of the *parousia* over against an extended period of waiting, which is what Conzelmann tried to address in his theory that Luke was attempting to explain an alleged "delay" of Jesus' *parousia*.

At the same time, there are words in verses 6b-7 that are not characteristically Lukan — a fact we will shortly discuss in dealing with the form history of the parable. Verse 8b, "But when the Son of Man comes, will he find faith on the earth?," is thought by many to be a Lukan addition. This is possible, though there is no pressing reason to assume it (unless, of course, one has already decided that verses 6b and 7 are not to be considered part of the original parable). Howard Marshall notes that "the saying itself is unexceptional as a teaching of Jesus," and yet wisely concludes that "it is not necessarily Lucan" (*Luke*, 670). Verse 1, however, is introductory, and so presumably Lukan. Furthermore, it needs to be observed that the similarity of the phrase used by the judge in verse 5, "to keep bothering me" *(parechein moi kopon),* and the words of the man in bed in 11:7, "don't bother me" *(mē moi kopous pareche),* suggest either a rather exact translation of an Aramaic expression or consistency in Luke's editing, or both.

In short, the evidences of Luke's editing do not require the conclusion that he forced the Parable of the Persistent Widow in 18:1-8 to fit an eschatological context. Every parable, of course, needs some context. But in spite of the similarities that exist between the parables in 11:5-8 and 18:1-8, we do well to work with the contexts Luke provides rather than go beyond the evidence in other directions.

The Form of the Parable

There are several significant differences in the form of the Parable of the Persistent Widow from that of the Parable of the Friend at Midnight. The narrative is not related *within* the dialogue, as it was in 11:5-8. In fact, our parable here does not contain dialogue, but is, rather, a soliloquy. The so-called "law of end stress," of course, is similarly operative here, and the outcome is unexpected and outrageous. Likewise, the focus is on just two people (the balance of emphasis being a matter of interpretation). But the characters are more sharply defined in this story about a widow and a judge than in the story about a host and a man in bed. And the characters of this story are at opposite ends of the social continuum in terms of power, which is a fact that not only is important to the story itself but also adds to its interest and memorability.

Status and Lukan Redaction

g of this story about a widow and a judge is clearly Palestinian, characters fitting into the social life known to Jesus. The Jesus gave the parable a "pink" rating, meaning that "Jesus probably nething like this" — though they considered verses 1 and 6-8 to be editorial inventions (cf. R. W. Funk, B. B. Scott, and J. R. Butts, *The Parables of Jesus: Red Letter Edition* [Sonoma, CA: Polebridge, 1988], 41).

If this parable had been given by Jesus as an encouragement during a period of persecution, it is easy to see why it would have been preserved by the early church and eventually selected by Luke. There is no reason why its position in Luke's Gospel could not reflect an original association with Jesus' eschatological teachings. People throughout biblical history — and since — have "waited" on God in times of trouble. For Luke to use this parable to address such a circumstance would hardly have been different from Jesus' original intention. And as for the closing comments in verses 6-8, their place in the tradition and editing are assessed variously. One might venture to say that any attempt to peel them away from the original parable and to construct their history differently must involve considerable speculation.

The main difficulty in construing this section as an original whole is the tension between God's delay (or patience), which is an acknowledged theme in Luke's Gospel, and the assertion that the elect will get justice "quickly" (v 8a). If this is Luke's way of glossing over the expectation of an imminent *parousia* by substituting the idea of an interim period, it is a clumsy way of doing it. But if this is a tension that is in accord with Jesus' teachings elsewhere in the Gospels — as well, of course, with God's ways in history as portrayed elsewhere in the Bible — our task is not to adjust our theory of transmission and redaction but to correct our theology and its application. That does not mean that we must see the entire framework of the parable as part of the original parable. Rather, such an approach suggests that the framework of the parable does not confront us with a severe disjunction caused by Luke's supposed misunderstanding and misapplication of Jesus' story.

The Story of the Parable

As we approach the interpretation of this story, we note that several of its aspects are rather obscure. Was the judge Jewish? Was the widow appealing to a Hellenistic court? Who was her adversary? Was she without relatives? Was the case about the inheritance due her as a widow? How large was the "town"? (Luke refers to it twice as a *polis*.) Was there some reason to state that both the judge and the widow were from the same town? Why did the woman not offer a bribe? Was she destitute? Why did she persist in pressing her case? Why did the judge not simply grant her request at the outset? If he feared no one, could he not have simply ruled in her favor to begin with? Were the judge and the widow adversaries, or friends, or, at least, of the same social class? A question even more pertinent to the interpretation is: If the judge had no fear of God and no "respect for people" (NRSV), why would he worry, as one interpretation proposes, about his reputation? Such questions have been discussed in detail most recently by William Herzog in his *Parables as Subversive Speech* (215-32). They need not all, however, be answered in order to construct an interpretation.

Some aspects of the situation, however, are clear enough. Widows were marginalized and vulnerable (cf. 1 Tim 5:3-16 for the response of the church). This woman did not have to be old or physically debilitated to be at a severe disadvantage. The fact that there was an adversary meant that the judge was not dealing with a financial matter that affected only her. The adversary does not figure in the structure of the parable, but he certainly does in the assumed background of the story. And the position and character of the judge are clearly delineated.

Jesus was painting the picture with bold strokes to emphasize the difference between the characters and the magnitude of the woman's effect on the judge. That does not imply that the scene or action is distorted. If it were an impossible situation, the parable would have had less authenticity; but if the woman's action and the judge's response were not outrageous, the parable would have had less impact. Without any further detail being given, we know that truth was on the widow's side. Furthermore, with Herzog, we can probably assume that her action of going beyond the bounds of what was customary was done so as to bring the teachings of the Torah about care for widows to bear on the situation (cf. *ibid.*, 230-32).

The widow's persistence had already become an affliction to the judge, but he fears that "eventually" or "at the end" *(eis telos)* she will "wear me out" (*hupōpiazē me*). This verb could refer to a blow by a boxer. It is questionable, however, that we should infer from this that he was afraid that she would in some way physically brutalize him. Is Jesus painting a scene so comic and outrageous that a judge is afraid of being physically attacked by a widow? The fact that the verb could also mean to give someone a "black eye" in a metaphorical sense has led to the possibility that this judge was afraid of losing his reputation. But if he already feared no one, how could this be so? It is probably better, therefore, to interpret the widow's actions and the judge's response in the context of a culture of shame and honor — that is, to see implied in the story the scenario that if she causes him to be known as someone who ignores a widow in need, such shame could overbalance any self-bestowed "honor" that he cherishes of being a "tough judge."

The Teaching of the Parable

It would seem that each character in the parable of 11:5-8 and the parable of 18:1-8 — both the petitioner and the one being petitioned — is intended to draw the hearer/reader's attention. At the same time, the ultimate focus in both parables is on the response of the second figure. By means of a lesser-to-greater argument, we learn that if even the man in bed or the unjust judge responds in spite of their reluctance, we can certainly count on God to respond.

But whereas in the midnight scene persistence is not a factor, in the judicial scene it is of utmost importance. The woman needs vindication. The situation is prolonged and heading toward a climax (recalling the phrase *eis telos*, "eventually" or "at the end"). So the "elect" cry "day and night." This element of prolongation has surfaced in the Parable of the Persistent Widow as being significant, and so the natural question now is whether God will take a long time to bring justice or vindication to those suffering in the period described in 17:22-37.

A further question that relates to the conclusion in verse 7 is the meaning of the interrogative clause *kai makrothumei ep' autois* (NIV: "Will he keep putting them off?"). The connective *kai* can have several nuances (such as "and," "ever," "although," or even represent a different meaning in the underlying Aramaic). Also, the verb *makrothumeō* ("have patience," "put off," "wait") can have several meanings related to the idea of waiting,

such as delaying or being patient or forbearing. Even the referent of *ep'*
autois ("for them") is not completely certain (cf. Marshall, *Luke*, 674-75,
for an analysis of the various proposed interpretations).

Given the vocabulary and grammar — coupled with the facts that
(1) God promises vindication, (2) a period of waiting seems inevitable
given the context, (3) the reference seems to be to the elect, and (4) part of
the answer is "quickly" — the question of verse 7b should probably be
read: "Will God delay doing anything for a long time?" Verse 8a provides
the answer: No, God will act "quickly" *(en tachei)*. But this expression
"quickly" functions not to measure the speed of God's response in "real
time," but to complete the strong contrast with the judge's methodical and
deliberate delay. The question then turns in verse 8b from how God acts
during the waiting period to how the hearers and readers respond, and
whether they will endure with respect to the faith: "However, when the
Son of Man comes, will he find faith on the earth?"

3. The Parable of the Pharisee
and the Tax Collector (Luke 18:9-14)

[9]To some who were confident of their own righteousness and looked
down on everybody else, Jesus told this parable: [10]"Two men went up to
the temple to pray, one a Pharisee and the other a tax collector. [11]The
Pharisee stood up and prayed about himself: 'God, I thank you that I am
not like other people — robbers, evildoers, adulterers — or even like this
tax collector. [12]I fast twice a week and give a tenth of all I get.'

[13]"But the tax collector stood at a distance. He would not even look
up to heaven, but beat his breast and said, 'God, have mercy on me, a
sinner.'

[14]"I tell you that this man, rather than the other, went home justified
before God. For all those who exalt themselves will be humbled, and
those who humble themselves will be exalted."

The Context of the Parable

As with the Parable of the Persistent Widow, Luke prefaces the Parable of
the Pharisee and the Tax Collector with an introduction to guide the

reader to its significance. And as do the two parables just discussed, this parable also features two strong figures. But the introduction of this parable draws attention particularly to the first figure, with a reference to those who are self-righteous and look down on others. Nonetheless, the conclusion in verse 14b, whether part of Jesus' saying or Luke's addition, refers to both attitudes — to both self-exaltation and self-humbling.

In Luke's introductory formula, "Jesus told this parable," the reader is informed that this is only a story and not about two actual people. But it has become so familiar that modern readers often forget this and do not allow for parabolic exaggeration. Jesus' original hearers, however, would have known these two characters well, and probably would have been eager to hear exaggerated descriptions — much as theological conservatives and theological liberals today all-too-often like to hear and tell stories about their heroes and villains. But Jesus reversed their roles, and so both his words of condemnation and his words of commendation would have come as a surprise to his original hearers. Those of us who read Luke's account in later times are not as knowledgeable, and so can easily miss the force and shock of the original telling. More than that, many of us who have read Luke's Gospel have only negative attitudes toward the Pharisees and warm feelings toward repentant tax collectors.

Dominical Status and Lukan Redaction

The originality of this parable may seem a foregone conclusion, and the tracing of any form history unnecessary. But some, in particular the Fellows of the Jesus Seminar, consider both the form and framework of this story to be a construction stemming from the latter part of the first century, "when the rivalry between Christianity and Judaism produced considerable acrimony" (Funk, Scott, and Butts, *The Parables of Jesus: Red Letter Edition*, 56). The judgment of Luise Schottroff ("Die Erzählung vom Pharisäer und Zöllner als Beispiel für die Theologische Kunst des Uberredens," in *Neues Testament und christliche Existenz*, ed. H. D. Betz and L. Schottroff [Tübingen: Mohr, 1973], 439-61) that this is a caricature of the Pharisees is often cited, either with disapproval (e.g., Marshall, *Luke*, 678), or, less often, with approval and even as a strong case (e.g., F. G. Downing, "The Ambiguity of 'the Pharisee and the Toll-Collector,'" 84-86).

But while *caricature* can imply unfairness, *exaggeration* (as just noted) is not only permissible but to be expected in a parable such as this. We need not assume that Jesus' intention was to criticize Pharisees and commend tax collectors, but to contrast two attitudes. And instead of doing this abstractly, Jesus makes up a story and selects two well-known types, one religious and one not, to facilitate the description and the shocking conclusion.

The Teaching of the Parable

To interpret the Parable of the Pharisee and the Tax Collector it is important, first, to observe the Pharisee's attitude: that he was confident of his own righteousness. This attitude on the part of certain Pharisees had already been condemned by Jesus in Luke 16:15, "You are the ones who justify yourselves in the eyes of people, but God knows your hearts." Such an attitude is also familiar from Paul's confession in Phil 3:4-6, where he lists the reasons he had for putting confidence in the flesh. But also it needs to be noted that with such an attitude, the Pharisees looked down on others. Their confidence in themselves called for an object of scorn, and this is a role for which the tax collector was an ideal candidate.

Jesus portrays the tax collector in an attitude of repentance in order to give the lie to the Pharisee's assumption. While readers of Luke's Gospel know that Jesus was strongly criticized for his association with "sinners," those who criticized him could have been put on the defensive if they objected to one of the sinners repenting in the shadow of the Jerusalem temple. For the Pharisee to go home unjustified, however, would have been unthinkable, even though the hypocrisy of some Pharisees was caricatured in Jewish literature of that period. Gerald Downing's extensive research into examples of prayers of both genuine and false penitence, which he presses into service to discredit the tax collector's prayer (cf. "The Ambiguity of 'the Pharisee and the Toll-Collector'"), needs, indeed, to be taken into consideration. But those examples must not be allowed to distract our attention from the focal point of the story in Luke: that what is missing from the Pharisee's prayer, but was present in that of the tax collector, was confession and repentance.

4. Conclusion

These three parables of Jesus on prayer have portrayed God as (1) the one who will maintain his honor and not allow us to be ashamed in approaching him in prayer (The Friend at Midnight), (2) the one who will not hesitate to vindicate those who cry to him, though he may seem to be delaying (The Persistent Widow), and (3) the one who accepts the prayers of those who come with confession and repentance (The Pharisee and the Tax Collector). An explication of how one can, like the tax collector, be "justified" had to wait until after Jesus' death and resurrection.

Selected Bibliography

Bailey, Kenneth E. *Poet and Peasant: A Literary Cultural Approach to the Parables in Luke*. Grand Rapids: Eerdmans, 1976.

Blomberg, Craig L. *Interpreting the Parables*. Downers Grove: InterVarsity, 1990.

Catchpole, David R. "Q and 'The Friend at Midnight' (Luke xi.5-8/9)," *Journal of Theological Studies* 34 (1983) 407-24.

Cranfield, C. E. B. "The Parable of the Unjust Judge and the Eschatology of Luke-Acts," *Scottish Journal of Theology* 16 (1963) 297-301.

Derrett, J. Duncan M. "Law in the New Testament: The Parable of the Unjust Judge," *New Testament Studies* 18 (1972) 178-91.

———. "The Friend at Midnight: Asian Ideas in the Gospel of St. Luke," in *Donum Gentilicum*, ed. E. Bammel, C. K. Barrett, and W. D. Davies. Oxford: Clarendon, 1978.

Donahue, John R. *The Gospel in Parable*. Philadelphia: Fortress, 1988.

Downing, F. Gerald. "The Ambiguity of 'the Pharisee and the Toll-Collector' (Luke 18:9-14) in the Greco-Roman World of Late Antiquity," *Catholic Biblical Quarterly* 54 (1992) 80-99.

Fitzmyer, Joseph A. *The Gospel According to Luke X–XXIV*. Garden City: Doubleday, 1985.

Green, Joel B. *The Gospel of Luke*. Grand Rapids: Eerdmans, 1997.

Herzog, William R., II. *Parables as Subversive Speech: Jesus as Pedagogue of the Oppressed*. Louisville: Westminster/John Knox, 1994.

Huffard, Everett W. "The Parable of the Friend at Midnight: God's Honor or Man's Persistence?," *Restoration Quarterly* 21 (1978) 154-60.

Johnson, Alan F. "Assurance for Man: The Fallacy of Translating *anaideia* by 'Persistence' in Luke 11:5-8," *Journal of the Evangelical Theological Society* 22 (1979) 123-31.

Marshall, I. Howard. *The Gospel of Luke: A Commentary on the Greek Text.* Exeter: Paternoster; Grand Rapids: Eerdmans, 1978.

Snodgrass, Klyne. "*Anaideia* and the Friend at Midnight (Luke 11:8)," *Journal of Biblical Literature* 116 (1997) 505-13.

Talbert, Charles H. *Reading Luke: A Literary and Theological Commentary on the Third Gospel.* New York: Crossroad, 1982.

CHAPTER 12

Strange Neighbors and Risky Care
(Matt 18:21-35; Luke 14:7-14; Luke 10:25-37)

SYLVIA C. KEESMAAT

IT IS TEMPTING when reading the parables of Jesus — especially when reading his parables about the forgiveness of debt, welcoming an outcast, or loving an enemy — to begin by ferreting out the context of the original hearers or the situation of the early church, but to leave a consideration of our own context as the last step — with, perhaps, the insertion of two paragraphs or so at the end of the exercise that make some vague connections to our contemporary world. There are good reasons for this impulse. After all, one cannot understand what Jesus was really saying without knowing his context and that of his listeners. It is also a safer way to read the parables, for it ensures that engagement between a text and its context do not become too uncomfortably close to our own world.

Such a reading, however, does a disservice both to the texts themselves and to the words of hope and challenge that they speak to the problems facing us as individuals, as churches, and as societies. So I want to begin this article with a brief reflection on some features of our contemporary context that set the stage for an engagement between these texts and our world. I will then explore the meaning of these parables in Jesus' context — although our own world will always be there, lurking in the background. Finally, I want to conclude with consideration given, once again, to some broader connections.

SYLVIA C. KEESMAAT

1. Our Contemporary Context: Setting the Stage

The parables we will be dealing with here are the parables of the Unforgiving Servant (or, the Forgiving King) in Matt 18:21-35, the Banquet in Luke 14:7-14, and the Good (or "Compassionate") Samaritan in Luke 10:25-37. All three of these parables raise issues that are pressing in our world today. The first deals with matters having to do with forgiveness and debt; the second, whom we welcome with gracious abundance to our tables; and the third, an enemy whom we not only hate but also find immoral and repulsive.

It does not take much imagination to see how these themes are played out in our contemporary contexts. Take the issue of debt. On a global level, less developed countries paid out over $2.9 trillion (US) in principal payments on their debts to the North between 1981 and 1997. This is about $1.5 trillion (US) more than — in fact, double — what they received in new loans. For every dollar that northern countries provide in aid to less developed countries, over three come back in the form of debt servicing. The funds to service these debts are diverted from basic services: health, nutrition, clean water, education, and housing. Indeed, cutbacks in such areas are required by the lending countries for further aid (cf. Canadian Ecumenical Jubilee Initiative, *A New Beginning: A Call for Jubilee*).

Closer to home, of course, the paying down of our national debt is central to the platforms of most of our political parties, with similar economic cuts to social services.

But that is not all, for we live in a culture where the ethos of forgiveness is not generally accepted or welcomed. Such an unforgiving culture is often reflected in our churches, where schism is more prevalent than unity. For instance, the church I grew up in, which is itself the result of a schism earlier this century in Holland, has recently had a group split off once again. And I do not need to say much about the lack of forgiveness in our personal lives and the violence and fragmentation that it creates for each of us. We know that reality too well. What do Jesus' parables say to such local and global contexts?

Or take the issue of welcoming the outcast and graciously sharing our abundance with them. Who are the ones whom we do not want to invite into our churches because they will threaten the purity of the community? Who are the ones whom we do not want to share our wealth with because they do not deserve it? Who are the ones whom Jesus is calling us to invite to the communion table, the ones we would not want to sit with or expose our children to? Who are the ones whom we are sure do not deserve to share our abundance because they cannot pay anything — those too schizophrenic, or too homeless, or too deeply entrenched in welfare? What do Jesus' parables have to say to this societal ethos?

Or take the issue of our enemy. In spite of so-called globalization, we continue to see an escalation of tribalism and nationalism in our world. Ethnic cleansing, racial genocide, these are the realities that face us daily as we look at the papers. And as immigration levels continue, these are the issues that we will face more and more in our neighborhoods and in our Christian communities. How do we deal with pluralism without hating others who are different than we are? How do we love those whose identity is tied up with a way of life we find repugnant, both morally and otherwise? How do we learn to love our enemy as a neighbor? What words of hope do Jesus' parables have for these perplexing and pressing problems?

When one puts the problems in these ways, it becomes apparent why Jesus spoke in parables rather than by means of such commands as "Your neighbor is anyone you meet in need," or "Love your enemy," or "Forgive one another." These complex political and social realities are deeply rooted in the worldview of our culture — in our assumptions about money and success, in our fears about our own security, and in situations of scarcity rather than abundance. And the realities of the first century were no less complex.

In such contexts, the parables of Jesus do far more than merely suggest a few ways to change one's behavior. Rather, Jesus' parables fundamentally reorder and reshape reality. They function to create a world for Jesus' hearers that presents a challenge to the prevailing worldview. For in telling these parables, Jesus is creating a new world for his hearers — the world of the new kingdom that he is inaugurating. As he invites his hearers to enter into the stories of his parables, he is inviting them to enter into that world and so to join him in the new kingdom and its vision. Furthermore, he is calling for a fundamental renunciation of who they are — a repentance, if you will — and a fundamental reorientation in how they view the world. And so we have before us three parables: the Unforgiving Servant of Matthew 18, the Banquet of Luke 14, and the Compassionate Samaritan of Luke 10.

2. The Parable of the Unforgiving Servant (Matt 18:21-35)

"How often should I forgive my brother if he sins against me?" asks Peter. "As many as seven times?" (Matt 18:21). "Not seven times," answers Jesus, "but seventy-seven times [or, perhaps, 'seventy times seven']" (v 22). The exact number, of course, is not the issue here. For both "seventy-seven" and "seventy times seven" are enormous numbers.

In the Old Testament the number seven is the number of fulfillment and, more importantly, the number of Sabbath. Every seven years debts are to be forgiven (cf. Deut 15). And every seven times seven is the year of Jubilee, when slaves are to be freed as well (cf. Lev 25). In fact, freeing from slavery in the ancient world was a matter of debt forgiveness, since one became a slave if one was unable to pay one's debts. An emphasis on "seventy times seven," therefore, would evoke the sabbatical forgiveness of Israel's past.

Also, it needs to be recognized that in the first century the language of the forgiveness of sins was a language that spoke to the deepest hopes of the people, for it was a language that signaled their return from exile (cf. Wright, *Jesus and the Victory of God*, 268). When Jesus forgave the sins of those who came to him for healing, he not only undermined the authority of the temple priests (who were the only ones authorized to perform the sacrifices that resulted in forgiveness), he also evoked the great promises of the dawn of God's new age as found in Israel's Scriptures. All three of the great visionary prophets, Isaiah, Jeremiah, and Ezekiel, describe God's restoration of the people in terms of a return to the land, where they will experience safety, fruitfulness, and forgiveness. The language used is that of a new exodus, for it is in the exodus that God has portrayed his way of dealing with this wayward people as being through forgiveness (cf. Exod 32–34).

Thus the description of the new covenant in Jeremiah 31 ends with the affirmation that "they shall all know me, from the least of them to the greatest, says the Lord; for I will forgive their iniquity and remember their sin no more" (v 34). Similarly, in Jeremiah's vision of restoration, God proclaims:

> I will bring [to Jerusalem] recovery and healing; I will heal them and reveal to them abundance of prosperity and security. I will restore the fortunes of Judah and fortunes of Israel, and rebuild them as they were at first. I will cleanse them from all their guilt of sin against me, and I will

forgive all the guilt of their sin and rebellion against me. And this city shall be to me a name of joy, a praise and glory before all the nations of the earth who shall hear of all the good that I do for them; they shall fear and tremble because of all the good and all the prosperity I provide for it. (33:6-11)

And while Ezekiel records the magnificent vision of sprinkling clean water on the people and giving them a heart of flesh for their heart of stone (Ezek 36:25), Isaiah prophesies a servant who will make many righteous by bearing their iniquities (Isa 53:11-12).

All of these passages were central to first-century expectations. They are echoed not only in the Gospels but also throughout Paul's letters (cf. Keesmaat, *Paul and His Story*). Likewise, the actions of the rebels who took over the temple during the Jewish revolt indicate that their expectations of God's new kingdom included the forgiveness of debt. For one of the first things that those rebels did was to burn the existing records of debt in the temple treasury (cf. Josephus, *War* 2.426-27). So when Jesus began not only to forgive sins but also to proclaim forgiveness as a defining characteristic of the kingdom and those within it, his hearers would undoubtedly have understood the fulfillment of God's great promises in the terms found in both the Torah and the prophetic literature.

In such a context, therefore, it is no surprise that Jesus launched into a parable about debt in response to a question concerning forgiveness. "The kingdom of heaven," he says, "may be compared to a king who wished to settle accounts with his servants" (v 23). Notice that the context here assumes that the king will be dealing with *all* of his servants. But he begins the process of accounting by first dealing with a servant who owed him ten thousand talents (v 24).

Considering the fact that Herod's annual income was nine hundred talents and that all the taxes collected in Galilee and Perea together amounted to only two hundred talents annually, ten thousand talents would be equivalent to millions of dollars of debt (cf. Ringe, "Solidarity and Contextuality," 203). The number, in fact, is so astronomical that it would have been impossible to repay. Thus, since the servant could not pay, his master ordered him sold — that is, the man along with his wife and children were to be sold into slavery (v 25). But when the servant promised the impossible, to try to pay off the debt, the king had compassion and released him and forgave his multimillion-dollar debt (vv 26-27).

The situation of an impossibly high debt was one that was altogether too common in the first century. As a number of studies have shown, the heavy burden of taxation in first-century Israel ensured that many farmers lost their land and therefore their income. Furthermore, not only was debt common, but the impossibility of emerging out of it was increasingly common as well.

Israel's Torah, of course, demanded that debt be forgiven every seven years. But some of the Pharisees had set up a legal fiction called *prozbul,* which enabled the holder of a debt to give the debt over to the courts. Because the debt was then no longer a personal debt, it did not have to be forgiven in the seventh year. One of the reasons given for this law was that creditors were not lending in the sixth year, since they knew that the next year they would have to forgive their loan. On the face of it, therefore, finding a way around debt forgiveness supposedly opened up credit. The end result, however, was the perpetuation of debt in the land, for such a law leads to increased incidence of foreclosure rather than forgiveness (for the relevant texts, see Neusner, *Rabbinic Traditions,* 1.217-22).

So Jesus set up a scenario here that was, on an initial hearing, entirely plausible and believable for first-century Jews. They knew all-too-well how such stories would unfold in their own situations: a lord or landowner decides to settle his accounts and forecloses on his debtors; those who owe him money end up losing their land — with the result that the debtors, along with their wives, sons, and daughters, end up becoming slaves.

Incredibly, however, in Jesus' kingdom this story turns out differently. The servant begs and pleads for time. Surprisingly, what is granted him is release from slavery and a total forgiveness of his debt. Coming after all those sabbath numbers, the overtones are unmistakable. This is a king who proclaims Jubilee for his servant. After all, the sabbath and jubilee legislation of Deut 15 and Lev 25 was for precisely this sort of situation — for an impossibly high debt that could not be paid off. Jesus' hearers would have heard, with ever increasing joy, that the kingdom Jesus proclaimed was, indeed, a fulfillment of the Mosaic law. Jubilee was finally being enacted!

The story, of course, could have continued by recounting further details about the king. After all, we have been told that the king wished to settle accounts with *all* of his servants. Presumably, therefore, he continued to deal with his other servants as he had dealt with the first, proclaiming a gracious release and forgiveness beyond anyone's wildest expectations or hopes. But that is not where the story goes, for its action shifts to the forgiven servant.

Now that the forgiven servant has experienced this great jubilee event — now that he has discovered that the world of his lord's kingdom is one of graciousness and forgiveness — how will he live in that kingdom? Now that he has discovered the true nature of the lord he serves, will he, in turn, display that nature to anyone else? Having discovered the graciousness that is at the heart of this kingdom, will he live out this "economy of grace" himself? Well, you know the answer. The forgiven servant, coming upon a fellow servant who owed him a few hundred denarii, which is approximately ten thousand dollars in today's terms, refuses to cut him any slack when he cannot pay and throws him into prison (vv 28-30).

This forgiven servant has not gotten the point. He has not figured out that now he lives in a kingdom that operates by completely different rules, by a completely different law, and so he acts as though he were still in the old regime. To put it in the terms of Israel's Scriptures, this servant is acting as though he is still in Egypt rather than the promised land. His failure to forgive someone else shocks his fellow servants — some of whom, presumably, have also just had their debts forgiven — and as a result they report him to the king (v 31). His final punishment is far worse than his original enslavement would have been (vv 32-34). So, says Jesus, your heavenly father will do to you if you do not forgive your brother and sister from the heart (v 35).

What kind of a world does the story of this parable create? One that is far beyond the expectations of most first-century Jews, but maybe not beyond their wildest hopes. For just as the language of forgiveness speaks of the restoration of the people and God's presence with them once again, so the language of debt forgiveness highlights the fact of a new order in which economic liberation is to be experienced and the people are to be slaves no more. Such a hope of wide-ranging forgiveness was deeply rooted in Israel's Scriptures.

Sadly, the interpretation of this parable throughout the centuries has tended to drive a wedge between the forgiveness of sins and the forgiveness of debts. The argument has often been summarized like this: "The Jewish people of Jesus' day expected a Messiah who would release them from bondage to the Romans and forgive all their debts. Jesus, however, proclaimed a more radical message than they could imagine, since he proclaimed forgiveness of *sin* rather than mere monetary debt. In pinning their hopes on the forgiveness of monetary debt, the Jews show how mistaken they were in their thinking." The end result of such a dualistic reading of the gospel message — and of such a misreading of first-century Judaism — is that many readers of this parable have been able to separate the forgiveness of sins and the forgiveness of debts, as if the former is a Christian concern and the latter is not.

But the evidence of Israel's Scriptures and the Christian Gospels is entirely otherwise. In fact, throughout the Old Testament and the story of Jesus' ministry these two features are always intertwined. In Israel's Scriptures, forgiveness of sin and redemption from slavery were the hallmarks of God's dealing with his covenant people. Moreover, forgiveness of debt was central to how such forgiveness and redemption were to be manifested in the community that God called together to bear his image.

In the year of Jubilee, as we noted earlier, there was to be a total economic leveling, which was to involve both the release of slaves and the return of lands to their original owners. Slavery and the loss of land were, of course, almost always the result of debt. Such laws were rooted in Israel's memory of God's redeeming action: because God released his enslaved people from Egyptian bondage, so Israel is called to image God by being a slave-releasing community (cf. Deut 15:15). In the new covenant reality to which God calls his people, forgiveness is to extend far beyond the personal sphere of life to the social and economic spheres as well. For not only does God's covenantal reign proclaim a radically new way of being in our "spiritual" lives, God's reign also proclaims a new beginning socially and economically. One cannot proclaim the reign of God and not practice that reign in every area of life.

When Nehemiah returned to the land with the Israelites who had been exiled, it became clear that this issue of indebtedness was one that was threatening the very fabric of their community. So Nehemiah proclaimed that all taking of interest was to stop and all debts were to be forgiven — that is, all fields, vineyards, and olive orchards were to be restored to their original owners (cf. Neh 5:1-13). Shortly thereafter, when the people pledged themselves once again to the covenant, there were four main things that they pledged themselves to: (1) no intermarriage, (2) no buying on the Sabbath, (3) the giving of tithes, and (4) the forgoing of crops and the forgiveness of debts every seventh year (Neh 10:28-39). Clearly the forgiveness of debt was seen as a defining characteristic of what it was to be the people of God.

Those who came into contact with Jesus seem to have interpreted his message in just this way. Zacchaeus, for example, on receiving Jesus into his home, promises to give half of his possessions to the poor and to return fourfold anything he had taken through cheating (Luke 19:1-10). The rich young man is told to sell all that he has, give the money to the poor, and follow Jesus in order to inherit eternal life (Mark 10:17-31). And both Matthew and Luke in their tellings of the Lord's Prayer explicitly link the forgiveness of monetary debt and the forgiveness of sin. Matthew does this by recording the prayer: "Forgive us our debts, as we forgive our debtors" *(opheiletas)* — commenting on this petition in terms of the forgiveness of sins *(paraptomata)*. Luke, even more strikingly, records: "Forgive us our sins *(hamartias)*, for we forgive all who are indebted *(opheilonti)* to us." The Greek word used for debt in both of these texts is one that means an economic debt. The forgiveness of sins, therefore, is linked explicitly to the forgiving of economic debts.

The early church, too, seems to have interpreted Jesus in this way. The experience of Jesus' followers at Pentecost is said in Acts 2:44-47 to have resulted in newly baptized believers selling all that they had in order to share with those in need. There is here an economic leveling that is fully consistent with the intent of Jubilee. And Paul's call to an economic sharing amongst the churches is rooted in the same ethos (cf. esp. 2 Cor 8 and 9; see also Jas 1:27; 2:15).

Clearly, then, Jesus has told a story that draws deeply from the Scriptures of Israel and that highlights the fact that the central features of the new age have dawned — that is, the forgiveness of sins and the forgiveness of debts. Moreover, in telling this story he has drawn his listeners into this new world of forgiveness and described a reality that they must either accept or reject. But there are other dimensions to the reality of the kingdom that are even more radical than what has been articulated here. Let us, therefore, move on to our next passage.

3. The Parable of the Banquet (Luke 14:7-14)

The Parable of the Banquet in Luke 14:7-14 also draws on the hopes and expectations of Israel. But it subverts and undermines those expectations in a totally unexpected way. Let us set the context and spell out the parable.

Jesus has been invited to dinner at the home of a prominent Phari-

271

see. While there, he launches into a criticism of those very people who had shown him hospitality. Here he is, the guest of a leading Pharisee. But he is so lacking in graciousness that he tells those gathered a parable that seems to undermine all of the protocols of his host's dinner etiquette. It is a strange parable of odd reversal: From now on your attitude at a banquet is to be that of the least, the lowest. In a social setting where rank — especially at a common meal — confirms one's social status in the community, such advice would have been regarded as absolutely crazy. It would completely undermine one's position in the community.

Jesus then continues to address his host and those at the table as follows:

> When you give a luncheon or a dinner, do not invite your friends or your brothers or your relatives or rich neighbors, in case they may invite you in return, and you would be repaid. But when you give a banquet, invite the poor, the crippled, the lame and the blind. And you will be blessed, because they cannot repay you, for you will be repaid at the resurrection of the righteous. (vv 12-14)

Remember to whom Jesus is here talking — to a leading, respected Pharisee. Now, one thing we know about the Pharisees is that they were a group within first-century Judaism who attempted to bring holiness to Israel by keeping in their own lives the laws of purity, especially as they pertained to table-fellowship, to eating together. Consequently, the presence of sinners or other "unclean" people at the table would threaten the very purity that the Pharisees were trying to maintain. Because so much depended on such a meal — that is, the purity and holiness of the nation itself — such threats carried far more weight than a mere breach of etiquette. The very status and future of the nation, as they viewed it, was at stake.

So what were some of these rules of purity? Well, one in particular is relevant to this passage. It can be found in Lev 21:16-20:

> The Lord spoke to Moses, saying: "Speak to Aaron and say: 'No one of your offspring throughout their generations who has a blemish may approach to offer the food of his God. For no one who has a blemish shall draw near — one who is blind or lame, or who has a mutilated face, or a limb too long, or one who has a broken foot or a broken hand, or a

hunchback, or a dwarf, or a man with a blemish in his eyes or an itching disease or scabs or crushed testicles.'"

These are the ones who were not permitted to offer the Lord's food by fire. They were, however, permitted to eat of the food, unless they were also in a state of ritual uncleanness.

Another indication of stringent requirements for meals can be found in the Manual of Discipline of the Dead Sea Scrolls. At Qumran the participants in such a meal sat according to rank. Gentiles were excluded, as were all imperfect Jews. No one was allowed who was "smitten in his flesh, or paralyzed in his feet and hands, or lame, or blind, or deaf, or dumb, or smitten in his flesh with a visible blemish" (1QSa 2.11-12; trans. G. Vermes, *The Dead Sea Scrolls in English*, 2nd ed. [Harmondsworth, Middlesex: Penguin Books, 1975], 120).

It is not entirely clear whether the laws found in Lev 21 or the Qumran Manual of Discipline were applied by the Pharisees to their table fellowship. What is clear, however, is that the Pharisees' stringent requirements for meal preparation and eating ensured that most of their fellow Jews — especially those who were wanting in some way — would have been excluded from table fellowship with them.

In such a context, Jesus' comments would undoubtedly have been seen as being more and more offensive. For not only does he begin by criticizing the behavior of his host and fellow dinner guests by pointing out their selfishness in seeking the best seats, he then goes on to criticize the fact of their presence and to suggest an entirely different guest list. Moreover, not only is it a different guest list, it is one that includes people who would be most likely to defeat the whole purpose of the meal — that is, people who would be on the list of "those who can defile the sanctuary." Such defilement was precisely what the Pharisees were trying to avoid.

But that is not all. For a holy meal that was prepared by clean hands and eaten by a holy people would anticipate, for a first-century Pharisee, the eschatological banquet that God will set before his people when they are restored in the land. And so just as debt relief and forgiveness were important parts of Israel's expectation for God's new age, so is also a time of abundant food and feasting.

A few obvious passages come to mind. Ps 23:5 is one such passage, where a banquet is prepared in the face of threat and an enemy. Likewise, Isa 25:6-9, where a banquet is set for all the nations — though, of course, enemies are to be excluded, as verse 10 tells us in speaking about Moabites being trodden down in a dung pit! And there are a host of other Old Testament passages, including some we have already discussed, that speak about an abundance of grain and wine in God's coming age of restoration.

Joel, for example, says that "the threshing floors shall be full of grain, the vats shall overflow with wine and oil" (2:24; see also vv 18-27), and, strikingly, that "the mountains shall drip sweet wine and the hills shall flow with milk" (3:18). Employing the same image of the mountains dripping wine, Amos goes further and evokes the image of the one plowing overtaking the reaper, and the treader of grapes overtaking the one who sows the seed (9.13). Such images of overabundance echo Lev 26:5, where an abundance is promised as a result of obedience to Torah.

Again, in Isa 55:1 the call of God is this: "Ho, everyone who thirsts, come to the waters! And you who have no money, come, buy and eat! Come, buy wine and milk without money and without price." Notice especially that this food is for those "without money." It is abundance for those who cannot buy wine and milk themselves. Jer 31:14 promises, "My people shall be satisfied with my bounty"; Ezek 34:29 promises that the people will "no longer be consumed with hunger in the land." And in that magnificent passage quoted earlier from Ezekiel 36, God connects forgiveness and abundance: "I will save you from all your uncleanness, and I will summon the rain and make it abundant and lay no famine upon you. I will make the fruit of the tree and the produce of the field abundant, so that you may never again suffer the disgrace of famine among the nations" (vv 29-30; cf. Hos 2:21-23).

Although not all of these passages are talking specifically about a banquet that is set for the people, they all highlight the importance in Israelite expectations of God's abundant offering of food and wine for his people in the new age. Jesus' actions of eating and drinking and providing food for the hungry (cf. Matt 14:13-21//Mark 6:30-44//Luke 9:10-17; Luke 7:31-35; John 6:1-13; Matt 15:32-38//Mark 8:1-9) would, therefore, have undoubtedly drawn to mind these promises of God's abundance in the eschatological age.

What would this have meant for those Pharisees who were eating and drinking with Jesus? It is clear that such a group, by its emphasis on the significance of meals as a preparation for the coming kingdom, would have been aware of these prophetic texts and have been attempting to work within the symbolic world that they present. But it is also clear that Jesus was completely undermining their expectations by insisting that the coming eschatological banquet will consist not only of the holy, but also will include the outcasts of society — that is, those found in the streets and the lanes, as the following parable of the Wedding Banquet in 14:15-24 (esp. v 21) makes clear.

In effect, Jesus is saying: God's new age has dawned; the kingdom has arrived; and the people who are enjoying my banquet are not those who were expected. Indeed, this parable of 14:7-14 follows shortly after a passage that states that not everyone who expects to enter the feast will be able to do so; that many will come from east and west, from north and south, to eat in this kingdom, but that the last will be first and the first will be last (cf. 13:22-30). So also the Parable of the Wedding Banquet of 14:15-24, which follows our passage, ends with the assertion that "none of those who were invited will taste my dinner" (v 24).

The implications for these Pharisees are clear. If they wish to partake in Jesus' new kingdom, they need to be willing to join the banquet with all kinds of people whom they had never expected to sit at table with. That is all it will take. But for this group, that is perhaps the hardest requirement of all. Even the forgiveness of debts would be easier than sitting and eating a meal with people who are not worthy — with people who are not whole or healthy, or with people who can contribute nothing to the meal.

The message of the Parable of the Banquet is uncompromising. God's new kingdom, which is taking form around the ministry and person of Jesus, is one where God's abundance is extended to those who would seem by their very presence to defile the whole meal. This parable offers a world where the ancient expectations of honor and shame are completely overturned — a world where reversals of the most uncomfortable sort are enacted. If the Pharisees want to be a part of this world, they need to be willing to eat with the "riffraff" and to risk that God's abundance is for those who would never expect it.

The decision to welcome Gentiles into the Christian community, as recorded in Acts 15, is the most radical evidence that the early church took the inclusive nature of Jesus' message seriously. For Gentiles were widely regarded by first-century Jews to be deeply immoral (cf., for example, Rom 1:18-32, which is commonly seen as a standard Jewish diatribe against Gentiles). Thus for Jewish Christians to welcome Gentiles into their fellowship was, indeed, to welcome people they would have least expected to be part of the new kingdom.

It is clear that early Christian communities often had considerable struggles regarding how to understand and embody this new kingdom established by Jesus (cf., e.g., 1 Cor 11:27-34 on eating together; also Gal 2:11-14 on Peter and the Gentiles). Nonetheless, it is equally clear that the early Christians came to appreciate, in large measure, the radical implications of the world that Jesus called his kingdom. Even so, we have not yet dealt with the most radical dimension of this new kingdom that Jesus proclaimed.

4. The Parable of the Compassionate Samaritan (Luke 10:25-37)

In some ways, the Parable of the Good (or, better, the "Compassionate") Samaritan of Luke 10:25-37 has been so domesticated that is hard to see anything new in it. It has been so domesticated that even the Jesus Seminar thinks that Jesus really did tell this story — though, of course, it doesn't believe the parable's context in Luke's Gospel to be authentic. I would like to argue, however, that not only is the context of the parable authentic, but that that context actually provides the key to the parable's meaning.

The context is this: a lawyer stood up to test Jesus. "Teacher," he said, "What must I do to inherit eternal life?" (v 25). Now let us be clear about what the lawyer was asking. He was *not* asking, "How can I get to heaven after I die?" Rather, the question of inheriting eternal life is a question about having a share in the coming of God's new age. It is a question about God's new kingdom. It is a question about resurrection from the dead: "some shall awake to everlasting life and some to shame and everlasting contempt" (Dan 12:2). And resurrection, of course, was the classic description of Israel's restoration in the land (cf. Ezekiel 37).

Throughout the Scriptures of Israel it is clear that obedience to Torah is central for the inheritance of the land (cf., e.g., Lev 26:3-13; Deut 30:15-20; Ezek 36:22-38; 37:24-28; see also *Psalms of Solomon* 14:1-2, 9-10). It is also clear that the inheritance of the whole of the earth was part of Israel's eschatological expectation (cf. Ezek 36:8, 12; Sirach 36:10; *Jubilees* 22:14, 15; 32:19; *1 Enoch* 5:7), when God would forgive his people's transgression and renew his covenant with them (cf. *Jubilees* 22:14, 15).

Ultimately, then, the lawyer's question was a question about the sort of kingdom that Jesus was inaugurating. Is it one where eternal life, and inheritance in the land, is rooted in God's Torah? Is it one that fulfills the eschatological hope of a new covenant with God's people Israel? Is Jesus really proclaiming something that is consistent with God's promises to Israel?

Unlike the other places where this question is asked in the Gospels (cf. Mark 12:28-31; Matt 22:34-40; Luke 18:18), here Jesus turns the question back on the lawyer. Jesus says to him, "What is written in the law? How do you read?" (v 26). The lawyer answers with a quotation from the *Shema:* "You shall love the Lord your God with all your heart, and with all your soul, and with all your strength, and with all your mind" (the latter is an addition to Deut 6:50); and he adds a quotation from Lev 19:18: "You shall love your neighbor as yourself" (v 27). "You have given the right answer," says Jesus; "Do this and you will live" (v 28). The lawyer has his answer: the kingdom that Jesus proclaims is one firmly rooted in the Scriptures and law of Israel.

But the lawyer doesn't stop there. He takes the matter further. For "wishing to justify himself, he said to Jesus, 'And who is my neighbor?'" (v 29). We need to remember that whenever we read the English word "justify" we are reading a translation of the same word in Greek as the word we translate "righteousness" — or, in this case, "being made righteous." A better translation, therefore, though somewhat more awkward, would be "wishing to find himself righteous, he said to Jesus, 'And who is my neighbor?'"

Why would this lawyer wish to be righteous? In first-century Judaism, and indeed throughout the biblical tradition, it is the righteous who will participate in God's new age. It is the righteous who will enter the kingdom; it is the righteous who will inherit eternal life. So the question of whether the lawyer is righteous is closely linked to his first question of how to inherit eternal life.

The question of who should be accepted as a neighbor was apparently much discussed in first-century Judaism. According to most mainstream texts of the time, the concept "neighbor" should definitely include one's fellow Jews, but not necessarily go beyond Jews. In fact, some texts make it clear that one's help should *not* extend beyond the bounds of the Jewish people — definitely not to "sinners" (i.e., Gentiles), since to help sinners would be to condone their sins (cf. Sirach 12:1-7).

The question was a very real one in first-century Judaism. But it also had certain expected answers. Jesus, however, responds to the lawyer's question in an unexpected way in his Parable of the Compassionate Samaritan, which begins: "A man was going down from Jerusalem to Jericho, and fell into the hands of robbers, who stripped him, beat him, and went away, leaving him half dead" (v 30). We are not told if the man was Jewish or not, although the assumption of the story seems to be that he was. All we are told is that he fell into the hands of robbers (Greek: *lēstoi,* "highwaymen; bandits"), with quite disastrous results.

Now highwaymen would not necessarily have been without the sympathy of many Jewish peasants. Such groups of bandits often consisted of peasants themselves, who were unable to pay off their debts or provide for their families, and so turned to robbing travelers. Often the spoils of their robberies were channeled back into the local villages and resulted in benefits for others. The presence of highwaymen was, in fact, widespread at this time, and they eventually became an important factor in the Jewish revolt against Rome in A.D. 66. So Jesus' hearers would probably have heard in the parable a story of what was for the day a fairly common occurrence on the seventeen-mile road that descended through the desert from Jerusalem to Jericho.

The pattern of violence of these highwaymen, however, is something that Jesus explicitly condemns in Luke 19:45, where he overturns the tables in the temple and utters the following word of judgment: "It is written, 'My house shall be a house of prayer,' but you have made it a den of robbers *(lēstoi)*." In so saying, Jesus suggests that the very heart of Israel had become a haunt of *lēstoi* or robbers. And, of course, Jesus is presented in the Gospels as having been crucified between two *lēstoi,* one on each side.

But the plot of Jesus' story thickens: "Now, by chance a priest was going down that road; and when he saw him, he passed by on the other side. So likewise a Levite, when he came to the place and saw him, passed by on the other side" (vv 31-32). There are good reasons why such behavior on the part of the priest might not have surprised Jesus' hearers. For in order to be able to accept the people's offerings and offer sacrifice in the temple, a priest could not risk the contagion of uncleanness. The man in the ditch was, after all, probably naked and unconscious. This means that there was no way to tell, in the first instance, if he was Jewish — or even, in the second, if he were still alive.

According to Torah, contact with a corpse resulted in the most serious type of ritual uncleanness that one could contract. It took seven days to purify oneself from the uncleanness of a corpse, with the burning of a red heifer being required as part of the process (cf. Lev 19). A priest, in fact, was not to defile himself with a corpse, except in the case of the death of his mother, father, son, daughter, brother, or virgin sister (cf. Lev 21:1-4). It may be, therefore, that this priest was taking the most prudent path. For if this man turned out to be dead, his temple service would have been impossible to carry out.

Similar concerns held for the Levite, whose task was to accept tithes from the people (cf. Neh 10:37-38). Touching a corpse would also have made him ritually unclean, and so prohibited him from temple service, until he could complete the seven-day ceremony for purification. In addition, the Levite probably took his cue from the priest's actions. For when traveling such a treacherous road, a traveler in the Middle East would have ascertained who else was on the road not only by looking ahead, but also by looking for the tracks of previous travelers and inquiring at villages on the way. And if the priest had been traveling in the opposite direction, they would have passed on the road (cf. Bailey, *Through Peasant Eyes* 46). But either way, the Levite could have surmised that the priest had passed by the man without helping him, and so, possibly, have used the priest's action (or, inaction) as a guide for his own.

On another level, of course, Jesus told this story in a context where there was considerable tension between Jewish peasants, on the one hand, and the priesthood and temple aristocracy in Jerusalem, on the other. His portrayal of the actions of the priest and the Levite would have served to confirm the animosity his listeners already had toward Jerusalem. On a social level, therefore, the point could be easily drawn: The priest and the Levite did not help; they do not concern themselves with the plight of the peasants at any time!

In such a rhetorical context it is clear where the story should go next. The hero should have been a Jewish peasant, who was traveling next on the road and, in spite of his lack of personal resources, helped the man who was robbed, beaten, and left to die by the bandits. But in his own inimical fashion, Jesus completely overturns the expectations of his hearers. For the next person to come along is a Samaritan (v 33a).

Not much needs to be said about Jewish-Samaritan relations in the first century. Animosity between the groups went both ways. Samaritans were classed by Jews in the same category as Philistines and Edomites (cf. Sirach 50:25-26). They had even been accused in Jewish tradition of secretly entering Jerusalem during a Passover season and defiling the temple by strewing human bones "in the porticoes and throughout the temple" (cf. Josephus, *Antiquities* 18.30). And within Luke's narrative, the Samaritans have already rejected Jesus at the outset of his journey to Jerusalem (cf. Luke 9:53). So by introducing a Samaritan into the story, Jesus was probably picking out a person who was considered by his audience to be one of the most odious characters possible.

It is, therefore, all the more striking that Jesus goes on to describe the Samaritan in ways that could only have heightened the offensive nature of the story. For, in the first instance, he speaks of the Samaritan as having *compassion* on the man (v 33b). In Israel's Scriptures the confessional statement about God that occurs most often is the one taken from Exodus 34:6-7:

> The Lord, the Lord, a God *compassionate* and gracious, slow to anger and abounding in steadfast love and faithfulness, keeping steadfast love for thousands, forgiving iniquity and transgressions and sin, but who by no means will clear the guilty. (See also Neh 9:17, 32; Pss 86:15; 103:8; 111:4; 112:4; Joel 2:13; Jonah 4:2.)

God's compassion and graciousness are depicted in the Jewish Scriptures as (1) the basis for God's deliverance (cf. Pss 40:11; 51:1; 69:16; 77:9; 79:8; 102:13; also Isa 63:15-16); (2) the basis for God's remembrance of his people (cf. Deut 4:13; 2 Kgs 13:23); (3) the basis for God's forgiveness (cf. Ps 78:38; 1 Kgs 8:50; Isa 49:13; Hos 2:21-23; Mic 7:19, as well as most of the references in the first parenthesis above), and, most importantly, (4) central to the restoration and reconciliation of God with his people (cf. Hos 2:19; Zech 1:16; also Zech 12:10).

This language is carried over into the portrayals of the ministry of Jesus, where we read that he had compassion on the people and began to heal them (Matt 14:14; 20:34; cf. Mark 1:41; Luke 7:13); that he had compassion and began to teach them (Mark 6:34); and that he had compassion and fed them (Matt 15:32//Mark 8:2). Oddly enough, in Luke the word occurs in only a few places: in the account of the raising of the widow's son (cf. 7:13), in our passage here (cf. 10:33), and in the description of the father when he sees his prodigal son returning home (cf. 15:20). Clearly, its use in the parables of the Compassionate Samaritan and the Prodigal Son must have had quite a strong effect in identifying the characters of the Samaritan and the father with Jesus and even God himself — which would, undoubtedly, have been totally unacceptable for Jesus' original hearers.

But matters get worse. For Jesus then describes the Samaritan as one who binds up the wounds of the man, after having poured oil and wine on them (v 34a). Again, this explicitly echoes the language used of God in Israel's Scriptures as the one who binds up the wounds of his people (cf., e.g., Isa 30:26; 61:1; Jer 30:17; Ezek 34:16; Hos 6:1; Ps 147:31). Likewise, the use of oil and wine, while medicinally helpful in softening the traveler's wounds and purifying them, echoes what the priest and Levite would have offered on the altar. Thus, overtones of sacrificial love are unmistakable in the story: it is the Samaritan who pours out the true offering acceptable to God (cf. Bailey, *Through Peasant Eyes*, 50).

Kenneth Bailey points out that the Samaritan did for the man everything that the priest and Levite should have done, but did not. He binds up the man's wounds, which was the very least the Levite should have done. He puts the man on his own donkey, which was the very least the priest should have done (remember that the priest as a member of the upper class would likely have been on a donkey). And he takes the man to an inn and pays for his immediate and continuing care, thereby explicitly countering the actions of the robbers who had robbed him and left him for dead (vv 34-35).

It is important to remember that Samaritans also followed Torah, and so the same risk of defilement from touching a dead body was present for this Samaritan as well — with such ritual "uncleanness" extending also to his animals and merchandise. Furthermore, he risked retaliation from the man's family. For in situations of violence, where revenge was commonly taken, an enemy (even one who helps) could easily become the object of a family's revenge. In addition, the robbers might still have been lurking around the place watching for other travelers. A Samaritan, who probably had more than one animal and some merchandise, was a prime target. Thus the risk of violence was high for the Samaritan.

Jesus' question to the lawyer at the end of the story reveals how he completely has revolutionized the original question, "Who is my neighbor?" "Which of these three, do you think, was a neighbor to the man who fell into the hands of the robbers?" (v 36). The lawyer replies, "The one who showed him mercy" (v 37a).

Notice that the lawyer does not respond by saying "the Samaritan." The identification of the one who showed mercy as being a Samaritan is so odious that the lawyer seems not to be able to name him. For this Samaritan was not only an enemy, he was a particularly hated enemy. Any self-respecting, pious Jew in a ditch would rather be left for dead than be helped by such a person. It is as if Larry Flynt, of *Hustler* magazine fame, had picked you up by the side of the road, softened your wounds with the massage oil he used for his erotic parties, and cleansed them with the wine that flowed at those parties. The Samaritan embodied this same kind of moral revulsion. If, in fact, the man in the ditch had been conscious, he would probably have refused help from such a hated enemy.

In this context, Jesus' question is startling: "Which of these three was a neighbor?" The question suggests not so much that the lawyer is to be a neighbor to his enemy, but that he is to allow an enemy to become a neighbor to him. But the question also implies that he is to follow the example of his enemy in learning what it is to be a neighbor!

There is, however, more than this to the parable. For, remember that the parable is set in the context of a question about the coming of God's rule and how the lawyer can be a part of that kingdom. As we have seen from the previous parables, God's world is a world where forgiveness in the broadest sense of the word is central. It is a kingdom of unexpected reversals, where the lowest members of Israel are the ones welcomed the most enthusiastically to the feast. And now, as the Parable of the Compassionate Samaritan teaches, it is a kingdom where the boundaries have been drawn even wider — where the most odious enemy is discovered to be one's neighbor, capable of such unexpected goodness that those who want to be righteous must follow the actions of those they most despise. That is the startling impossibility of this parable. In order to be righteous, the lawyer is called to go and do the likes of what an immoral Samaritan would do (cf. v 37b).

5. Some Observations and Conclusions

Jesus was preaching such a radical redefinition of the kingdom of God in these parables that it is no wonder that certain people began to seek ways to kill him. His message presented a threat to everyone. To wealthy landowners, who had no desire to forgive the debts of their slaves; to the Pharisees, who were concerned about the holiness of Israel and the purity of the nation; to priests and Levites, who could not risk losing their temple positions through possible uncleanness; to the average Jewish peasant, who could not imagine that righteousness would be exemplified by immoral heretics, whom they must now not only love but also emulate. This is the world that Jesus' three parables created: one of profound joy and liberation for slaves, debtors, the poor, the crippled, the lame, the blind, and the hated — but also one that was a profound threat for the wealthy, the landowners, the prestigious, the healthy, and the acceptable.

Which brings us, of course, to the question of our place in such a world. How do we respond to Jesus' radical redrawing of boundaries? Where do we fit in this story? How does it become ours?

One thing is clear: Our very claim to be followers of Jesus places us firmly on the list of those who should be most challenged and threatened by Jesus' parables. This is often hard for us to comprehend, for the contexts are so different. We live in a much larger world, a global world, where the debts people suffer from most are national not personal, where a lack of forgiveness results in nuclear detonations in Asia, where those who can't return our dinner invitation live not only in our cities but are concentrated in the south, and where our most odious enemies are not only in some other nation but also next door.

In such a context, what does Jesus' message proclaim? How do these parables invite us to repentance and to live in such a radical kingdom? Who are we? Are we people who, in spite of the forgiveness of our debts (both "spiritual" and "economic"), continue to insist on payment from others — whether that be holding a grudge in our homes or churches, or holding the debts of others individually or nationally over their heads? Or do we practice God's gracious forgiveness in our churches, homes, and world, joining in with initiatives that seek to forgive the debts of poor people and the poorest nations? Are we proclaiming this new world of radical forgiveness or denying it?

Or are we people who, invited to the banquet, insist on our proper place at the table, arguing that we've worked hard to get where we are? Do we resent providing food for those who don't deserve it, the "riffraff" of society, who are too poor to make a contribution? Do we invite only those who deserve to participate in our abundance and our feasts? Or do we proclaim a different kingdom, a different world, where all are welcome, regardless of ability or status, to share in the abundance we have to offer? Do our churches model what it is to share our abundance with those who have less? Is such an economics of generosity evident in our church budgets? In our investment portfolios? Do we proclaim a kingdom where the banquet is only truly *complete* when the poor, the sick, the outcasts are being fed as well? Do we proclaim a world where God's abundance is extended to all, without discrimination? Or do we deny such a world?

Do we respond to Jesus' Parable of the Compassionate Samaritan with a refusal to let the identity of the one who showed mercy pass our lips, because he is so repugnant to us? Do we live in fear of defilement from those abandoned and vulnerable, from the unclean? Are we piously afraid of being hampered in the "real" work of the Lord? Are we afraid that if we help, if we risk pollution, we too might be attacked — if not by robbers, then perhaps by our brothers and sisters? Do we avert our eyes as we walk down the street and cross to the other side? Or do we drive by in hermetically sealed automobiles so that we do not actually have to encounter the sight of the one on the side of the road?

Or are we willing to be despised as the enemy, even as we pour out our resources and time and very selves? Are we willing to bear the blame of the situation in the first place? Are we a people willing, in the end, to bear a cross? Do we proclaim a world of such radical compassion and healing? Or do we deny it?

In a world of crippling international debt, which is literally paid with the lives and health of the poorest of the poor and the sacrifice of the world's ecosystems, these parables proclaim a radically alternative world characterized by Jubilee. In a world in which the very truth of the gospel is continually undermined by scandalous schism and enmity in the church, Jesus tells stories that can only be heard and understood when the listening community is prepared to be permeated by a compassion that manifests itself in gracious forgiveness.

The world found in these parables is one in which the most marginalized in our society — the homeless, the mentally ill, AIDS victims — are the guests of honor at Jesus' banquet. And the story of a despised enemy becoming a compassionate neighbor offers a kingdom of embrace in the face of the violent exclusion that characterizes the tribal conflicts and ethnic cleansings that wreak havoc throughout our world. This is the kingdom that Jesus invites us to in these parables. Do we dare enter it?

In the end, what these parables mean for us today has everything to do with how we respond to Jesus' command to the lawyer. When he says to us: "Go and do likewise," do we regard our sacrificial participation in the new world of the kingdom as a profound threat or as a deep-seated joy in the gracious abundance of our God?

Selected Bibliography

Bailey, Kenneth E. *Poet and Peasant: A Literary Cultural Approach to the Parables in Luke.* Grand Rapids: Eerdmans, 1976.

————. *Through Peasant Eyes: More Lucan Parables, Their Culture and Style.* Grand Rapids: Eerdmans, 1980.

Capon, Robert Farrar. *The Parables of Grace.* Grand Rapids: Eerdmans, 1988.

Fitzmyer, Joseph A. *The Gospel According to Luke,* vol. 2. New York: Doubleday, 1985.

Keesmaat, Sylvia C. *Paul and His Story: (Re)Interpreting the Exodus Tradition.* Sheffield: Sheffield Academic Press, 1999.

Koenig, John. *New Testament Hospitality: Partnership with Strangers as Promise and Mission.* Philadelphia: Fortress, 1985.

McDonald, J. Ian H. "Rhetorical Issue and Rhetorical Strategy in Luke 10.25-37 and Acts 10.1–11.18," in *Essays from the 1992 Heidelberg Conference,* ed. S. E. Porter and T. H. Olbricht. Sheffield: Sheffield Academic Press, 1993, 59-73.

————. "The View from the Ditch — And Other Angles: Interpreting the Parable of the Good Samaritan," *Scottish Journal of Theology* 149 (1996) 21-37.

Neusner, Jacob. *The Rabbinic Traditions About the Pharisees Before 70,* 3 vols. Leiden: Brill, 1971.

Ringe, Sharon H. "Solidarity and Contextuality: Readings of Matthew 18.21-35," in *Reading from This Place.* Vol. 1: *Social Location and Biblical Interpretation in the United States,* ed. F. F. Segovia and M. A. Tolbert. Minneapolis: Fortress, 1995, 199-212.

Sanders, E. P. *Judaism: Practice and Belief 63 BCE–66 CE.* London: SCM; Philadelphia: Trinity Press International, 1992.

Volf, Miroslav. *Exclusion and Embrace: A Theological Exploration of Identity, Otherness and Reconciliation.* Nashville: Abingdon, 1996.

Wilder, Amos N. "Story and Story-World," in *The Bible and the Literary Critic.* Minneapolis: Fortress, 1991, 132-48.

Wright, N. Thomas. *The New Testament and the People of God.* Minneapolis: Fortress, 1992.

————. *Jesus and the Victory of God.* Minneapolis: Fortress, 1997.

CHAPTER 13

"Everyone Who Hears These Words of Mine": Parables on Discipleship
(Matt 7:24-27//Luke 6:47-49; Luke 14:28-33; Luke 17:7-10; Matt 20:1-16)

MICHAEL P. KNOWLES

NOTWITHSTANDING THE enormous volume and complexity of modern parables research, any discussion of specific parables must begin with the simple observation that their purpose is essentially pragmatic. Nowhere is this clearer than in the case of parables that specifically focus on discipleship. For whether at the level of their original audience, in the context of the Gospel writers and the audiences for which they wrote, or as they apply to audiences of a subsequent age, parables are intended to provoke, to challenge, and to elicit a concrete response to Jesus' invitation to discipleship.

A parable is an extended metaphor that typically illustrates significant features of God's character and conduct, and sets out consequences for human conduct, by reference to commonplace features of everyday experience. The compelling appeal of parables, however, derives from the fact that their familiarity — dealing with such common matters as farmers, rulers, seeds and weeds — is often confounded by unexpected reversals or outcomes. The listener (or reader) is drawn by the power of a good story, only then to discover that the narrative leads him or her in unexpected directions or to unanticipated conclusions.

286

The approach taken here, in concert with a variety of commentators today, is that the meaning of any given parable need not be limited to a single main point. When they want to make a single point, teachers (Jesus among them) tend to favor the precision of propositional language: "You have heard it said, . . . but I say to you"; "Whenever you pray, do not be like the hypocrites," and so on. The purpose of parables is, to be sure, generally didactic. But it would be a mistake to suggest that the restrictions of propositional speech must always apply to the language they employ. Rather, it is the nature of narrative in general and of metaphoric language in particular to be resonant and allusive, suggesting a range of possible meanings. The parables to be examined below each address specific issues. And they assert one or two main premises. But they do so with all the richness of a well-told story, inviting the interpreter to explore various secondary or supportive meanings that are suggested by the story's specific details.

Broadly speaking, parables move from the familiar (based on depictions of human experience) to the unfamiliar (conveying assertions about God), and back to the familiar again (implying consequences for present conduct). This process will become evident in each of the following parables of discipleship: the Parable of the Two Builders (Matt 7:24-27//Luke 6:47-49); the paired Parables of the Tower Builder and the Warring King (Luke 14:28-33); the Parable of the Unworthy Servant (Luke 17:7-10); and the Parable of the Laborers in the Vineyard (Matt 20:1-16).

1. The Parable of the Two Builders
(Matt 7:24-27//Luke 6:47-49)

In both Matthew and Luke, the Parable of the Two Builders, which is a parable about "foundations" and the fate of structures built on them, illustrates the contrast between those who hear the words of Jesus and act on them, on the one hand, and those who hear but fail to act, on the other. Likewise, in both Gospels this parable occurs at the end of parallel blocks of teaching material — as the conclusion of Matthew's Sermon on the Mount (Matt 5:1–7:29) and as the conclusion of Luke's Sermon on the Plain (Luke 6:20-49) — thereby pressing home the urgency of an obedient response.

The differences between the portrayals of this parable are largely matters of narrative detail. In the simpler narrative structure of Luke's

Gospel, two individuals are depicted who choose to build on a floodplain (translating the Greek *ho potamos* of 6:48 in its literal sense as "the river"). The one builder, knowing the danger of the location, carefully excavates the site to bedrock, lays stone on stone, and so establishes a structure that will be strong enough to withstand the onslaught of seasonal flooding. The other builder, however, exercises no such foresight, but erects his home carelessly, or in haste, on sand. The rising river carries the structure away, "and the ruin of that house was great."

In Matthew's more complex narrative structure, the houses that are built face not one, but three consecutive threats: rain, floods, and wind. Matthew also specifies what is merely implicit in Luke — that is, that the two builders are a "wise man" and a "foolish man," respectively (in both cases, *anēr*, "male"). The explicit references to "wise" and "foolish" builders, together with the gender specificity of the story, suggest that this parable anticipates that of 25:1-13, the Parable of the Wise and Foolish Bridesmaids, where the wise are likewise distinguished from the foolish by their foresight and provision for future need.

While the general intent of the Wise and Foolish Builders is clear, at least two questions remain: To whom is the parable addressed?, and, What situation of crisis might the flood represent? For the majority of interpreters, the flood represents either the trials and difficulties of daily life or the "Great Trial" of final judgment. The first school of thought takes its cue from the great fourth-century Christian diplomat, preacher, and bishop John Chrysostom (c. 345-407), for whom the rain and floods represent "all the ills in our life that anyone could mention," whereas the rock on which the house is founded is Christian doctrine, "setting one above all the waves of human affairs" (*Homily* 24.3). A similar ethical emphasis (although using the metaphor of a tree rather than a building) is found in a parable attributed to Rabbi Eleazar ben Azariah (c. 90-130 CE), who was an approximate contemporary of the evangelist Matthew:

> He whose wisdom is more abundant than his works, to what is he like? To a tree whose branches are abundant but whose roots are few; and the wind comes and uproots it and overturns it, as it is written, *He shall be like a tamarisk in the desert and shall not see when good cometh; but shall inhabit the parched places in the wilderness* [Jer 17:6]. But he whose works are more abundant than his wisdom, to what is he like? To a tree whose branches are few but whose roots are many; so that even if all the

winds in the world come and blow against it, it cannot be stirred from its place, as it is written, *He shall be as a tree planted by the waters, and that spreads out his roots by the river, and shall not fear when heat comes, and his leaf shall be green; and shall not be careful in the year of drought, neither shall it cease from yielding fruit* [Jer 17:8]. (*Mishnah Aboth* 3:18)

On such an ethical reading — which, it should be noted, the parallel drawn from Rabbi Eleazar ben Azariah suggests would have been entirely appropriate to a Palestinian Jewish context — the Parable of the Two Builders affirms that the discipline of a righteous and obedient life is sufficient to sustain the pious in times of adversity and affliction.

But a number of contextual indicators also point to the appropriateness of an eschatological reading. For a start, the mention of a destructive flood recalls the time of Noah, in keeping with the rabbinic principal that the origins and end-time of creation mirror one another (or, as in the German formula, *Urzeit = Endzeit*). Jesus himself is portrayed as emphasizing this correspondence: "For as the days of Noah were, so will be the coming of the Son of Man. For as in those days before the flood . . . they knew nothing until the flood came and swept them all away, so too will be the coming of the Son of Man" (Matt 24:37-39; cf. Luke 17:26-27). Furthermore, the Matthean context of the parable — particularly the accompanying material of 7:13-23 (note esp. the expression "on that day" of v 22), but also its parallels with the Parable of the Wise and Foolish Bridesmaids in 25:1-13 — conveys unmistakable eschatological overtones. And references to "foundations" and building metaphors that appear elsewhere in the New Testament consistently imply final judgment (e.g., 1 Cor 3:10-15; Col 1:23; Eph 2:19-20; 1 Tim 6:18-19; 2 Tim 2:19).

One of the implications of the Parable of the Two Builders seems to be that in matters of faithful discipleship, appearances are often deceiving. The inherent strength or instability of the two houses remains hidden until the moment of crisis, at which point the worth of the builder's method is quickly revealed. A similar principle is operative not only in the Parable of the Bridesmaids but also, implicitly, in such diverse parables as the Sower and the Seed (Mark 4:3-8 *par.*), the Talents (Matt 25:14-30), the Pounds (Luke 19:11-27), the Sheep and Goats (Matt 25:31-46), and the Rich Man and Lazarus (Luke 16:19-31). Any one of these parables might illustrate the Pauline injunction: "Therefore, do not pronounce judgment before the time, before the Lord comes, who will bring to light the things now hidden in darkness and disclose the purposes of the heart" (1 Cor 4:5).

But the specific focus of this parable is, first of all, on the teaching of Jesus, and then, concurrently, on the response that his teaching demands. Implied here is not only the remarkable assertion that the acceptance or rejection of Jesus' words entails eschatological consequences, but also that Jesus possesses the authority to command such obedience. Jesus' insistence on "these words of mine" (Matt 7:24, 26//Luke 6:47, 49) implies an authority beyond even that of Israel's prophets. Indeed, his telling of the parable aptly illustrates the more prosaic editorial comment that follows in Matt 7:28-29: "Now when Jesus had finished saying these things, the crowds were astonished at his teaching, for he taught them as one having authority."

The Matthean presentation, moreover, includes at least one additional feature of note. For the language of "building on the rock" (*ōikodomēsen . . . epi tēn petran*) of 7:24 anticipates that of Peter's commissioning in 16:18: "On this rock I will build my church" (*epi tautę tę petrą oikodomēsō mou tēn ekklēsian*). In both passages the premise is much the same — that is, that even the greatest affliction ("the gates of Hell" in 16:18) will not prevail. For Matthew, it seems, the point is not simply that Jesus and the obedient follower each build on solid foundations. These two formulations also recall — and, indeed, provide a counterpoint to — the traditional Jewish concept of the temple as having been founded on a rock that stands at the gateway to both heaven and the underworld. Thus in the context of Jesus' ministry, the Parable of the Two Builders conveys a challenge to "build a house" on a foundation equivalent to that on which God's own house is set (with the Hebrew noun *beth*, "house," referring to both kinds of structures).

Even more to the point, since Matthew and Luke probably wrote in the immediate aftermath of the fall of Jerusalem and the destruction of its temple — the city and "house" of God — they doubtless both could attest to the fact, to quote Luke, that "the ruin of *that* house was great." The historical context of the evangelists' own day, therefore, suggests that those who acted (or failed to act) on Jesus' words would have already faced a crisis of testing, a crisis that only those with secure foundations could withstand.

To whom, then, was the Parable of the Two Builders likely addressed? There is nothing in the parable to indicate an audience other than that suggested by its contexts in Matthew and Luke. Together with the sermon of which it is part, the parable is directed in the first instance to "the disciples" (Luke 6:20). Yet it is also given "in the hearing of the people" (Luke 7:1; cf. Matt 5:1-2; 7:28-29). In other words, the parable speaks to any and all who will hear (or read) Jesus' teaching, and it is to them that the temporal and eternal consequences of an appropriate response is pressed home. Discipleship, therefore, is first and foremost a matter of positive, obedient action — action that turns out to be foundational for life, both in the present age and in the age to come.

2. The Paired Parables of the Tower Builder and the Warring King (Luke 14:28-33)

From the building of houses we turn to the building of a tower. The comparison is not arbitrary, for in Luke's Gospel the vocabulary of "laying a foundation" *(themelios theinai)* is unique to the two parables of 6:47-49 and 14:28-30. Thus, whereas Matthew's language pairs the wise and foolish builders (7:24-27) and the wise and foolish bridesmaids (25:1-13), Luke's language juxtaposes the building of houses (6:47-49) and the building of a tower (14:28-30).

Commentators usually agree that the paired parables of "the Tower Builder" and "the Warring King" have always belonged together, and were not juxtaposed at some later stage in the transmission of early Christian tradition. They begin with a challenge to the audience: "Who among you?" In the Gospel tradition, Jesus is often depicted as using this rhetorical device to command assent. For example, he asks: "Who among you would not rescue their livestock on the Sabbath?" (paraphrasing Matt 12:11// Luke 14:5). The answer is obvious. So he concludes: "Of how much more value is a human being than a sheep! Therefore it is lawful to do good on the Sabbath" (Matt 12:12). The question "Who among you?" is intended to elicit agreement from the hearer *a fortiori* — that is, given the logical necessity of the anticipated response, how much more, by implication, must the legal or spiritual corollary apply.

The context of these two parables in Luke's Gospel allows for little ambiguity as to either their meaning or their intended audience. Large crowds were accompanying Jesus. Perhaps fearing that they had failed to grasp the radical nature of God's reign, or its drastic implications for discipleship, Jesus issues a blunt, twofold challenge: Whoever does not hate the members of his or her own family "cannot be my disciple," and whoever does not take up his or her own cross — that is, is not prepared to die — "cannot be my disciple" (Luke 14:25-27). The parables that follow illustrate his point.

In the first, someone sets out to build a tower. Will that person not reckon in advance whether he possesses sufficient resources to complete the task? Otherwise the would-be builder will reap the mockery and scorn of the onlookers. In the second, a king contemplates the cost of going to war, weighing the chances of a successful campaign against an opponent who commands an army twice the size of his own. If his forces are insufficient to ensure victory, will he not negotiate terms of surrender?

The second parable heightens the imagery in at least two ways. The subject of the first is, at least rhetorically, any one of the listeners ("Which *of you*, desiring to build a tower . . ."); whereas in the second, the protagonist is a king — a man of wealth, stature, political and military power. The second parable also presents a more drastic consequence. For if the tower builder risks mockery and shame, the king stands to lose his army, his kingdom, perhaps even his life. "So therefore," concludes Jesus, "whoever of you does not renounce all that he or she has cannot be my disciple."

The role that one assigns to the tower has a significant impact on the meaning of the passage as a whole, since archaeological evidence allows for a number of possibilities (cf. "Towers" in *The Anchor Bible Dictionary*, 6 vols., ed. D. N. Freedman [New York: Doubleday, 1992], 6.622-24). If the tower was to be simply a dwelling place, then the builder's ridicule and shame is compounded by his inability to establish a settled existence. He and his family must continue to live in tents, as transients and nomads. Yet isolated stone houses of this sort were, it seems, comparatively few in Palestine. Alternatively, if the tower was to serve an agricultural purpose, then the parable suggests that the builder's pride may be overtaken by his poverty. Towers often functioned as lookouts from which a shepherd would guard his flock or a farmer his vineyard (cf. Mark 12:1 *par.*). They also served as storehouses to safeguard the fruit of the harvest. In either case, the builder discovers that despite his dreams of agricultural plenty, he lacks enough field stones — free for the taking though they might be — to build himself a tower.

The apparent complexity of the building process, however, where the foundation must first be laid, does not favor a simple field structure being here in view. As a third option, therefore, it should be noted that ancient towers frequently served a military and defensive function (cf. the Tower of Siloam referred to in Luke 13:4). Such towers needed to be either sufficiently strong to withstand an enemy onslaught or sufficiently high to afford a view from afar.

On this latter interpretation, the builder's inability to complete the task again reflects his lack of resources, not to mention his lack of foresight. Perhaps he could not afford the masons or the stone. Perhaps he found his authority insufficient to compel his subjects to complete the task (which would account for their scorn). In any event, he comes to realize that his resources are unexpectedly lacking. Moreover, a military interpretation of the tower intensifies the parallelism within the doublet. For in the parable of the tower, the builder is expecting an enemy assault and so takes measures to protect himself, thereby assuming a defensive posture. In the subsequent parable the warring king contemplates initiating a battle, and thus assumes an offensive stance.

Both parables envisage a coming crisis, a time of testing. The logic of the narrative, however, suggests that in both instances the "crunch" comes in the midst of discipleship, as part of a process that is still underway, rather than at some more distant end point. Luke appears to favor parables with a midpoint crisis — such as the Prodigal Son (15:11-32), the Shrewd Manager (16:1-13), and the Persistent Widow and the Unjust Judge (18:1-8) — whereas in the Matthean parables the crisis often comes at the end. In any event, those who hear must not only seek to follow and obey, but must consider carefully the cost of doing so (cf. Luke 13:24).

Without pressing the details of the narrative too hard, it is not difficult to see in these paired parables two different aspects of discipleship. As A. M. Hunter has observed: "In the first parable Jesus says, 'Sit down and reckon whether you can afford to follow me.' In the second he says: 'Sit down and reckon whether you can afford to refuse my demands'" (*Interpreting the Parables,* 65). On the other hand, any differences in emphasis between the two parables appear to be overpowered by the force of Jesus' concluding pronouncement: "So, therefore, whoever of you does not renounce all that he or she has cannot be my disciple."

The renunciation of all of one's possessions is consistent with Luke's emphasis on the demands of discipleship, although the degree of commitment that such a total renunciation implies has led some to ask whether this requirement was originally directed only to the inner core of disciples. But if Luke's narrative context serves as any guide, such an explanation is unnecessary. Rather, in the manner of Joshua insisting "You cannot serve the Lord, for he is a holy God" (Josh 24:19), thereby bearing witness against the possibility of Israel's apostasy, Jesus in Luke's Gospel seeks to dissuade his listeners from too easy a view of discipleship. Similar challenges come quickly to hand throughout the Lukan portrayals, however harsh they may sound to modern ears. In 9:57-62, for example, to one who offers allegiance, Jesus holds out only the prospect of homelessness (vv 57-58); in response to filial piety, he replies, "Let the dead bury their own dead" (vv 59-60); and rather than allowing for family leave-taking, Jesus declares a prospective disciple unfit for the kingdom (vv 61-62).

The conclusion in the two parables of 14:28-33 is similarly uncompromising. Jesus' point is that either following him or refusing to follow will cost one's all. The issue facing his hearers (and Luke's readers) is not one of risk management, or even of being willing to forsake "house or wife or brothers or parents or children, for the sake of the kingdom of God" (18:29). Rather, losing all appears to be unavoidable in any case. The only question is whether one will lose all as a follower of Jesus and for the sake of God's reign, or as one who refuses to follow and obey. Which, in other words, is the more promising course of action?

The events of Jesus' own life, as well as those of the evangelist's day, bear out the logic of such an assertion. In retrospect, these paired parables must be set against (1) the controversy that Jesus' ministry had already begun to evoke, (2) the emergence of official opposition, and (3) the increasing likelihood that judicial consequences would soon ensue. Whatever difficulties might await the disciples in a later day, Jesus' own imminent destiny clearly justified the need to renounce earthly bonds and obligations. Were this not enough, the narrative detail of an overwhelmingly superior force rising to meet the challenge of a weaker king could not have failed to recall, once again, the recent folly of the Jewish insurrectionists (cf. Luke 19:41-44).

Luke's audience, of course, was predominantly Gentile and Hellenistic, if not actually Roman. Nonetheless, contemporary political developments within the Roman empire amply underscored the point that the followers of Jesus of Nazareth could be faced with the need to renounce all. Luke's own community, in fact, may have faced the threat of material loss on account of their confession of Jesus, rather than Caesar, as *Kyrios,*

"Lord." These two paired parables, therefore, would have had great significance for those that the evangelist addressed. But also, because of a current, widespread perception that Christian discipleship is a "low-risk," "low-cost" endeavor, these two parables pose a telling challenge to the Western Church today. Set in any of these historical contexts, both the parables themselves and Jesus' personal example make the cost of faithful discipleship unmistakably clear.

3. The Parable of the Unworthy Servant (Luke 17:7-10)

The Parable of the Unworthy Servant in Luke 17:7-10 bears several key resemblances to the paired parables of the Tower Builder and Warring King. It, too, is uniquely Lukan; it challenges the audience, "Who among you . . ."; it is apparently addressed to disciples (cf. 17:1, 5); and it presents the conditions of discipleship in a decidedly uncompromising manner.

The situation that this parable describes is simple enough. No servant (or "slave," since the Greek noun *doulos* encompasses both possibilities) can expect to serve his or her own needs first. Rather, it is the essence of servanthood (not to mention slavery) to place the requirements of one's master above one's own, however inconvenient doing so may be. The same, Jesus implies, is true of discipleship.

The rhetorical genius of the parable lies in its adoption of different perspectives on the situation to make its point. The first three verses assume the perspective of the master — or, rather, they invite the listener to assume such a perspective:

> Who among you having a servant plowing or keeping sheep, will say to him when he comes in from the field, "Sit right down to eat"? Will he not say to him, "Make me something for supper, and when you are ready, serve it to me until I have eaten and drunk; and afterwards you can have your meal"? Does he owe the servant anything for having done what was asked of him? (17:7-9)

The translation "make me something *for supper*" reflects the use of the verb *deipnein,* which refers to serving the main meal of the day — that is, the *deipnon* or principal meal eaten in middle to late afternoon.

It is well within a servant's job description to prepare and serve his master's main meal. Nor is the master in any way indebted to the servant for having completed his daily chores. Verse 9, which is often translated "Does he *thank* the servant," can be literally rendered "Does he [the master] have *charis* toward the servant?" While "thank" is an appropriate translation (as in 1 Tim 1:12; 2 Tim 1:3), it does not convey the full force of the question: Has the servant found *charis* — that is, grace, favor, or credit — in the master's eyes for having served as expected?

Does the master owe the servant anything? Of course not! Both the absurdity of the question and the syntax of verse 9 indicate that no right-minded employer would act in such a manner. Questions in Greek can be worded to anticipate either a positive or a negative response. The question posed in verse 9 is emphatically of the latter variety. Accordingly, any right-minded listener would be expected to agree that servants simply serve, and that there would be no point in anyone thinking otherwise.

Having thus won agreement from the audience, verse 10 springs the rhetorical trap — no longer assuming the perspective of the master, but addressing the audience as servants or slaves: "So too with *you*, when *you* have done all that you have been commanded, say, 'We are unworthy servants; we have only done what was required of us.'" If they agree from the perspective of the master, how much more must Jesus' hearers (and Luke's readers) agree if they are really only servants. And if such service and submission are required in human relationships, how much more are they required in our relations with God, who is the heavenly Master (whose agency is implied grammatically by the use of the passive voice), and in our obedience to all that God commands.

Notwithstanding Jesus' controversies with certain Pharisees of his day — and *contra* some stereotypes of Judaism that have arisen among Christian commentators — this parable affirms a foundational principle of piety that seems to have been current among many of Jesus' contemporaries. The outlook in question is exemplified by an aphorism recorded at the very beginning of the "Sayings of the Fathers" *(Pirqe Aboth)*, which is the oldest section of the Talmud, and is attributed to Simeon the Just, who is said to have lived in the third century BCE: "Be not like slaves who serve the master for the sake of receiving a reward, but be like slaves who serve the master *not* for the sake of reward, and let the fear of heaven be upon you" (*Mishnah Aboth* 1:3; cf. also the saying attributed to Johanan ben Zakkai, a first-century CE rabbi, in *Mishnah Aboth* 2:8: "If you have accomplished much in Torah, claim not merit for yourself, for to this end you were created"). The piety of the earliest Jewish sages, therefore, declared that since God is God, Israel's obedience must be a matter of divine initiative and human obligation, rather than one of human initiative and divine obligation.

And this is the point of the proposed reply in Jesus' parable: "We are unworthy servants; we have only done what was required of us." Commentators differ on the meaning of *achreios*, which can be translated as either "worthless" or "unworthy." The first option seems to run counter both to the logic of the situation (for the servant's labors prove his worth) and to the general tenor of Jesus' ministry (above all, his openness to social outcasts, cf. Luke 19:10). The second option, on the other hand, appears more appropriate in its suggestion of a lack of merit, or an inability to command the master's (God's!) favor. For nothing is due a servant for having done what was expected. Or to quote John Calvin:

> The object of this parable is to show that all the zeal manifested by us in discharging our duty does not put God under any obligation to us by any sort of merit; for, as we are his property, so he on his part can owe us nothing. (*Harmony on Matthew, Mark, and Luke* 2.194)

John Drury notes that many of Luke's parables derive their "vivacity" from an "adventurous handling of hierarchical relationships: father and son, steward and lord, plaintiff and judge, master and servants" (*Parables in the Gospels,* 151). Such parables begin with the assumption that the divine-human relationship is similarly hierarchical, then proceed to reverse conventional expectations. The parable of the Watchful Servants in 12:35-38, for example, concludes with the unthinkable: the master, having returned home from a wedding celebration, seats the servants and serves them. Jesus later applies this reversal to himself: "Who is the greater, the one who reclines at table, or the one who serves? Surely the one who reclines. Yet I am among you as one who serves!" (22:27).

The remarkable feature of the Parable of the Unworthy Servant here in 17:7-10, however, is that it offers no such reversal. Rather, the master insists, in thoroughly conventional fashion, on obedient submission — with Jesus insisting in verse 10 that no less obedient submission is due to God. Taken by itself, the first half of the parable denies the follower any role in setting the terms of discipleship. This applies as much between Jesus and his disciples as between Israel and God. And the second half denies the possibility that service for God is intrinsically meritorious. But, it must be asked, to whom is such an admonition addressed?

In Jesus' day the role of a disciple was not simply to learn, but also to act as a servant. A disciple's service involved performing a variety of essential, yet menial, tasks for the teacher. Thus two of Jesus' disciples fetch a donkey for him to ride on (cf. Luke 19:29-35), and Peter and John prepare the Passover meal (cf. Luke 22:8-13; also 8:3). Only responsibilities considered degrading were excluded (which probably explains John the Baptist's comments in Luke 3:16).

Yet Jesus' disciples are portrayed as sometimes thinking that their association with their master allowed them some special status, or somehow accrued to their benefit. Thus, for example, they are presented as attempting to keep a non-disciple from using Jesus' name (Luke 9:49 *par.*), seeking special favors from Jesus (Mark 10:35-37 *par.*), and arguing among themselves as to which of them was the greatest (Luke 22:24 *par.*). Insofar as the disciples act as servants to Jesus, the intent of the Parable of the Unworthy Servant may well be to point out that such service does not constitute a claim on his favor, much less a claim on God's favor. And without wishing to impose the Christology of subsequent ages, the parable allows for a creative ambiguity as to the identity of the landowner, who may be either God (as Jewish piety would anticipate) or Jesus (as the disciples might expect) — or, more remarkable yet, both.

The continued existence of slavery as a social institution sustains the relevance of servanthood as a metaphor for Christian discipleship, and, in turn, contributes to the parable's ongoing currency. Well beyond his own day, Paul's words apply alike to slave and free: "Whoever was called in the Lord as a slave is a freed person belonging to the Lord, just as whoever was free when called is a slave of Christ" (1 Cor 7:22; cf. Rom 6:22; Gal 3:23-47; Eph 6:6; 1 Pet 2:16; note that Paul and other early Christian leaders also applied the metaphor to themselves, Gal 1:10; 1 Cor 9:19; James 1:1). Similarly, the Pauline emphasis on unmerited grace (e.g., Eph 2:8-9) and his metaphorical appeal to "redemption" (e.g., Rom 3:24; Eph 1:7; cf. 1 Cor 6:20; 7:23), which may reflect the slave market (cf. *Anchor Bible Dictionary* 6.655), lend further support to the parable's uncompromising description of discipleship: that discipleship is not self-determined, and that one is not compensated according to one's merits, but on some other principle.

4. The Parable of the Laborers
in the Vineyard (Matt 20:1-16)

From parables unique to Luke we turn to a parable unique to Matthew —
and here one that supplies precisely the kind of unexpected reversal that
the Parable of the Unworthy Servant failed to provide. For in the Parable of
the Laborers in the Vineyard of Matt 20:1-16, workers hired at different
hours throughout the day expect to be compensated proportionately; but
much to their astonishment, they all receive the same wage.

This parable has enjoyed (or suffered) a long history of imaginative
exegesis. As interpreted by Irenaeus (c. 130-200), who had been instructed
by Polycarp and was from about 178 the Bishop of Lyons:

> The first call to the workers represents the beginning of the created
> world, while the second symbolizes the Old Covenant. The third call
> represents Christ's ministry. The long lapse of time in which we now live
> is the fourth call, while the final call symbolizes the end of time. (*Against
> Heresies* 4.36.7)

Origen of Alexandria (c. 185-254), the greatest scholar, teacher, and writer
of his day, was even more specific:

> The first shift of workers signifies the generations [from Adam] to
> Noah; the second, those from Noah to Abraham; the third, those from
> Abraham to Moses; the fourth, those from Moses to Joshua; the fifth,
> those up to the time of Christ. The householder is God, while the
> denarius represents salvation. (*Commentary on Matthew* 15.32)

At the same time, Origen offered a "deeper and more mystical" interpretation, namely that the various hours of calling represent the various stages
of human life (*ibid.*, 15.36). Viewed in this way, John Chrysostom of
Antioch (c. 347-407), who in his latter years was Bishop at Constantinople,
declared that the parable teaches that even in old age it is not too late to
draw near to God (*Homily* 64:3-4).

Reformation exegesis, on the other hand, largely rejected the Church
Fathers' search for allegorical meanings in the minor details of the para-
bles. Commenting on the workers and their labors, Calvin insisted that
Christ's "one aim [is] continually to incite his people to keep going"; yet,

also, that the parable demonstrates the sovereignty of God: "He pays those whom He has called the reward which seems good to Him" (*Harmony on Matthew, Mark, and Luke* 2.264-67).

But separate identities for each group hired at the various hours — that is, at six and nine A.M., at noon, and at three and five P.M. by Western reckoning — are rendered unlikely by two considerations. First, the reference to the vineyard, which was a stock metaphor for Israel (cf. Isa 5:1-7; Jer 12:10; Mark 12:1-10 *par.*), makes it probable that all of the laborers are to be understood as Jewish, and not both Jewish and Gentile (as would be required for them to represent, collectively, the entire history of salvation). Second, resolution of the narrative requires only two groups, "the first" and "the last," rather than the literal five mentioned earlier. Payment to those hired at the various midday hours is omitted to avoid any diminishment of the intended contrast between those who thought they had earned more and those who knew they deserved less.

The image of the twelfth hour, at which time payment is rendered, is a stock metaphor for final judgment. And in the context of Matthew's Gospel, this eschatological dimension provides a possible explanation as to why the apparently shortsighted landowner needs to return so many times for additional laborers. Quite simply, he needs ever more workers because the final ingathering proves so much more plentiful than even he could have imagined. The situation perfectly illustrates Jesus' admonition to the disciples in 9:37-38: "The harvest is bountiful, but the laborers few. So beg the Lord of the harvest to send out workers into his harvest." For in the logic of the kingdom and its proclamation, the few scattered seeds have generated such a disproportionate increase that the landowner must take extraordinary measures to gather in the full yield.

Those hired last are paid first. They receive a denarius, which was the standard wage for a full day's manual labor. Both this reversal in the order of payment and the amount paid are essential to the creation of tension — not just in terms of labor relations, but also in terms of the tension inherent in the narrative of the parable itself! For having toiled all day long, those still waiting in line naturally expect some kind of bonus. As they see it, natural justice requires a proportional system of recompense. But the landowner insists on fulfilling the exact terms of their contract, which was to pay them what he considered "just" (*dikaios*, v 4) — that is, a full day's wage (cf. vv 2, 13).

So when the grumblers accuse the owner of unfairness, the only injustice in the situation is their own selfishness. Hence the appropriateness of the owner's challenge (which is altogether obscured by most translations): "Is your eye evil because I am good?" The earliest workers have received their just reward. But they show themselves to be estranged from the larger graciousness of the one who had engaged their services. Therefore the landowner's words imply dismissal: "Take what is yours and go."

Distinctive features of this Matthean parable emerge in comparison with the following frequently-cited (although considerably later) rabbinic parallels. An anonymous Tannaitic parable of the third century CE (at the earliest) comments on the statement "And I will have regard for you" of Lev 26:9 as follows:

> It is like a king who hired many laborers. And along with them was one laborer that had worked for him many days. All the laborers went also. He said to this one special laborer: "I will have regard for you. The others, who have worked for me only a little, to them I will give small pay. You, however, will receive a large recompense." Even so both the Israelites and the peoples of the world sought their pay from God. And God said to the Israelites: "My children, I will have regard for you. The peoples of the world have accomplished very little for me, and I will give them but a small reward. You, however, will receive a large recompense." (*Sifra* on Lev 26:9; cf. *Ecclesiastes Rabbah* 5.11.5)

From a similar scenario, this parable derives a conclusion exactly opposite that of Jesus' Parable of the Laborers in the Vineyard, for in the rabbinic parable the faithful within Israel are rewarded in proportion to their piety.

More closely resembling the parable in Matthew's Gospel is the following, which is said to have been told by Rabbi Zeira at the funeral of Rabbi Abun ben Hiya, who died about 325 CE at a relatively early age:

> It is like a king who hired many laborers. But one was outstanding in his work. What did the King do? He took him away and walked up and down with him. When it was evening, the laborers came to receive their pay, and he gave him, with them, the full amount of his wage. Then the laborers murmured and said, "We have worked the whole day, and this man has worked only two hours." Then the king said, "This man has done more in two hours than you have done in the whole day." So has Rabbi Abun learned more in the Law in twenty-eight years than a clever

301

student could have mastered in a lifetime. (*Jerusalem/Palestinian Berakoth* 2:8, cf. *Song of Songs Rabbah* 6.2.6)

Even here, however, the emphasis is on the laborer's ability to accomplish much in proportionately less time than the other workers, which is in line with the rabbinic dictum: "Some obtain and enter the kingdom in an hour, while others reach it only after a lifetime" (*Babylonian Abodah Zarah* 17a).

Rabbinic doctrines of merit and grace were multifaceted, just as they have been in much of Christian theology. On the one hand, sayings such as those of Simeon the Just and Johanan ben Zakkai, cited above, emphasize the centrality of divine grace. On the other hand, one must weigh such opinions as that of Rabbi Tarfon (c. 50-120 CE), a contemporary of the evangelist Matthew: "If you have studied much in the Law, much reward will be given you; and faithful is your taskmaster who will pay you the reward of your labor" (*Mishnah Aboth* 2:16) — or that attributed to Rabbi Akiba, the leading rabbi of the early second century CE: "The world is judged by grace, yet all is according to the excess of works" (*Mishnah Aboth* 3:16; cf. also further statements attributed to R. Akiba in *Mishnah Aboth* 3:17 and to R. Hananiah ben Akashya in *Mishnah Makkoth* 3:16). By comparison, Jesus' parable does not focus on issues of wages or "merit" *per se*, but uses them only as a narrative vehicle for emphasizing the owner's — which is to say, God's — unmerited generosity. Perhaps, as well, there are overtones in Jesus' parable of God having compassion on those who cannot otherwise make adequate provision for themselves.

In its form in Matthew's Gospel, the moral of the story is that "the last will be first, and the first last" (cf. esp. v 16). This has led to speculation that the parable refers to Jews and Gentiles — or, perhaps, to Christians of Jewish and Gentile origins, respectively. Or, keeping matters strictly within Israel, perhaps it should be seen as referring to scribes and Pharisees, on the one hand, in comparison to sinners and social outcasts, on the other. Certainly Jesus' notorious familiarity with "sinners" earlier in Matthew's Gospel had given rise to scorn and indignation on the part of the religious authorities (e.g., 9:10-11; 11:19). Tax gatherers and prostitutes could hardly commend themselves with pious works. Yet Jesus seems to have welcomed such marginalized persons readily enough.

In the Matthean Parable of the Two Sons (21:28-32), who are called to work in their father's vineyard, Jesus concludes by declaring to the "chief priests and elders of the people" (v 23): "Truly, I say to you, the tax collectors and the prostitutes go into the kingdom ahead of you" (v 31). Likewise, a reference to sinners and outcasts suits not only the central motif of "good" and "evil" in the Parable of the Laborers in the Vineyard (cf. v 15), thereby emphasizing the owner's perspective on what is "just" or "righteous" (cf. vv 4, 13), but also the eleventh-hour laborers' own explanation of why they have "stood idle" all day: "Because no one has hired us." So while the latter laborers themselves attest that no one else thought them capable of accomplishing anything useful, the owner replies: "Go, *even you (kai humeis)*, into the vineyard" (v 7).

But however fitting such an interpretation may be, we must not overlook the fact that the proverb about "the first" and "the last" in Matthew's Gospel not only concludes the parable of 20:1-16, but also appears in 19:30 — and so, in effect, introduces it: "Many who are first will be last, and the last will be first. *For* (an explanatory use of the conjunction *gar*) the kingdom of heaven is like a landowner . . ." (19:30–20:1). In 19:30 the proverb is applied to disciples who have abandoned all to follow Jesus. It suggests that those who have nothing with which to commend themselves can yet look forward to a rich recompense in God's kingdom (so 19:27-29). And if this is the meaning of the Parable of the Laborers in the Vineyard as well, then the disciples are portrayed as those who have been hired last in the day and rewarded more on the basis of God's generosity than on the basis of their own accomplishments.

Yet a third interpretation is also possible, based on the fact that the disciples did not always share the generosity of spirit exhibited by their master (cf., e.g., Matt 19:13-14). Perhaps it was the disciples who felt that they had "labored long and borne the heat of the day" in the service of their rabbi. Particularly if the disciples were liable to an inflated sense of their own importance, the Parable of the Laborers in the Vineyard might have served to redirect their attention to the gracious generosity of their teacher as the only basis for their own present standing.

In a sense, however, the same lesson applies to all three comparisons — whether "the first" and "the last" be understood as referring to "Pharisees" and outcasts generally, to "Pharisees" and the disciples of Jesus, or to disciples who had followed Jesus for longer or for shorter periods of time, respectively. For in the end, the identity of the laborers is less important than the character of the landowner, and what it implies about the character of God. In each case, the parable illustrates contrasting perceptions of the laborers' relationship to the master. Those hired first are given what "belongs to them" — that is, their wages are their due, for they have earned them. But the owner's resolution of the matter points to a deeper truth: that the fulfillment of his contract with the remainder of the workers is based less on their rights than on *his* right to be gracious and "just" (v 4). And this, as demonstrated time and again by the histories of both Israel and the church, is the difference between a contract and a covenant.

5. Conclusion

To some extent, all of Jesus' parables address questions of discipleship — that is, they all concern issues of how one should live in response to God's reign. The Parable of the Two Builders in Matt 7:24-27 and Luke 6:47-49 insists on the need for obedient action, portraying in dramatic fashion, as well, the consequences of a failure to act. The paired Parables of the Tower Builder and the Warring King in Luke 14:28-33 press the matter further, asserting that discipleship will cost one's all. But, according to the Parable of the Unworthy Servant in Luke 17:7-10, obedient service does not accrue to one's merit. Rather, as in the Parable of the Laborers in the Vineyard of Matt 20:1-16, the master offers the same reward to those who have served little as to those who have served long. Why? Because, to expand another metaphor, the kingdom is characterized by the character of the King: God's reign, which obedient discipleship acknowledges, is characterized in its entirety by God's own graciousness and generosity.

Nor, finally, can we omit from consideration Jesus' own role as the teacher and teller of parables. Many in his original audience, we are told, heard a certain divine authority in his words. They perceived something of God's own voice in the stories that he told. Others reacted to what they perceived as a pretension to authority. And that same range of options remains open to those who encounter — or, more accurately, are encountered by — Jesus' parables today.

In keeping with recent discussions that focus on a philosophy of language, it is helpful to approach the parables of Jesus recorded in the Synoptic Gospels as instances of "performative utterance" — that is, as words that intend to effect the reality of which they speak. For the parables still carry with them a challenge to hear the voice of Jesus in the words of the evangelists, and to hear in Jesus' words the voice of God. How individual readers hear these words — and whose voice they hear within them — is, precisely, a question of discipleship.

Selected Bibliography

Bailey, Kenneth E. *Through Peasant Eyes: More Lucan Parables, Their Culture and Style.* Grand Rapids: Eerdmans, 1980.

Blomberg, Craig L. *Interpreting the Parables.* Downers Grove: InterVarsity, 1990.

Crossan, John Dominic. *In Parables: The Challenge of the Historical Jesus.* New York: Harper & Row, 1973.

Danby, Herbert. *The Mishnah: Translated from the Hebrew with Introduction and Brief Explanatory Notes.* London: Oxford, 1933.

Drury, John. *The Parables in the Gospels: History and Allegory.* New York: Crossroad, 1985.

Funk, Robert W. *Parables and Presence.* Philadelphia: Fortress, 1982.

Gundry, Robert H. *Matthew: A Commentary on His Handbook for a Mixed Church under Persecution.* Grand Rapids: Eerdmans, 1994.

Hagner, Donald A. *Matthew* (WBC 33), 2 vols. Dallas: Word, 1993, 1995.

Hunter, A. M. *Interpreting the Parables.* London: SCM, 1960.

Jeremias, Joachim. *The Parables of Jesus,* trans. S. H. Hooke. 2nd rev. ed. New York: Scribner's, 1972.

Jones, Ivor H. *The Matthean Parables: A Literary and Historical Commentary* (NovTSup 80). Leiden: Brill, 1995.

Kissinger, Warren S. *The Parables of Jesus: A History of Interpretation and Bibliography.* Metuchen, NJ, and London: Scarecrow, 1979.

McArthur, Harvey K., and Johnston, Robert M. *They Also Taught in Parables. Rabbinic Parables from the First Centuries of the Christian Era.* Grand Rapids: Zondervan, 1990.

Sider, John W. *Interpreting the Parables: A Hermeneutical Guide to Their Meaning.* Grand Rapids: Zondervan, 1995.

Via, Dan O., Jr. *The Parables: Their Literary and Existential Dimension.* Philadelphia: Fortress, 1967.

Index of Subjects

Index of Modern Authors

Index of Scripture and Other Ancient Literature